Harrogate Terriers

THE 1/5TH (TERRITORIAL) BATTALION
WEST YORKSHIRE REGIMENT
IN THE GREAT WAR

John Sheehan

Pen & Sword
MILITARY

First published in Great Britain in 2017 by
PEN & SWORD MILITARY
an imprint of
Pen and Sword Books Ltd
47 Church Street
Barnsley
South Yorkshire S70 2AS

Copyright © John Sheehan, 2017

ISBN 978 1 47386 812 0

Printed and bound in England by
CPI Group (UK) Ltd, Croydon, CR0 4YY

Typeset in Times New Roman
by CHIC GRAPHICS

Pen & Sword Books Ltd incorporates the imprints of
Pen & Sword Archaeology, Atlas, Aviation, Battleground, Discovery, Family
History, History, Maritime, Military, Naval, Politics, Railways, Select, Social History,
Transport, True Crime, Claymore Press, Frontline Books, Leo Cooper, Praetorian Press,
Remember When, Seaforth Publishing and Wharncliffe.

For a complete list of Pen and Sword titles please contact
Pen and Sword Books Limited
47 Church Street, Barnsley, South Yorkshire, S70 2AS, England
E-mail: enquiries@pen-and-sword.co.uk
Website: www.pen-and-sword.co.uk

Contents

4

* * *

List of Sketch Maps

Foreword

'Ordinary' men doing extraordinary things is the theme underlying this book. Not mawkish pity for a generation lost, but an admiration for the achievements of a battalion of men who gradually transcended their civilian backgrounds to become a formidable body of trained soldiers. Their tale reflects the progress of the whole British Army during the war, as it was gradually hammered into shape, until finally emerging victorious in the Advance to Victory of 1918 – a series of British victories that has never been matched. All this achieved by 'ordinary' men.

Unlike so many battalion histories, which dissipate their energies in detailing the origins of the war and background to each offensive, this book concentrates on the 'doings' of the 1/5th West Yorkshires, only supplying enough of the background to allow us to fully appreciate what was happening to 'our' unit. This allows John Sheehan to flesh out the picture and as a result it soon becomes a body of men that we really care about. We follow the progress of individuals: endearing characters are introduced, memories and experiences shared and – far too often – their poignant deaths recorded. Sheehan does not shy away from recording the initial inexperience and trepidation of the men, indeed most of the 'Saturday Night Soldiers' failed to sign up for overseas service in August 1914 – at least until their brigadier pointedly asked them, 'Whether the friends who came to visit them in camp had come to see men ready to sacrifice themselves for their country or boys playing at soldiering?' That did the trick and next day most had volunteered.

Initially, the bulk of the men came from Harrogate and York, with a strong regional West Yorkshire identity that shines through these pages. There are many vivid quotations from letters and personal experience accounts. Few could forget the warning words uttered – as only a Yorkshire man could – by Private Walter Mellor during a German gas attack at Ypres on 19 December 1915, 'Hey up lads, it's gas!'

The unending trickle of daily losses from snipers and shells is shocking. Even worse is the pain of the outright slaughter at Ypres and the Somme – and at times there is blunt criticism of the generals. This is inevitable in a book recording the stories of a relatively small group of men, in a war fought by millions; a worm's eye view of the war with no time to consider the manifold tactical problems of fighting the Imperial German Army. The roller-coaster progression to the British war-wining 'all arms battle' tactics of 1918, required numerous painful sacrifices. It is always difficult to accept losses when one has come to identify with the victims.

To return to the theme of the book: the men of the 1/5th West Yorkshires collectively learnt their new trade as soldiers even as they fought, suffered terrible casualties and were regenerated with drafts from home. From barely-trusted ingénues, they showed their courage during the vicious fighting at Schwaben Redoubt on the Somme on 28

September 1916. Their professional skills blossomed amidst the patrols and raids in the Laventie sector in 1917. Yet there was a loss of innocence too, and Sheehan notes that accounts become less optimistic as the realities of war hit home. The 1/5th West Yorkshires then endured a terrible ordeal in the muddy hell of the Battle of Poelcappelle on 9 October 1917. They were rebuilt, only to be torn to shreds again amidst a brave fight against the German attacks at Wytschaete Ridge on 25 April 1918. The losses and replacement drafts greatly diluted the Harrogate core when the battalion was once again rebuilt. Although the final battles of October–November of 1918 may have been great victories, the casualties brought misery to yet more homes.

And after the war, after victory? They went home and resumed their lives. Soldiers no more, but many scarred physically or mentally, by all they had undergone. This beautifully illustrated book is a welcome tribute to a fine body of men.

Peter Hart
Author and oral historian at the
Imperial War Museum, London

Preface and Acknowledgements

In the centre of Harrogate, on the corner of Commercial Street and Strawberry Dale, stands an imposing Victorian gothic drill hall built out of York stone. Constructed in the grand manner, it has a turret with castellated battlements and a large dedication stone laid by Colonel Kearsley on 22 May 1894. This building was clearly intended to play a significant role in the civic life of Harrogate and the army locally. Nowadays the only remaining military presence is the Army Cadet Force, which drills there a couple of times a week, and in the daytime it is used as a furniture warehouse.

In the summer of 2012, I started researching the history of the building and immediately chanced upon a rich seam of local history which also turned out to have national significance. From 1908 the Strawberry Dale Drill Hall had been the home of E Company, 5th Battalion (Prince of Wales's Own) West Yorkshire Regiment, which was renamed the 1/5th Battalion prior to its arrival on the Western Front in early 1915.

Strawberry Dale Drill hall, Harrogate.

Dedication Stone.

Formed as a part-time unit of the Territorial Force, the 1/5th Battalion went on to play a role in some of the most famous and horrific battles of the First World War, and this book is an attempt to trace its progress from Yorkshire to Laventie, Ypres, the Somme, Passchendaele, Wytschaete, Cambrai, Valenciennes and the post war occupation of Cologne. It tells the story of the soldiers involved, and explains how their battalion fits into the wider history of the First World War.

This objective would not have been possible without the assistance of many individuals and organisations, whose kindness and patience still seems to me astonishing in a world where time is money. The organisations include Leeds University Library (Liddle Collection), Harrogate Library, York Central Library, the Western Front Association (WFA), The Imperial War Museum, The Pump Room Museum, York Minster Library and Leeds City Museum. Don Jackson and Hannah Rogers have been particularly kind in identifying original source material, including unpublished photographs, nominal rolls and personal diaries from the archives of the wonderful York Army Museum (YAM).

I would like to thank Matt Jones, Roni Wilkinson, and Irene Moore at Pen & Sword, as well as Peter Hart (oral historian at the Imperial War Museum) for taking the time to provide an excellent foreword to the book.

Others have also been exceptionally generous with their time and artefacts. Chris Noble, a WFA member, is the author of the Wetherby War Memorial website, and I am very grateful to him for his expertise and wise counsel. Colin Chadwick is the author of the Pateley Bridge War Memorial site and has helped a great deal. I would also like to acknowledge here the encyclopaedic Harrogate People and Places website, curated by Tony Cheal, which was the portal through which I first entered the world of the Harrogate Terriers.

Fraser Skirrow, author of the excellent *Massacre on the Marne (The Life and Death of the 2/5th Battalion West Yorkshire Regiment in the Great War)* encouraged me and provided some very useful materials which have helped make the book what it is. Michael Wilson, Ronald Pickup, Andrew Volans, Mark and Jeremy Swinden are the authors of self-published works which have been of great value. In particular, Mr Wilson has kindly permitted me to quote some letters from his father, Arthur (Peter) Wilson, to illustrate the experience of the infantryman in 1915 and 1916, and Lyn MacDonald kindly allowed me to use extracts from her seminal work: *1915 The Death of Innocence*.

I have worked hard to identify and contact all other copyright holders, but in some instances without success. I would therefore like to hear from any unacknowledged copyright holders so that I can make the appropriate acknowledgement.

Other individuals who have helped me steer a course through the history of the 1/5th Battalion include John Snowdon, Tom Cruikshanks, Richard Tillett, Richard Taylor, Jason Dainty, Maureen Sullivan, Brian Skinner, Tony Greveson, Chloe Wilson, Laurie Holmes, Tim Waddington, Kirsty Farthing, Janet Lea, Ken Haywood, Patrick Ryde, the current owners of the Chateau Les Trois Tours in Flanders, and Anthony Rogers.

My father (who sadly passed away in June 2016) provided expert technical advice on writing and my mother helped compile the index and appendices. Finally, and most importantly I need to acknowledge the practical help, endless support, and saintly patience of my wife, Vicky. She had no idea what she was getting into when she agreed in late 2013 that I 'should write a book'. I am forever grateful.

What follows is the result. It is the history of the 1/5th Battalion Prince of Wales's Own West Yorkshire Regiment in the Great War, told where appropriate from the perspective of the Harrogate Terriers who served with it, and this book is heartily dedicated to their memory.

Harrogate – June 2016

ENGLISH CHANNEL

HOLLAND

Nieuport

CALAIS

BOULOGNE   DUNKIRK   OSTEND

Boesinghe
Passchendaele
YPRES   Broodseinde
ARMENTIERES   Wytschaete   GHENT
Laventie   ANTWERP
Merville   Fauquissart
Neuve Chappelle   LILLE
La Bassee   BRUSSELS
Loos
Vimy
ARRAS
Ransart
Foncquevillers   Hannescamps   VALENCIENNES
Thiepval   Avesnes-Le-Sec   MONS
ALBERT   CAMBRAI
R. Somme   BELGIUM
PERONNE

NOYON   FRANCE

Compiegne

Soissons

R. Aisne

SEDAN

0 10 20 30 40
    Miles

RHEIMS

- - - -   Front Line 15 April 1915

-·-·-   Front Line 11 November 1918

···········   National Border

VERDUN

THE WESTERN FRONT
15th APRIL 1915 and 11th NOVEMBER 1918

The Western Front [Sketch Map 1]
*Showing some key locations in the story of the 1/5th Battalion and the positions of the front line
on the day of its arrival and the last day of hostilities, respectively.*

13

Note on Army Organisation

An Approximate Characterisation of Army Rank and Structure

Officers:

General	Army	c.200,000 men
Lieutenant General	Corps	50,000 men
Major General	Division	16,000 men
Brigadier General	Brigade	4,000 men
Lieutenant Colonel	Battalion	1,000 men
Major		
Captain	Company	250 men
Lieutenant		
Second Lieutenant	Platoon	60 men

Warrant Officers:
Regimental Sergeant Major (RSM)
Company Sergeant Major (CSM – formerly Colour Sergeant)

Non-Commissioned Officers:

Sergeant		
Corporal		
Lance Corporal	Section	15 men

Infantry Units of the 49th West Riding Infantry Division (TF)

146 Brigade (formerly 1st West Riding Brigade)
1/5th Battalion West Yorkshire Regiment
1/6th Battalion West Yorkshire Regiment
1/7th Battalion West Yorkshire Regiment
1/8th Battalion West Yorkshire Regiment

147 Brigade (formerly 2nd West Riding Brigade)
1/4th Battalion King's Own Yorkshire Light Infantry
1/5th Battalion King's Own Yorkshire Light Infantry
1/4th Battalion York and Lancaster Regiment
1/5th Battalion York and Lancaster Regiment

148 Brigade (formerly 3nd West Riding Brigade)
1/4th Battalion Duke of Wellington's Regiment
1/5th Battalion Duke of Wellington's Regiment
1/6th Battalion Duke of Wellington's Regiment
1/7th Battalion Duke of Wellington's Regiment

Introduction: Who Were The Harrogate Terriers?

On 12 October 1938, the *Harrogate Herald* reported a funeral:

The cremation took place at Stonefall Cemetery on Monday, of Arthur Herbert Alderson, of 11 St Clement's Road, Harrogate, who passed away at the Ministry of Pensions Hospital, Leeds, on Thursday. Mr Alderson, who was 50 years of age, suffered a severe wound in the left leg during the War, and some weeks ago this became infected, necessitating amputation. A man of quiet and unassuming disposition, he was regarded with affection and esteem, and his passing has cast a gloom over his colleagues in the Municipal Offices, where, for 32 years he was associated with the Education Department.

Mr (Arthur) Alderson enlisted with the Harrogate Pals (5th West Yorks) in August 1914, and was promoted to the rank of Sergeant. He went to France in 1915, and in the following year, during the Somme battle, he received his wound. He was a member of the Comrades' Association, and always made a point of being present at the annual dinner. In his younger and more active days he was a keen cricketer, and in later years was an enthusiastic spectator at the Harrogate cricket ground.

He leaves a widow and two sons to whom deep sympathy will be extended.

Arthur Alderson [Ackrill]
Arthur Alderson pictured on enlistment in 1914.

Arthur Alderson appears to have been an ordinary man, like so many thousands of others born in the 1880s and 1890s, whose lives were changed and in many cases ended, by the juggernaut of the Great War. As such, he characterises the 'Saturday Night Soldiers', or 'Terriers' of the 1/5th Territorial Battalion, who fought together as volunteers from York, Harrogate and the northern West Riding of Yorkshire.

In the autumn of 1914, Arthur and his comrades were sometimes known locally as 'Harrogate Pals' because the local townspeople and media felt a very strong connection to the erstwhile occupants of the Strawberry Dale Drill Hall and the men and boys recruited by the Harrogate Defence League. But they were not 'Pals' in the accepted sense because the 1/5th Battalion was a pre-existing Territorial unit, and never pretended to be a Pals battalion of Lord Kitchener's 'New Army'.

Flag Day [Ackrill]
The 10th Harrogate Baden Powell Scouts collecting in December 1914 'to provide a good Christmas Dinner for the boys of the 1-5th and 2-5th West Yorks.

In fact, the connection between town and battalion was already long established when the war started in August 1914, even though York had always provided the main recruiting pool and headquarters depot. By August 1915, with the 1/5th Battalion now in the trenches at Ypres, the relative strength of recruiting in Harrogate meant that Harrogate men now accounted for more than half the battalion, with those who came from York, Ripon and Knaresborough making up the remainder.

As the war rolled on, the make-up of the battalion continued to change as men died and were invalided out in their droves. On three occasions the 1/5th was virtually wiped out: on the Somme, at Passchendaele and then at Wytschaete. As a result, the 1/5th Battalion naturally diversified as casualties were replaced from all over Yorkshire and then increasingly from across the United Kingdom, even including some conscripts after 1916.

Furthermore, the profile of the battalion gradually became more professional and battle hardened, developing from expendable trench fodder in 1915 (as place-holders for the Regular Army and Kitchener's New Army), into a potent offensive force in its own right by late September 1916. However, the 1/5th always remained true to its Territorial heritage and West Riding roots, which can be traced at least as far back as the creation of the West Riding Rifle Volunteer Corps in 1859, where this story begins.

Chapter 1

West Riding Volunteers

'Well done! Harrogate!'

Military Bloodline of the 1/5th Battalion West Yorkshire Regiment
In the first half of the nineteenth century the United Kingdom was dotted with small militia units whose job was to defend the country against any invasion attempt. Military men of influence, including the aged Duke of Wellington, regarded these sparse forces as insufficient for the task and, at the height of an invasion scare in 1859, the War Office invited the lord lieutenants of each county to raise their own Rifle Volunteer Corps (RVCs) for the defence of the realm, at local expense.

There was an immediate and vigorous response to the call, with the creation of many local RVCs across the land. Twenty years later, they were clustered together at local level, and in 1887 the RVCs were converted into 'volunteer battalions' (VB), and formally incorporated into the regimental structure of the British Army. In 1908, the VB were themselves scrapped, and replaced with a new Territorial Force (TF), which included the 5th Battalion (Prince of Wales's Own) West Yorkshire Regiment.

This was the military bloodline of the 1/5th Battalion. Its cultural and demographic heritage, on the other hand, lay rooted in the towns and countryside around York, in the northern West Riding of Yorkshire.

West Riding Heritage
By 1908, when the 5th Battalion was formed, the city of York had a long and important military history, centred on the cavalry barracks at Fulford. The civilian inhabitants of the city had long been used to seeing soldiers mixing in the markets, route marching on the Knavesmire and drinking in local inns. They were also familiar with the pageantry and patriotism of Military Sunday which, from 1885, involved a service at the Minster followed by a parade through the streets of the city.

Military Sunday was symbolic of the inter-connection between military and civilian York, important as an expression of civic pride as well as local economic power, which was considerable. The success of the North Eastern Railway (NER), under the stewardship of George Hudson and then George Leeman, had helped deliver wealth for a few and work for tens of thousands after 1840. Nineteenth century York was also home to minor manufacturing industries including iron works, glass manufacture and notably, confectionery, as Terry's of York and Joseph Rowntree dominated the domestic market.

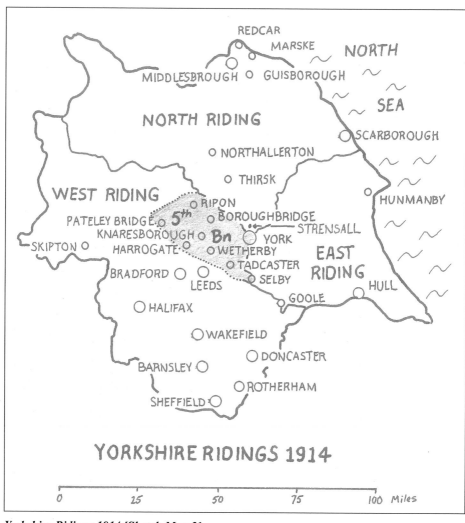

Yorkshire Ridings 1914 [Sketch Map 2]
Showing the heartland of the 5th Battalion West Yorkshire Regiment around York and Harrogate.

Guided by non-conformist religious ethics and a keen social conscience, the powerful Rowntree family was uncomfortable with militarism in any form, but their substantial influence did not prevent York becoming, and remaining, the centre of gravity for the Volunteer movement in the northern West Riding until the end of the century.

Nearby Ripon, Knaresborough, Selby and Pateley Bridge shared certain characteristics with York. They were minor industrial centres in their own right, with cottages, mill terraces and factory chimneys. They too had military connections centred on York, and Selby even had its own version of Military Sunday. However, none of these places had much in common with the tourist town of Harrogate, except geographical proximity.

The health-giving spa waters that made Harrogate famous had been discovered in 1571 and over the following 300 years the town grew as it developed a thriving tourist trade, providing hospitality and cures to genteel invalids. Middle class professionals, including doctors and lawyers, flocked to Harrogate in the 1800s to build their businesses on the needs of the wealthy sick. The town also gained a modern civil infrastructure with fine municipal and private buildings and a social structure to match. As the local economy grew, so did the town's population, more than doubling between 1891 and 1911, and this created the conditions necessary for a successful Territorial company, born out of the 16th Rifle Volunteer Corps, based at the Strawberry Dale Drill Hall.

The Victorian Volunteer Army in York and Harrogate

In 1859 the Lord Lieutenant of the West Riding approved the creation of the 1st Yorkshire West Riding Rifle Volunteer Corps. The new RVC was established initially in York with four companies of up to one hundred men each, a fifth company being added in 1862. Local RVCs were also formed between 1859 and 1864 in Harrogate (16th Corps), Knaresborough (17th Corps), Ripon (27th Corps), Tadcaster (31st Corps) and Wetherby (33rd Corps).

In 1860 the 1st Administrative Battalion was founded in York to form an umbrella and focal point for these outlying corps, although they remained fiercely independent of any central authority. Tellingly, the motto of the Harrogate Corps was 'Loyal yet Free'. By September 1861 their collective strength was 550 officers and men, with the majority attached to the five

Claro Rifles Badge [Dixon Pickup]
Silver plate officer's pouch badge.

York-based companies. The Harrogate and Knaresborough Corps knew themselves collectively as the 'Claro Rifles', and wore this title proudly on their badges and buttons.

From the start, the Volunteer movement was imbued with the amateur spirit which came naturally to civilian gentlemen turned evening soldiers. The RVCs often resembled private military clubs for the wealthy, as membership fees were levied to allow the corps to remain independent of central authority. Volunteers were also expected to provide their own weapons and uniforms. This was a recurring cost as kit changed with fashion. Initially the uniforms of the West Riding RVCs were mid-grey, later changing to a scarlet tunic with sky blue facings, then scarlet/white about 1888 and scarlet/buff in 1904.

The transposition of the Victorian class structure onto the early Volunteer movement was apparent at every level. The aristocracy played a self-consciously gracious role, with Earl de Grey of Ripon, the honorary colonel. Lower down the social order,

1st VB Officers Outside Colliergate Drill Hall 1898. [YAM]
Front Row - from fifth from left:- Lt. Col. Francis H. Anderson, Lt. Col. George Kearsley, Lt.
Col. W.A White, unknown, Capt. Cecil E. Wood. [Identified by Author]

Lieutenant George Sutton and Ensign Henry Wood, both of the 1st (York) RVC, were formally titled 'Gent' in the *London Gazette* which publicised their commissions in 1860. Wisely, their fresh-faced enthusiasm was tempered by the professional experience and know-how of Captain George Briggs, formerly of the 1st Dragoon Guards, who was commissioned to lead the 1st RVC as its first commandant, supported by Captain James Meek. This mixed composition of gentlemen amateurs and ex-professionals was typical of Volunteer Corps around the United Kingdom in the second half of the nineteenth century, and was to remain characteristic until the melting pot of the First World War necessarily blurred the distinction.

It was common for RVCs to have no fixed home of their own in the early years. From its formation, for example, the 1st RVC was forced to parade and drill in full view of the public and off-duty regular soldiers in Parliament Street, York. They were not taken terribly seriously, even after the construction of a new drill hall by the battalion officers and men at 28A Colliergate in 1871 (now Barnitt's hardware store).

In 1880, further military reforms created clearer lines of command by bringing local RVCs into a formal battalion structure. The corps based in Harrogate, Knaresborough, Tadcaster, Pateley Bridge and Selby were converted into companies and formally drawn (with the York companies) into a single unit, headquartered at the Colliergate Drill Hall in York. Together, they became the 1st Volunteer Corps, which was renamed again in 1887, becoming the 1st Volunteer Battalion, Prince of Wales's Own (West Yorkshire) Regiment, known for short as the 1st VB.

The changes had considerable impact in the ranks. In the early days only bandsmen had been excused joining fees, but after 1880 men of the urban and agricultural working classes were now able to enlist as the financial restrictions were eased for riflemen, although they had no hope of rising to officer level. For example, William Mawson, a 16-year-old linen weaver from Knaresborough, had joined the Claro Rifles as drummer boy in 1860. He served for thirty years without exceeding the rank of sergeant, despite his apparent efficiency.

Overall, the 1st VB retained a degree of financial independence, which allowed the battalion to reflect the social, political and economic structures of York, Harrogate and Ripon. The importance of social standing is illustrated by the relative careers of Colonel Francis H. Anderson VD and his groom, Sergeant William Henry (Harry) Fearn.

Born in 1853, Francis Anderson was the son of a leading York solicitor. He was commissioned ensign in 1872, aged 19, rising swiftly to the rank of lieutenant in 1873 and then captain in 1879. He became major in 1896, lieutenant colonel in 1901 and took command of the 1st VB in 1905. It is striking that Colonel Anderson's military career as a volunteer mirrored his rise through the ranks of the family law firm as he established himself in the commercial life of the city.

When he retired in 1908, Anderson was said to be at the head of one of the strongest and most efficient battalions of infantry in the north of England. According to his obituary in the *Yorkshire Herald*, he *'devoted all the time that could be snatched from the claims of an extensive legal practice to the encouragement of volunteering.'*

Harry Fearn, on the other hand, was the son of a white-smith and char woman. His father died in 1901 following committal to a debtors' prison and was buried in a

1st VB Officers outside Colonel Kearsley's Tent - Isle of Man Camp 1899. [YAM]
Left to Right:- Lt. Alexander Stoddart, Lt. Col. Francis H. Anderson, Lt. Pickering, Lt. Col. W.A. White, Capt. Richard Cattley, Lt. Col George Kearsley (seated). [Identified by Author]

Scarborough Camp 1901. [YAM]

1st VB Exercising the Freedom of the City of York in 1906. [YAM]
Military Sunday on Duncombe Place with York Minster behind.

pauper's grave. Harry was working as a butcher when he joined the 1st VB, aged 18, in 1902. He was given the role of groom to Colonel Anderson and served for twelve years before the Great War, with only one promotion: to the rank of lance corporal. During his subsequent time on the Western Front with the 1/5th Battalion, Harry continued to work with the battalion's horses and mules in the transport section. This involved bringing munitions and supplies to the front, often under heavy shell fire. Like William Mawson before him, Harry rose to the rank of sergeant, was awarded the Territorial Efficiency Medal on 20 November 1917 and the Military Medal on 10 November 1918. He was never commissioned, however.

The same social dynamics were at play in the battalion's outlying companies. In Tadcaster, the 31st RVC was formed in 1864, under the command of Captain Charles Shann and Lieutenant John Bromet, both men of social rank.

In Ripon, the Kearsley family was prominent in local economic and political life. Following the family tradition, George Kearsley was elected mayor in 1881. By 1894, he was officer commanding the 1st VB, and made a substantial impact on the history of the battalion. He opened a series of drill halls and recruited very successfully, not least in Pateley Bridge, where K Company was formed in 1900 to accommodate more than a hundred local volunteers.

In Harrogate, the 16th RVC drilled in the old Town Hall when it was first formed, the Victoria Baths from 1871 and then in premises in James Street, with a rifle range constructed at Birk Crag on the western outskirts of the town. The 16th Corps was incorporated into the 1st VB as F Company in 1887 and in 1893 there was an appeal for funds to build a new drill hall on the junction of Commercial Street and Strawberry Dale. This building was dedicated on completion by Colonel Kearsley in 1894.

As a sub-plot to the growth of Harrogate during the Victorian era, the development of the Claro Rifles (and the 16th RVC in particular) had a significant influence in shaping the social structure of the town. It was an engine of social mobility, helping ambitious young men to improve their standing and influence, or to match financial success with social status. Like the town, the 16th RVC started small in 1860 but grew fast, with local dignitaries like Richard Dyson, buildings inspector of the Harrogate Corporation, playing a key role as corps paymaster. The Reverend Horatio James was honorary chaplain and shooting prizes were donated by Mr Robert Ackrill. The first captain was John James Harrison, a banker of Devonshire House, High Harrogate. In due course he was succeeded by Major Holt who arranged for the promotion of his protégé, Henry Dury, to the rank of lieutenant.

The Volunteer Movement was described by the *Harrogate Advertiser* in 1893 as *'one of the strongest bulwarks of our constitution'*. Even ladies were represented by 'Mrs Captain Reynard', enthusiastic patroness of the 16th RVC since its formation, and donor of various cups and shields presented as prizes in rifle shooting and drill competitions. She opened the battalion's annual ball and was often present to encourage the volunteers. Watching them march past at Knaresborough, knee deep in mud, the *Harrogate Advertiser* reported that: *'the ringing cheer came from the lips of Mrs Reynard, she waved her handkerchief and cried, 'Well done! Harrogate!''*

Captain Wood and the war in South Africa

The Second Boer War broke out in 1899. Following a series of early military disasters, and as if to test the professionalism of the Volunteers, the War Office decreed in 1900 that each Volunteer Battalion should provide a single company of 116 officers and men for active service, in support of the regular troops. The 1st VB contributed, as required, the composite 1st Volunteer Service Company, which went out to form part of the 2nd Battalion, West Yorkshire Regiment early in 1900.

This company was commanded by Captain Cecil Ernest Wood, a future commanding officer of the 1/5th Battalion on the Western Front. He had trained initially as a sea cadet on HMS *Worcester* on the Thames and came to York in the early 1880s to take up a position as a timber merchant's clerk. Wood joined the 1st VB and was gazetted lieutenant in 1886, aged 19. By 1899 he was in command of D Company.

Captain Wood was one of many who volunteered for service in South Africa and on 24 February 1900 he was temporarily commissioned into the Regular Army for the purpose. One of his junior officers in the 1st Volunteer Service Company (and a future commanding officer of the 1/5th Battalion at the Battle of Passchendaele) was Lieutenant Hugh D. Bousfield, a solicitor from Leeds who had served with the 3rd VB (Leeds Rifles) in the 1890s.

South Africa was a proving ground for these young Volunteer officers and Captain Wood's personal diary gives some glimpses of actions involving artillery fire and trench warfare, as well as difficult weather conditions. He turned out to be a brave and accomplished commander and was mentioned in despatches. The whole experience of serving in a regular battalion and leading men into battle was, perhaps, critical in preparing him for events fifteen years later, and for the first day of the Battle of the Somme, in particular.

The Haldane Act

Following Cecil Wood's return from South Africa in 1902, the 1st VB flourished and by 1905 it had expanded to thirteen companies under the overall command of Lieutenant Colonel W.A. White.

Nationally, though, the Volunteer Movement was under threat. Despite the protestations of the venerable Colonel Anderson, who was consulted on these matters by the Secretary of State for War, Sir Richard Haldane, the Territorial and Reserve Forces Act (1907) brought an end to the Volunteer Battalions and in their place created the Territorial Force (TF) on 1 April 1908. Newly formed local County Associations were to run the Territorial units, but absorption of former Volunteer Battalions into the TF now brought them firmly under central military control.

The Haldane Act, as it became known, was wide ranging. It adjusted the balance and structure of the British Army, including regulars and reservists, as well as volunteers. At local level, the West Yorkshire Regiment was reorganised so that its two existing regular army units, the 1st and 2nd battalions, were now supplemented by two special reserve units (3rd and 4th battalions) which incorporated the remnants of the ancient county militia.

1st VB Officers at Aldershot Camp 1902. [YAM]
Middle Row (seated) - from left:- Capt. Robert Cattley, Lt. Col. Francis H. Anderson, Lt. Col. John Husband, Rev. Smith. The group also includes Captain William Oddie. [Identified by Author]

The four West Yorkshire Volunteer Battalions were formally disbanded. In practical terms they were converted into newly formed Territorial Force battalions. The 1st VB became the 5th Battalion, headquartered in York. The 2nd VB became the 6th Battalion, based in Bradford. The 3rd VB and 4th VB became the 7th and 8th Battalions (Leeds Rifles) respectively. Together the four new battalions formed the 1st West Riding Infantry Brigade, which in turn formed a part of the West Riding Infantry Division. The White Rose of Yorkshire was adopted as the divisional symbol.

The Haldane Act also created the Officers' Training Corps (OTC), which absorbed some volunteer companies. This was controversial. In 1908 Captain Wood complained to the West Riding County Association that the five York-based companies of the 5th Battalion had been reduced to three by the uncoupling of the St John's College and St Peter's School Companies to become OTCs. This act had reduced the establishment of the York-based 5th Battalion (and Captain Wood's span of command) from 500 men to 300, at a stroke.

At national level, the Haldane Act created the British Expeditionary Force (BEF) of six Regular Army divisions drawn from across the regiments. This was the spearhead, designed to go overseas at very short notice, in time of emergency. The formal plan was that the Reserves would provide support to the BEF overseas, with the Territorials staying behind to guard the United Kingdom and provide coastal defence.

Officers of the 5th Battalion, West Yorkshire Regiment

Led by Colonel John Husband and his second-in-command, Major George Lumsden, twenty-six officers of the 1st VB joined the 5th Battalion on 1st April 1908 (listed in the appendix). Twelve of these were eventually to embark for France with the 1/5th Battalion in April 1915, and to this extent the command structure of the battalion through to 1918 (and beyond) was steeped in the history of the 1st VB and the Volunteer culture nurtured by Colonel Anderson.

Major William Oddie. [Ackri Oddie was a Pateley Bridge solicitor and long term volunteer who was to comman the 1/5th Battalion at the Seco Battle of Kemmel.

These twelve gentlemen officers were of a type, fitting the mould cast by Francis Anderson and George Kearsley in the nineteenth century. Frederick Thompson, Donald P. Mackay, Henry Scott and John 'Jack' Peters were solicitors based in York. William Oddie was a solicitor in Pateley Bridge. Mackay and Scott had both attended St Peter's School and may have graduated from the 1st VB training company there. Mackay is recorded to have served later with the Leeds University Officer Training Corps (OTC) as a law student and was commissioned into the 1st VB in 1903.

5th Battalion Officers outside Colonel Husband's Tent – Redcar Camp 1908. [YAM]
Left to Right:- Lt. Donald P. Mackay, Lt. Henry C. Scott, Lt. Charles Moody (seated), Lt. Col. John C. Husband, (seated), Major George Lumsden, Capt. Robert Cattley.

5th Battalion Officers at Redcar Camp 1908. [YAM] *The territorial spirit is characterised by commanding officer John Husband (far right), leading a practical joke on John Foxton, as Henry Scott looks on (far left). [Identified by Author]. The photograph also includes Donald Mackay and Geoffrey Sowerby.*

1st VB Officers in Tin Baths. [YAM]

Charles Whitworth and Percy Williamson were Harrogate men. Whitworth (whose diary entries are referred to below) was a barrister, while Williamson was a medical practitioner. Alexander Stoddart was a doctor and sometime President of the York Medical Society. He had joined the 1st VB in 1896. Robert Cattley had been medical officer of health in York from 1894–1900, and was subsequently a research medic at the Leeds University and Leeds Infirmary.

Geoffrey Sowerby, John Foxton and Rupert Lansdale were also solidly middle class, though perhaps lacking the professional stamp of their medical and legal comrades. Sowerby was a land surveyor employed in the Railway Estate office in York, Foxton was a farmer near Pocklington and Lansdale a superintendent brewer from Ilkley. By 1908 Cecil Wood was a wealthy timber merchant in his own right.

Other Ranks

Outside the officer cadre, the transition from 1st VB to 5th Battalion was problematic, with many old sweats declining to re-enlist. Having already suffered the loss of two companies to the OTC, Captain Wood was now concerned to see the three remaining York-based companies suffer a sharp decline after 1908, with numbers falling to about 160. It was clear that many volunteers did not want to be part of the new TF structure, and that they were being discouraged by their employers and trade unions from taking part in the new form of part-time soldiering. Captain Wood and his brother officers of the York-based companies wrote to local business leaders in a bid to calm fears and encourage enlistment:

> *'The terms of service are exceedingly light, and such as can be complied with by nearly every working man, with a minimum of personal inconvenience, whilst the advantages derived from discipline, drill and musketry, coupled with an annual training under canvas, far outweigh the small sacrifices of time necessary under the regulations which are required to make himself an efficient Territorial.'*

Wood also wrote personally to the secretaries of local football clubs, asking them to send in recruits, promising that a career as a Territorial would not adversely affect their performance on the football field.

Despite the reticence of many veteran volunteers, a hard core of 1st VB soldiers still followed their officers into the 5th Battalion in 1908 and some stayed long enough to serve with the 1/5th Battalion. Albert Pook, for example, was the longest serving of the 1st VB to be killed on the Western Front. He had been a municipal clerk in the town clerk's office in York, and was 35 years old when he lost his life on 12 October 1918 at Cambrai, less than one month before the war ended.

In addition to its middle class officers and enthusiastic part-timers, the 5th Battalion inherited from the 1st VB some ex-regulars as warrant officers and NCOs to give it much needed backbone. Fred Raynor had been forged into a hardened professional soldier in the 2nd Battalion, West Yorkshire Regiment, which he had joined as a 17 year old in 1896. Having fought in South Africa, he left the Regular Army after ten years' service to become colour sergeant with the 1st VB in 1906. In 1911 Fred was based at the Colliergate Drill Hall, York, subsequently transferring to the Harrogate Drill Hall. By the outbreak of the Great War he had become a Harrogate local, drilling the Terriers of the 5th Battalion, and was known locally as 'Sergeant Raynor from Strawberry Dale'.

Sgt-Maj. Fred Raynor.
[Ackrill]

Fred Raynor was a regular soldier and father figure to the Harrogate Terriers of E Company.

New Blood

About 750 boys and men enlisted in the 5th Battalion between its formation in 1908 and the outbreak of the First World War. These numbers were not sufficient to prevent a contraction of the battalion, overall, but alongside the veterans of the 1st VB who decided to stay, these new men were to be the core of the 1/5th Battalion in April 1915 when it embarked for the Western Front. They included a few trained men like John 'Jack' Radford and many raw recruits like Arthur 'Peter' Wilson and Edward Iredale.

Jack was a brave and hugely modest individual. He served with distinction in South Africa as a volunteer with the Imperial Yeomanry. On returning home to York in 1902 his neighbours on Wellington Street turned out to welcome him, but hearing of the waiting party he took various back routes to avoid the celebrations and sneaked in through his back gate. He enlisted in the 5th Battalion in 1912, aged 30.

Well educated at St Peter's School and a clerk at Beckett's Bank in Knaresborough, 18-year-old Peter Wilson joined the 5th Battalion in early 1914. He wrote many descriptive letters home and kept a diary of his experiences on the front line with the 1/5th. He was an enthusiastic and brave soldier, destined to become battalion intelligence officer on the Somme, before joining the Royal Flying Corps (RFC) as a pilot in 1917.

Seventeen-year-old Edward Iredale also kept an interesting diary. He was a working class boy from Tadcaster where he worked at the John Smiths

Private Peter Wilson. [Michael Wilson]
Peter was a bank clerk who sought adventure and found it on the Western Front with the 1/5th Battalion and later in the Royal Flying Corps.

brewery. He studied at night school to complete his education and played football at weekends. On 29 April 1914 he was passed fit to join the 5th Battalion and attended his first 'Terriers' Supper' on 1 May. Edward was promoted swiftly through the ranks after war was declared, ultimately achieving the rank of company sergeant major. He was awarded the Military Medal for going out into no man's land to bring in a wounded man at Ypres in November 1915. Wounded during this episode, he recovered but was later killed in action on the Somme in August 1916.

These new recruits were almost all from the battalion's traditional heartland in the northern West Riding, but fewer than half were now from York, confirming a significant shift away from the city as the main recruiting ground. Harrogate was gradually becoming the new centre of gravity.

Culture and Training

Despite Haldane's intention of professionalising the 'Saturday night soldiers' of the TF, the 5th Battalion remained a relatively amateurish outfit after 1908. New recruits were commonly very young, like Peter Wilson and Edward Iredale, and were generally attracted by the prospect of fellowship and outdoor activity rather than the notion of active service overseas, which was actually precluded by their terms of service.

A handful of ex-Regular Army drill sergeants like Fred Raynor and John Sim were expected to help bridge the experience-gap. These old soldiers were certainly feared as well as respected by the young recruits, and the peace-time training schedule was made as intensive as possible to make up for the drain of experienced men. Two nights per week, on Tuesdays and Fridays the companies of the 5th Battalion paraded, drilled and were lectured by their officers. On Saturday afternoons training was at the local rifle range, for musketry practice over 200-500 yards. There were weekly route marches too.

However, there was a general lack of expert leadership and role models, as officers had insufficient time to attend specialist courses. They led by personal reputation rather than the authority bestowed by their rank, which yielded variable levels of discipline. Many NCOs lacked experience too. In 1909, 38 per cent of them were under twenty years old, nationally. The effect of the training regime was therefore limited, as in 1910 more than one in three Terriers failed their annual musketry test, and in 1913 it was felt by Lord Scarborough (chairman of the West Riding County Association) that the Territorial Force was still unfit for war after its first five years' training. In essence, the 'Saturday night soldiers' of the 5th Battalion remained enthusiastic amateurs rather than semi-professional soldiers.

Annual Camp

One of the benefits of TF membership was the annual camp, which usually lasted a fortnight. Captain E.V. Tempest, author of the *History of 6th Battalion West Yorkshire Regiment (Volume 1)*, records that *'men joined the battalion as a relief from the monotony of civil life, as an outlet for high spirits, and as a means of spending a healthy holiday with good comrades.'* The West Riding County Association was keen to maximise attendance by feeding the men well on roast meat and vegetables, at a time when many were otherwise living on meagre rations. It was certainly a pleasurable experience for the young men who generally worked hard all year round. Sleeping fifteen to a bell tent was no hardship, when at home in York and Harrogate two or three families of ten or twelve commonly occupied four room houses.

The 5th Battalion attended annual camps at Redcar (1908), Guisborough (1909), Ramsey (1910), Marske (1911), Hunmanby (1912) Aberystwyth (1913) and Scarborough (1914). These were not without unfortunate incident, though. In September 1909, Viscount Haldane was forced to answer questions in Parliament on the recent death of the Reverend Nigel Hodgson during the mock battle held at Guisborough. Hodgson was killed by a shot fired from the field occupied by the 5th and 8th Battalions, West Yorkshire Regiment. Somehow live ammunition had been

5th Battalion Arrives at Guisborough Camp, 1909. [Tim Waddington]

**Postcard from Guisborough Camp 1909. (Front)
[Chris Noble]**
Showing a view of the camp.

**Parading the Colours at
Guisborough camp 1909. [YAM]**
*Colour Party includes Lt. Henry C.
Scott (front left), Lt. Donald P.
Mackay (front right). CSM F. Davies,
CSM F. Milner and Sgt. A. Erned.*

**Postcard from Guisborough Camp
1909 (Back). [Chris Noble]**
*Sent by Stanley Mellor to his wife
on 25th July 1909.*

5th Battalion at Aberystwyth Camp 1913. [Chloe Wilson]
Shows Harry Waddington ('Sergeant Wadd') far left.

Postcard Photo of Redcar Camp 1908.

loaded into a rifle instead of blanks. This indicated serious disciplinary and training issues and damaged further the reputation of both battalions, as well as the TF as a whole.

The camp held in Aberystwyth in 1913 was also eventful. There was a 25-mile route march and it was so hot that one man from the Leeds Rifles was said to have been driven to suicide. A mock invasion from Ireland involved the firing of live shells for the first time by the Divisional Artillery. Unfortunately a shell landed in a local farmyard, killing a pig.

The West Yorkshire Regiment

Notwithstanding their part-time status and relatively parochial outlook, the Terriers of the 5th Battalion were deeply proud of the history and culture of their regiment, originally titled the 14th Regiment of Foot. King George III had conferred on the regiment his motto *Nec Aspera Terrent* (difficulties be damned), and his own White Horse of Hanover motif in 1765. The Regimental Quick March was the song: 'Ca Ira', which was adopted after the 14th Regiment of Foot saw action against the French Revolutionary Army at Famars, near Valenciennes in French Flanders, in 1793.

These cultural icons were important in binding the men of the new Territorial battalions to their history, being owned by the veterans and new recruits alike. The white horse cap badge is prominent in many of the photographs of 1/5th Battalion soldiers which have survived. It is known that 'Ca Ira', was whistled by the men of the 1/5th Battalion on their arrival in France in April 1915, although it is doubtful that any of them understood (or even knew) the words.

The White Horse of Hanover. [Author]

Chapter 2

Mobilisation
(August 1914–April 1915)

'The local Battalion, as it may be termed,
want more Pals.'

Embodiment

On Monday, 27 July 1914, eight days before the United Kingdom entered the First World War, the 1st West Riding Infantry Brigade held its last peacetime annual camp, at Scarborough. The day before, at first light, a special train had collected E and F companies from Harrogate and Wetherby, H Company from Ripon, and G Company from Knaresborough, to take them to York. A, B, and C companies from York and D Company from Selby were waiting for them at York Station. United on the platform, the khaki-clad soldiers of the 5th Battalion were issued with their scarlet 'walking out' uniforms, and horses for the company commanders were loaded aboard the train for Scarborough. On arrival at Scarborough station at 8.30am, the battalion paraded and then marched to camp on the racecourse.

The days started at 5am, with reveille, followed by coffee and biscuits at 5.30am, adjutant's parade at 6am, breakfast (bacon and coffee) at 7.30am, and colonel's parade at 8.45am. There was a further inspection most days, of feet and rifles, for example. This was followed by manoeuvres in the morning and some free time in the afternoon, for games and letter writing. Dinner was meat, potatoes and tea. Two companies were detailed to night outpost duty from 8pm to 4am. Otherwise, bed was at 10pm.

The summer bank holiday fell on Monday, 3 August, one week into the annual camp, but the carefree atmosphere in Scarborough was now tempered by an underlying tension. The Archduke Franz Ferdinand had been assassinated in Sarajevo on 28 June and the holiday weekend was unusually quiet, with the threat of war discouraging the hordes of people who would usually have travelled to the coast for a day or two. Following a catastrophic series of events that culminated in the German invasion of Belgium, a proclamation was issued by the War Office on 3 August ordering territorial battalions to clear their training camps and 'embody' at their drill halls.

More than seventy years later Peter Wilson described events to author Lyn MacDonald as the 5th Battalion made its way to Scarborough Station:

I was marching behind the Colonel who was on his horse, and I had four men each side of me with fixed bayonets. Well, being Battalion Orderly Corporal I was carrying dispatches and my rifle was put in a truck, so that I was marching through Scarborough with these four armed men around me, while I was carrying the boxes. One old girl looked out of her door and she was standing there in her nightdress and she shouted out, "Yon little lad's off to prison."

By 8pm on 3 August, the 5th Battalion was ready to entrain for York. With patriotic airs sung by the crowds, accompanied by the battalion band on fife and drum, the Terriers left Scarborough on two trains, arriving in York in the early hours of 4 August.

That night Reservists and Territorial Battalions crossed the country in all directions. During the hours of darkness fifty troop trains passed through York Station, most without stopping, and all were cheered from the packed platforms. Miniature Union Flags were waved and thousands of hastily penned letters were flung from the carriage windows. Few had stamps but all were dutifully collected from the tracks and posted for payment on delivery.

On arrival at York, the city-based Terriers of the 5th Battalion were allowed to spend the first night of the 'world war' at home. The outlying companies were marched to billets at the Colliergate Drill Hall, and Park Grove School. They were observed by the Press to look remarkably fit. From York the battalion divided, with the outlying companies returning to their home drill halls for embodiment on the morning of 4 August. During the day, they were joined by those men of the 5th Battalion who had missed the annual camp and who had received formal notices, by telegram, to report at their local drill hall for embodiment, in their uniforms with a spare shirt and pair of socks.

Twelve hours after arriving back in York, with the 5th Battalion embodied, Colonel Wood received the order to call in the outlying companies from their local drill halls. At 11pm that night the British Empire declared war on Germany.

Mobilisation

The British Army mobilised on 5 August 1914; that morning the outlying companies of the 5th Battalion made their way back to York, with the 300 men of E and F companies arriving from Harrogate by special train. Edward Iredale and the Tadcaster contingent arrived at 8.30am. Camped outside the Colliergate Drill Hall, the Press noted that the Terriers were all carrying rifles, and two machine guns were seen to be in their possession. The *Yorkshire Herald* later reported that:

Large and excited crowds gathered round the barracks of the fifth Battalion of the West Yorkshire Regiment (Territorials) quite early this morning in anticipation of seeing the Battalion depart. Between 8 and 9.30am a small quantity of baggage was sent away and a quantity of fodder taken in for the horses. The utmost enthusiasm exists among the members of the force. They await orders.

The rumour was that they were heading for coastal defence duty at Fleetwood, Hull, or Tilbury. In fact, the 1st West Riding Brigade was to head 30 miles south of York, to Selby, on 10 August. Its orders were to guard the North Eastern Railway Bridge over the River Ouse, and the great arms magazine of the Northern Command. They were on one hour's notice to move in the event of a German invasion on the Yorkshire or Lincolnshire coastline. Within a year they would be at the front.

Things did not go very well at Selby. On arrival at its 'war station', there was some confusion as 5th Battalion set up camp in the wrong field. Inevitably, nerves were on edge, and trigger fingers twitchy. On 17 August, ten rounds were fired from the railway bridge into the funnel of the Ammonia, a Goole-based steamboat working its way up the Ouse. When challenged by the 5th Battalion sentry, the boat's captain did not respond. He stopped his engines but the craft continued to drift forward on the tide, causing the

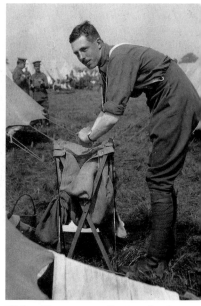

Walter Freeman washes in a bucket at Strensall in August 1914.

sentry to open fire, luckily with no casualties. In a separate incident, a G Company sentry fired four bullets into a wooden advertising hoarding 200 yards from the railway bridge, having mistaken the over-sized man in the poster for an enemy invader. Around this time the night train from King's Cross to Edinburgh was also fired at as it passed through Selby and suffered damage to its roof.

Apart from sentry duty, the 5th Battalion engaged in special training exercises and route marches, carrying packs with 100 rounds of ammunition. According to Brigade Staff Captain Charles Whitworth, this caused the men 'great discomfort'. By the end of the week, 112 men of the brigade were reported sick, forty with sore feet and the others with other assorted minor injuries.

The casual spirit and lack of discipline which had characterised the pre-war Territorial battalions (and embarrassed Haldane in the House of Lords) now became an operational concern. Captain Whitworth noted 'men not behaving in a very soldierly manner – measures taken to remedy this state of affairs'. This included 'trouble-makers' being combed out and sent back. The battalion was sifted for the unfit, as well as the obviously under-age, who were also rejected.

After a few days, the initial invasion scare eased and on 19 August the 5th Battalion returned to York to be re-equipped. Initially they slept in scattered billets around York, with G Company in the North Eastern Railway carriage works at Holgate, and others in Park Grove School or under canvas at Bustardthorpe on Knavesmire Common. Activities included practising emergency entrainment, firing at Zeppelins and attending divine service, the Archbishop of York officiating. Edward Iredale was visited by his

THE 5TH WEST YORKS. ON KNAVESMIRE.

NEW RECRUITS
A retired captain (well known in York) repeats as private
Standing (left to right)— W. Oxlade, R. Fernie, and R. Savage
Sitting—L. Briggs, and R. Hall

'The 5th West Yorks on Knavesmire'. [Yorkshire Herald]
Left to right: W. Oxlade, R. Fernie, R. Savage, L. Briggs, R Hall.

parents in York, and went home for the afternoon on Sunday, 30 August.

The following day, the 1st West Riding Brigade moved from its ad hoc billets in York to Strensall Camp, north of the city, where the 5th Battalion occupied the huts (which appear in the background of some group photos below), and the other battalions bivouacked. They would be based here for the autumn and winter of 1914-15.

Swelling the Ranks

When the 5th Battalion embodied on 3 August, it numbered 561 officers and men, equivalent to only 62 per cent of its establishment. A major feat of recruitment and organisation saw numbers increase to 814 by 2 September, then to 834 on 20 September, stabilising through the winter at about 950. The local media played its part in the recruitment drive. On Thursday, 6 August, with the war only two days old, the Harrogate Advertiser announced:

> HARROGATE COMPANIES, 5th WEST YORKS. REGIMENT,
> *Are open to recruiting for ex-soldiers, ex-Territorials, ex-Volunteers, age not to exceed 35. Must be physically fit: they will have to report to the DRILL HALL, COLLIERGATE YORK. Information about railway warrants can be obtained at the Harrogate Police Station any time after 11 a.m. August 6th. On August 12th the Harrogate Companies will be open to recruiting for men who have never served previously.*

This was aimed at men like Gordon Lund, who had been a career soldier. Born in 1877 in Plompton Mill, he had fought in South Africa with the King's Own Yorkshire Light Infantry (KOYLI) and also served in India. He left the army at some point between

37

Parade of National Reserves before leaving Harrogate. [Ackrill]

1911 and the outbreak of war, and was 37 years old in 1914 when he enlisted in the 5th Battalion.

Similar announcements were made in York, Ripon and Knaresborough, resulting in R. Fernie, formerly captain and adjutant in the 19th Hussars, re-enlisting as a private in the 5th Battalion. In Selby, Sergeant T. Kenny, local school attendance officer and ex-Regular colour sergeant, also joined the ranks.

The next step was the immediate call up of about 100 National Reservists (Class II) on 8 August. A complex creature, the National Reserve List generally comprised men under 50 years old with military experience who were fit for home defence duty. They included time-expired Territorials and ex-Regular soldiers, like George Elsworth.

George joined the Regulars of the 2nd Battalion, West Yorkshire Regiment in February 1885, at the age of 18. He served in South Africa and India, and was awarded one of only two gold medals by the town of Harrogate, for Royal service, in 1901. In 1914 he was 47 years old.

By 9 August, about 150 trained ex-soldiers like George had enlisted in the 5th Battalion. In many ways the presence of these older men helped to steady the raw recruits, but they also brought problems, as Captain Whitworth recorded on 9 August 1914:

Mobilization proceeding regularly – as far as serving Territorials go – but 5th W.Y. Regt. is having difficulty with National reservists. Many of these men are old NCOs of regular army and demand to be taken back in old grades – this is impossible – some are bad characters and are inclined to be insolent to and play the 'old soldier' on Territorial officers. This will soon be put in order.

'E' Company at the Majestic Hotel, Harrogate. [Ackrill]

Officers and NCOs of E Company at the Majestic Hotel, Harrogate. [Ackrill]
Left to right, front row: Unknown, CSM W.E Rathke, Lt. Walter H. Freeman, Capt. John C. Peters. 2nd Lt. Charles E. Foulds, Sgt John Sim, Sgt Swain.
Back row, Cpl E. Scott (4th from left) L/Cpl G. Elsworth (far right).

In addition to the Reservists and old soldiers, by 9 August, about seventy-five untrained new recruits had been posted to the 5th Battalion. These included men like Fred Kelley, who was 32 when war was declared. The son of a Wetherby Police sergeant, he was brought up in Otley before moving to Harrogate to work as a solicitor's clerk in 1903. He was well known in the town as player and then secretary and honorary treasurer of the Harrogate Old Boys Football Club, and a member of St Luke's Cricket Club. His father-in-law, Edwin Wright, had been a drummer with the 1st VB so the family link with the local Terriers was already strong when Fred enlisted in the 5th Battalion.

The Harrogate Defence League
On 8 August 1914, the Harrogate newspapers had carried Lord Kitchener's famous call for a mass citizens' army. Willing recruits were to report to the Drill Hall in Strawberry Dale, where Colour Sergeant H. Dalby of the 5th Battalion, a soldier with thirty years' experience, was in charge of proceedings.

Scenes outside Strawberry Dale Drill Hall on 4 August 1914. [Harrogate Advertiser]

That night, 2,000 local people attended an enthusiastic meeting of the Harrogate Civilian Rifle Club at the Winter Gardens. The *Advertiser* reported that with the town's mayor in the chair (Alderman J. Sheffield) supported by 'a number of influential gentlemen', the Harrogate Defence League was formed and Mr F. Kelley JP was appointed its commanding officer. Without any formal connection to the War Office, the County Association, or indeed the Army, the Harrogate Defence League was a group of leading citizens whose self-appointed role was to organise recruitment in the Army locally, and that meant the local E and F Companies of the 5th Battalion.

The approach of the Harrogate Defence League was simple, but effective, involving rousing speeches at public entertainment events and in the street. On at least one occasion Mr Kelley sent four motor cars draped in the flag of St George, with two loud speakers each, to hold impromptu open air meetings.

Mr Fred Kelley J.P. [Ackr Commanding Officer of the Harrogate Defence League

Formal enlistment for the 5th Battalion was based at York, so the Harrogate Defence League set up a local recruiting depot at Westminster Chambers, off Parliament Street, where prospective recruits were given a number. The process is unclear but it seems likely that they were then collected and taken to York by train or motor car after 12 August to attest formally, and to enlist at the Exhibition Buildings which had been set up as the general recruitment office. Here they would identify their preferred unit as the 5th Battalion West Yorkshire Regiment and report to the Colliergate Drill Hall, ten minutes' walk away.

Recruits Leaving Westminster Chambers. [Ackrill]
Fred Kelley's first batch leaving for York by motor car.

Harrogate Recruits in York. [Ackrill]
The caption in Ackrill's Harrogate War Souvenir 1914 reads: 'An interesting Photo of the Harrogate Pals Company, taken outside the Exhibition Buildings, York'.

Harrogate Territorials on Active Service. [Ackrill]

Perhaps surprisingly, Harrogate outstripped York as a recruiting centre for the 5th Battalion once war had been declared. By reference to casualty records it seems that by the mid-summer of 1915, about 35 per cent of its strength came from Harrogate, 30 per cent from York, 13 per cent from Selby with the remainder from elsewhere in the West Riding. This was a matter of significant civic pride in the spa town, and on 15 September 1914 the *Harrogate Advertiser* reported that:

> *The 5th Battalion of the West Yorkshire Regiment (our local Territorial Unit) has now been selected for foreign service... (it) has been brought up to full strength. The Harrogate Defence League has enrolled 136 for that. They have not had orders where to go as yet, but they are expected shortly. The men are drawing their 3s 1d per day.*

At the end of the year it was reported that:

> *The League has justified its existence... by the fact that it has now enlisted (at time of writing) 274 members for the Harrogate pals Companies.... Including the 200 or so pre-war Territorials of 'E' and 'F' Companies, it appears that Harrogate had by the end of the year supplied about 500 soldiers to the 5th Battalion.*

Recruitment in Pateley Bridge, Knaresborough, Ripon, and Selby

Immediately prior to the outbreak of war, the Pateley Bridge detachment of F Company contained only five Terriers. This changed swiftly as twenty local men joined or re-joined the battalion. One of these was Edwin Swires, who enlisted in York on 10 August 1914, aged 19. Wounded and gassed twice at Ypres in 1915, he was killed at the Battle of Passchendaele in October 1917.

In Knaresborough, 72-year-old Sergeant William Mawson recruited eighty men during August and September 1914. Recruiting meetings were held in Knaresborough, Ripon and Wetherby, where local grandees and representatives of the military deployed their best oratory. Fred Kelley often attended too, to push the cause of the 5th Battalion. On 15 August, at a public meeting in Knaresborough, so many attended that the meeting had to be repeated outside the hall at the Market Cross.

Some local rivalry is discernible behind the rhetoric of the recruitment drive. In November 1914, the *Harrogate Herald* noted a degree of resentment in Knaresborough.

It has been considered an injustice to the town that so many who have volunteered and have enlisted at the Harrogate Barracks or recruiting stations,

Pateley Bridge Territorials at Strensall Camp York 1914. [Colin Chadwick]
Left to right, back row: Walter Bradbury, Rowland Light, Henry Walker, W. Richmond, Edward Stoney.
Third Row: Edwin Swires, Robert Wilmot, W. Gibson, William Chadwick, James Fieldhouse (Ripon).
Second Row: E. Richmond, J. Storey, Thomas Kirkbright, T. Thackery, H. Storey.
Front Row: R. Brown, Harry Waring, Herbert Heaton, B. Calvert.
Standing left, Robert Bland; Right, George Raw.

have had their names entered as among the recruits from Harrogate instead of from Knaresborough.

The article failed to note that Harrogate was suffering the same fate in respect of its local recruits who were travelling to York to enlist. These included Francis Yates, who was 21 when war was declared. The *Harrogate Advertiser* later summed up his talents by reporting that:

He was a very popular employee at the Kursaal up to the outbreak of war when he enlisted a year last August. He had been at the Kursaal for ten years, starting as programme boy and working his way to be assistant stage manager. Yates gained the trust of those whom he served and he was looked upon as a most intelligent worker. He showed an aptitude for music and applied himself to learning the cello, and was making excellent progress with his studies and bid fair to become a really capable player. He played the bells in the orchestra when such works as Tchaikovsky's "1812" were rendered. He travelled with the Harrogate municipal orchestra, when three or four years earlier the orchestra, under Mr Julian Clifford, went on tour. Yates was a well-built young man who could hold his own in athletics. He played for several local clubs at Association football, including West Park, and was also a useful cricketer, and in fact he was useful in all outdoor games.

In addition to advertisements and stirring speeches at public meetings, there were other enticements to enlist. Peter Wilson was paid an allowance by Beckett's Bank for the duration of his service. On 22 August 1914, the *Rothwell Courier and Times* reported that in Tadcaster, John Smith's Brewery: '*intend paying 10s. per week to the wives of Reservists and Territorials in their employment who are on active service, and 2s. for each child, while 10s. per week will be paid to the dependants of unmarried Reservists.*'

Recruitment in York
The 5th Battalion had more competition in York where there were a number of local military regiments to join. Family links counted for a lot, though. For example, Charles Boldison joined the 5th Battalion West Yorkshire Regiment because his brother Arthur had served for seven years and was now a lance corporal. Arthur Mason joined the 5th Battalion because his brother was already serving as a corporal; both were Rowntree's employees.

Overall, military recruitment in York started briskly, at hundreds of men per day, and then dropped off sharply by mid-August 1914, which perhaps explains why Harrogate men soon formed the majority of the 5th Battalion's strength. The Lord Mayor of York, Henry Rhodes Brown, had set up a recruiting committee in early August 1914, although from the start it lacked the dynamism and élan of the Harrogate Defence League. In late August a public meeting at the York Guildhall considered forming a York Pals Battalion, along the lines proposed by Lord Derby in Liverpool, but there was a lack of appetite for this and the proposal was rejected.

Arthur Mason. *[Yorkshire Herald]*

Charles Mason. *[Yorkshire Herald]*

Charles Boldison.
[Yorkshire Herald]

On 26 August 1914, the *Yorkshire Herald* reported an average of only thirty-four recruits per day in the city, and that 93 per cent of these came from outside the boundaries. There are no background statistics, or any explanation of the methodology to allow a modern re-appraisal of this figure, but there is no doubt that substantial numbers of recruits from Harrogate, Knaresborough, Ripon and Pateley Bridge took the King's shilling in York, and many of these joined the 5th Battalion.

Imperial Service

Appointed Secretary of State for War on 5 August 1914, Lord Kitchener knew that a mass citizen army was needed to support the relatively small BEF on the Western Front, in what was to be a long and brutal conflict. His 'New Army' would take time to recruit and train, so the Territorial Force was needed to help plug the gap by freeing up British troops overseas, or by going to the Western Front itself. This was a leap of faith for Kitchener, given the well-documented inefficiency of the under-resourced TF. There was also a legal issue as Territorial soldiers could not be ordered to serve outside the United Kingdom without signing an agreement to do so. On 10th August it was decreed that a unit could only be designated for 'foreign service' if 80 per cent of its officers and men signed the agreement, and ten days later the required proportion was reduced to 60 per cent.

On 11 August 1914, the commanders of all Territorial units were asked how many of their officers and men would volunteer, if needed. Captain Whitworth records that in the 1st West Riding Brigade, about half the officers and only 15 per cent of the other ranks were prepared to go. He was shocked by this lack of enthusiasm, and particularly critical of the 5th Battalion, observing that 'The two Harrogate Companies showed up very badly.'

Local Officers and NCOs of the 5th West Yorks at Strensall. [Ackrill]
Left to right, back row: Unknown, John Sim, Unknown, Ernest Scott, Unknown, Gordon Lund, K. Newstead.
Middle Row: Howard Horner, Pierce Mandeville, Cecil E. Wood, Donald P. MacKay, Alwyne P. Dale, Fred Raynor.
Front Row: Chris Topham, Harry Westerman, Arthur Calverley, William Wilkinson. [As identified by the author]

On 20 August Colonel Wood reported a slight improvement, as by then twelve officers and 118 other ranks of the 5th Battalion had formally agreed to serve overseas, but this still compared badly to the 6th Battalion which had 306 volunteers. The 7th and 8th battalions had 226 and 202 volunteers respectively. Brigadier General McFarlan decided that if any battalion was needed at the Western Front, the 6th should go, with its ranks made up of soldiers from the other battalions who had volunteered individually for foreign service. This was embarrassing for the 1st West Riding Infantry Brigade and the 5th Battalion in particular. The County Association therefore decided to get involved, under pressure from the War Office, and on 1st September its secretary, Brigadier General Mends, addressed the assembled battalions of the 1st West Riding Brigade at Strensall. According to Whitworth:

> He pointed out the urgent need for more men to back up the gallant efforts of
> our expeditionary Force [and] drew attention to the fact that in the 3rd W.R.
> Inf. Bde. all the Bns had volunteered whereas in this Brigade only one Bn (6th

46

W.Y.) had done so as yet & asked the soldiers whether the friends who came to visit them in camp had come to see men ready to sacrifice themselves for their country or boys playing at soldiering. He left it to the men to turn over in their minds what he had said.

This harsh rhetoric had the desired effect, for the very next day Colonel Wood reported to Brigadier General McFarlan that 710 out of 814 officers and men of the 5th Battalion had now volunteered. The battalion was therefore qualified for foreign service and honour was saved. Within nine months they would be going to the Western Front to hold the line in France and Flanders while Kitchener's New Army was still pulling itself together ready for the 'big push' in the summer of 1916.

Home Service

When the 5th Battalion formally volunteered for foreign service on 2 September 1914, more than 100 of its members had yet to sign the agreement, whilst others would prove unsuitable for active service overseas following the 'radical weeding out of the unfit' planned by Captain Whitworth. Fraser Skirrow explains in *Massacre on the Marne* that one young officer, Second Lieutenant Arthur Green, was upset that his father refused him permission to volunteer. Private Edward Iredale avoided any such inconvenience by claiming that he was 19 years old, when he was only 17, on 16 September 1914. As such he was passed fit for active service overseas.

The 'foreign service' men needed to be separated from those who would be staying at home, so that equipment and training could be organised efficiently, with resources focused on the men heading to the front. Within hours of volunteering, Colonel Wood was notified that his battalion would be divided into a 'service corps' and a 'home defence corps', preliminary to the formation of a shadow reserve battalion in due course. Work started on dividing the 5th Battalion in two on 11 September. They were

1/5th Battalion Band.
The photograph shows the 1/5th band at an unknown location, under the probable direction of Bandmaster Sergeant Arthur Helps.

known as the 'first line' and 'second line' respectively. On 15 September the *Harrogate Advertiser* announced that:

> *A new regiment of reserves in the 5th West Yorkshire has been started, for which the Harrogate Defence League has already taken 36 men. Other names are wanted as Mr Fred Kelley and his band of supporters are hoping to form another "Pals" company for this reserve regiment.*

The 5th Reserve Battalion was formally created on 28 September 1914 under Lieutenant Colonel Bottomley, who transferred from the 6th Battalion to take command. At least eight officers (and an equivalent number of NCOs) transferred from the 5th Battalion to its second line, to form a core. They had considerable experience and were steeped in the history of the 5th Battalion. Captain Bower and Captain Pearson had both served as company commanders with the 1st VB, and Harold Pearson had fought with Captain Wood in South Africa. Captain Alwyne P. Dale, York solicitor, and officer formerly commanding the Knaresborough Company, also transferred to the Reserve as he was deemed medically unfit for foreign service.

The Reserve Battalion moved from Strensall to Harrogate on 24 November 1914, where they became known locally as the 'Beechwood Boys', after the hotel where they were billeted.

Beechwood Hotel. [Ackrill]
The Beechwood Hotel no longer exists.

On 7 January 1915 the 'double company' system was adopted whereby the 5th Reserve Battalion was converted into a structural replica of its parent. At the end of the month both battalions were restructured again, from eight companies to four (plus headquarters detachment) which was more suitable for battlefield organisation. Commanded by a major or a captain, each company was sub-divided into four platoons numbered 1–16, under a lieutenant or second lieutenant (subaltern), and eight sections, each commanded by an NCO.

On 4 February 1915 the 5th Battalion was renamed the 1/5th Battalion, and the Reserve became the 2/5th Battalion. A second Reserve, or 'third line', was by then already in existence and was renamed the 3/5th Battalion. The primary role of the 2/5th and 3/5th Battalions was to supply drafts of men to replace losses suffered by the 1/5th (until the 2/5th Battalion went to the Western Front in its own right in January 1917). This became more important after the 1/5th arrived at the front in April 1915, and soldiers began to be killed, wounded, and to come home on leave, or to train for their commissions.

A hefty proportion of these replacements were Harrogate men recruited in the autumn of 1914 and throughout 1915. Among the first to transfer across were William Jennings, Joseph Wrather, Herbert Calvert, Fred Fairburn, James Robinson, and George Mackridge; all were recruited by the Harrogate Defence League. They were slightly older, on average, than those who stepped forward on the outbreak of war, and generally had family responsibilities which may have disinclined them to volunteer during the initial clamour.

The first draft went across from the 2/5th Battalion in Harrogate to the 1/5th Battalion at Strensall on 4 January 1915. More followed, so that by 14 January 190 men had been transferred. In March and April a further fifty-nine went across, and then on 29 June 1915, ninety-nine men were sent from the 2/5th Battalion to the 1/5th Battalion which was by then camped at Proven, outside Ypres. Harrogate led the campaign to replace these newly trained men, with the York authorities following. In June 1915, a hundred Terriers of the 2/5th Battalion toured the spa town to find new recruits and the *Harrogate Herald* carried the following notice:

YOUR COMRADES ARE COMING
FOR YOU

RECRUITS URGENTLY
REQUIRED
FOR
5th BTN. THE PRINCE OF WALES
OWN
(WEST YORKSHIRE) REGIMENT.

The *Harrogate Advertiser* reported that 600 locals were already fighting at the front with the West Yorkshires and that more were needed, announcing that: '*the local Battalion, as it may be termed, want more Pals*'.

*Harrogate Defence
League Newspaper
Notice.*
*Fred Kelley used every
means to attract recruits
to the 5th Battalion.*

As part of the campaign, Lieutenant G.S. Chadwick addressed a crowd in James Street, where a French Boy Scout called Jean Dolfus drilled a squad of recruits. In the evening he did so again at the Kursaal. The men from the 2/5th were then entertained to dinner by the mayor at Grove Road School and paraded on the Stray before departing with thirty new Harrogate recruits. On 28 July, W.H Breare in the *Harrogate Herald* claimed that sixty men had been recruited in a single day in Harrogate as part of the campaign. He went on to say that:'we soon shan't have a man to prop a lamp post.'

Training for War in Strensall and York

During September 1914 Colonel Wood attempted to instil some fitness and discipline into the disparate ranks of old Territorials and new recruits of the 5th Battalion. An 11-mile route march was attempted in stifling heat on 3 September, with 106 men of the brigade falling out, twenty-one of whom were deemed to be 'malingerers'. Captain Whitworth noted haughtily that: 'This incident shows that as yet discipline is only skin deep. The physique of a large proportion of the men leaves much to be desired.'

A week later the exercise was repeated, when only four dropped out. Entrainment and other schemes were practised, with the officers who had served in South Africa showing the value of experience in battlefield command. The basics of combat were also taught, as hundreds of new recruits were trained in musketry, whilst machine-gun sections practised on the range.

All ranks were vaccinated against typhoid, but an infected sample incapacitated the whole brigade for days as soldiers were laid low with headaches and painful sores. Forty-eight hour leave was granted to the sick to ease the strain on the MO.

Leave was also granted for other pressing reasons. On 5 September Lieutenant John Foxton was allowed forty-eight hours to get married at Selby, to his austere looking

5th W. Yorks Machine Gun. [Janet Lea]
Undated postcard showing the machine gun section of the 5th battalion.

Wedding Party At Selby. [Yorkshire Herald]
Left to right: Lt. John Peters, Mr H Foxton (Best Man), Lt Arthur Gaunt, Lt. John Foxton, Captain Henry C. Scott, the Bride Miss Edith Poskitt in the centre.

wartime bride, Miss Poskitt. They spent a very brief honeymoon in Scarborough before Foxton returned to Strensall. On 19 September Colour Sergeant Birbeck got married and Private M. Franklin 'tied the knot' ten days later.

The late autumn and winter was mainly spent in brigade exercises on the Knavesmire and at Copmanthorpe. This included large amounts of what Edward Iredale calls 'trenching'. In October and November the 5th Battalion spent at least two

5th Battalion at Birk Crag Rifle Range. [Illustrated History]
Birk Crag Rifle Range was on the western outskirts of Harrogate.

Knaresborough Platoon at Strensall. [Michael Wilson]
Front row left to right: Walter Malthouse, Peter Wilson, William Mumford [Identified by author].
Also includes Francis Peacock (back row far right) and Bert Mumford.

short periods training on the Stray and at Birk Crag Range in Harrogate, billeted in the Majestic Hotel. For entertainment they went to the pictures at the Kursaal and the Empire. There was a series of invasion scares in early November, and on 16 December 1914 they were alarmed to hear the shelling of Scarborough by the German navy.

It seems that Colonel Wood had achieved some success in his training programme by 11 November, when Brigadier General McFarlane inspected the battalion and commented within Captain Whitworth's hearing that there had been an improvement since he had last seen them. Three weeks later Major General Baldock inspected the battalion as to fitness for active service.

He returned again in the New Year to observe night-time trench digging and repair. The battalion trained hard in miserable weather, including snow, with early morning parades and physical jerks, followed by lectures. They also carried out route marches in pitch darkness.

By early February a degree of efficiency was achieved, and a weekly half-holiday was granted by General Baldock for battalion sports and leisure activities. Captain Whitworth may not have agreed, dryly observing that this was 'by order of the W.Y.R. Division who are evidently arriving at the opinion that all work and no play makes Jack a dull boy.'

Coastal Duty and Embarkation

On 24 February 1915, the 1st West Riding Brigade was detailed to coastal defence duty. The 1/5th Battalion headed for Sutton-on-Sea on the Lincolnshire coast, where they spent the days scanning the horizon for evidence of impending invasion and monitoring the locals for signs of espionage. A series of strange incidents occurred, with lights in the night sky later turning out to be Zeppelins heading in from the Belgian coast.

Trench digging continued but there is no evidence of training in the use of the weapons which would become an essential part of trench warfare, such as the rifle grenade or trench mortar. The 1/5th Battalion were equipped and trained to occupy trenches but little more, and this would not change until 1916.

Regimental sports were held on the shore for relaxation. These carried their own dangers, and the 1/5th suffered its first death on active service, when Private Smith Fryer almost drowned at sea and was saved by his comrade, 16-year-old Edwin Tattersfield. Sadly, Smith did not recover and died at home on 7 April 1915. Tattersfield survived the war and was discharged on 8 August 1919.

On 31 March 1915, Colonel Wood learnt that the 1/5th Battalion would soon receive orders for the Western Front. The excitement was palpable as the battalion proceeded to Gainsborough on 9 April where the West Riding Division was already concentrating. Kit was checked and renewed and mules arrived from South Africa with new limbers to supplement battalion transport. Further medicals were held, with inoculations for all ranks, before the journey to Folkestone.

On 13 April, Colonel Wood received a telegram from the Lord Mayor of York wishing the battalion well. He replied as follows:

Officers and men of the 1st 5th West Yorkshire Regiment thank you and citizens of York for your good wishes, which we greatly appreciate. Please also thank everyone for their kindness to the Battalion when stationed at York. All ranks will do their best to maintain the glorious traditions of the City of York and the West Yorkshire Regiment.

The transport and machine-gun sections went ahead, embarking at Southampton on 14 April. They sailed on the SS *Archimedes*, arriving at Le Havre, and moving north to meet the rest of the battalion at Boulogne on 16 April.

There had been no time for embarkation leave, and there was only limited room for civilian well-wishers on 15 April, as the main part of the battalion left Gainsborough on two trains heading for Lincoln, Cambridge, then Liverpool Street Station. Along the route, flag waving locals saluted them as they steamed past. The 1/5th Battalion arrived in Folkestone the same evening for the short sea crossing to Boulogne aboard the SS *Invicta*, escorted by two destroyers.

Chapter 3

Into Battle
(April–June 1915)

'We were all friends in the Territorials'

Disembarkation

Late on Thursday, 15 April 1915, the 26 officers and 906 other ranks of the 1/5th Battalion paraded on the Boulogne dock-side and marched off through the dark streets of the town to St Martin's rest camp where they arrived just after dawn. Nearly twenty-four hours since they had last woken from sleep, the men were paraded again then dismissed to the vast field kitchens of the camp for a breakfast of bully beef, hard biscuits and tea. The remainder of the first full day in France was spent resting in camp, washing, eating and in excited preparation for the next leg of their journey to the front.

Early on 17 April, the 1/5th Battalion paraded, had breakfast and then marched four miles in the early spring heat to Pont de Brique station just outside Boulogne. Followed by French vendors, they bought oranges for 1d each. At Pont de Brique they boarded a troop train headed due east towards the front. Officers' horses and baggage were loaded aboard, and with forty-three men to each cattle truck meant for only forty, the whole process was not complete until about 11.30am. When the overloaded trains eventually rumbled out of the station, their destination was the town of Merville. The 70 kilometre train journey took more than eight-and-a-half hours and on arrival the 1/5th Battalion had to march a further two miles to the sleepy settlement of Le Sart, where they were to spend the next few nights on straw in local barns.

The battalion was now only 15 miles from the front line, where it ran between Armentières and Neuve Chapelle, in the Fleurbaix sector. The general feeling was one of excitement and a desire to get to grips with the enemy; the men of the 1/5th would not have to wait long to see their first battle.

The West Riding Infantry Division (to be renamed the 49th (West Riding) Infantry Division in May 1915), incorporating the 1st West Riding Brigade (to be renamed 146 Infantry Brigade), was to have an active role in the next big attack, planned for 8 May 1915. They had been brought to Merville to help outnumber the enemy in this sector and to support the battle-hardened 7th and 8th divisions in the main assault on Aubers Ridge. Merville was strategically important as the main railhead for troops arriving in the Fleurbaix sector and it had already received the close attention of enemy artillery.

The town's church was a pile of rubble and few streets looked as they had before the war started. Farms had been raked by gunfire and as a result the 1/5th Battalion were billeted in the remains of wrecked barns, using open latrines. This amused the local peasantry who had stayed despite the danger, simply because they had nowhere else to go.

Fauquissart

The newly arrived Terriers were keen to experience the front line for themselves and on 19 April veterans of the 7th Division came out of the front line to accompany a party of eight subalterns and twelve NCOs into the firing trench. The Terriers were collected from Le Sart and led eastwards along lanes of corduroy track covering muddy fields, which led to the trench network itself around the village of Fauquissart. They spent twenty-four hours at the front where they could observe the German front line and the village of Aubers about a mile beyond. Less visible were the German snipers and machine gunners, hidden all over the ridge, with a good view of the British front line and support positions.

Lieutenant Colonel Wood and the other battalion officers took their turn in the front line on 20 April, leaving the Adjutant, Captain Sidney Wilkinson, in charge at Le Sart. As author of the battalion war diary, Wilkinson recorded that the officers found their initial experience of the firing line to be 'instructive'. He was a regular soldier and a Cambridge graduate, who had transferred into the 5th Battalion as adjutant in February 1913, and as such he was keen not to seem overawed by the prospect of engagement with the enemy.

Fauquissart April 1915. [Sketch Map 3]
Showing the E Lines and F Lines positions with altitude in metres.

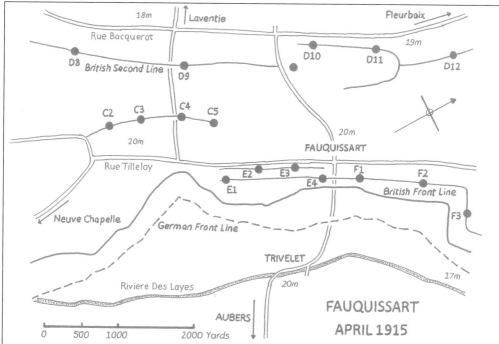

Fauquissart Trenches from the Air. [Tempest]
Taken from a balloon, this photograph shows at the bottom the Fauquissart cross roads where E Lines and F Lines meet, looking south east towards the bend in the road at Trivelet. The British and German trench lines are clearly visible. Their lines can also be discerned from modern aerial photographs at certain times of year.

On 22 April the battalion moved its base from Le Sart to within 11 miles of the front line at La Gorgue, near Estaires. This gave easier access to the front and ten platoons (up to 480 other ranks) were taken forward for instruction by the Grenadier Guards. The next day a further ten platoons saw the front line, at Fauquissart. Within a fortnight of disembarkation at Boulogne, all officers and men of the 1/5th had experienced at least twenty-four hours in the front line under supervision.

Into the Trenches

Fauquissart was a very quiet sector in the British line where, it was said, there was 'nothing to shoot at but rats'. The countryside seemed undisturbed as bodies of dead soldiers were hidden by the grass and flowers which still grew in no man's land. Fleurbaix was regarded by the General Staff as a nursery for newly arrived troops to acclimatise to the front line.

However, on their second night the peace was shattered as the 1/5th Battalion was shelled for the first time. It was a terrifying experience for the newly arrived Terriers, but made little impression on their veteran escort from the Border Regiment. The soldiers had their own shorthand for describing the different types of artillery ammunition. 'Whizz Bangs' were fired from a German 77mm field gun. 'Moaning Minnies' and 'Rum Jars' were 25cm Minenwerfer (trench mortars) which sent large containers of explosive spinning across no man's land. 'J.J.s', were large shells named after Jack Johnson, the world champion heavyweight boxer.

Shells contained high explosive or shrapnel, described as 'bullets'. In April 1915 British soldiers had yet to be issued with steel helmets, whilst in the Fleurbaix sector there were relatively few dug-outs for protection. Some of the fire trenches had been dug in late 1914 and repaired many times since. Due to the high water table in this bleak part of the Pas de Calais, they were often little deeper than shallow ditches at their foremost point and a man of average height could not stand up straight without exposing his head and shoulders to enemy snipers. Soldiers were instructed to remove the wire from caps, to make them less of a clear target for snipers.

Captain Lansdale was an early victim to a German sniper, as described by Peter Wilson to Lyn MacDonald:

We went more or less straight into the trenches in front of Aubers Ridge, about ten days before the battle. Of course it was all quiet then compared to what came later, with just the odd bit of shelling and sniping, and we went in batches to get accustomed to it. The very first night we were there my company commander, Captain Lansdale, was shot in the neck. He hadn't been in the trenches half an hour and out he went! He wasn't killed or even very badly wounded, though I remember we were horrified seeing him streaming with blood. I wasn't far away when it happened, but it could only have been a flesh wound. Anyway, out he went, and that was our first casualty. Strangely enough, he came back several months later, again as our Company Commander, and he hadn't been in the trenches another night when he was shot in the shoulder! We couldn't believe it! His total service on the trenches didn't even amount to a day and he ended up with two wound stripes! We thought it was a great joke the second time it happened – of course we were a bit blasé by then – but the first time he never got anywhere near the battle of Aubers Ridge. We had another Company Commander for that show.

Arrival and departure from the front line usually took place after dark to avoid attracting enemy fire. Screens had been erected at Fauquissart to hide troop movements along the roads behind the front line, but as time went by it became clear that the enemy had sound intelligence, allowing the German artillery and snipers to give the 1/5th a 'hot' reception every time it went forward. Ration parties carrying food and other items up to the firing line in front of Fauquissart were clearly in sight of German snipers in Trivelet, who molested them daily. Occasional respite was gained by requesting that E Battery of the West Riding Artillery send over some 18-pounder shells, which forced the German snipers to keep their heads down.

Colonel Wood was frustrated by his inability to retaliate in kind, because the 1/5th lacked sniper rifle sights and binoculars. Wood wrote to his brother and the father of Captain Donald Mackay (one of his company commanders) to ask for their help. They jointly placed a notice in the *Yorkshire Herald*, requesting financial assistance.

ADDITIONAL EQUIPMENT FOR 1ST/5TH WEST YORKS
'Sir – A letter has been received from Lt. Col CE Wood, commanding 1st/5th West Yorkshire Regiment, in France, asking for 40 magnifying sights for rifles and 40 field glasses or telescopes.

Feeling sure the friends of the Battalion will wish these requirements to be supplied immediately, and after consultation with the West Riding Territorial Association, the sights have been ordered and we appeal for gifts or loans of field glasses and donations to pay for the sights and such glasses as may have to be purchased.'

We have ascertained that the cost of the sights and field glasses would be upwards of £300.

Field glasses and donations may be sent to either of us.
Yours obediently
John Wood
Donald S. Mackay

The battalion diary records few successful attempts at sniping over the following months. They also still lacked training in basic weaponry (some of it defensive) such as rifle grenades and trench mortars, which were now arriving at the front. The Yorkshiremen would have to train themselves using trial and error. In the absence of proper grenades they made their own bombs out of jam tins and gun cotton.

The 1/5th Battalion in the Front Line

On 27 April the West Riding Division formally took over responsibility for the IV Corps front line from the 7th Division. Major General Baldock ordered the 1st West Riding Brigade, including the 1/5th Battalion, to occupy the forward positions around Fauquissart known as E Lines. The battalion machine-gun section went with them. Platoons from the three other West Riding battalions of 146 Brigade took up supporting positions behind.

For the first time without the chaperones of the 7th Division, and on their own, soldiers of the 1/5th Battalion were directly facing the enemy across 180 yards of flat level ground, sodden and intersected by drainage ditches, some of which were 6 feet wide and 4 feet deep.

Major General T.S. Baldock.
[Laurie Magnus]

Fortunately, the enemy did not seek to take advantage of the front line being held by new arrivals, and the only casualties during this period were two men sick and one horse dead from pneumonia.

Lance Corporal T.H. Doherty, describing his unit as '5th West Yorks Territorials – York Detachment' proudly wrote to the *Yorkshire Herald* to confirm he had been under fire. The *Herald* reported that an anonymous Selby Territorial of the 1/5th Battalion had already had a narrow escape when his rifle was *'smashed by a (sniper's) shot'*, although he himself had escaped unscathed.

On 1 May the battalion marched back to billets in Estaires for the night, then the next day to Bac St Maur, near Fleurbaix where the new divisional headquarters had been set up by Major General Baldock. The billets here were said to be 'highly insanitary', which was disappointing for soldiers who had just spent their first few days in the front line.

Rest and Training

Out of the front line trenches, the Terriers slept under a single blanket on the straw covered floor of a ramshackle barn, or under the stars in good weather. Letters from home began to arrive from Tuesday, 20 April, and this lifted the spirits which had started to dip after the initial excitement of having reached the front before the war was all over. Packages of food and titbits were also received by the lucky ones. Invariably, food was shared within the platoon, including eggs, butter, Bovril and chocolate. Bread, wine and beer were available, at a cost, from the locals.

Church parade was held by the battalion chaplain on Sundays, usually in a barn at Bac St Maur. Rifles were stacked outside, although soldiers wore their bandoliers and kept their respirators close, just in case. Afterwards, cigarettes were distributed to the men by the Padre, Reverend Whincup (informally named 'Woodbine Willie'), and then there would be more letter and postcard writing.

Training continued where it had left off in England amounting to little more than exercise and drill. Route marches took place in the hot sun and intermittent rain. Shirts would itch and boots form blisters. Smoking and talking, singing and whistling would be allowed from time to time to make the journey pass quicker. During the march and when resting, soldiers occasionally watched air duels between the Royal Flying Corps and German flyers. These were matters of wonder and awe at a time when few soldiers had seen an aeroplane. Shells exploding at a distance provided the constant soundtrack.

At rest stops and around camp, French civilians engaged in pidgin conversations, exchanging news and gossip, including sketchy anecdotes about the conduct of the war in general. It was known at the time that there were thirty-six British divisions on active service, and that these were supplemented by Colonial troops, including the Indian Corps which had been involved in the fighting at Neuve Chapelle. News also filtered through from Gallipoli and even the Eastern Front.

The Battle Plan

The forthcoming attack on Aubers Ridge was intended by General Sir Douglas Haig to put right the failed attack at Neuve Chapelle, two months earlier. A precise artillery bombardment was planned to punch a hole in the German defences at Rouge Bancs. The infantry would drive through this narrow gap to Fromelles, then on to the Haute

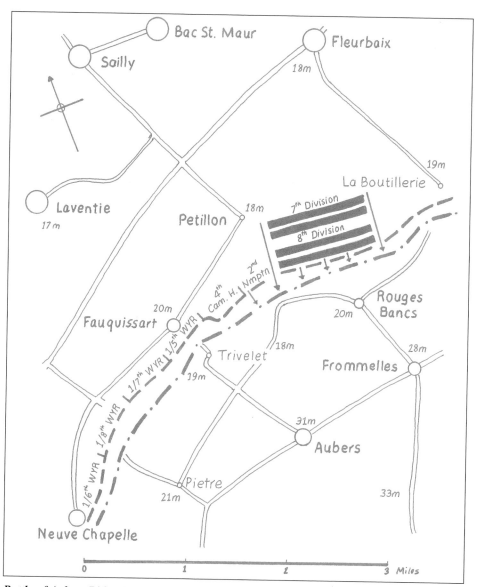

Battle of Aubers Ridge 9 May 1915. [Sketch Map 4]
Showing the position of the 1/5th Battalion relative to the main attack on Rouge Bancs and Fromelles by the 7th and 8th Divisions, and the 2nd Northamptons.

Deûle Canal, leaving the way clear to an advance on the strategically critical town of Lille.

The plan was hopelessly over-ambitious, given the lack of artillery ammunition which eventually gave rise to the 'shell scandal'. There was no real element of surprise as troop build-up had been fairly obvious to the enemy who worked hard to reinforce and strengthen front line defences, including thicker barbed wire entanglements, concrete bunkers and wider, deeper, breastworks to protect the front line trenches.

These were much more impressive than they had been during the battle of Neuve Chapelle, with breastworks heightened and the sandbag wall made wider and stronger. Machine-gun posts were set behind the German front line, and in shallow trenches in no man's land, to produce deadly enfilade fire at knee height, creating a virtually impassable killing zone in front of the German wire. Critically, the number of German troops present had increased by 50 per cent since the Battle of Neuve Chapelle and there was nowhere near enough heavy artillery to destroy the German front line defenders.

Preparing for Battle

On the night of 4 May the 1/5th Battalion was once more detailed to occupy the firing trenches at 'E Lines', the other battalions of 146 West Riding Infantry Brigade again behind them in supporting positions. This time the enemy was aware of the front-line build up, and the march into the trenches was affected by heavy shelling and machine-gun fire which caused the Yorkshiremen to march bent double. There was also a thunderstorm which drenched them and caused the guides from the departing 25 Infantry Brigade to lose their way, leaving the 1/5th Battalion standing waiting at the rendezvous, dripping wet. On arrival at the front line trenches they crammed into dugouts to sleep in full kit and equipment. Combined with humid conditions, this storm helped turn the trenches into a muddy morass.

The soldiers of the 1/5th Battalion occupied this position for eight days without a break. Significantly, it put them in the front line 800 yards to the right of the 'grand

1/5th Battalion Headquarters at Fauquissart, 1915. [Ilustrated History]
Lieutenant Colonel Cecil Wood is seated on an upturned tub in front of his HQ. The hole in the roof was probably used for observation. Surgeon Major Stoddart wears a Red Cross arm band. Between Wood and Stoddart stands Major William Oddie. [Identified by the author]

slam' attack on Rouge Bancs. To the south the French artillery bombardment could be heard loud and clear, preparing for their co-ordinated assault on Vimy Ridge and Notre Dame de Lorette.

There was much to do in preparation for battle. The 1/5th Battalion was heavily occupied for days repairing the communication trenches through which the first waves of attacking 7th and 8th Division troops would pass on their way to the grid of new assembly trenches, just behind the jumping off trench, which also needed to be dug.

It was also necessary to maintain the appearance of normality to prevent the enemy suspecting that a major assault was in the offing. This involved occasional harassing attacks. On 7 May rifle fire was kept up on enemy trenches and trench mortar bombs were sent over by the 1/5th Battalion. These were hopelessly inaccurate, with only one doing some damage to the enemy trench parapet. In return, there was a direct hit from an enemy shell which collapsed a trench parapet wall and two German aeroplanes strafed the British trenches.

Lance Corporal E. Scott. [Ackrill]

That morning Ernest Scott was wounded, as reported by the *Harrogate Advertiser*:

This was about half past four in the morning. Rations had been brought in during the night, and they were issuing them to the sections. A shell came over about thirty yards from Scott, and that did no damage. Then another shrapnel shell burst near-by and Scott received a bullet through the cheek which injured the jaw at the back. He could with the aid of a looking glass see his back teeth through the hole in his cheek. He had his wound dressed at the dressing station and was sent down to the Territorial Hospital at Estairs. From there he was taken on to the Merville Hospital, and it was at Merville that he met the Canadian wounded just from the charge during which the Canadians covered themselves with glory. He was next taken on to Boulogne. He left the latter place at 3 o'clock in the afternoon and arrived in England at 5 o'clock. The Hospital Train carrying them on leaving the ship went on to London, where half the train with serious cases was left, and they were sent to Birmingham, where he remained three weeks. At the end of that time he was granted furlough, and came home to Harrogate. Scott has also been troubled with Rheumatism. Scott, who lives in Bolton Street, Harrogate, worked for JW Rudd, joiner and contractor, up to the outbreak of war. His furlough was up last Thursday.

Labours also included breaking up night time German wiring parties by firing at them in no man's land. According to Sergeant Charles Volans, at 2:20am every night the whole battalion would turn out to fire furiously across no man's land, in the expectation of preventing any night time assault by the enemy.

Colonel Wood also sought to obtain intelligence on the state and strength of the enemy by sending out his own listening parties. This was done at the dead of night, with an NCO and a few soldiers getting within 100 yards of the enemy lines. Peter Wilson said it was a 'terrible business' with British and German star shells lighting the sky and rifle fire aimed into no man's land from both sides. The star shells also showed up the bodies of Scottish troops still hanging on the wire from the Battle of Neuve Chapelle, and the soaked ground was laden with the unburied corpses of their comrades.

The Battle of Aubers Ridge

As night fell on 7 May, the enemy artillery sent over a few shells, which had little effect except to blow some sandbags off the trench parapet. Then news came through that the attack planned for the following day had been postponed twenty-four hours. This late change of plan was caused primarily by the approach of adverse weather conditions including mist, an easterly wind favourable to German gas, and light rain. The postponement came too late to stop the first wave of the 8th Division entering the support trenches, where they lay awake until the next morning.

Contrary to expectation, 8 May turned out to be a fine day. German spotter aircraft were seen overhead, examining and photographing the British troop build-up, and the Yorkshiremen released tension by firing their rifles at the planes. Sidney Wilkinson records that the enemy trenches opposite must have changed hands overnight, as the accuracy of the sniping had now improved. Throughout the day, in preparation for 'the do', the 1/5th Battalion erected trench ladders and cleaned their weapons. Carrying the rudimentary gas masks, which had now been issued to all ranks, there was not much sleep to be had in the overcrowded trenches that night.

Shortly after 4am on Sunday, 9 May, streams of light in the eastern sky led to a beautiful dawn, accompanied by the swooping of skylarks. At 5am the birds were scattered and silenced by a terrific bombardment of the German lines at Rouge Bancs, slightly to the left of the 1/5th position. Peter Wilson wrote in his *Dewar's "White Label" Whisky* diary: *'Terrific bombardment started at dawn. Awful shelling with deadly accuracy... The bombardment the greatest of the War.'*

The noise of shells whizzing overhead and exploding all round was deafening, with clouds of dust and earth being thrown into the air. For the unseasoned Terriers of the 1/5th, waiting in the trenches of the front line only three weeks after arriving in France, the sight and sound must have been terrifying. They now had a ringside view of the assault from their position in the E Lines. The men of the 8th Division went 'over the top' immediately after the British artillery bombardment switched from shrapnel to high explosive at 5.30am, with the 1/5th Battalion supporting them from the right flank with rifle fire.

An anonymous artilleryman described the bombardment and first wave of the assault in a letter published by the *Yorkshire Herald*:

For half to three-quarters of an hour the British shells pounded the German lines, and the front parapet crumbled, and broke and gaped in patches under the steady fire. But the barricades were stoutly built, and when the guns lifted their fire further back, there were still defences stout enough for the infantry to tackle. But there was no hesitation when the time came. Suddenly the British parapet swarmed with struggling khaki figures. The open space between the trenches filled with running figures. A ragged line swept across the open and straight for the German parapet.

...the appearance of these figures on the British parapet was the signal for a sudden outbreak of rolling rifle fire and the murderous, machine-like whir of the machine guns. From British to German trench the space was anything up to 200 yards wide – 300 yards of whistling, pelting bullets and bursting shrapnel storms.

The lines were rent and torn, battered and beaten out of shape. It was no longer a charging line; it was a series of disjointed links of a broken chain, but a chain whose remnants still pushed on in the teeth of death. The running groups wilted and withered. Men fell in clumps and clusters, the dead lying crumpled where they fell, the wounded hobbling and staggering and crawling back to shelter from the scourging bullets. Right to the foot of the German parapet the attack pushed, but there it stayed and died.'

During the initial assault, the 1/5th Battalion fired their rifles furiously across no man's land in support of the attack, whilst they had orders to defend their trench against counter-attack at all costs. Emotions were mixed, with the shock of the sight and the terror of knowing that they could be ordered to follow across and be thrown into the cross fire at any moment. Their heads and sometimes shoulders appeared over the parapet from time to time, to get the best shot and this made them vulnerable. Lance Sergeant Sidney Batters appeared in the sights of a German rifle and he was shot in the head. A pre-war Territorial and a confectioner living in Brook Street, York, Sidney had become a close friend of Sergeant Volans, also from York, who helped bury him later a mile behind the front line.

Stanley Rutherford was also hit and wounded in each hand and below the shoulder; injuries indicative of being struck by a bullet when standing tall on the firing step, aiming his rifle. Luckily for Stanley, the wounds were not life threatening and he was treated by the 3rd Field Ambulance, West Riding Division, at Estaires before being transferred to the Field Hospital at Merville by the motor ambulances. Corporal J. Buckley from Knaresborough was also hit and suffered non-fatal wounds. Many others considered themselves lucky to hear bullets whistling past their ears and embedding in the sandbags of the trench wall behind them – if you heard a bullet it had missed you.

Following the apparent failure of the first wave, there was a further artillery bombardment, and a second wave went over the top. Against the odds, handfuls of soldiers made it across their own and the German wire and into the enemy trenches, waving their flags to indicate success. Where this happened, though, they were cut off from each other and their support and had to retire to their own lines the next morning.

Friendly Fire

In the mid-afternoon, once the scale of the disaster was apparent and staff officers were considering what to do next, the men of the 1/5th Battalion felt the true force of their own artillery, when the trench occupied by D Company was hit by a British 40-pound shell fired from a worn out 4.7inch gun, aimed at the German rear. The gun was of the type originally designed for naval defence. It had done good service in the war in South Africa, but was now discarded by the regular artillery as obsolete, which is why it was being used by the Territorial artillery as a 'hand-me-down'. One particular flaw was that the firing ring would fly off as the shell left the barrel, thereby destabilising it and making it inaccurate.

The blast caused the trench parados to collapse, burying Private Walter Malthouse, a Knaresborough man. He was killed by the explosion and three others were badly wounded. Peter Wilson described to Lyn MacDonald the death of his best friend:

> '*Of course we were standing to all day, ready to go, but about three o'clock in the afternoon we were stood down and told we could rest a bit in the trench, and it was fairly clear that nothing much else was going to happen. Well of course we were exhausted, and I got down in the trench next to Walter and I dropped off right away. All of a sudden there was an almighty explosion, right in the trench, a direct hit just a little bit further along from where we were. I was right next to Walter – touching him even. I was stunned of course, but when I got my wits together I could hardly believe it. I was covered in blood – saturated – and I really thought I'd bought it. But it was Walter's blood. I didn't*

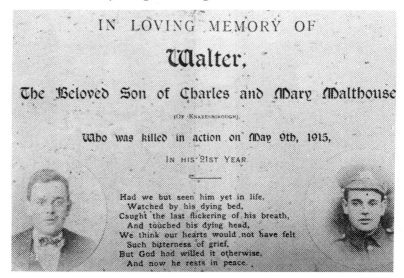

IN LOVING MEMORY OF

Walter,

The Beloved Son of Charles and Mary Malthouse

(OF KNARESBOROUGH).

Who was killed in action on May 9th, 1915,

IN HIS 21ST YEAR.

Had we but seen him yet in life,
Watched by his dying bed,
Caught the last flickering of his breath,
And touched his dying head,
We think our hearts would not have felt
Such bitterness of grief,
But God had willed it otherwise,
And now he rests in peace.

Walter Malthouse Memorial. [Ackrill]
Grief stricken parents Charles and Mary Malthouse had a printed memorial prepared for their son, Walter; Peter Wilson's best friend.

have a scratch myself. Walter had taken the full blast and somehow or other it hadn't touched me. He was blown to bits. A terrible sight. I don't think there was a bit of his body bigger than a leg of lamb. I gathered up what I could, put him into a sandbag and later on when it got to dusk, a few of us got out of the trench and buried him a little way behind, about twenty-five yards back, because we couldn't go far. I had my prayer book and I read the burial service – the whole thing, prayers and everything. We had several men to bury of course but we saw that they got a proper burial. We were all friends in the Territorials, joined together, been together all along...'

The three men wounded by this wayward shell were all from Harrogate. Leonard Holland had been recruited by Fred Kelley and the Harrogate Defence league in September 1914. He recovered from his wounds only to be killed seven months later at Ypres.

Twenty-seven-year-old James Newton of Wedderburn Road came from a well-known Harrogate family. He had been a steam driver before enlisting, and his father had been an Army padre with 24 years' service. According to the *Harrogate Advertiser*, James suffered three or four wounds, and he '*had a miraculous escape, the man next to him (Malthouse) being blown to pieces, whilst he was buried with debris and wounded caused by the bursting of a shell on the top of the trench.*'

James Newton. [Ackrill]
Wounded by a British shell on 9th May 1915.

James was transferred via the Casualty Clearing Station to Stobhill General Hospital, Glasgow.

Sydney Toas, of 39 Grove Road, was the third Harrogate man wounded by the British shell. He wrote home to explain his situation:

My Dear Mother – I hope you got my pc [post card] *letting you know that I am wounded. At present I am in a Canadian hospital miles from the fighting, thank the Lord. It is grand to sleep in a bed with a mattress on, if only you can lay on one side. I got wounded in the big attack on Sunday afternoon by a shrapnel shell bursting on the trench. I got hit on the buttock, left side and left arm, between elbow and shoulder and keep having a lot of pain now and again, but other fellows are worse than me. Don't write to old address any more, but the one underneath. Trusting you are well and that you keep so. Excuse writing as I can only lie on my right side.*

Don't send anything only letter. I may not be here long.
Your Loving Son
Syd
P.S. I have lost everything I possessed, even handkerchiefs.

Following the failure of the initial attack, the staff wisely cancelled the bayonet attack planned for 7pm, and the repeat assault planned for the following day could not be carried out because there simply was not enough available artillery ammunition left. It is possible that these decisions saved thousands of lives, including those of hundreds of Yorkshire Territorials. Nonetheless, by the end of the day 11,000 British soldiers were killed, wounded or missing. The groaning of wounded soldiers in no man's land between Fauquissart and Rouge Bancs was heard all night.

Sydney Toas. [Ackrill]
Wounded by 'friendly fire'.

As General Haig admitted two days later, the artillery bombardment had been too brief and inaccurate to be effective against German barbed wire or trenches. Also, the strength of the German positions and defences had been hopelessly underestimated. The machine-guns remained lethal and the German wire impenetrable except in a few places where the lanes through it were so narrow that troops had to bunch together, presenting a clear target for enfilade fire. The German defensive bombardment, on the other hand, was accurate and potent enough to inhibit soldiers leaving the 'jumping off trenches' and kept the soldiers of the 1/5th Battalion crouching and lying down, when not firing their rifles.

The bombardment continued overnight, killing Private John Wain at 4am the next morning. Charles Volans reported that Wain had *'the top of his head blown off, one hand and his foot fearfully damaged. Of course he was killed instantly...'* John was a painter from Layerthorpe in York. A few days later Charles Volans himself suffered a bullet wound in the thigh and was evacuated on a stretcher amidst a hail of bullets to the advanced dressing station, then repatriated via the Stationary Hospital at Boulogne.

After the Battle

Having suffered fewer losses than the battalions of the 7th and 8th Divisions, the West Ridings were detailed to take over the front line for a period. The 1/5th Battalion was selected as the first Territorial Battalion of the West Yorkshire Regiment ever to relieve a regular battalion on active service when it moved north of Fauquissart, towards Petillon, to occupy the F Lines from 12 May 1915.

F Lines included a right-angle turn directly towards the German front line at the point later known as Red Lamp Corner, which instantly reduced no man's land from 300 yards to a mere 70 yards. Due to the proximity of the opposing lines, the German barbed wire here was supplemented by a line of *chevaux de frises*, which were movable bundles of barbed wire interwoven with sharpened stakes.

Including their time in F Lines, the 1/5th Battalion occupied the front line for eleven days unbroken, which was almost double the length of the usual six-day relief, and

German Front Line

F1 towards Fromelles. [Author]
The flat, featureless terrain of No Man's Land, viewed from the British trench lines at F1. The man in the distance is standing on the German front line.

claimed to be a record for British Territorials (and Regulars) at the time. On Sunday, 16 May they retired to Bac St Maur for two days' rest.

Petillon Trenches

At 7.15pm on 18 May, the 1/5th marched to the front line at Petillon, about 1,000 yards north east of Fauquissart, to relieve the 7th Battalion, Middlesex Regiment. On arrival it was pitch dark and raining. The trenches, which had been the jumping off point for the attack on 9 May, were found to be in an awful state, virtually impassable with mud. The battalion came under occasional shrapnel fire which hampered the repair work they were doing under the direction of the Royal Engineers.

Then, on Wednesday, 19 May, George Exelby was killed. As later reported by the *Harrogate Advertiser*:

> *Private George H. Exelby, son of Mr. and Mrs. G.A. Exelby, Oatlands Mount, and Grandson of the late Mr. John Exelby of Kingswood House, Harrogate, has, we regret to say, been killed at the front, presumably by a sniper. Private Exelby enlisted at the outbreak of war, and went out with the 1-5th [sic] West Yorks. The news of his death, although not officially communicated yet to his parents is too circumstantial not to be true. The following letter from Private Barber, a fellow apprentice of Private Exelby, and a great friend, has been received by Mr Spencer, manager of the firm of Scott and Sons, Oatlands Mount, to whom both privates Exelby and Barber were apprenticed:-*
>
> *Dear Mr. Spencer – Just a few lines to let you know I have received your letter, and that I am very well under the circumstances. I have been going to*

write to you, but have kept putting it off as we have been in the trenches for 11 days at a stretch and under very heavy bombardment on Sunday May 9th, but George and I came out alive. Then we had three days rest then in again to some fresh trenches, only 70 yards from the Germans, so you have to look out, and there are dead both at the back and front of us that we cannot get to bury. You will have heard the sad news about George. He was on sentry at a small bridge that you have to cross and was shot through the back, and it must have gone through his heart, because he died before they could get him out. I could not get to see him, as he was a good way off, so did not get to know until it was too late. They buried him the same night behind our headquarters, and put a little wooden cross to mark the spot. I could not believe it at first, but I have sent a few lines to his mother, and I will leave it to you to tell her more. We were together nearly all Monday afternoon

*George Exelby. [Ackrill]
Sniped 19 May 1915 near Petillon.*

talking about when we got back and what we should have to tell you all. Then I saw him for the last time on Tuesday night as we were going to the trenches, but not to talk to as his company went on before ours. We used to see each other sometimes in the trenches, so I shall miss him very much, and only wish George was knocking about.

    Yours sincerely
    HARRY BARBER

Two days later the 1/5th Battalion lost Drummer James Milner of North Street, York. He was a confectioner by trade and like so many of his comrades, a pre-war Territorial.

The weather turned warmer towards the end of the month, as the battalion marched into Brigade Reserve at Rue du Quesnes. Whit Sunday (23 May) was a very hot day, according to Peter Wilson, who also records that he attended Holy Communion at Bac St Maur with Bob Anderson. He had a close hair cut, and then gloried in the 16 Platoon victory over 14 Platoon at football. Walter Mellor wrote some locally purchased postcards, two of which have survived. They were censored by Major Robert Cattley.

The relative peace was shattered when 18-year-old Arnell Johnson, grocer's assistant from York, was shot by a sniper while carrying sandbags across an open field on 25 May.

The 1/5th returned to the trenches at the end of May. The heat had started to dry out the land and trenches, so that the stink of dead bodies became unbearable after heavy shelling. It was now sixteen days since the massacre in no man's land and men still lay where they had fallen. This hit morale hard, despite the good news stories around the apparent triumph in the Dardanelles and the fact that Italy had joined the war on the Allied side.

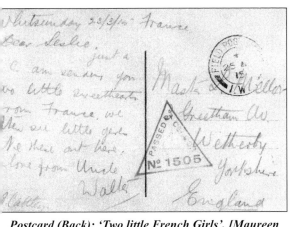

Postcard (Back): 'Two little French Girls'. [Maureen Sullivan]
Walter Mellor wrote to his nephew, Leslie, in Wetherby on Whit Sunday 23 May 1915. The postcard was censored by Robert Cattley.

Postcard (Front): 'Two little French Girls'.
[Maureen Sullivan]

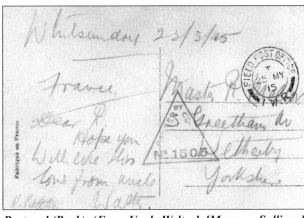

Postcard (Back): 'From Uncle Walter'. [Maureen Sullivan]

Postcard (Front): 'From Uncle Walter'. [Maureen Sullivan]
Another postcard from Walter Mellor dated 23 May 1915.

The inspection by Field Marshal Sir John French on 9 June was not viewed with the enthusiasm of the appearance of the Commander-in-Chief in the previous month, and was privately regarded by Peter Wilson as 'very troublesome'. Relationships with comrades were also suffering as the men of the 1/5th were again not impressed with the condition of the trenches and headquarters left to them by the 1/6th Battalion. Captain Wilkinson reported the filthy conditions to the brigade staff, and also complained that the Bradford men had done little to improve safety either.

Ernest Harrison. [Yorkshire Herald] Sniped on 9 June near Petillon.

The same day Ernest Harrison from York and Harry West from Tadcaster, were killed. Ernest was in D Company; he was shot through the neck by a sniper. He was said by Lance Corporal J. Carling to have died instantly. A few days earlier, Ernest had saved the life of his best friend, Frank Smith, who was struck by cramp when bathing in the river.

The next day Private Harold Field, from Selby, died of his wounds at the casualty clearing station at Estaires. Private George Thompson suffered the same fate on 31 May. A letter from Walter Franks to the *Claro Times* discloses the developing and real impact of life in the trenches, and F Lines in particular:

> *We are at present in the trenches, but expecting to be relieved on June 3rd. I am glad to say that up to the present our platoon (9th) has only lost one (Wilde), and one wounded (Ramus). Other platoons of our regiment have not been quite so lucky. The report about Dr Wilkinson is not true and he is quite well. I don't know how people get the news; it baffles me completely. I shall be glad when the War is over. People in England have no idea what it is like out here. It is a very grand country where we are just now. Our billets, when we come out of the trenches, are right out in the country.*

Born and bred in Harrogate, Wally was 38 years old when he wrote this letter; it gives the impression of a man who is scared and sickened by the conditions in the line and the way in which rumours spread. The last two sentences do not sit well with the rest of the letter, suggesting that they might have been added to relieve the concerns of a loved one, or the Army censor. The 'report about Dr Wilkinson' is something of a mystery, but Norman J. Ramus is known to have survived the war, having risen to the rank of corporal.

For the 1/5th Battalion there was little action in the last week of May 1915, with the boredom of inactivity in the trenches interspersed for some by overnight wiring duty in no man's land, and ditch digging in the heat of the day. Fatigues also included re-building parapets and bridges over trenches.

On 29 May poison gas equipment was seen in the German trenches. Since the use of chlorine on 22 April 1915 against the BEF and the French, at the Second Battle of

Ypres, all ranks were aware of the dangers of this particular weapon, and the need to predict when it was likely to be used. At Petillon in May and June 1915, the German Army used tear gas with the potential to incapacitate troops and soften them up for infantry attack. All ranks were ordered to wear their gas helmets during morning stand to. At this early stage in the war these were pieces of gauze worn across the nose and mouth, sometimes soaked overnight in tins used as urine receptacles.

June Days

A routine developed in the first fortnight of June 1915. As the 1/5th moved between support, reserve and front line firing trenches around Petillon, the tremendous heat was punctuated by a thunderstorm which flooded the dugouts. Most nights, patrols were pushed out into no man's land to rebuild and strengthen barbed wire defences and to listen for enemy activity. Artillery duels took place most days.

In the middle of the month there was a spurt of activity with reports of bombs dropped on marching troops by German aeroplanes and heavy enemy shelling. On Sunday, 13 June Peter Wilson wrote home, describing one of the bombardments:

We had a rather hard time this time in the trenches and have had very little sleep. And to our surprise in the last two days the Germans bombarded or trenches and several shells fell around us. One hit the very dugout I was residing in and shook the abode like the wind does a tree. I wondered what was up and very soon went out into the trench, which was up to the boot tops in mud, and ready for what might come. Well, Whizz-Bang-ETC. came and very soon shrapnel was bursting and falling all over like Old Harry. A shell bursts at one place and we all rushed in the opposite direction and before we had gone 20 yards one burst about 10 yards away in a rotten ditch and covered several of us with mud and filth, which possessed an odour one seldom enjoys. We quickly retraced our steps but the shells seemed to follow us and I thought it best to take cover behind the parapet and trust to luck – which we did with success, for in less than five minutes the boom of our heavy guns sent volleys of shells with deadly accuracy right into the German batteries and soon one could walk about in ease with only rifle fire to molest us.

Major Cattley was wounded about this time, suffering a severe concussion to the head which in the view of Dr Stoddart (who attended him at Boulogne Stationary Hospital) would take six weeks for recovery: in fact, he did not return to the front until 24 July 1916 (and was wounded again two months later).

On 18 June 1915 the 1/5th Battalion retaliated to good effect using rifle grenades and a converted anti-aircraft gun nick-named 'Archibald', which had been carried into the front line trench. Fifteen shells hit the enemy trenches, silencing a German mortar.

Half an hour later, the enemy retaliated, causing three casualties. Joseph Cahill, aged 22, was killed instantly. He had been a chocolate confectioner from Margaret

Street, York. Harrogate men Edward Ramsey and George Elsworth were both fatally wounded. The *Claro Times* reported that:

Edward Ramsey. [Ac

> *Mrs M. Wynne of 9 Grove Street, Starbeck, received official intimation on Wednesday morning that her son, Private Edward Ramsey, of the 1/5th West Yorkshires, had been killed in action on June 18th… A letter from Private Ramsey was received from the front on Saturday, the 19th inst, in which he stated he was quite well. He evidently had been killed the day before his letter was received at his home.*

George Elsworth died of his wounds on 20 June in the casualty clearing station at Estaires. He had been a bath chair driver, tending to the needs of Harrogate's genteel health tourists, and lived near Strawberry Dale with his wife and adult son, who was a chauffeur.

The same day, 24-year-old Second Lieutenant Edward 'Ned' Irish was the first officer of the 1/5th to be killed in action. A former chemistry student from Liversedge in Leeds, he was hit by a 'chance bullet', according to Captain Wilkinson. Colonel Wood wrote to Ned's father, describing his son's death:

Edward Irish. [Leeds University]
The first officer of the 1/5th battalion to be killed in action, on 20 June 1915.

> *He was shot in the head just before noon whilst superintending the mending of the wire in front of his post and was not conscious from the moment he was hit until he passed away. In him we have lost an exceedingly good and hard working officer, who knew his work and did it thoroughly. We shall miss him and I hope you will accept the sincere sympathy of my brother officers and myself in your sad loss. He is buried beside some of his comrades, who have gone before him, in the little cemetery behind the trenches, where General Lowry Coles and many other brave men are laid to rest.'*

The Leeds University OTC Roll of Honour obituary notes that:

> *Second Lieutenant E. Irish came from Batley Grammar School to the University in 1910. In 1913 he obtained a graduate scholarship in Chemistry and stayed for a post-graduate course in leather industries. He was just looking forward to starting his industrial career when the call to arms came, and being a Sergeant in the O.T.C., he was soon gazetted to the 5th West Yorks. By temperament and from the special character of his abilities Irish was one of the best soldiers the University has produced.*

Ned's younger brother Harry, who was a bank clerk until he was commissioned, joined the 1/5th Battalion in June 1916 and was awarded the Military Cross, before being blinded at the Battle of Passchendaele in October 1917.

Thomas Coleman was killed on 22 June 1915, probably by the blast of a trench mortar. He had been a fishmonger in Harrogate. The next day, Frederick Long of York was also killed by a trench mortar.

On 25 June, two months after arrival at the front and just as the 1/5th Battalion was to be pulled out of the line and redeployed, the first batch of home leave came up and about seventy men went back to England for a few days. The battalion was then withdrawn from the Fleurbaix Sector and sent north to the trenches near Boesinghe at the northern end of the Ypres Salient, where they would spend the rest of the year.

Chapter 4

Summer in the Salient
(July–December 1915)

'...his noble death has robbed Harrogate
of a worthy citizen'.

Fleurbaix to Ypres

The journey from Fleurbaix to Boesinghe took six days. It involved a series of route marches of up to 15 miles each day, resting for ten minutes in every hour. The men carried 50lbs of kit in tremendous heat, with lice (referred to as 'Jaspers') adding to the discomfort. After crossing the border into Belgium, the weather turned and on 29 June the 1/5th Battalion marched in pouring rain for five-and-a half-hours along slippery country roads to Proven, three miles north-west of Poperinghe. Peter Wilson described it as marching in a 'Turkish Bath'. Three of his boot nails worked into his foot, and Captain Wilkinson recorded that sixty men were suffering from sore feet, 'not bad ones'.

On 1 July the 1/5th Battalion was reinforced by the draft of ninety-nine men and four subalterns sent out by the 2/5th Battalion. They had left Thoresby Park two days earlier with Captain Claude 'Bully' Bulmer in command. A further draft of twenty men would follow on 15 August. These drafts comprised mainly Beechwood Boys recruited in the late autumn and winter of 1914-15, who had trained in Harrogate. They moved to Matlock in March 1915 and then went under canvas at Doncaster Racecourse. Their arrival at the front meant that more soldiers in the 1/5th Battalion were now from Harrogate than anywhere else. They brought gossip and news from home, as well as footballs supplied by W.H. Breare, editor of the *Harrogate Herald*.

The new draft was inspected by Colonel Wood and then allocated to companies over the next three nights, as the 1/5th Battalion recovered from their march in scattered billets around Proven, some under canvas. There were inspections on consecutive days by Sir Herbert Plumer and Sir John Keir, General Officer Commanding VI Corps, to which 146 Brigade now belonged.

Leave passes were granted to go into Proven, a very pleasant village, to taste the delights of eggs and other luxuries. This was followed by three days' rest, interspersed with occasional route marches. Sunday, 4 July dawned a hot day, with Holy Communion held in shirt sleeve order in a field near Watou. There was also the

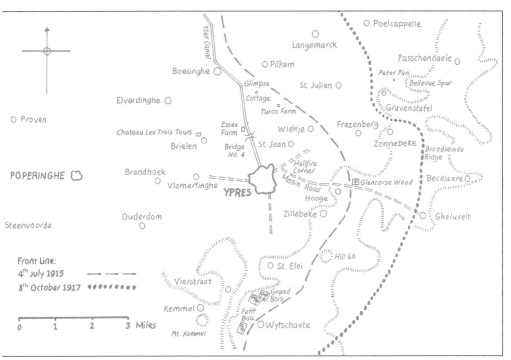

The Ypres Salient between the Second and Third Battles of Ypres. [Sketch Map 5]
Showing the front line from July 1915 to October 1917 and some key locations in the story of the 1/5th Battalion including Turco Farm (1915), Bellevue (1917), Broodseinde and Wytschaete. (1918).

opportunity to wash clothes, bathe in buckets, and burn the lice out of shirt seams. Mail was received and sent.

The distant dangers of warfare returned on 5 July when a stray shell landed nearby. The *Harrogate Advertiser* reported that:

> *Private Arthur Johnson of the 1-5th West Yorks Regt., son of Mrs Johnson, House Farm, Beckwithshaw near Harrogate, was seriously wounded on July 5th by shrapnel in the left arm, thigh, knee, and back and is now an inmate of Queen Mary's Military Hospital, Whalley. One bullet struck a cigarette case in his pocket and no doubt this was the means of saving his life. His brother, Lance-Corporal Allan Johnson, was with him at the time, and is now in the trenches in Belgium.*

The next day the 1/5th Battalion marched through Poperinghe, then past hop and tobacco fields towards Elverdinghe, where they bivouacked in a wood for their last night before entering the Ypres Salient. They were now close enough to the front line to smell tear gas and that night they saw a group of 200 German prisoners being marched to the rear. In the distance they could see the ruins of the Cloth Hall in Ypres and the continuing destruction of the town by German artillery.

Bridge 4. [Michael Wilson]
Peter Wilson sketched Bridge 4 from the west bank of the Yser Canal, where he also once saw the famous cartoonist Bruce Bairnsfather sitting on a stool, drawing.

On 7 July, the 1/5th Battalion left for the front line trenches at dusk, heading first to Essex Farm, a dressing station nestled into the west embankment of the Yser Canal. Essex Farm was the last staging post for the front line, where John McCrae had written the poem 'In Flanders Fields' during the Second Battle of Ypres. Here, mule-drawn ration limbers mustered to allow parties from forward battalions to collect their food and take it to the troops in the trenches.

From Essex Farm they crossed the Yser Canal, breaking step to walk across the famously rickety Bridge 4 and into the Salient. They probably made their way along Coney Street Trench, as far as La Belle Alliance Farm, then turned north up Gawthorpe Road to the front. Over the next six months, the 1/5th Battalion would make its mark in this sector by naming support and communication trenches after landmarks at home, including The Pump Room, Clifford's Tower, and Knaresborough Castle.

The front line was divided into three parts in this sector, respectively named Glimpse Cottage, Lancashire Farm and Turco Farm. Sub-divisions were made by a simple alpha-numeric reference system, with Glimpse Cottage running from E27 to F30, Lancashire Farm from E23 to E26, and Turco Farm from D18 to D22.

Turco Farm
The destination that night was Turco Farm and the front line at D19 and D20, otherwise known as Willow Walk and Canadian Dug-outs, with Morteldje Estaminet on the right at D18. Immediately behind the German front line trench the ground rose to a height

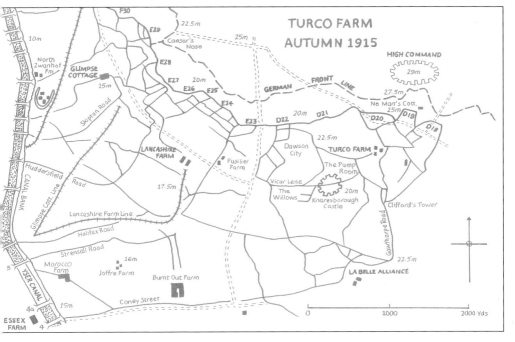

Turco Farm Autumn 1915. [Sketch Map 6]
Showing southern part of the Boesinghe sector, including High Command Redoubt, Caesar's Nose, The Pump Room, Glimpse Cottage, Lancashire Farm, La Belle Alliance and Essex Farm.

High Command from Willow Walk. [Author]
High Command Redoubt is at the crest of the gentle ridge, looking from D19.

of 90ft, giving German snipers and machine gunners a commanding view of the entire British front line and support area. From the ridge, informally named the High Command Redoubt, the enemy could see all the way back to the canal.

Only 70 yards wide at this point, no man's land was squeezed between Willow Walk and the foot of the High Command ridge; having changed hands a number of times during the Second Battle of Ypres a few months earlier. It contained a number of British listening posts and remained hotly disputed. Gas attacks were a regular occurrence and machine-gun, artillery and rifle fire constant. Colonel Wood was ordered by the commander of the 49th Division, Major General Baldock, to 'hold at all costs, and not a single inch of ground is to be lost'.

The relief pattern was six days in the front line alternating with six days in reserve, until 10 September. This meant that the 1/5th and the other battalions of 146 Brigade occupied the Salient for two months without a formal period of rest: an unprecedented record.

Baptism of Fire

The first relief in the front line started on 8 July 1915, when the 1/5th Battalion found that the trenches were not in too bad a state; deeper and narrower (for protection against heavier shell fire) than those in Fleurbaix.

Immediately they came under terrific fire from enemy artillery and the next day, Turco Farm was targeted by 'aerial torpedoes' and tear gas shells. Saturday, 10 July was quiet, but this only meant a pause in the shelling which allowed the enemy snipers to get to work from their positions on the High Command Ridge. Some even climbed into ruined trees, 500 yards behind their own front line to spot unwary Yorkshiremen through telescopic sights. Peter Wilson was narrowly missed by a high velocity sniper's bullet while sitting on a latrine bucket.

Private John Brown of B Company was less lucky, killed instantly by a sniper's bullet in the head. He was buried that night on the Canal Bank, with Colonel Wood officiating. Like many others to follow, his grave was lost at some point in the following three years of conflict, as the ground was turned over by constant shelling. His name is inscribed on the Tyne Cot memorial to the missing.

On Sunday, 11 July, the 1/5th Battalion came under artillery fire again. At Morteldje Estaminet, 60lb trench mortar bombs blew holes in the trench parapet walls. The 1/5th Battalion retaliated but only succeeded in demonstrating their lack of expertise with rifle grenades: no apparent damage was done to the German trenches. Later that day the Yorkshiremen suffered another sustained attack by rifle grenade, trench mortar and whizz bang, with six killed and eleven wounded in two explosions.

Three of the dead were York men. They were all chocolate workers, probably friends from pre-war days who were standing in a group when the shell burst nearby. Walter Lea, aged 23, had enlisted shortly after the creation of the 5th Battalion. Also 23, Henry Lund had joined up on the outbreak of war, as had John Wetherill, who was four years older. John and Henry were chocolate moulders and Walter was a labourer.

Private William Haley, a dental assistant from Harrogate, was also killed that day, probably in the same blast. His company commander, Geoffrey Sowerby, reported that he bled to death from a severed artery in the neck.

William Haley. [Ackri
Bled to death on 20 Ju
1915 at Turco Farm.

Later that day George W. Macey and Alfred H. Thornton, both from Selby, were killed, probably by a whizz-bang. George was 20 years old, and a brickyard labourer who lived in Bondgate with his parents and four younger siblings. He enlisted in the 5th Battalion in 1911.

Lance Corporal Fred Kelley, of Chatsworth Grove Harrogate – no relation to the founder of the Harrogate Defence League – was also fatally wounded by a shell blast on 11 July, although his death was somewhat unexpected and possibly all the more tragic for that. He had received what appeared to be a minor wound in the buttock, causing Charles Whitworth to write to Fred's wife:

Your husband wishes me to write and tell you that he has had a slight wound. It is only a flesh wound, but he thinks if he wrote himself (and he is quite able to do so), you would think he was worse than he is. To the best of my knowledge it is only a slight wound, and he is quite cheerful. It may be that the doctors may send him home for a few days; if so, I'm sure you will have a happy time together ... Again, I assure you he is quite fit...

Fred Kelley. [Ackrill]
Died of his wounds at Boulogne.

Whitworth was wrong. Soon after receiving his letter, Mrs Annie Kelley received a telegram from Territorial records office in York on 15 July saying:

Regret to inform you that No. 2012 Lance-Corporal F Kelley 1-5th West Yorks, is dangerously ill at No.2 Stationary Hospital, Boulogne, suffering from gunshot wound to buttock. Regret permission to visit him cannot be granted.

That evening a second telegram arrived telling her of his death. The *Claro Times* reported that Fred Kelley was *'always courteous and obliging, with a genial temperament which made him popular with all, his acquaintance was a privilege, and his noble death has robbed Harrogate of a worthy citizen.'*

Charles Bishop.
A father figure from Huby.

Arnold Day and Charles Bishop were killed on 13 July. Charles was 38 years old and a coachman by trade. He was a father of five from the village of Huby, located between Harrogate and Leeds. His brother Maurice also enlisted in the 5th Battalion. Second Lieutenant John C. Walker wrote to Charles's widow to say that: *'He was a grand example to my younger fellows, and a good soldier who died like a true English gentleman.'*

Arnold Day was the only son of Edward and Adah Day, of South Drive, Harrogate. According to the *Advertiser*, he was:

a young man of fine physique and great promise in his profession. Day was the first Bradford Journalist to respond to his country's call on the outbreak of war, and last September he enlisted in the 5th West Yorks, at Harrogate... for about seven years he had been a member of the reporting staff at the Bradford Daily Telegraph, and his charming nature made him quite a personality in Bradford newspaper circles, whilst he was an esteemed member of the National Union of Journalists.

In honour of Arnold, the *Bradford Daily Telegraph* published a touching poem from a colleague in the Manchester Guardian:

Arnold Day. [Ackrill]
Journalist and 'personality ▪
Bradford newspaper circles

Good-Bye
(To Arnold E. Day)

Good-bye! The toil is done
Thy crown is won
Night's pitying eyes shine over ended pain
And not in vain
The strife endured, the given life; 'tis gain to freedom's cause.
And though in England's homely island soil thou mayest not lie,
Yet hast thou laid a stone of that defence whereby
Shielded from war's aggression, men unborn
Shall build on new foundations toward the dawn.

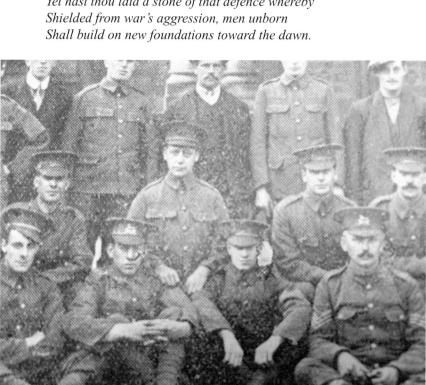

Pals at the Exhibition Centre. [Ackrill]
Arnold Day (bottom left) with other ne recruits at the Exhibition Buildings, Yo in September 1914.

Arnold Day and Charles Bishop were killed on the day the 1/5th Battalion came to the end of its first, costly, six-day in the Boesinghe trenches. There was the usual pattern of German mortar bombs and rifle grenades landing on the communications trenches behind Turco Farm, followed by British trench mortars retaliating, this time putting four bombs into the enemy trench opposite No Man's Cottage. At midnight the 1/5th was relieved by the 1/6th West Yorkshires and they marched back to brigade reserve positions on the east bank of the Yser Canal, adjacent to Bridge 4.

The Canal Bank

For the next six days the 1/5th Battalion lived in shelters dug into the east bank of the canal. The weather varied day by day from warm sunshine to rain and on pleasant days the men were able to swim and fish, although the enemy had opened the sluice gates further up the coast and the water level had dropped, leaving an appalling stench.

H.F. Swann. [Ackrill]
Shot and wounded on the Canal Bank.

The war was still close, though, as the canal was within range of enemy rifle shot. Private H.F Swan, of Dragon Parade, Harrogate, was shot in both legs, suffering a shattered right thigh. He was processed through the Casualty Clearing Station and base hospital on 15 July and arrived at Beckett's hospital in Leeds on 27 July.

Turco Farm II

On 19 July the battalion returned to the front line at Willow Walk and the Canadian Dugouts, where Peter Wilson said there was 'nothing but mud, flies and water'. There was an enthusiastic exchange of all types of small munitions daily, from rifle grenades and trench mortars to heavy trench mortars. Mercifully there was no gas, but the heavy death toll continued, with nine men lost.

John Fraser of Knaresborough Road, Harrogate, was a machine gunner who was shot and killed on 20 July. Also sniped on 20 July was Selby man, Frederick G. Walker. Three more men from Selby, including Horace Bradley (an old sweat and veteran of the 1st VB), John 'George' Castle, and Gilbert Connell, a ship-fitter by trade, were killed the

John Fraser. [Ackrill]
Machine gunner killed on 20th July 1915.

next day, along with Henry Parker from York. George Castle was hit in the neck by a sniper's bullet and expired while being attended to by Peter Wilson. Peter himself was shot in the arm the same day, but his wound only kept him from the trenches for four days, which he spent in hospital.

Over the next three days there were further exchanges of trench artillery, with the

1/5th Battalion now sufficiently skilled to score a number of hits on German trenches. On the morning of 22 July they observed in the German front line a small explosion from one of their trench mortar bombs which caused sandbags to fly about, and they heard whistles blow, calling for stretcher bearers. That evening another hit started a small fire in the German trench opposite Morteldje Estaminet. Two days later, six heavy trench mortar bombs were sent over 'with excellent results, blowing up timber and sandbags'. Along with timbers and ballast, Captain Wilkinson dryly adds that 'a German also went up with the debris'.

George Timmins. [Ackri Jeweller at Ogden's Harrogate.

The next day, Albert Seal from York and George Timmins, apprentice jeweller from Harrogate, were both killed. George was shot by a sniper and, according to Sergeant A. Hendry of the Signal Section, he died almost instantaneously.

George had been a pre-war Terrier who worked at Ogden's Jewellers, in James Street. His younger brother Herbert also enlisted in the 1/5th Battalion and was taken prisoner in March 1917.

Also serving with the 1/5th was the 20-year-old heir to the jewellery business, James Robert (Jimmy) Ogden. Jimmy had been recruited by the Harrogate Defence League in September 1914. In the Salient he went out on a number of wiring parties into no man's land with Knaresborough men, Peter Wilson and Francis Peacock. He was also well known for receiving 'a succession of sensational food parcels', entirely in keeping with the social and financial standing of his family. Jimmy was discharged from the 1/5th Battalion on Christmas Day 1915, and commissioned in the KOYLI. He survived the war and went on to manage Ogden's in Harrogate.

The enemy was aware that a relief was due on Monday 26 July and, knowing that two battalions would therefore be present in the front line in the late evening, they bombarded Turco Farm and its communication trenches with trench mortars and whizz-bangs, causing some damage to the parapets. Their intelligence was accurate, as the 1/6th Battalion had just arrived and the 1/5th Battalion was making ready to leave.

This was when an enemy sniper hit Private William Jennings, as described by Captain Jack Peters in a letter to William's mother

We were just leaving the trenches at the time, after a strenuous six days, for a well-earned rest, and your son was packing up his kit to be ready. He was in a dangerous place, and must have been seen by a German sniper as he was hit in the head and died instantly. It may perhaps be some consolation to you that he cannot possibly have suffered any pain. He was buried last night in a little cemetery behind our line of trenches, alongside other fallen comrades of the 1-5th West Yorkshires, some of them Harrogate men. Lieut. Col. Wood officiated at the simple service and his friends Pte. Inman and Pte. Hunt, and his platoon officer, Lieut. Ellison, were also present.

Chateau Les Trois Tours. [Author]
Showing the bridge where Major General T.S. Baldock was wounded by blast.

Chateau Les Trois Tours

Relieved from the front line, the 1/5th Battalion crossed back over the Yser Canal and out of the Salient. They headed further west for about a mile, past Brielen to the picturesque Chateau Les Trois Tours. This had been headquarters of the 49th Division until Major General Baldock was wounded in the head on 8 July, by a shell blast while he was crossing a bridge. Major General E.M. Perceval assumed command of the division (which he retained until 1917) and immediately moved divisional headquarters to Hospital Farm.

This left Chateau Les Trois Tours vacant for use as billets for the Divisional Reserve, and the 1/5th Battalion arrived there at 2am on Monday, 26th July. The officers stayed in the Chateau, and the men in dug-outs in the grounds, which had been fortified with concrete bunkers at each corner. There were some opportunities for fishing in the moat, at the risk of Sergeant-Major Raynor's wrath, and baths too. Cricket matches were held whilst individuals read and wrote their post on the lawns. Reserve inevitably involved fatigues too, with three large working parties sent out to dig third line defences on Tuesday, 27 July.

A bunker in the grounds of Chateau Les Trois Tours. [Author]
Bunkers were constructed at each corner of the chateau's grounds.

Chateau Les Trois Tours stables. [Author]
Six horses were killed and one wounded here, by a bursting shell in July 1915.

Captain Wilkinson records that on the morning of Friday, 30 July, a German 4.9mm shell landed 'on or near 8 horses', killing six and wounding one of them. Three men were also wounded by the blast.

Turco Farm III

At 10pm the next day, the 1/5th Battalion arrived back at Willow Walk and Canadian Dugouts to relieve the 1/6th West Yorkshires, for their third tour at Turco Farm. This time they knew what to expect in terms of lethal artillery bombardment.

At 11am on Sunday 1 August 1915, Corporal Harry Beetham Holmes was wounded for the first time in the leg and buttock by a whizz-bang which also collapsed three dugouts. This was a 'blighty wound' which took him back, via No.1 Canadian General Hospital in France, to the Royal Bath (Military Auxiliary) Hospital in Harrogate, where he stayed seven months. On 24 November 1915, W.H. Breare wrote in the *Harrogate Herald* that Harry had been in to see him *'looking extremely well. Just a little paler, but full of life, and spirits as ever.'*

While a patient at the Bath hospital, Harry organised the hospital concert party which performed around Claro District and finally at the Harrogate Grand Opera House (now Harrogate Theatre), raising £200. By March 1916 he had recovered and returned to the battalion in time for the first day of the Battle of the Somme; he was killed three months later.

Wilfred Sunderland.
[Ackrill]
Wounded in the right arm, left shoulder and both legs.

Around the time that Harry Holmes was wounded at Turco Farm, Fred Bean from York died of his wounds and Alexander Tuppen, a pre-war Territorial from York was also killed in action. He was watching the German front line over the parapet, then turned to talk to Harold Simpson. A sniper spotted the movement and shot Alexander in the back of the head. Quartermaster Sergeant John Dobson was wounded, as was Wilfred Sunderland, who suffered shrapnel in the right arm, left shoulder and both legs. Twenty-one years old, and a nurseryman before the war, he had lived in Plantation Avenue, Harrogate, with his parents and five siblings. He had played rugby for Harrogate and enlisted with the 5th Battalion in the autumn of 1914. After recovering from his wounds in a London hospital he transferred to the 12th Battalion West Yorkshires, with whom he was awarded the Distinguished Conduct Medal (DCM) for consistent bravery. He was killed in action at the Battle of Cambrai on 21 November 1917.

Monday, 2 August 1915 was a highly eventful day for the 1/5th Battalion. In the morning and then again in mid-afternoon, they exchanged fire with the enemy, suffering 'much damage' including collapsed parapets. About 8am a German minenwerfer bomb exploded in the trench near brothers Robert and Herbert Calvert, from New Park in Harrogate. The story is told in a letter to their mother from J. Sidney Hobson, Wesleyan chaplain, dated 3 August:

I was talking with Robert this morning, and told him that I would write and let you know that he was wounded in the side by a German "Whizzy Bang" about 8 o'clock yesterday morning. The wound is not a dangerous one, and when I saw him he was comparatively easy and quite cheerful and bright. He was taken to a clearing hospital by the Red Cross motor about 9.30 this morning, and from the clearing hospital he will be sent to a base hospital, and probably before long he will be in England. Unfortunately a piece of the same shell that wounded Robert hit Herbert, and it is with very severe regret that I have to report that Herbert was killed whilst doing his duty. I wish I could write in such a way as would give you a little comfort in what must be a terrible loss to you. I know that no sympathy, however sincere, can make the heavy blow a light one. Herbert has finished his work; he has done his duty like the brave man that he was, and he has truly died the death of a hero, and entered upon the hero's reward...

Herbert was the older brother, aged 21, and had been a fireman on the North East Railway before enlisting. Robert must have suffered badly, waiting more than 24 hours in the front-line trench and at the forward dressing station with shrapnel in his side, before being taken to the CCS and then on to a base hospital on the coast.

Frank Kitson was also killed on 2 August. It is impossible to identify the type of round which landed on the 14th Platoon and took his life, because there was a series of whizz-bangs and minenwerfer hits on the Turco Farm trenches that day. Platoon Sergeant Jonathan Patrick and Second Lieutenant Noel H. Cope both wrote to Mrs Kitson to express their sympathy, Sergeant Patrick noting that her baby boy had lost his father.

Herbert Calvert. [Ackri A 21-year-old engine fireman killed by a 'whi. bang' at Turco Farm.

On 2 August the 1/5th Battalion captured its first German prisoners. They were three soldiers from the '237th Landsturm Regiment' [sic] who walked across no man's land and surrendered about 9pm. This account from the battalion diary differs slightly from that of Edward Iredale, who said that the three Germans were spotted lying in front of the British wire and put up something of a fight before being overpowered by the party of wire menders who encountered them.

Captain Hunt, the brigade major recorded that: *'All come from Lorraine and sympathies entirely French. Much useful information obtained.'*

Frank Kitson. [Ackrill] Killed on 2 August 1915.

Rain

After days of shelling and destruction the weather changed on Tuesday, 3 August. It rained for two days solid, forcing both sides to divide their energies between staying dry and defensive duties, which still included keeping bayonets fixed all day, and 'stand to' between 9pm and 3.30am every night. The water rose in the trenches, turning them to knee-deep mud and causing walls and dugouts to collapse. The only place to stay out of the mud was on the fire step, so soldiers huddled for hours under their greatcoats, cupping cigarettes under their hands to retain some warmth. It was utterly miserable.

Edward Baker. [Ackrill] *Ted Baker stayed in the firing line for fear that others would think he was 'trying to shirk the dangerous part'.*

When the rain eased on 5 August, it left a morass which made trench warfare even harder to endure and much more dangerous. That afternoon, the Germans sent over the heaviest artillery bombardment that Edward Iredale had experienced. He said that *'many of our chaps had their nerves completely shattered by the terrific explosions.'* The Yorkshiremen attempted to retaliate, but the slushy mud in the bottom of the trench destabilised the mortar, making it hopelessly inaccurate. The German trench artillery, from dryer ground, scored more hits, destroying the battalion machine-gun emplacement and collapsing dug-outs weakened by rain. Ted Baker of D Company, Arnold Day's friend, was killed in one of these dug-outs. He was hit on the head by a falling beam and buried under the collapsed roof. Second Lieutenant Kenneth Mackay, his platoon officer, sent Ted's ring to his parents, who lived on Otley Road, Harrogate. The brief funeral service was conducted by Colonel Wood.

Ted had served three-and-a-half years as a Territorial in the 5th Battalion before rejoining on the outbreak of war. Well respected as a good leader by the men and the other NCOs, he was a devout Methodist who was sought out by others for support and solace. One of his comrades wrote that:

I was a good deal with Ted when we were resting the last six days, and I told him I should have liked his transfer to come off before we went into the trenches, but he said he would rather go in this time as some might think he was trying to shirk the dangerous part. That was just like him all the while out here – always cheery and cheering others up. Many a time I have felt depressed and have just gone to Ted. Because I knew he would encourage me....

Late on Friday, 6 August the 1/5th Battalion was due back into Brigade Reserve on the Canal Bank. This coincided with the attack of the British 6th Division at Hooge, to the south. The platoons of the 1/5th Battalion, which were holding the front line, were ordered back into the communication trenches while the artillery duel took place, acting as a feint intended from the British side to indicate an infantry attack in the Boesinghe sector. During the exchange, Frank Pennington from York was killed.

Company Sergeant Major (CSM) John Sim was also wounded in the arm. Thirty-seven years old, he was an old soldier and veteran of the 1st VB. In 1911 he lived in Mayfield Terrace, Harrogate, just round the corner from the drill hall on Commercial Street, with his wife Jane and four children.

Over the following fortnight the 1/5th Battalion rotated twice through the Canal Bank and Turco Farm, relieving the 1/6th Battalion on each occasion. They suffered four deaths during this period and a number of wounded, mostly from minenwerfer rounds which were regarded by Edward Iredale as much more effective than the British alternative. The wounded included one of the Bean brothers and Robert Eastwood from Harrogate.

Swimming races were held on the Yser, within enemy rifle range, but drinking water was scarce, with each soldier rationed to one bottle per day in the August heat. On 11 August Lieutenant Colonel Wood went into hospital suffering from an unidentified illness. It must have been serious as on 20 August he was evacuated to England, only returning on 23 September. It is very likely that Major William Oddie took interim command of the battalion.

Lancashire Farm

On 24 August the 1/5th Battalion moved back to the front line at Lancashire Farm, a relatively quiet part of the Salient. At the end of the month, Sergeant Gilbert Tolley demonstrated his expertise with a machine gun by hitting a German officer and two soldiers. He was awarded the DCM for conspicuous gallantry, and skill as a sniper. The citation read that: *'Serjeant Tolley has silenced a number of the enemy snipers, one of whom especially harassed the Company. He has shown himself to be absolutely fearless and always devoted to duty.'*

On 3 September the rain returned with a vengeance. Peter Wilson spent the day and evening out on the canal bank and was wet through despite the recent issuing of Wellington boots to NCOs and some of the men. Returning to the Lancashire Farm trenches the next night he found that he was up to his thighs in water and that the dug-outs were unusable. Edward Iredale reports his dug-out falling in, and having to construct a new one in the rain before being able to get some sleep.

Gilbert Tolley. [Ackrill]
An 'absolutely fearless' sniper.

The only comfort was the rum ration, which tested, and sometimes defeated, Edward's Wesleyan principles and teetotal ethic. At least it helped him sleep.

On Sunday, 5 September, Peter Wilson's diary reads: *'30 yards from Germans. One man in Co sniped. Trenches in awful state all mud & water. Over Wellingtons at knees with mud.'*

The sniped man was Private Ernest (Nobby) Abrams, of C Company. He was shot while rebuilding a collapsed dug-out. His brother-in-law, George Winter, wrote to his own sister, Nobby's wife:

We came to the trenches on Saturday night, and on the Sunday morning, after 'standing to arms', which is from dawn to daylight, I went into my dug-out , intending to go to sleep, when Ernest came and told me they were going to build a dug-out, as there were not plenty for all. Not many minutes later, Harry Waddington came running out and told me Ernest had been shot through the head by a sniper. I went to him at once, but he was unconscious, and died an hour later. He was buried at 6 the same night, and Corporal Kitchen of Wetherby, Bandmaster Pearson, and myself attended the funeral. The service was conducted by Captain Thompson and the now Regimental Sergeant-Major Raynor, late of the Drill hall, Harrogate. I am asked by many friends in the Company to convey to his family their deepest sympathy. We get relieved tomorrow, and go back to billets for a twelve days' rest, and Ernest was looking forward to it, as we intended to have a good time, but his death has quite upset me, and I do not think the rest will do me any good now. I am too upset to write any more now, but will do so later.

Also on 3 September, Private Stephen Royce died in hospital in Le Havre from wounds sustained at Turco Farm. His funeral was conducted by an officer of the 1/5th, with four other ranks present, including Private Harold Kirk of Harrogate.

Ernest Abrams. [Ackrill]
Sniped at Lancashire Farm.

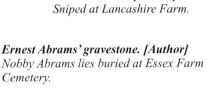

Ernest Abrams' gravestone. [Author]
Nobby Abrams lies buried at Essex Farm Cemetery.

91

On Tuesday, 7 September the weather improved but the water remained. Spirits were lifted briefly by the sight of a Royal Flying Corps airman shooting down an enemy plane. Normality returned, though, when Francis Peacock from Knaresborough was shot through the head by a sniper.

It was around this time that Private Willie Spinks from Grove Park, Harrogate, was wounded. As part of a ration party, he had worked his way back to Essex Farm to collect the food brought forward by limber. He was said by the *Claro Times* to have had a remarkable escape from death as the enemy artillery found the location of the handover and driver and wagon were both blown to pieces.

Francis Peacock. [Ackrill]
From Knaresborough - sniped on 7 September 1915.

Francis Peacock Gravestone.
[Author]
Francis Peacock lies buried in Essex Farm Cemetery.

Coppenolle Hoek

On 9 September 1915, the 1/5th Battalion left the Salient their first real rest since their arrival in France. They were to stay at No.1 Rest Camp, Coppenolle Hoek, a wood three miles from Poperinghe.

The men slept in fifteen-man bivouacs, did some light work and endured a couple of route marches. The battalion was also inspected by General Sir Herbert Plumer who handed out gallantry decorations. More in keeping with relaxation, there were rugby matches against the Leeds Rifles, with the 1/5th victorious against the 1/8th by one try to nil. Three men had to be carried off and five lost their shirts. There were also

Nurses of Royal Bath Hospital Harrogate, [Ackrill] where Harry Holmes recuperated.

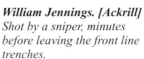

William Jennings. [Ackrill] Shot by a sniper, minutes before leaving the front line trenches.

A ward at the Royal Bath Hospital at Christmas time. [Ackrill]

'first rate' boxing matches with 'blood flying about' according to Peter Wilson. Holy Communion was held on the Sunday morning and men took trips into Poperinghe for delights both civilised and illicit. Wilson mentions in his diary visiting the 'Cathedral' [sic] and noting that the brass and marble had been removed to Paris for safe keeping, a timely reminder that the retention of Ypres was no foregone conclusion.

There were visits to cafés for steak and chips, and to see the 49th Division concert party ('The Tykes') sing 'Sister Susie', 'Charlie Chaplin's Walk', and 'Roses of Picardy'. Both Wilson and Iredale describe the performance as 'very good', while Brigade Intelligence Officer Captain Tempest gives a more poignant description of the role of the concert party in maintaining morale:

> *Such songs… were certainly a better narcotic than the vile wine, weak beer or copious whisky which usually characterised other "magnificent evenings" in reserve billets, and which were inevitably followed by a headache, or an "orderly room". The most noticeable feature about every Tykes' concert near the line : the pathetic eagerness to be amused, and to forget everything : the intense way the men took their pleasures : in many cases the slight hysteria : in all cases the occasional look of staring or gloom : which, though only momentary, expressed more than the average onlooker knew.*

Rest was also an opportunity for Major Oddie to review the structure of the battalion, in the absence of Colonel Wood, as some men were lucky enough to return to England on leave on 15 September. B and D companies swapped their sergeant majors and NCOs were redistributed between the platoons in preparation for the return to the Salient on 20 September. This was prompted, in part, by the fact that on 11 August one of the A Company sergeants, a long serving pre-war Terrier and member of the 1st VB, was convicted by District Court Martial in Poperinghe of being drunk on duty. He was reduced to the ranks and transferred to C Company as a private. There, he was subjected to three months Field Punishment No.1, described by Robert Graves in *Goodbye To All That* as being:

> *stood spread-eagled to the wheel of a company limber, tied by the ankles and wrists in the form of an X. He was obliged to stay in this position – Crucifixion they called it – for several hours every day so long as the battalion remained in billets, and then again after the next spell of trenches.*

The brutality suffered by British soldiers in the First World War was not inflicted exclusively by the enemy.

Chapter 5

Mud and Gas
(September–December 1915)

'Still alive after eight months.'

Angry Germans

On 25 September the French and British Armies attacked in Champagne and Artois, supported by diversionary activity all along the line. At Boesinghe, this involved the throwing of thousands of phosphorous smoke bombs into no man's land and bombardment of the German trenches by rifle grenade. The enemy retaliated with shelling of the canal bank, causing the 1/5th Battalion eight casualties.

The next evening, the 1/5th Battalion relieved the 2/8th West Yorkshires at Glimpse Cottage, opposite a kink in the German front line known as Caesar's Nose. Between the tip of Caesar's Nose and the British line ran the vestiges of an old communication trench, dating from the time before the Second Battle of Ypres when the whole area was in British hands. The old trench had since been blocked off on the British side to form a bombing sap. This meant that opposing soldiers were only 25 yards apart and, according to Peter Wilson, they regularly said 'good morning' to each other.

When news arrived of fifty enemy guns and 28,000 prisoners taken at Champagne, on 28 September Colonel Wood ordered that the bombers from Pateley Bridge should scrawl this information on an oilsheet placard and hoist it out of their sap for the enemy to see from Caesar's Nose. The German reaction was immediate and violent, with a furious bombardment destroying communication trenches, trench parapets and dugouts occupied by the Yorkshiremen. In places the bombing sap itself was blown in.

Then at 9.55am, a German raiding party of one officer and ten men climbed out of their end of the trench and rushed across no man's land to tear the notice down and take it back. Two German soldiers jumped into the bombing sap occupied by William Chadwick from Pateley Bridge and bayoneted him in revenge. Also in the sap was 20-year-old Harry Waring, also from Pateley Bridge. Harry appears to have been a large man and the invaders clambered out of the sap before taking him on. Three of them were hit by rifle fire as they returned across no man's land.

The *Pateley Bridge & Nidderdale Herald* reported the incident as follows:

Mr J. Chadwick of Pateley Bridge, has received information from the record office and also from Mrs Wood, wife of Colonel Wood, that his son, Private W. Chadwick of the 5th West Yorkshires has been wounded. It appears that the West Yorks put up a board stating the gains in France for the Germans to read. The Germans were only ten or twelve yards away. About eight o'clock in the morning about a dozen Germans rushed for the board and into the sap head. There were only two bombers in the sap at the time and one was some distance away down the trench. The Germans were on the other bomber (Private Chadwick) before he could get to his bombs and stabbed him in the shoulder and neck. Chadwick was removed to Boulogne Hospital and later to the hospital at Havre, where he is progressing favourably. The knife or dagger was secured by one of the officers, who has sent it to Chadwick's parents at Pateley Bridge.

William Chadwick had been employed as a stone worker in a local quarry when he enlisted at Harrogate on 9 August 1914, aged 18, at the same time as seven other men from Pateley Bridge: Thomas Thackery, Walter Bradbury, Harry Storey, Edwin Swires, John William Metcalfe, Harry Walker, and Ben Calvert, all of whom elected to join the local 5th Battalion. After recovering from his wounds in 1916, William transferred to the newly formed Machine Gun Corps, where he served until discharged on 18 December 1918, due to sickness. He was wounded and gassed a total of five times. Upon leaving the Army, he was employed as a gardener and chauffeur at Bewerley Hall, near Pateley Bridge.

William Chadwick. [Col Chadwick]

Lull

Things quietened down until mid-November. Casualties were less frequent, with the *Harrogate Advertiser* reporting that Private W.D Charles from Harrogate and Private W. Beck from Knaresborough had been wounded and were in separate hospitals in Belgium and France respectively. Private Beck was said to have *'been hit in the upper part of the face with a fragment of shrapnel shell fired from a trench mortar.'* The wound however, was *'not serious'*.

The day that William Chadwick was knifed, William Hardwick died from wounds, and Gilbert Johnson, originally from Staffordshire, and Cecil Yates, the budding musician and sportsman from Harrogate, were both killed. Cecil was shot in the head by a sniper and took two hours to die, without regaining consciousness.

Unfortunately, in September, the battalion suffered two (apparently) accidental wounds. On the 26th, Second Lieutenant Lee shot his finger off with his revolver, having just returned from hospital, and, on the 28th, Bertram Sandbrook shot Arthur Hudson in the leg.

On 8 October there were further casualties during a ration fatigue and on 11 October, George Raw from Pateley Bridge was killed. The same day, Lieutenant

Bernard Brown and Corporal Harry Storey were wounded.

On 12 October, 300 shells dropped on Skipton Road communication trench in just over an hour. Many were duds and the only damage was to a machine-gun emplacement. Edward Iredale noted that *'several of our chaps were suffering from shock owing to the heavy bombardment.'* The next day, the 1/5th Battalion supported an artillery bombardment with machine-gun fire leading to a retaliatory bombardment which killed 18-year-old William Mumford, a pre-war Terrier from Knaresborough.

Following a further week in Divisional Reserve, the 1/5th returned to Turco Farm on 24 October. This was a very quiet relief, although William Smith from Harrogate was killed on the last day. Peter Wilson sadly recorded that, presumably for want of a human target, a German sniper had shot the old black dog which had roamed the trenches for weeks. The first fortnight of November was spent at Coppenolle Hoek, resting, training, laying railway track and building huts.

On 24 November 1916 Private W. Anderson from Knaresborough was shipwrecked when the SS *Anglia* struck a mine off Folkestone. The story was told in the *Harrogate Herald* nine days later:

Pte. W. Anderson (5th West Yorks), son of Mr and Mrs T. Anderson, Calcutt, Knaresborough, who was on the mined hospital ship Anglia, which was sunk on Wednesday, had a miraculous escape from drowning. In a brief letter sent to his parents yesterday from a hospital where he is located at Epsom, Private Anderson states that immediately after the explosion he was immersed along with a large number of the wounded and invalided soldiers, but remembers little beyond striking out, swimming for himself...

Private Anderson, who was formerly captain of Scriven Football Team, was coming home on sick leave and was just recovering from an attack of influenza and

Escaping the HMHS *Anglia*. [Illustrated London News]

rheumatism in his arm, which had been aggravated from his exposure and the fact that he was hauled into a boat by the affected arm. He states he has lost his money, clothes, and everything he possessed. Anderson's two brothers (one a sergeant) are also in the 5th West Yorks.

Trench Life in the Salient

Unfortunately, the BEF was not prepared in time for winter in the Salient. Since the autumn rains had started early in August, there had not been time to put in the A-frame and duck-board structure necessary to keep the trenches usable during the winter. They were now knee deep in water with some trenches no more than isolated outposts, 50 yards apart, joined by impassable ditches full of water. To move between posts men had to climb out and run along the parapet, at the mercy of snipers.

Trench-foot was on the rise, with the generals unable to do anything but threaten criminal sanctions for failure to look after one's lower extremities properly. There were not enough Wellington boots to go around, so as each battalion was relieved in the Salient, they left their boots in a huge pile at Essex Farm. Within minutes, a battalion on its way back into the Salient would hunt through the pile for matching pairs, not always successfully. There was no hope of a dry pair.

In mid-November hostilities flared up again, culminating in the phosgene attack of 19 December. High Command Redoubt was a continued threat and efforts were made during November and early December to destroy it, or at least reduce the danger it posed to this part of the British line. Artillery exchanges increased in their frequency, as both sides fought the conditions as well as each other.

Around this time, some interesting letters home give an insight into trench life in the Salient. Private Roland Alderson wrote to his parents, describing the death of 1st VB veteran, Sergeant James Atkinson, from Tadcaster, and 19-year-old Daniel McNichol from York, on 18 November:

Dear Mother and Father, Thanks very much for your letter and parcel, which arrived safely last night (Sunday). The box was somewhat bent, but the contents were all right. I will write Miss Wade as soon as I can, but we haven't had a great deal of time these last few days. We have had a most exciting time lately. We went out of the trenches last Wednesday night, and were billeted in a farm a mile or two back. There were no civilians there. That night was all right, and on the following afternoon some of our guns started, and the Germans replied very quickly. The first shell or two dropped on the road near us, and then they got on to the farm where we were and of course we had to clear out, and whilst doing so they dropped one or two right among our chaps, and our platoon sergeant was killed, others wounded. One of them has since died. It was marvellous there were no more hit. I was lucky in being practically out of it, as when they started I was at the other end of the field in which the farm stood, and saw all the shells burst. Most of the chaps were in the barns and had a very anxious time. The stretcher bearers and one or two of the others were looking after the wounded whilst the shelling was going on, and I think they have been recommended for the DCM. They certainly deserve it, especially one of the stretcher bearers, called Humpherson. He is one of the best chaps in the Battalion, and whenever there is a call for SB's, I'll bet he is the first there every time, and it doesn't matter whether he is in danger himself or not, he sticks at it. I certainly hope he gets it.

When things quietened down again we got orders that if a certain battery of ours opened fire we had to clear, as they (the Huns) always retaliated. However, we were left in peace that night, but about breakfast-time next morning they started again, but luckily for us the first shell was a "dud", and we all got clear away without incident. We were very glad to get away from that billet, as you feel like a rat in a hole when they shell you. It's much better in the trenches, as you have a bit of protection there. We nearly got straffed going in the trenches. The Germans put 12 shells over in quick time, but it must have been our lucky day, as only one got hit in the waist, but they were too near to be pleasant. However, we are still smiling and are once more in reserve after two days in the front line. Our Platoon was in a detached post and could only get to the rest of the company at night by going over the top; but things were all very quiet. When we were coming out they spotted us and started potting at us, and we had to crawl into a trench on our hands and knees, which is no joke with a white ... the ground and full pack on, but we ... all right, and that's the main thing. The weather is fine at present, and there ... keen frosts at night, but the trenches are in a rotten condition, which, of course, has not helped, as there has been a terrible lot of rain lately. Today it has been foggy, and it is very thick tonight.

Arthur and George are all right, as is "your humble", but it's hard work keeping your feet warm, but they do all they can for us from getting trench feet; but it is a hard thing to prevent nowadays. I hope mine keep all right. I think that's about it this time. Hoping you still keep well, and with love from the three of us. We have not had snow yet, and don't want it.

Unfortunately, brave stretcher bearers like Humpherson were not always available, and others, like Peter Wilson, had to fill in. He was nearby when a sergeant in the bombing sap at Glimpse Cottage was hit by a machine gun bullet.

A beastly German sniper, not 50 yards away, had found his human target and the bullet struck the unfortunate fellow just a fraction of an inch above his left eye. The few fellows around seemed quite unable to attend the poor man – they were probably unable to attend the wounded as even many strong men are. I hastily placed the wounded man into a comfortable position and I knew if I stood erect – I could get potted as well – as the place was in a sap in advance of the firing line, sandbagged up to the shoulders which is used as an advanced post. Having torn open the field

Henry Scott's dugout. [Sketch British Library]

dressing, I also applied some iodine to the wound, which was a cruel gash and bled badly. I think the bullet must have scorched his eye, but I was delighted to think that the bullet had not penetrated his brain.

The intense artillery exchanges began to have a psychological effect. The first formally recorded case of shell-shock in the 1/5th Battalion was Private Wallace Rennie, who was diagnosed when transferred to hospital in London. Edward Mitchell from Harrogate had also been repatriated and was said to be suffering from 'Trench Fever' at St Bartholomew's Hospital in London.

Conversely, Captain Henry Scott demonstrated his phlegmatic attitude towards the dangers of life in the Salient. He wrote to *The Sketch*, with a photograph showing the inside of his dug-out on the Canal Bank, adorned with pages torn from the summer issue:

> *Dear Sir – Enclosed memories of your summer number may interest you. They have adorned my dug-out for five months though twice in peril – once from the wall falling in after a surfeit of rain, and, only yesterday, from a shell bursting within three yards. We are looking forward with feeling to the pleasure of your Christmas number. Yours, Still alive after eight months.*

Ben Thorpe wrote a vivid letter to his brother:

> *Your parcel received on Thursday. We were just saying we were getting sick of jam and bread for tea when it arrived, and, needless to say, it soon "went west", and we didn't leave a crumb, so you can imagine how the contents were appreciated. The chocolate was very acceptable, as I was absolutely stony at the time and couldn't buy any, so it arrived in the "time of nick". Tell Mr Tom Smith (Royal Oak) how grateful I am for the cigarettes and packs of playing cards, which were just what we required, as we only had a pack with the ace-of-spades badly marked, and when we were dealing them out we could tell who got it, and it used to be, "He loves me not, he loves me", until somebody got it, and then there was a shout, so we all knew where it was.*
>
> *I was very sorry to hear of the death of my old boss, Mr Ackrill. He will be greatly missed at the office by the whole of the staff. He was a good boss, and his breezy manner and jolly style made him popular with them all. I saw Fred's letter in the Knaresborough Post, and he seems to have had a warm time, but am glad to see he has got through all right. We will keep having casualties, and no wonder, as it is about as warm as any part of the line here. We could not have lost more, if we had gone over the top once or twice. As to recruiting, they may as well bring in conscription and have done with it instead of diddling about as they are doing.*

Norman Richardson.
[Ackrill]
Grateful recipient of a mouth organ from the editor of the Harrogate Herald.

Norman Richardson wrote to W.H. Breare to thank him for the mouth organ supplied by an anonymous donor:

Just a line to let you know I have received your paper all right. Well, we are still sticking to the work in the trenches. It is surprising what a difference a mouth organ makes to chaps; the more so when they are nearly fagged out. It seems to put new life into them, and they all get into step, and before they know they are at the billets. For instance, the first rest we went to while we were on the march somebody passed a mouth organ along, and I started playing it until we arrived at our rest billets. Some of the chaps said: "Well, if it had not been for the mouth organ we should not have landed." It just shows what a big difference it makes to a chap when he is nearly done up. Well, I will not waste any more of your time, so will close. Wishing you and your paper every success in the future. In the dug-out there are some Tommies who like to hear the mouth organ, so I am just going to give them a tune to keep them alive.

Some other members of the battalion received very little from home. On 3 October, Peter Wilson wrote to his parents:

I should be greatly obliged if you would send my next parcel to a comrade who is greatly neglected. Nobody writes to him and he never gets a parcel. I feel so sorry for him and he always gets a very welcome share from my parcels. His address is Pte. C. Carter 3021 16 Platoon D Co. 1/5 W. Yks. B.E.F. France. The poor fellow is also unable to write and has been seriously neglected at home... he has five other brothers serving and a father.'

Charles Henry Carter.
[Ackrill]
From Bilton. Received no parcels from home because his four brothers, step father, and five cousins were also serving.

Charles Henry Carter, from Bilton near Harrogate, and his brothers Joe and Arthur, were all serving with the 1/5th Battalion. Two other brothers were also serving, along with their step-father and five cousins. Little wonder that Charles's mother was unable to send much from home.

On 19 November Sam Meekosha of the 1/6th Battalion won the 49th Division's first Victoria Cross for digging out at least ten buried men under heavy shell fire at Turco Farm. He was to transfer to the 1/5th as an officer in 1917. That afternoon the 1/5th Battalion relieved the 1/6th, with B Company holding the front line trenches, such as they existed, on the right of 146 Brigade's sector.

The artillery exchanges continued and on 21 November 23-year-old Private James McTiernan was wounded. He was caught in the blast of a bursting shell, probably shrapnel, which wounded two others. He was too badly wounded to be taken back to Essex Farm and was carried directly into the B Company officers' dugout where Captain Hughes, the Medical

Joseph Carter. [Ackrill]
Brother of Charles and Albert: all three serving with the 1/5th Battalion.

Officer, surgically removed part of his intestine. However, the MO could not save James, who died due to previous loss of blood. In civilian life, he had been a mill worker from Volta Street, Selby, where he lived with his nine brothers and sisters in five rooms.

More excitement followed that night as A Company relieved B Company in the front line. A patrol of Yorkshiremen was sent out to listen for activity in the enemy trenches and they encountered a group of Germans, near No Man's Cottage. The two parties threw grenades at each other, and two members of A Company were wounded, including Private John Knowles who suffered a bad injury to his right arm. John was brought in from no man's land by Edward Iredale, and he eventually made it back downhill to the Battalion HQ officers' mess at La Belle Alliance. When he arrived, Colonel Wood was briefing Lieutenant Colonel Moxon of the 1/5th KOYLI, who were due to relieve the West Yorkshires at Turco Farm in the next rotation. Captain Hughes, who was also present, immediately set about amputating John's arm, with the assistance of Colonel Moxon, but they could not save him.

Edward Iredale was the other wounded man and he was evacuated to the 14th Stationary Hospital at Boulogne, via the dressing station at Essex Farm. He had two operations to remove shrapnel from his leg and was eventually repatriated on 7 December 1915. He was later awarded the Military Medal for his bravery in trying to save John Knowles and recommended for the DCM and a Russian decoration, but these were never awarded.

 On 22 November, the 1/5th Battalion withdrew to the west bank of the canal, returning to Turco Farm trenches on 1 December. This time three platoons from D Company were ordered forward to hold D19 and D20, just as a major artillery bombardment of High Command Redoubt started, supported by machine guns of the King's Royal Rifles on the right. The shallow elevation of the British machine guns, aimed from behind Willow Walk at the redoubt, meant that bullets were striking the parados and parapet of the front line trench at D19 and the Yorkshiremen had to be withdrawn for their own safety.

Over the following days the German occupiers of High Command Redoubt worked hard to repair the damage done, whilst the 1/5th Battalion laboured to thwart them, with frequent patrols and night time machine-gun volleys to scare off repair parties.

On 13 December, Corporal John Richardson of the signal section crawled out to make repairs at five separate points on the line, under heavy artillery fire. His heroism was recognised in a letter from Divisional Commander, Major General Perceval, and on 1 August 1916, at Hedeauville, he was presented with the Military Medal by General Sir Hubert Gough for his bravery. In a letter to his parents, he reported that: *'I got the medal for keeping up communication during the attack. We were very heavily shelled but came through alright.'*

John Richardson had been a Terrier since early 1913, employed by the York Corporation electricity offices as a clerk.

Phosgene

Chlorine gas had been used on the Western Front since the Second Battle of Ypres, and mustard gas would be used later on in the war. Both could be fatal under certain circumstances, but phosgene, on the other hand, was usually lethal. The newly designed 'PH' gas helmet, which had been distributed to the 1/5th Battalion at Fleurbaix in June 1915, was specifically designed to deal with phosgene, but was effective only if used promptly and correctly.

By 10 December intelligence reports confirmed that cylinders containing chlorine and phosgene had been dug into the German front line trenches from Boesinghe to Pilckem, with the intention of releasing the gas and floating it across no man's land as soon as the wind was favourable.

On 17 December the 1/5th Battalion moved into Turco Farm. D Company was in the front line at D19 and D20, B Company was in support at the Pump Room and Clifford's Tower, C Company at Battalion HQ (La Belle Alliance), and A Company in reserve on the east bank of the canal. All four companies were in the path of the deadly new gas.

That night the shelling stopped and the next day was unusually quiet, allowing work on the trenches to continue uninterrupted. According to Everard Wyrall, 'an eerie stillness charged the atmosphere overnight', as gas masks were checked in anticipation and sentries sniffed the air.

Then, in the early hours of 19 December, a breeze came up from the north-east, blowing down the ridge from the High Command towards Turco Farm. The taps were opened and the deadly mixture was released along three miles of front line. From the German trenches it floated downhill, across no man's land into Willow Walk and Canadian Dugouts, reaching as far as the canal bank and beyond for a distance of ten miles. As the gas rolled down the hill, it was closely followed by an artillery barrage. The primary victims were the 49th Division, including the 1/5th Battalion at Turco Farm.

Rowland Casebourne, the new adjutant, described the beginning of the attack in the battalion war diary:

At about 05:40 the sentries in D.20 heard a shout which was immediately followed by the firing of coloured rockets all along the German line. These seemed to be the signal for the gas to be turned on for the hiss of escaping gas was heard most distinctly + as a dense white vapour it was soon blown across to our own trenches by the prevailing N.E. wind. Warning was at once sent to H.Q. by telephone and by runners and this message was the only one that was got through by wire from D20 as the terrific bombardment delivered by the Germans immediately after the gas had got into our trenches cut the wire from D19 and D20 as well as at the WILLOWS. Prompt measures were taken to meet the gas which got to HQ at LA BELLE ALLIANCE by 5.15am. Communication was kept up with Brigade HQ throughout the attack which lasted about an hour but the Coy on the CANAL BANK was cut off immediately notification had been got through to them. The enemy did not take any advantage of their gas far beyond three small parties which were caught between the lines by one MG and rifle fire. No advance was made by the Germans who kept up a heavy bombardment all day...

There was no German plan to attack behind the gas, but small parties of enemy soldiers followed the gas cloud as it drifted across no man's land, so they could observe the effect of the fumes and grab prisoners and equipment.

The *Yorkshire Herald* printed an anonymous account of the attack, confirming that there had been warning of a gas attack for some days and that smoke helmets were to be carried night and day with goggles kept in good order. On the morning of the attack, the 'special correspondent' reports that all were standing to, sniffing the air as the delicious smell of lilac drifted across:

> *A white mist came creeping along the ground towards us. It was about 12 inches high but gathering volume from the German trenches. When it reached us it was a wall of grey-green vapour, some seven feet in height. Only when the officer commanding screamed incoherently for the men to don their gas masks did they do so, becoming "500 black-a-veiled demons peering at each other through the mica eye pieces".*

Norman 'Norrie' Beech, a gents' outfitter from Harrogate, and his comrade James Atkinson, had just brought their machine gun back into the trench from its night time position in no man's land when the phosgene was released. As the 'gas gongs' (made of York treacle tins) were sounded by the sentries, Norrie and James reacted by hefting their gun back over the parapet into no man's land, and carried it up the rise so that they could fire directly into an approaching party of German soldiers. In their hurry, the pair did not have time to put on their gas masks and were both awarded the DCM for beating off the attack.

Norman Beech. [Ackrill] Photographed on enlistm in 1914, Norrie Beech w awarded the DCM for bravery with his machine during the phosgene atta

An hour after the red rockets had been fired, signalling the release of phosgene, green rockets were sent up, ordering the German artillery to commence firing gas, high explosive and shrapnel shells into the British rear areas. It was behind the front line, at the Canal Bank and La Belle Alliance, where most damage was done because the soldiers of A and C companies were less well prepared than their comrades in D and B companies, further forward. Some of those on the Canal Bank were asleep in their dug-outs as the phosgene arrived and the gas shells exploded around them. Twenty-two year old Walter Mellor, from Wetherby, recorded his experience in a letter to the *Rothwell Courier & Times*:

> *I was lying in my dug-out with some other chaps, and had a presentiment that something was going to happen, especially as the Germans seemed unusually quiet. I awoke with a start, as the rifle fire was heavy, and sat up. I said, "There's something going off." I put my head outside the dug-out, and I smelled that infernal gas (it haunts me still). I said, "Hey up, lads, its gas," and out I dashed to wake our chaps up with my respirator in my hand, ready to put on.*

The chaps were in dug-outs further away, and by the time I got to them the gas was fully on us. I remember well it was choking me slowly, but I got to them and got them out. I say this quite modestly – very likely they would never have awakened again if I hadn't got to them. I was just about done, and when I came to I was soaked to the skin, and plastered like a kiddie having a mud bath. However, here we are, here we are again! I am still alive and kicking but it was a teaser, I can tell you. Gas rolls over the ground just like green vapour, and turns our buttons green just like a penny that's been in the fire.

Charles Winterburn, also of Wetherby, confirmed that Walter: *'jumped out of his dug-out and ran down the trenches in his stockinged feet to warn us of the gas, and I am sure he saved many lives in doing so.'*

The gas had affected C Company particularly badly at La Belle Alliance, so Colonel Wood hurriedly adjusted the reliefs, sending them back to the relative safety of the canal bank. A Company was sent forward to D19 and D20, and D Company to HQ. This was all done during the day under continuing and heavy artillery fire. Captain Lansdale from Knaresborough, Second Lieutenant Griffiths, and the Adjutant, Rowland Casebourne, were all sent to hospital, suffering from the effects of gas.

There were many other acts of bravery in the chaos. Second Lieutenant James Jameson was awarded the Military Cross for conspicuous gallantry and devotion to duty following the incapacitation of Captain Lansdale:

When his Captain was injured early in the day he took command, and set a fine example to his men. Although himself suffering considerably he stuck to his work, and at one time carried bombs to a bombing party, going across the open to do so.

Badly gassed at La Belle Alliance, Second Lieutenant John Walker (from Thirsk) also refused to succumb, insisting on accompanying his company to the canal bank, against the orders of MO Captain Hughes. However, on arrival there he was killed by a shell blast which collapsed his dug-out.

John C. Walker. [Steve Billings]
Disregarded medical orders to stay with his company.

Sergeant M.C. Morton and Private A.W. Cooke were both awarded the DCM for gallantry on 19 December 1915. Matthew Morton was born in Tadcaster, and was a widowed house-painter based in York. He had served in the 5th Battalion as a pre-war Territorial, along with his brother Albert (who survived the war). Later in the war Matthew transferred to the Royal Flying Corps as a pilot and was killed when his plane crashed in April 1918. His DCM citation records that on 19 December 1917:

He set a fine example of cool bravery all day during the enemy attack. He took messages over ground where others had been wounded, and volunteered and took charge of an isolated and important bombing post, where his presence did much to steady the men.

James Atkinson. [Ack Awarded the DCM for taking his machine gun into No man's Land without a gas mask du the phosgene attack.

Cooke's medal was conferred for *'conspicuous gallantry when, though wounded in the head, he volunteered to carry bombs to a bombing post, and, in order to save time, went across the open in full view of the enemy. While crossing, he was seriously wounded, but handed over the bombs to the post.'*

On 23 January 1916, General Plumer presented the Military Cross to Jameson, and the four DCMs to Morton, Beech, Atkinson and Cooke. In doing so, he said:

I come here today to present Military Crosses and DCMs which on the recommendation of the Commander-in-Chief, His Majesty the King has been graciously pleased to award for gallantry in the recent gas attack.

Whether your acts were the most gallant of the many performed on that occasion that has been brought to my attention it is hard to say.

I look upon you and talk to you as representatives of the whole Corps who behaved with gallantry and I should like you to pass on to your comrades or those who may be under you what I have to say today.

No longer now does the Gas attack have the same terrifying effect it had in the earlier days of the War. A gas attack can be overcome as it has been, but only by great steadiness, by the implicit obedience to the orders of the commanders, and by real discipline. The Corps Commander and the divisional Commanders have reason to be proud of the way their troops met the attack. The Commander-in-Chief has personally expressed his appreciation and, as commander of the Second Army I endorse his remarks. The matter of selection of recipients of the awards is a very difficult one, as the number of awards is limited. As I have said, the number here today do not all represent the total number of the acts of personal devotion. You are here today not only as individuals, but as representatives of the units to which you belong.

We are proud of you. You have brought credit on your Brigades, on your Divisions, and on your Corps.

Explain to your comrades when you return what I have said, that you are the representatives of many who performed gallant deeds, for which only a limited number of awards can be given.

New Year awards were also made in early 1916 to reflect specific acts of gallantry on other days in the Salient, as well as consistent bravery. Captain Sowerby and Captain

Williamson received the Military Cross. Sergeants John Sim and R.T. Hastings, both veterans of the 1st VB, were mentioned in General Haig's first New Year Despatch in 1916, as was Private Joseph Abbott, grocer's assistant from Dacre Banks.

In addition to Gilbert Tolley, three other men were awarded DCMs. The citations act as appropriate illustrations of the constant dangers of life around Turco Farm and the steadfast spirit needed to withstand the strain. Private Harry Usher, from Harrogate, *'remained at his post alone in the telephone office of his Company Headquarters when the front line had been withdrawn on account of the enemy's heavy trench mortars, shells bursting within 10 yards of the line.'*

John Sim. [Ackrill]
Mentioned in Despatches.

CSM John Nicholson received his for: *'conspicuous gallantry on all occasions, especially when in charge of wire parties. He has also performed excellent work in repairing parapets under heavy fire, and has invariably shown a marked devotion to duty.'*

CSM Gordon Lund, one of five brothers from Plompton Mill, all serving, was decorated for *'putting up parapets damaged by shell fire, when a machine gun was firing on the spot. He has invariably exhibited great bravery and devotion in the performance of his duties.'*

He was badly gassed on 19 December and repatriated to England for recuperation, returning to his battalion in 1916, only to be killed on the Somme.

According to the *Yorkshire Herald*, on 1 December 1917:

Harry Usher. [Ackrill]
Signaller Harry Usher stayed at his post alone under heavy artillery bombardment.

Corporal Fred Tomlinson has gained distinction for conspicuous gallantry in action. Thirty-five years of age he enlisted on November 6th 1914, and went to the front with his unit on April 15th 1915. In the December following he received the Distinguished Conduct Certificate for bravery in rebuilding the damaged parapet of a trench under heavy fire. For splendid service during a gas attack on Dec 19th 1916 [1915] he received the Military Medal…

He was employed in the smith's shop in the carriage works of the North Eastern Railway, previous to the outbreak of hostilities, and was for eighteen months on special duty with the railway section of the Royal Engineers. He is married and his wife and two children reside at 16 Bedford Street, The Groves, York.

Casualties

Including Lieutenant Walker, twenty-four men of the 1/5th Battalion lost their lives as a direct result of the gas and artillery attacks of 19–20 December 1915. Fifteen of these were killed, and nine lived long enough for their passing to be recorded as their having died of wounds.

The eight men killed on 19th December were:

John Walker	(Thirsk)
Robert Wilmot	(Pateley Bridge)
John Heavisides	(Ripon)
William Pybus	(Ripon)
Robert Daniel	(York)
Percy Mason	(Ripon)
Richard Wilson	
James Cahill	(Harrogate)
Charles Kilvington	(Harrogate)

James Cahill. [Ackrill] Gave his life on 19th December 1915 He wa from Starbeck.

On 20 December the enemy artillery bombardment continued, taking a further toll. Also, the delayed effects of exposure to phosgene became evident. It was not uncommon for men to drop dead the next day having shown no other signs of ill health. This is why forty further casualties were sent to hospital the day after the attack. All around, the ground was littered with crystals looking like hoar frost, which released harmful amounts of gas if disturbed. The six men killed on 20 December were:

Robert 'Bob' Wilmot. [Ackrill] Gave his life on 19th December 1915.

Ronald Marshall. [Ackrill] Gave his life on 19th December 1915.

Samuel Penrose. [Yorkshire Herald] Gave his life on 19th December 1915.

108

Samuel Penrose	(York)	
Richard Tute	(Selby)	
Robert Cousins		
Ronald Marshall	(Harrogate)	
Walter Dawson	(Harrogate)	
Edwin Buckborough	(Harrogate)	

Eleven died in the following days and weeks. They were:

Leonard Holland	(Harrogate)	d. 21 December 1915
George Pink	(York)	d. 22 December 1915
Benjamin Baines	(York)	d. 27 December 1915
Alfred Pounder	(York)	d. 27 December 1915
Ernest Gomersall	(Harrogate)	d. 1 January 1916
William Ferguson	(York)	d. 7 January 1916
Selwyn Lupton	(Harrogate)	d. 10 January 1916
Alfred Clark		d. 27 January 1916

George Pink. [John Snowdon]
Painter and decorator at York City Asylum.

News of a big gas attack hit the local and national press before Christmas, as the dreaded telegrams started to arrive. It was the New Year before the details began to emerge. On 8 January 1916, the *Pateley Bridge & Nidderdale Herald* reported the death of Robert Wilmot, and the events of 19 December.

HARROGATE AND DISTRICT MEN ATTACKED BY GAS

On Sunday, December 19th a regiment containing many Harrogate and District men were attacked by the Germans with the deadly gas. Private Robert Wilmot, son of Mr Tom Wilmot, Park Street, Pateley Bridge succumbed to the gas. Mr Wilmot received the following from Major Oddie:

"I am sorry to tell you that your son died in action yesterday morning. We were resisting a big German gas attack, and were successful in doing so, but of course had to pay the price, and you are one of the sufferers. Your boy was badly 'gassed' shortly after 5am and never got over it. It will be some consolation to you to know that he died as he was sitting in the trench, and according to his Captain did not suffer; he simply laid back his head and passed away. I would have liked to have attended his funeral, but it was impossible for me to get away. He has been buried in a small graveyard, close to some of his pals, two miles from here. Sympathising with you in your loss etc."

Private Wilmot, it may be remembered was one of the first three that left Pateley Bridge. He went along with Lance-cpl Geo. Raw & Private Rowland Light. Lcpl Raw was killed some weeks ago. Wilmot was only about 19 years of age and previous to going out worked for Mr Atkinson at Glasshouses Mill.

The *Yorkshire Herald* reported the deaths of four York-based soldiers of the 1/5th Battalion. Twenty-six-year-old Samuel Penrose was a pre-war Territorial and

Lijssenthoek Military Cemetery. [Author]

Beechwood Boy who disembarked in France in August 1915. His parents were informed of his death on Christmas Eve. Before the war Samuel had been a chemist's assistant in Micklegate, York. Benjamin Baines, from Middle Eldon Street, had been a smith employed by the North East Railway in the Holgate carriage works for thirteen years. Aged 32, he left a widow and two children. Alfred Pounder was 20 years old, from Blossom Street and a newly promoted lance corporal. He had been wounded in the chest and abdomen, presumably by shrapnel in the artillery attack which followed the gas release. Before the war he had been a clerk with the NER. Thirty-five-year-old Robert Daniel was a widower who worked as a blacksmith before enlisting with the 5th Battalion on the outbreak of war.

Harold Leyland from Harrogate was a prominent local pianist. Along with Benjamin Baines and Alfred Pounder from York, he died at the huge Casualty Clearing Station at Lijssenthoek, near Poperinghe, about 12 miles west of Ypres. All three would have been evacuated there via Essex Farm Dressing Station and Elverdinghe, on the light railway. On arrival at Lijssenthoek, they were probably assessed as too unwell to be repatriated. Nurse M. Wharton, sister in charge, reported that Alfred was 'in a most critical condition', but that he died peacefully.

The *Herald* also reported the death of 26-year-old Ernest Gomersall, an Association Footballer from Harrogate, who was wounded in the right side of the head and shoulder. He made it as far as the coast, but died in Boulogne. The death of Walter Dawson, a YMCA member, was reported in the *Claro Times* and *Harrogate Advertiser*. He was wounded in the leg, probably on 19 December, because he had time to write a letter saying he would be home by Christmas, before he died the next day. The telegram reporting his death read: *'Regret report death of 2235 Pte. Walter Dawson, 1-5th West Yorks, December 20th, at 22 General Hospital, Wimereux. Cause, gunshot wound thigh. – Territorial Records, York'*

Robert Eastwood. [Ackrill]
Wounded twice.

The local newspapers reported some of the men of the 1/5th Battalion who had been gassed. These included Edwin Swires from Pateley Bridge; Roy Holmes, Gordon Lund, John 'Jack' Kell and Edward Blackstone from Knaresborough; Owen Metcalfe and Walter Mellor from Wetherby. From York, brothers James Snowden, 26, a Rowntree's worker, and Robert Snowden, 21, NER cleaner, were both reported gassed and recovering in hospital in England.

From Harrogate, the list included Guy Wilkinson, Joe Carter, Arthur Carter, Charles Carter, Fred Martlew, R.M. Stamp, George Lawson, Norman Richardson, Joseph Tipling, Allan Johnson, Roy Purchase, Walter Pickard, H. Gledhill and Drummer J. Ellis. Swires had already been wounded once previously and was in hospital in Nottingham, with Gledhill, Purchase, Pickard, and Metcalfe reported to be in hospital in France with most of the others affected.

Harry Waddington. [Chloe Wilson]
'Sergeant Wadd' recovered from his wounds in time for the Battle of the Somme.

The wounded were also listed. Charles Inman saw his comrade, James McNicholas, from Knaresborough, have his right hand blown off by a whizz-bang. He *'bore his injury bravely and was quite cheerful as he left ... for the hospital.'* Robert Eastwood was wounded for the third time, this time very badly, having been shot through the thigh and body. He was in Lincoln Hospital. Harry Waddington, known to the men of his platoon as 'Sergeant Wadd', had been wounded in the head and was lying in

Selwyn Lupton. [Ackrill]
Received his 'blighty one' on 20th December at Turco Farm but died at Wharncliffe Hospital, Sheffield, three weeks later.

hospital at Boulogne on 30 December. He would recover to serve with the 1/5th on the Somme.

Selwyn Lupton made it back to Yorkshire before passing away in Sheffield. He wrote to his mother to say that he had had a piece of shrapnel removed, and that he was 'going on all right', but died on 10 January 1916. His coffin was collected by a detachment of Sherwood Foresters, and escorted by train to Harrogate, where he was buried with full military honours in Harlow Hill Cemetery.

Christmas 1915

Over the next few days, the 1/5th Battalion remained in the Salient, but the men were not required to do much by officers who were themselves lethargic and recovering from the effects of the gas. Rations were hard to come by as the wagon lines and tramways had been destroyed by shell fire and the weather. Everything had to be brought forward by pack horse, and bearer parties of exhausted soldiers.

On Christmas Eve, George Cartmel of the 1/5th Battalion's machine-gun detachment was killed by a single sniper's bullet. He had lived in Valley Drive,

Harrogate and worked at Messrs England & Robinson, Ironmongers, of Parliament Street.

Christmas Day is described in the battalion war diary as 'very quiet'. There was no intention of repeating the famous informal truce of 1914. A single shell fell on a dug-out at La Belle Alliance, three men being slightly injured.

The last day in the Ypres trenches was 29 December, all companies clearing up prior to departure. Enemy artillery bombarded them all day until 8pm, especially B Company who were occupying D21. John Holmes and Leonard Bracewell were both killed in the afternoon. John Holmes was a veteran of the 1st VB and had served under Cecil Wood in South Africa. He was a joiner in York before re-enlisting on the outbreak of war as a time-expired soldier. Drummer Bracewell had joined the 5th Battalion in 1909 as a 15-year-old cadet and was well liked as a cheery soul. He had worked at Waddington's piano factory in Stonegate and lived on the Hull Road. Captain Frederick Thompson had arranged home leave for him just before the phosgene attack and he had returned to B Company on Christmas morning.

From Turco Farm, the remaining men of the 1/5th Battalion marched back over Bridge 4, and turned right past Essex Farm for the last time, heading for Elverdinghe where they boarded London Transport buses. They spent the night in camp near Poperinghe, marching six miles to the French border at Houtquerque, and then a further five miles to Wormhoudt, roughly half way between Ypres and Calais, arriving on New Year's Day 1916.

Chapter 6

The Somme
(January–June 1916)

'The soft thud of the bayonet'

Leaving Ypres

When the men of the 1/5th Battalion marched out of the Ypres Salient, they were bedraggled and disorientated. Their bodies were dirty and infested with scabies and lice. Trench foot was rife and in some cases acute. For example, Private William Sharp was invalided back to England with trench feet in January 1916 and did not return until 3 June. Clothes were caked in mud and reeked of gas. Personal kit was incomplete and mixed with that of other soldiers.

To aid recovery, the battalion spent the first four weeks of 1916 resting at Wormhoudt, then on the Channel coast at No.6 Rest Camp, two-and-a-half miles east of Calais. With a relatively relaxed daily routine involving baths, parades and inspections of clothing and weapons, the mud of Ypres was washed away and kit began to resemble its intended form. Item by item, the battalion was re-equipped, with new limbers and horses arriving. There was some relatively gentle platoon-based training, including drill, musketry and physical training intended to re-instil the skills and discipline lost during months of living minute to minute in slushy ditches. This included the 43-mile route march from Wormhoudt to Calais in the middle of the month. At Calais, there was the opportunity to train on the sandy beach and dunes. As the men recovered their strength and discipline, training progressed from the basics at platoon level, to company-based exercises. There was also technical instruction in bombing, signals, musketry and fire tactics. The men also practised attacking from taped trenches for the first time. This foreshadowed events six months later and indicated their changing role from defensive occupiers of trenches to a unit capable of supporting, and even carrying out, a co-ordinated assault.

The culture and atmosphere of the battalion was also changing. Until this point in its history, the 1/5th Battalion was proudly a band of Territorials from the West Riding, with groups of brothers, cousins, friends, former neighbours and work-mates willingly facing hardship together. The phosgene attack had removed the amateur feel to operations, as well as some of the good humour, and replaced it with a more professional, fatalistic outlook.

The battalion numbered 14 officers and 553 other ranks when it left Ypres, barely half its normal wartime establishment. Drafts were needed to bring the battalion up to strength, which also affected its profile. These would include a few Regular soldiers and recruits from as far as Exeter and East London and, although most were still from Yorkshire and the North East of England, the West Riding voices were now sprinkled heavily with other regional accents. By the summer, the gulf between old stagers and new recruits, even those who had seen action in other units, began to appear and this may have affected the battalion's efficiency, as well as its easy atmosphere.

Army changes

Lieutenant Colonel Wood was still in command of the 1/5th Battalion, although he took some weeks blighty leave at the end of January, returning on 13 February. In his absence, Frederick (now Major) Thompson commanded the battalion. There had been changes at higher level, too, although these were on a more permanent basis. Sir John French had been recalled as commander-in-chief of the BEF on 19 December 1915, the day of the phosgene attack, to be replaced by Sir Douglas Haig, an ascetic Scotsman who was one of French's main critics. Major General Perceval still commanded the 49th Division, following Major General Baldock's incapacitation at Chateau les Trois Tours, but 146 Brigade was now commanded by recently promoted Brigadier General Michael Goring-Jones, who was from Shropshire and had served in India before the war. Having taken over from Brigadier General MacFarlane, Goring-Jones handed out certificates of merit to NCOs and men of the 1/5th Battalion and expressed satisfaction at their appearance when he inspected them on 26 January 1916.

The experience of nearly eighteen months of war had led to some structural lessons being learned across the BEF. Scouts were now organised as a separate section in the battalion, under the intelligence officer. The organisation of machine gunnery was also rationalised. The Machine Gun Corps, flippantly known as 'The Suicide Club', was founded in October 1915, and each battalion of 146 Brigade provided four machine-gun sections to be amalgamated into a newly formed 146th Machine Gun Company (MGC) on 27 January 1916. By 9 February 1916 it was fully equipped with sixteen Vickers guns.

The 1/5th provided two officers, Second Lieutenants S. Armitage and W.A. Anderson to the 146th Company MGC. Two NCOs, Robert Barrett and Harry Steel, also transferred across. Barrett, from New Park, Harrogate, was a technical man employed before the war by the Harrogate Road Car Company. Steel was from Boroughbridge and had been a tailor and pre-war Territorial with the 5th Battalion. He was later killed with the MGC on 19 February 1917, at Ransart, succumbing to chest and abdominal wounds. Each company in the 1/5th Battalion retained a single machine-gun section, equipped during the late winter and early spring with the new, lighter, Lewis gun. Each gun still required a team of six and could consume half a ton of ammunition in a single hour, with a sustainable rate of about 250 rounds per minute.

The Somme

The first fatality of the New Year came on 1 February 1916, when John C. Robinson

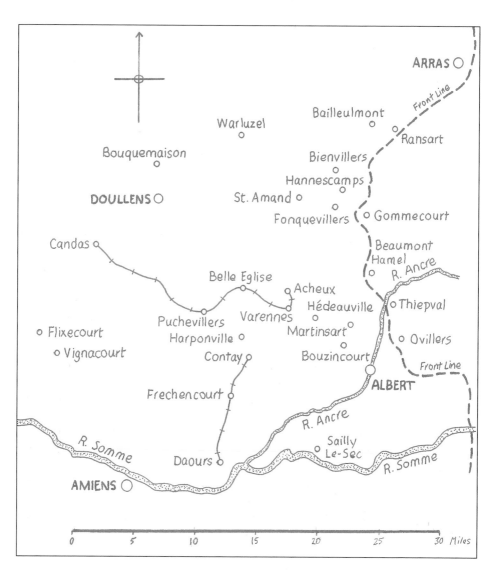

The Somme Rear Areas [Sketch Map 7]
Showing the route of the River Somme and the River Ancre, the Candas-Acheux and Contay-Daours railways, and other key locations in the story of the 1/5th Battalion in 1916 and early 1917.

from Sunderland was killed. It may have been due to a transport related incident, as the 1/5th Battalion left Calais for the Somme that day. Such incidents were not unknown, given the dangers attached to shifting large amounts of heavy equipment on and off limbers and trains, with minimal thought for safety. The divisional diary records also that the floor of a horsebox collapsed, killing one animal and injuring several others.

116

When the 1/5th Battalion entrained, the destination was secret, but by the time they steamed out of Calais station it was generally known that they were heading for the hitherto quiet zone of the Somme. This was good news for all who dreaded a return to the Salient. They were certainly cheered by their ability to secure a plate of egg and chips with a cup of coffee for a franc in Ailly-sur-Somme, near Amiens, where they arrived thirteen hours after leaving Calais. Here they spent the next few days under canvas, resting and continuing to practise musketry, scouting and further attacks from trenches.

In mid-February 146 Brigade moved forward to the support area around Martinsart and Bouzincourt. West of the River Ancre and three miles behind the front line at Thiepval, these villages were relatively peaceful and still occupied by civilians, sheltered as they were from enemy machine-gun fire by the dense cover of Aveluy Wood. The Yorkshiremen were put to work under the direction of the Royal Engineers.

The Battle Plan

On arrival at the Somme in early February 1916, the 49th Division came under the orders of Fourth Army, commanded by General Sir Henry Rawlinson, which would carry the main attack on the first day of the battle. At the time, the Allies were considering with Marshal Joffre a huge Anglo–French attack, with the objective of seizing the chain of German fortified villages and redoubts on the ridge north of the River Somme, and the plain to the south. This had been agreed in principle at the end of December 1915, following an inter-allied conference at Chantilly where a co-ordinated allied strategy was agreed for 1916.

On 21 February 1916, however, the German Army landed a weighty blow against the French at Verdun, further south, which almost succeeded in breaking the French line and caused Joffre to request urgent assistance from the British. A heavy counter punch, such as that being planned by the Allies on the Somme, would help by drawing off enemy troops giving the French a chance to recover and counter-attack. However, the contribution of the French Army would now be greatly reduced as it was heavily committed at Verdun, and the attack would need to be a mainly British affair.

General Haig put Rawlinson in charge of planning the 'Big Push', although the two men would have conflicting tactical objectives. In early April 1916 Rawlinson submitted a plan which took account of the lessons of 1915 in respect of artillery, including the need to ensure sufficient heavy guns to utterly destroy the German front line, allowing it to be taken at minimal cost in lives. This meant artillery bombardment of the enemy lines to a depth of 1,250 yards. Having gained possession of the enemy front line, the BEF would then be well placed to smash up German counter-attacks, before wheeling the artillery forward to repeat the exercise on the German second line trenches, and so on. This conservative strategy of 'bite-and-hold' appeared to draw on the experience of Aubers Ridge and Loos, where the relative lack of effective heavy artillery had allowed German machine gunners to survive the preparatory bombardment and massacre the advancing British infantry.

Sir Douglas Haig responded to Rawlinson's plan by asserting the need to bombard the German lines to a depth of about 2,500 yards, to enable a reserve force (including infantry and cavalry) to break through entirely when the opportunity arose, and roll up the German Army into a pocket near Arras. Notwithstanding the relative merits of this more expansive approach (which are a matter of considerable controversy), it involved doubling the depth of artillery attack, thereby halving the intensity of the onslaught. The result was to be a huge preliminary bombardment of one and a half million shells which would be too diluted to destroy fully the German defences in the front line, or at any depth. In the words of Gary Sheffield, 'too few guns were given too much to do'. In his masterly work, *The Chief*, Professor Sheffield quotes Major General 'Curly' Birch, artillery adviser at GHQ: 'Poor Haig – as he was always inclined to – spread his guns.' In many places the German wire and front line defences would remain intact and as a result the BEF was destined to re-live the failures of 1915, but on a gigantic scale.

Thiepval Wood

Thiepval Wood was to have considerable significance in the Battle of the Somme, as the assembly point and main supply line for the series of attacks aimed at Thiepval village and the Schwaben Redoubt between 1 July and 3 September 1916. When the 1/5th arrived in the Thiepval sector, the wood was a dense green canopy rising away from the marshes on the east bank of the River Ancre. It was hemmed in to the north-east and south-east by the German front line and the ridge along which it ran.

To the north east of the wood, the ground rose on the right to the Schwaben Redoubt, located on a ring contour at the top of the ridge, 600 yards beyond. The *Feste Schwaben* was protected by a forward trench system and heavy belts of barbed wire. German trench lines traced the crest of the ridge, joining the Schwaben Redoubt to Thiepval village, and the Leipzig Redoubt 1,000 yards to the south. The village was itself heavily defended, with machine-gun posts dominating no man's land.

Either side of the village, no man's land sloped down to the British front line which skirted Thiepval Wood. This was roughly the centre point of Rawlinson's 16-mile offensive, so there was much digging to do, as miles of trenches, forts and dumps needed to be constructed. The arrival of the 1/5th Battalion was not coincidental and fatigues once more took precedence over much needed training.

On 13 February, four officers of the 1/5th Battalion – Second Lieutenants Pearson, Dresser, Prest and Robinson – entered Thiepval Wood for the first time, to familiarise themselves with the trenches there. This enabled them to help co-ordinate five consecutive nights of working parties, directed by the Royal Engineers. It is possible that the Yorkshiremen helped to dig the assembly and communication trenches which they themselves were to occupy on the morning of 1 July 1916: the first day of the battle.

Minenwerfer

The enemy hurled occasional mortar rounds and machine-gun fire into Thiepval Wood to disrupt the work. This caused a handful of casualties, but there were no deaths in 146 Brigade until a heavy German mortar round struck on 20 February, just as the 1/5th

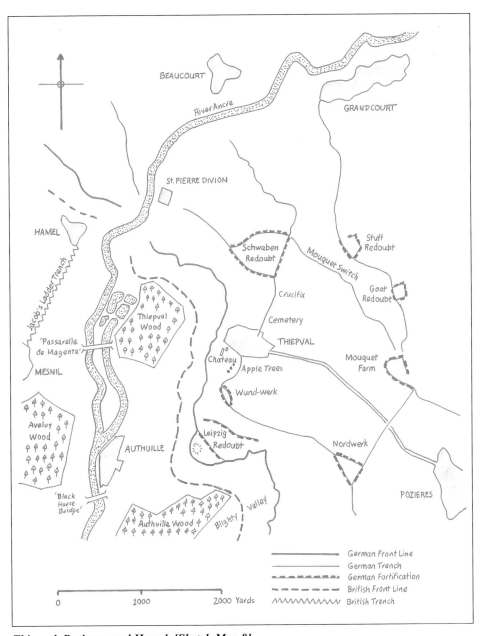

Thiepval, Pozieres, and Hamel. [Sketch Map 8]
Showing Aveluy Wood, Thiepval Wood and the strategic significance of the Pozières Ridge.

Battalion was relieving the 1/6th in the front line trenches. As B Company arrived at the head of a communication trench just behind Hammerhead Sap, the Minenwerfer (which was probably sited near the crossroads just behind the German front line in Thiepval village) fired its bomb. The missile exploded in the midst of the Yorkshiremen, collapsing the trench and virtually wiping out a platoon of sixteen men. Five were killed, including 15-year-old Alfred Dalby, from Oatlands, Harrogate. He had been an apprentice at Messrs Slater & Co in West Park, and was probably the youngest member of the 1/5th Battalion to die during the Great War. He was far too young to have been at the front at all.

The others who lost their lives included 22-year-old Hubert Moyser from Nunnery Lane, York, who was reported to have enlisted soon after the outbreak of war. He had been a cleaner with the North Eastern Railway. Donald Mackay, commanding B Company, and only 30 years old himself, wrote to Hubert's mother to confirm that *'no man could hope for a finer death than that of the private soldier who dies at his post.'* The Reverend F. Hood attempted to provide further comfort by assuring Hubert's mother that he had attended Holy Communion that morning and joined the prayer remembering the people left at home. Herbert Munday, Richard Robinson and Dennis Tate from Malton were the others who lost their lives. The *Harrogate Advertiser* reported

Alfred Dalby. [Ackrill]
Fifteen years old when he w
killed by a Minenwerfer at
Hammerhead Sap.

on 3 March 1916 that Lance Corporal Gregg was wounded, somewhat seriously, in both shoulders and the leg.

Over the following two days, having buried their comrades in the valley on the south-eastern edge of Thiepval Wood, the 1/5th Battalion repaired this and other damage under continuing trench mortar fire. Two men were wounded on 22 February, and the next day Harold Horsfield was killed by a rifle grenade. His lengthy obituary in the *Yorkshire Herald* encapsulates the life and death of a Yorkshire Territorial:

Mr and Mrs Henry Horsfield, of 25 Russell Street, Scarcroft Road, York, have received official intimation that their son, Private Harold Horsfield of the 1/5th West Yorkshire Regiment, was killed in action "somewhere in France" on February 23rd. He was a member of the Territorial Force prior to the outbreak of war, and when war was declared he was encamped with his company at Scarborough. He was called up for service, and after being stationed in Strensall and in York, he was allowed to resume his work as an apprentice in the instrument making department at the works of Messrs Cooke, of Buckingham Works, York. He was called to the colours again in November 1915, and went to Clipstone Camp. He crossed over from Southampton to Le Havre on Christmas Day. After being employed at the base for some weeks, he went into the trenches on Sunday February 20th, and his death was reported three days later. Private Horsfield, who was familiarly known as "Lal" was only 18 years of age but was well liked by all with whom he came in contact.

A letter by G. Clarke, serving with the 1/5th West Yorks states:- "Dear friend and brother – It is with great sorrow that I write these few lines to you. I have no doubt you have got to know of the loss of your dear son before this reaches you. Accept my deepest sympathy, also to Mrs Horsfield and family. He died a soldier's death – at his post. One thing, I hope will comfort you, and that is to know he had a very nice burial in a pleasant valley beneath a wooded slope about 200 yards behind our front line. I, personally, made his grave, and laid him in, with a nice turf to rest his head on. Your other son bore up well. Colonel Wood took his hand, and asked him to accept his deepest sympathy in the loss of his brother. We have had bad luck since we came in here on Sunday night, six deaths in all, and 30 wounded. I wish the job was over. I keep well, I am pleased to say. I trust you are well also, and Mrs Horsfield, and that you will bear your sad loss as lightly as possible. Once again, accept my deep sympathy, and believe me, yours sincerely."

Another son of Mr and Mrs Horsfield, Private Percy Horsfield, will be 21 years of age next month, and went out to France in April last with the 1st/5th West Yorkshire Regiment. He has been wounded, gassed, and suffered from trench feet. He has been in hospital three times, but so far as is known is all right. Prior to enlisting, he was employed as a designer and engraver by Mr. William Hewitt, of City Chambers, Clifford Street, York.

The day after Harold Horsfield was killed it snowed heavily. The frost ensured that conditions for trench works were impossible for the next few weeks. Every time there was a thaw, the trench walls collapsed, but then re-froze before they could be repaired. The ground eventually thawed properly at the beginning of March, when the 1/5th Battalion was again in the front line between Hammerhead Sap and Foxbar Street, facing Thiepval. Just as they had been at Ypres, the Yorkshiremen were again close enough to their enemy to greet each other with shouted insults.

Preparations for the Big Push

The attack was to involve massive numbers in terms of men and materiel. The preliminary artillery bombardment would use 1.5 million shells, all of which needed to be brought forward from the rear. On the return journey, it was expected there would be 10,000 wounded per day. Roads and railways had to be built to handle the two-way traffic, and casualty clearing stations as well as graveyards needed to be provided.

In the second week of March 1916, the 1/5th Battalion was five miles to the rear, at Harponville, where Captain Percy Williamson was appointed town major, responsible for keeping good order and discipline. The men were put to work in earnest, building roads at Puchevillers and Belle Église, with detachments of four officers and 250 other ranks assisting the Royal Engineers on a daily basis. In the second half of March and the first week of April, they helped build the Daours–Contay railway, at Béthencourt, digging cuttings and sidings and humping sleepers and rails. The whole battalion was at Vignacourt in the second half of April, where daily fatigue parties of 100 men were used to dig and construct new railway sidings.

When they were not working, the officers and men of the battalion were usually training. The Fourth Army training school at Flixecourt was attended by officers, including Colonel Wood and Rowland Casebourne. Junior officers attended field engineering courses and sniping school. Trench mortar training was attended by parties of one officer and four other ranks. Lectures were given to officers in German words of command and, memorably, on the use of the bayonet by Major Campbell of the Black Watch. Captain Tempest recalls Major Campbell in vivid terms:

He detailed the whole science of butchery, and seemed to enjoy describing the most horrible details of bayonet fighting. He explained in a quiet blood-thirsty voice exactly how to pierce the liver or kidneys or "lights" of the enemy, and described with a ghoulish gurgle the soft thud of the bayonet as it was pulled out of the quivering body of a German.

Percy Williamson. [Ackrill] *Territorial veteran and doctor from Harrogate.*

Throughout the spring specialist training was given by battalion NCOs in musketry, signalling, bombing and scouting. The battalion trained at company level in bayonet fighting, attacking taped trenches, practising artillery (diamond) formation and night attack schemes. There was also training at battalion, brigade and even divisional level, with companies taking turns to play the enemy. Signalling efficiency was tested, with messages sent over a course of ten miles, alternately by signal and runner. The signal took one hour and the runner two hours. The test seemed worthwhile at the time, but did not simulate the actual chaos of Thiepval Wood on 1 July, where messages would take hours to cover a few hundred yards, if they arrived at all.

When they were neither working nor training, a degree of relaxation was possible, with The Tykes playing to cheering crowds at the Salle des Concerts at Vignacourt. There were frequent sports matches. Anniversary dinners were held by officers to celebrate the passing of a year since disembarkation. In Albert, silk post-cards were bought and sent and fresh vegetables were available to supplement the diet of bully beef and biscuit. During the spring, most officers and other ranks had the opportunity to go on home leave. For a week or two, individual soldiers were allowed back to Yorkshire, but generally travelled in groups with an officer. Corporal Frederick Preston used his leave to get married in Knaresborough. Not all were so lucky. Private Willie Spinks, for example, served at the front sixteen months from disembarkation until he was killed, without getting back to England once.

Some postcards purchased in Amiens and elsewhere were saved for sending later. On 21 June, on a rest day in Bouzincourt, George H. Skinner (known as Herbert) sent his sister a postcard confirming receipt of her letter, saying he was in the best of health and hoping she was too. Second Lieutenant Dresser (or Herbert himself) censored the

'Knaresborough War Wedding'. [Ackrill]
Miss Daisy Thoseby and Corporal F.V.Preston (5th West Yorks).

postcard by cutting out the legend giving the location of the school in the picture. Nine days after writing the card Herbert Skinner was killed on the first day of the Battle of the Somme. Although he was originally listed as missing, his body was later found and ultimately buried at Connaught Cemetery, just outside Thiepval Wood (unfortunately his name is incorrectly engraved as E.H.

Postcard from Herbert Skinner (Front). [Brian Skinner]
Shows a school, probably in Amiens, with identifying legend
removed by (or for) the censor.

Herbert Skinner. [Ackrill]
Gave his life on the first day of
the Battle of the Somme.

123

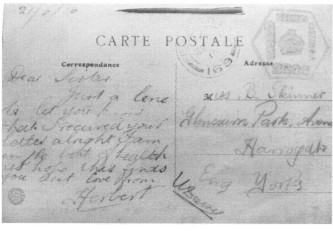

Postcard from Herbert Skinner (Rear). [Brian Skinner]

Herbert Skinner
Grave. [Author]
Connaught CWGC
Cemetery, Thiepval.

Skinner). Herbert's mother refused to accept his death until the end of her days. The inscription at the foot of his grave simply reads 'Loved by all'.

Hygiene was a constant challenge, with frequent scabies inspections and the whole battalion bathed weekly, if possible. These efforts achieved a degree of success and Colonel Wood was personally congratulated by Major General Perceval on 7 June on the state of personal cleanliness within the battalion.

Inspections by senior officers happened with regularity to build and maintain morale. Major General Perceval inspected on 6 March and Brigadier General Goring-Jones inspected every few weeks. On 29 March, Field Marshal Lord Kitchener inspected the 1/5th Battalion on the Bethencourt–Frechencourt road, on his way back from the Allies' conference in Paris. He presented DCMs to NCOs and men for acts of gallantry in the Ypres Salient. Kitchener was a true inspiration to the troops and when HMS *Hampshire* sank on 5 June, his death dampened morale considerably. Memorial services were held and officers wore crepe bands for days.

In the King's Birthday Honours in the *London Gazette*, of 3 June 1916, the Military Medal for general gallantry was awarded to Private A.J. Allen, Sergeant W. Broughton and Private F. Brown, who were formally decorated by General Perceval on 1 August. In his speech, the general commented that King George V had said that: *'In any other war most of the deeds performed in this one would have won the Victoria Cross, and that it was impossible adequately to reward everyone as every soldier in his army was a hero.'*

From February 1916 onwards, a steady stream of drafts, increasing in numbers, arrived to replenish the brigade. Having received drafts from the Beechwood Boys of the 2/5th and 3/5th Battalions West Yorkshire Regiment, and units from other regiments such as the East Yorkshire and West Riding Regiments, the 1/5th Battalion numbered 30 officers and 607 men on 31 May 1916. It was still well under strength and weak by comparison with the other three battalions of 146 Brigade. From May 1916 there were five further drafts of new men totalling 348 men. All went through the process of being inspected by the Medical Officer and addressed by Colonel Wood, before being allocated to companies.

According to Rowland Casebourne, the 175 men who arrived on 19 June *'were regular soldiers from garrison battalions mostly at MALTA and elsewhere. The men are old some of them but look fairly hard and in most cases have previous service in this war.'*

One of them was 29-year-old Lance Corporal Michael 'Mick' Jackson. He had enlisted at the age of 14 and served twelve years in the Regular Army, seven of which were on the North West Frontier in India. On returning to York in 1913 he placed himself on the National Reserve list and took a job with Rowntree's. As a Reservist he was called up on the outbreak of war and found himself quickly in France, where he was invalided out with neuritis in May 1915, and returned home just as the 1/5th were seeing their first real action at the Battle of Aubers Ridge. Initially unfit to serve on the front, he was posted to the West Yorkshire Garrison Battalion in Malta, but eventually found himself at Thiepval with the 1/5th Battalion.

It was a challenge to integrate these new men as they had missed out on all the training and rehearsals the 1/5th had undertaken recently, as well as the Ypres experience which had tempered the fighting edge of the battalion and bonded the old sweats together in the way only a common experience can.

Key officers also returned to the battalion, including Ronald Wood, now promoted to captain and Andrew Clubb from Divisional training school. Captain Barnet S. Bland also returned to take command of C Company, and be battalion bombing officer. Nicknamed 'Barnie', his father was headmaster of Ripon Grammar School; Barnie was a doctor who was educated at Cambridge where he played hockey for his college.

Ronald Wood. [YAM]
Attending to his kit, probably at Scarborough in 1921.

There were further developments in kit in the weeks before the assault, now planned for 29 June, or 'Z' (Zero) Day. The huge numbers of infantrymen involved in the attack could lead to confusion, as units inevitably became mixed in no man's land and the enemy trenches. Therefore, all Terriers had the letter 'T' sewn onto their right sleeve near the shoulder and the back of the collar. Soldiers of the 1/5th Battalion had a green T, 1/6th Battalion a yellow T, 1/7th Battalion a red T, and the 1/8th Battalion a blue T. Steel helmets had first been issued in 1915 but were not generally worn. In early 1916, they were redistributed to officers and men with the expectation they would now be donned. On 5 August 1916 the *Yorkshire Herald* reported as follows under the headline 'Tommy's Tin Hat'.

Tommy Atkins does not seem to share the official enthusiasm about the new helmet. I was talking to a batch of wounded men with bandaged heads, says a correspondent.

"They give you an norful headache, and bullets go through them as easy as winking," said one, and added ruefully, "But the officers won't let you sling them at the back of your head, nor boil your rations in 'em, nor use 'em as a dinner gong, nor even make rude remarks about 'em." They had to admit, however, that nothing but bullets did go through them; but being as conservative as your average schoolboy, they wouldn't be enthusiastic about them.

Soldiers returned from leave with weapons they had fashioned or purchased at home, including knives and knuckledusters. Some arrived back with steel waistcoats as body armour. Generally these were discarded as it was not good form to go into battle with a greater level of protection than one's comrades. Cameras had long been contraband and battalions were inspected, with officers asked to sign undertakings that they were not in possession of such items; 49th Divisional Orders in November 1916 warned that:

No officer, soldier or other person subject to military law is permitted to be in possession of a camera, to take photographs, or to send photographs or films through the post. Any officer, soldier or other person subject to Military law who disobeys this Order will be placed in arrest and the case reported to General or Army Headquarters.

This explains why so few photographs were taken of the 1/5th Battalion in the front line.

A panorama shot of Thiepval Wood from Mesnil Martinsart. [Author]

126

The Eve of Battle

On 15 June battalion officers reconnoitred the assembly trenches in Aveluy Wood, where the brigade would await the call to the front line on the eve of the attack. Three days later there was a divisional conference to discuss the likelihood that the battalion could break through the enemy lines; it was recorded that: *'All ranks full of spirits at the prospect of having a big fight and pushing the Germans back finally.'*

On 27 June Colonel Wood addressed the 1/5th Battalion, setting out their role in the forthcoming attack. It was expected that as the assault troops of the 32nd Division and 36th Division seized Thiepval and the Schwaben Redoubt respectively, the 49th Division would follow in their wake, picking up the attack at the second or third objective beyond St Pierre Divion, with the German line already broken. As such, the 49th Division was a mobile reserve.

The plan for the 1/5th Battalion was that it would be divided into three parts. Nine officers and forty-eight men under Captain Donald Mackay were to stay in the rear at Bouzincourt, as a 'second echelon' which could be drawn upon to replace casualties. Two officers with eighty-seven men would withdraw with the transport. This would leave the bulk of the battalion, numbering twenty-five officers and 725 other ranks under Colonel Wood (with Major Thompson his second-in-command), to move forward and assemble in the reserve trenches at Aveluy Wood. It was intended that as Thiepval Wood was vacated by the first waves of attackers, the Yorkshiremen would move across the Ancre into Thiepval Wood and beyond in support of the main attack.

As Colonel Wood spoke, the artillery boomed out and the eastern sky glowed orange. The assault had been postponed by forty-eight hours due to inclement weather, and 'Z' day was now 1 July 1916. Following his speech, the battalion geared up for the assault. Feet were checked by NCOs, kit was also inspected, including clothing, equipment, smoke helmets and field dressings. Two further small drafts were received, bringing the battalion up to 940 all ranks. Casebourne records that Brigadier General

Goring-Jones inspected the battalion again on 26 June and gave the men 'a very stirring address'. His speech probably relied on the content of intelligence briefings that the German artillery had been defeated at Verdun, that the British bombardment of the German front line had destroyed everything in its path and that the German soldier was sick of the war. According to Captain Tempest, it was this unrealistic level of confidence which led the sign-writers to label the bridges on the Ancre 'Thiepval–Bapaume–Berlin'.

At 9.30pm on the last day of June, the Yorkshiremen of 146 Brigade headed east towards their reserve positions in Aveluy Wood. The civilians who had come to their doors and windows to cheer them into Varennes had melted away. There was no direct road, so special tracks were laid across country between Hedeauville and Martinsart. Each was lit every 500 yards by lamps of a certain colour so that battalions knew which one to follow to its allocated assembly trenches, to arrive before sunrise. In this way steady columns of thousands of soldiers moved east towards Thiepval, mainly dividing between heading for Thiepval Wood or Aveluy Wood, depending on their allotted place in the attack.

At 9.30pm on 30 June, with the artillery pounding all around, Colonel Wood led the battalion into the narrow assembly trenches of Aveluy Wood. The men were in marching order and weighed down with full pack. Little rest was had due to the noise, the lack of space and abundance of kit, as well as the intense excitement of knowing the big push was now only hours away.

Field Service Postcard (Front)
To George B Gledhill, in the 1/5th Bn Transport Lines from his Brother.

Field Service Postcard (Rear)

Chapter 7

The Big Push
(July–August 1916)

'Our colonel tried to point out that this was impossible.'

1 July 1916

By 3am the 1/5th Battalion had arrived in Aveluy Wood. At 7.30am General Rawlinson's week-long artillery bombardment on the German front line fell silent and on the other side of the Ancre whistles sounded and the first wave of British troops went over the top. The Battle of Albert had begun. The Ulstermen of the 36th Division rose from the long grass north-east of Thiepval Wood and advanced at speed over the Schwaben Redoubt before the German machine gunners had time to climb out of their deep dugouts. Half an hour later the attackers had control of the Mouquet Switch lines, 300 yards beyond.

As soon as the smoke cleared, though, the enemy machine gunners recovered and got to work on the British support battalions as they emerged from Thiepval Wood. The machine gun in Thiepval Cemetery, in particular, was to dominate this critical ground for the rest of the day with enfilade fire, choking off the supply of reinforcements to the forward units. As a result, by mid-morning, the first wave of Ulstermen was cut off in the German reserve positions, and a fighting withdrawal was inevitable because the divisions on either side had not made sufficient progress.

On the south-eastern edge of Thiepval Wood, the Salford Pals and Tyneside Commercials of the 32nd Division were unable to make any progress at all. They had attempted a frontal assault on Thiepval. In this part of the line the enemy was prepared and German soldiers stood on their parapets, waving the Salford Pals up the steep rise towards them and into the deadly cross fire of the machine guns. Most were cut down a few seconds after going over the top and the few that made it into the German trenches were killed or beaten back. On their right the Tyneside Commercials were slaughtered in no man's land, which was bombarded by German artillery for the rest of the day. By mid-morning the British front line trenches near Oblong Wood were filled with dead and dying soldiers. Crucially for events in the afternoon, the communication trenches leading back into Thiepval Wood were also blocked with stretcher parties and confused, lost, soldiers.

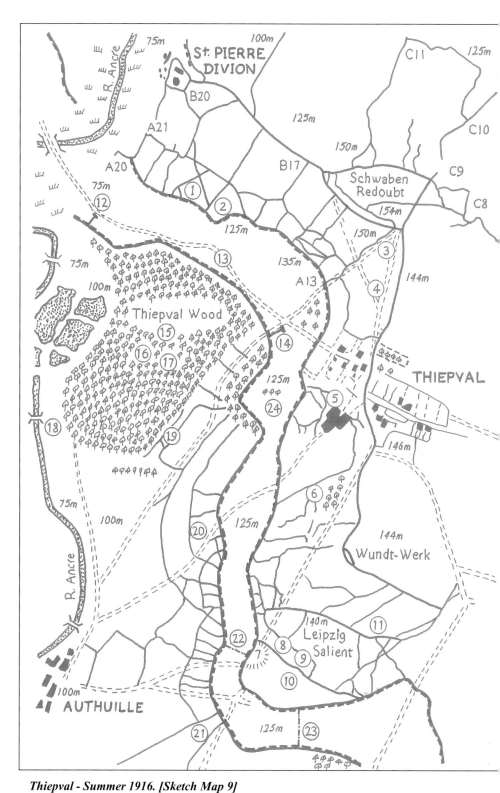

Thiepval - Summer 1916. [Sketch Map 9]
Showing British and German positions from St. Pierre Divion to Authuille. The German lines are sub-divided by an alpha numeric system. For example, the northern end of the German front line rests on the River Ancre at point A20.

The 1/5th Battalion Enters the Battle

The initial success of the 36th Division, and the unfortunate misconception that the 32nd Division had seized Thiepval, led the Corps staff to call 146 Brigade forward at 8.58am from its reserve positions. Unaware that a disaster was unfolding, and in full marching order, the 1/5th and 1/6th Battalions calmly trooped out of Aveluy Wood about 10am, along the railway on the west bank of the Ancre and across the Passarelle de Magenta into the 'rear entrance' of Thiepval Wood.

Their progress across the marshes was initially delayed by heavy artillery and machine-gun fire over the river crossings, mainly from the direction of the high ground at Thiepval Chateau. They saw numerous dead men from both sides floating in the Ancre, as artillery shells exploded and machine-gun bullets whistled all around. Thiepval Wood was also under heavy artillery bombardment and machine guns strafed the trees. About 11.30am, the 1/5th Battalion reached its allocated assembly position in the narrow trenches at Ross Castle, near the centre of the wood. Here they lay for three hours, under gas, high explosive and shrapnel attack, waiting for the order to advance. Gradually it dawned on them that things were not going as expected for the 32nd and 36th Divisions and the disappointment was stunning.

The Attack on Thiepval Village

The machine guns in and around Thiepval were clearly dominating the battle and had to be put out of action. As part of the reserve, 146 Brigade was detailed to make the assault and at 2.22pm the 1/5th and 1/6th Battalions were ordered to send out officer patrols to reconnoitre the village, with a view to attacking it from the west.

It was impossible for the patrols to carry out this task properly and report back to Ross Castle in time, because the front line trenches at the eastern edge of the wood were now clogged with the dead and wounded of the 32nd Division and under constant artillery bombardment. Had they succeeded, the patrols would have reported that the deep valley, or re-entrant, between the south-eastern edge of Thiepval Wood and the British front line was totally dominated by enemy machine guns. After all, if the Salford Pals and Tyneside Commercials had failed to climb across no man's land at 7.30am, after a week's artillery bombardment, the two West Yorkshire Battalions had no chance now, even though they were to have the benefit of a half hour artillery barrage starting at 3.30pm.

Key to Sketch Map 9:

1. The Triangle	*10. HindenburgTrench*	*19. Johnstone's Post*
2. The Pope's Nose	*11. Lemberg Trench*	*20. Thiepval Avenue*
3. Thiepval Crucifix	*12. Peterhead Sap*	*21. Oban avenue*
4. Thiepval cemetery	*13. Sunken road*	*22. Fifth Avenue**
5. Thiepval Chateau	*14. Hammerhead Sap*	*23. Eighth Avenue**
6. Pommiers (Apple trees)	*15. Ross Castle*	*24. Oblong Wood*
7. Granatloch (Quarry)	*16. Gordon castle*	*(*Constructed after 1 July*
8. 'H' sap	*17. Belfast City*	*1916)*
9. K' Sap	*18. Passarelle Magenta*	

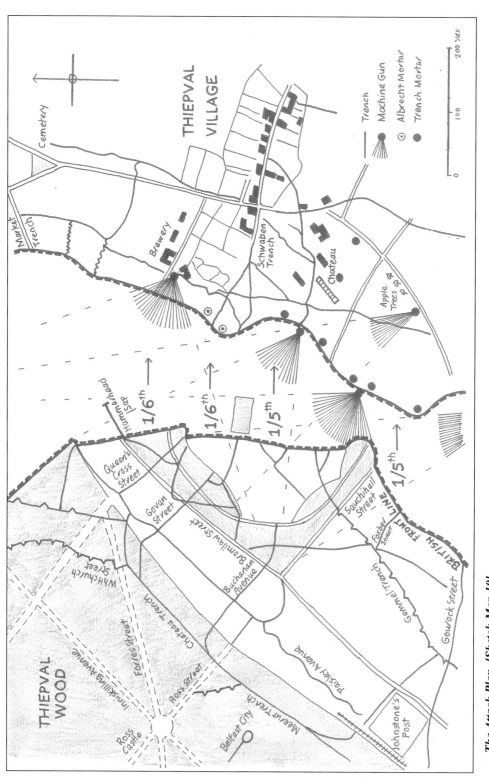

The Attack Plan. [Sketch Map 10]

Anyway, events had taken on a momentum of their own and, without benefit of reconnaissance, Major General Perceval ordered the attack on Thiepval to take place at 4pm. At 3.35pm Lieutenant Colonel Wood was summoned to Brigade HQ at Belfast City for a briefing, accompanied by his company commanders: Frederick Thompson, Barnet Bland, Walter Freeman and his own son, Ronald Wood. Together, they were given their orders and told they had just enough time to carry them out. Colonel Wood disagreed. According to Ernest Radband of the 1/5th Battalion, whose words are reported in Martin Middlebrook's seminal *The First Day On The Somme*:

> I was an officer's servant and had to go with him to a conference where the Brigadier (I think) met all our officers. He informed them that we had to be at the row of apple trees in Thiepval Village at 4 o'clock. Our Colonel tried to point out that this was impossible in the time. The answer was "Those are the orders". We moved off, got into the first communication trench and found it full of prisoners. We turfed them out and proceeded towards the front line.

Critically, the written order, issued at 3.30 by Captain G.R. Sandeman, the Brigade Major, stated that communication would be by runner. In other words there was no hope of effective instant communication between Brigade and Battalion HQ over the coming hours.

The 1/5th and 1/6th were each to attack uphill on a frontage of 300 yards, with the dividing line between them running due east and west through the Thiepval cross-roads. The Leeds Rifles were in support and reserve. The 1/6th Battalion was to go over the top on the far side of the hedge adjacent to Oblong Wood, while the 1/5th Battalion was ordered to attack from in front of Johnstone's Post, with a strong bombing party on its flank to deal with the machine gun in Thiepval Chateau. If successful in taking Thiepval, both battalions were ordered not to go beyond the village but to concentrate on the east side. In the face of utterly overwhelming odds, it appears that success was contemplated by the staff, even if Colonel Wood knew it was utterly impossible.

A half-hearted artillery bombardment had already started on the enemy front line before Colonel Wood left Belfast City. He had less than twenty minutes to get back to

Line of Attack 4pm 1 July 1916. [Author]
Showing the south east face of Thiepval Wood, the photo is taken from the German front line in front of the site of Thiepval Chateau.

his battalion, assemble them from the trenches and dugouts around Ross Castle, brief the platoon commanders and move them all more than 150 yards through clogged trenches to the eastern edge of Thiepval Wood. Once out of the wood, the 1/5th and 1/6th battalions came directly in view of the enemy machine guns with ground still to cover before reaching the British front line trench.

The communication trenches to the front line were completely full of British soldiers and clearly unusable so Colonel Wood ordered his men to climb out and advance in the open across the valley, on the double and in extended order in full view of the German machine guns and snipers who stood, head and shoulders above their parapet. Three men were killed and fifty-three wounded that day, many of the casualties occurring before they had even reached the British front line trench.

It is unlikely that either the 1/5th or 1/6th Battalion were ready to attack by 4pm, when the weak bombardment lifted, although the 1/6th Battalion arrived at the front line a few minutes before the 1/5th battalion, probably because they had less distance to cover from their assembly trenches around Ross Castle. They were cut down mercilessly as they mounted the trench parapet and advanced up the hill, with every third man a casualty, including their commanding officer, Colonel Wade. Private James Wilson of the 1/6th Battalion left a record of events at the edge of the wood:

We went forward in single file, through a gap in what had once been a hedge; only one man could get through at a time. The Germans had a machine-gun trained in the gap and when it came to my turn [I] paused. The machine-gun stopped, and thinking his belt had run out, or he had jammed, I moved through, but what I saw when I got to the other side shook me to pieces. There was a trench running parallel with the hedge which was full to the top with the men who had gone before me. They were all either dead or dying.

As Colonel Wood had predicted, the attack was clearly impossible. Before the 1/5th Battalion was able to get beyond their jumping off trench, orders were received cancelling it. From the chaos, the fragmented elements of the 1/5th began to make their way to Johnstone's Post to re-organise and await further orders.

Lieutenant Colonel Wood and the Schwaben Redoubt
Just as the attack on Thiepval was cancelled, to the north the 36th Division was now struggling to hold the Schwaben Redoubt in the face of sustained counter-attack, and calling for urgent reinforcements from the reserve, the 49th Division. Brigadier General Goring-Jones, commanding 146 Brigade, immediately agreed to help, but he was based at Belfast City and did not know that the 1/5th Battalion was now completely dislocated and out of touch. After all, its platoons were still spread out and mixed with the 1/6th Battalion as well as the remains of the 32nd Division in the bloody front line trenches on the edge of Thiepval Wood.

It is impossible to be certain about events on the night of 1 July 1916, as the evidence is fragmented and some places contradictory. At 4.30pm, we know that

Labels on image: Chateau, Leipzig Salient, Johnstone's Post, Aveluy Wood, Thiepval Wood, GERMAN FRONT LINE, BRITISH FRONT LINE, GERMAN FRONT LINE, COLONEL WOOD'S ROUTE FROM JOHNSTONE'S POST TO THE SCHWABEN REDOUBT, MARKET TRENCH, GERMAN SECOND LINE

View from the Schwaben Redoubt. [Author]
Showing Colonel Wood's probable Route from Johnstone's Post into the Schwaben Redoubt.

Goring-Jones issued the order for Colonel Wood and his men (with two companies of the 1/7th Battalion) to support the 36th Division in the Schwaben Redoubt. However, it appears from the *Illustrated History* (which gives the clearest picture of events) that Wood did not receive the written order until four hours later, once the fragmented 1/5th Battalion had succeeded in organising itself at Johnstone's Post. Colonel Wood read that the 1/5th Battalion was to advance to the Crucifix north of Thiepval, and then to support the defence of the Schwaben Redoubt by occupying the trench running between points C8 and C11. In effect, he was required to enter and hold the German reserve trenches beyond the far parallel of the Schwaben Redoubt. To get there he would have to move north-east from Johnstone's Post, along the valley floor parallel to the south-east face of Thiepval Wood, then out into no man's land (probably via Hammerhead Sap), following the re-entrant and crossing up towards the old enemy front line somewhere near point A13, and then into the Schwaben Redoubt at the top of the hill.

From the relative safety of Johnstone's Post, situated in a gully on the south-eastern corner of Thiepval Wood, Colonel Wood sent out scouts to reconnoitre, probably after the moon had set at 8.40pm, but they were soon forced back by shelling and machine-gun fire. It appears that Brigadier Goring-Jones was aware of the danger but declined to cancel the order, given the desperate situation in the Redoubt. He sent the 1/5th forward.

The whole battalion struck out from Johnstone's Post in a single column, with 50 yards between each company. None of the company commanders had been able to guarantee finding their way to the objective, so Colonel Wood and his HQ staff took the lead, followed in sequence by B, C, D and A companies. Star shells lit the sky brightly from time to time but this just accentuated the darkness otherwise and the

135

companies soon closed up to avoid losing touch. On their left and behind them, Thiepval Wood was still under intense artillery bombardment, including gas shells. As the column moved out into no man's land, under shell fire, they picked their way past the dead and the wounded, as well as withdrawing soldiers heading in the opposite direction.

Frederick Thompson.
Major Thompson, a York
Solicitor and pre-war
Territorial, was killed in th
Schwaben Redoubt with
Colonel Wood.

The Battalion HQ staff and leading platoons of B Company worked their way uphill along the re-entrant towards the crucifix under heavy artillery fire, as the German guns were pounding the Redoubt and the Ulstermen who were still occupying it. On the way across no man's land, Colonel Wood's leading party of about thirty officers and men lost touch with the remainder of the column, most of which had already fallen back to Johnstone's Post. Somehow, one platoon of C Company was caught out on the open; they lay in the long grass for the whole of the next day, only returning to Johnstone's Post the following night. Robert Hopper and Andrew Clubb were wounded in their attempt to keep up with Colonel Wood, Clubb taking shrapnel bullets in the right shoulder and left hand.

Entering the German trench system, Wood was joined by two machine-gun teams from the 146th Machine Gun Company, under the command of Second Lieutenant Bellerby who came from York. He later reported that there was no sign of any other British unit and together they took up the best defensive positions they could under the circumstances, and waited. As the German bombardment ended about 11pm, a concerted enemy counter-attack developed and started to work its way towards them from Thiepval on the right and St Pierre Divion on the left. By 3am the 36th Division was under enormous pressure in the Redoubt and was withdrawing back to Thiepval Wood. Colonel Wood's party appears to have been unaware of this and spent an uncomfortable night, isolated and at severe risk of being cut off.

Rowland Casebourne.
[Sphere]
The Adjutant, Lieutenant
Casebourne, was killed o
July 1916, as part of the
Battalion HQ detachment
with Colonel Wood in the
Schwaben Redoubt.

After sunrise on 2 July, Wood realised that he was probably alone and that his position was untenable. He decided to work his way towards St Pierre Divion. Heading west along the German trench system, his party came under heavy shell and bomb attack and suffered further substantial casualties. Using bombing blocks, made of corrugated iron or any other material to hand, with Bellerby's machine guns operating in tandem to cover their withdrawal, they fought their way as far as point A20 during the course of the day. The fortunate ones then escaped, one by one, over open ground into Peterhead Sap.

In effect, Colonel Wood had led his party in a giant loop from Johnstone's Post, via Hammerhead Sap, the crucifix and the German trench lines, as far as the east bank of the Ancre and back across no man's land into the British front line at the north-west tip of Thiepval Wood. The battalion diary is clear that Colonel Wood made it into the Schwaben Redoubt but the possibility cannot be excluded that this is an error and that his party penetrated only as far as the forward German trenches, and a small British enclave in the German lines known to the enemy as the *Meissennest*. On any view, chaos reigned for sure and at no point did he know where the enemy and the remnants of the 36th Division were located. It seems certain that he could not have understood the ebb and flow of the battle going on all around.

Robert E. Hopper. [Ackrill] Wounded in the Schwaben Redoubt.

Losses were heavy, especially among officers, with Major Thompson, Captain Casebourne, and Second Lieutenants Arthur Lee and James Jameson killed. Of the seven officers said to have penetrated the Schwaben Redoubt, only Colonel Wood and Second Lieutenants Dresser and Clough survived, with Dresser badly wounded.

2 July 1916

When Colonel Wood arrived back at Johnstone's Post after dark on 2 July, it was apparent that the rest of the battalion had fallen back there the night before, without having reached the German lines. There is no record of his reaction. Barnet Bland had taken temporary command and was joined by Donald Mackay and the second echelon during the day. For those who had already returned to Johnstone's Post there had been little rest. The 1/5th Battalion was immediately detailed to stretcher-bearing duties and other fatigues in support of the 36th Division. This was a grim task, made worse by the lingering gas, the continuing artillery bombardment of Thiepval Wood, and the inhuman noise described by Everard Wyrall as: *'a wail that rose and fell, interminable, unbearable. All along the muddy roadway they lay – the wounded; hundreds of them; brown blanket shapes; some shouting, some moaning, some singing in delirium, some quite still.'*

These scenes continued throughout the following day; 146 Brigade was withdrawn at dusk to the assembly trenches they had occupied on the eve of the attack in Aveluy Wood.

Colonel Wood was suffering from shell shock when he returned from the Schwaben Redoubt and unable to reassume command. He was admitted to hospital the next day. With the only major in the battalion missing (Frederick Thompson), it was thought necessary to bring in a new commanding officer from another battalion. The 1/5th Battalion diary baldly states on 2 July that Major H.D. Bousfield assumed command. Hugh Bousfield had served with the 1st Volunteer Service Company, under Captain Wood, in South Africa and therefore had close links with the battalion. After a period in temporary charge, he was promoted lieutenant colonel and formally appointed battalion commander.

Thiepval Casualties

Four officers and nineteen men of the 1/5th Battalion were killed in the first five days of the Big Push. Adjutant Lieutenant Rowland Casebourne, aged 39, was from Durham, and had served in South Africa. He was commissioned into the 3rd Battalion West Yorkshire Regiment in March 1915 and then transferred, as a lieutenant, to the 1/5th on 4 November 1915 to replace Captain Wilkinson.

Major Frederick Thompson was 33. He had been a York solicitor and originally served as a volunteer with the 1st VB. Second Lieutenant Arthur B. Lee was a bank manager's son from Ilkley, and (Temporary) Lieutenant James L. Jameson was the son of a vicar from Pickering. James had been a prefect at Ripon Grammar School under Charles Bland (father of Captain 'Barnie' Bland), where he was a member of the science society and played rugby, hockey and cricket. On leaving school James went to Leeds University,

James Jameson. [Ripon Grammar School]
Taken in 1910 when James was aged 15.

where he joined the OTC, and was later absorbed into the establishment of the 1/5th Battalion as a second lieutenant on 21 April 1915. He remained a keen rugby player and member of Headingly Rugby Club.

Ripon Grammar School Cricket XI 1913.
James Jameson, middle row centre, Charles Bland, top left.

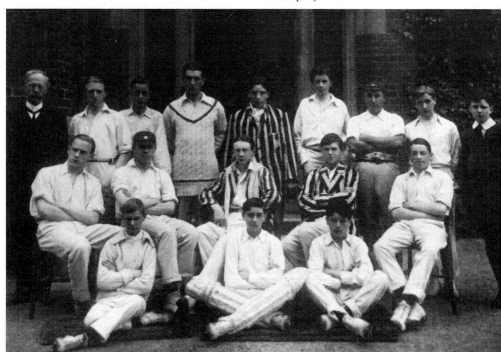

Less is known about the other ranks who were killed. Fred Wharton had only arrived at the front a fortnight earlier with one of the June drafts. He had trained with the 3/5th Battalion at Clipstone Camp, having enlisted in October 1915. He was a painter with the North Eastern Railway and lived in Nunnery Lane, York. Thomas Triffit and John Mitchell were also from York. Triffit, aged 31, was a clerk from Heworth Green, and a leading chorister at All Saints Church.

Alfred Thirkell, Gordon Lund, Herbert Skinner, Thomas Walker and Francis Henderson were all Harrogate men. Ernest Walker was a grocer's boy from Wetherby and the other soldiers who lost their lives in the first three days of the 'big push' were all West Riding men from Bradford, Leeds, and Sheffield, except Henry Heslop and Robert Carver who were from Durham.

Overall, 108 men were wounded on 1–3 July. These included Wetherby men, Fred Barton and Harry Skelton. Sergeant Sydney Rathmell was from York. A keen footballer, he was with the 1st VB from 1906 and served with the 5th Battalion while working at Rowntree's in Haxby. On 1 July he suffered shrapnel wounds to the head, and was repatriated to hospital in Southport. He told the *Yorkshire Herald* that: *'I feel that the public of York ought to be proud of their Territorials for the grand work done by them on the big push.'*

Sydney later returned to action with the 2/5th Battalion when it arrived at the front in February 1917. He survived the war.

Also wounded at Thiepval were C.W. Barnes, Willie Scott, John Binns, Arthur Cowan, Fred Fairburn, William Burton and W. Walker, all from Harrogate. Scott was shot through the

James Jameson. [Headingly RFC] James newly commissioned in 1915. He was killed on 2 July, possibly while attempting to escape from the Schwaben Redoubt into Peterhead Sap.

C.W. Barnes. [Ackrill] Wounded at Thiepval.

Willie Scott. [Ackrill] Wounded at Thiepval.

Gordon Lund. [Ackrill] Old soldier Gordon Lund had served in the second Boer War and was 37 years old when he enlisted in the 5th Battalion in August 1914.

John Binns. [Ackrill]
Wounded at Thiepval.

Fred Fairburn. [Ackrill]
Wounded at Thiepval.

thigh. Binns was evacuated to hospital in Wolverhampton where he recovered, to return to the front with the 2/6th West Yorkshires. On 6 September 1917 he died of wounds in a later battle. Fairburn was wounded in the arm and repatriated to be treated at Lord Derby's hospital in Warrington. He recovered from his wounds but was killed at Passchendaele on 9 October 1917. Burton was wounded by shrapnel when he was leaving the trenches, but recovered well in hospital and returned to action with the 1/5th Battalion, surviving the war.

Leonard Swales of Pateley Bridge was probably wounded on the first day of the Somme and repatriated. He died at home on 7 August 1916 and was buried in his home town.

The Leipzig Salient

Following Colonel Wood's return from the Schwaben Redoubt, the 1/5th Battalion retired from the front line to Martinsart, exhausted and downhearted. They needed to reorganise and there was the continuing job of supplying burial parties for the hundreds of dead in Thiepval Wood. Barely able to draw breath from this grim and back-breaking work, one week later they were back in the front line again, but this time south of Thiepval Wood, east of Authuille.

Facing the bristling Leipzig Redoubt, 146 Brigade was to occupy and hold the front line between Mersey Street and Thiepval Avenue. They were now part of General

Hubert Gough's Reserve Army whose role was to 'contain' the enemy and to consolidate the shallow gains made around Ovillers. These included the western rim of the Leipzig Salient, which had been taken at bayonet point on 1 July by the 3rd Worcesters and was still in British hands. The front line occupied by 146 Brigade therefore included this section of (formerly) German front line.

It was now joined to the old British front line by two shallow trenches hurriedly dug across no man's land. Just beyond was the Granatloch, a chalk quarry, now fortified and skirted by the Hindenberg Trench or Fort Hindenburg as it was known to the troops. Four hundred yards further uphill, into the Salient, beyond Fort Lemburg, lay the Wundt-Werk. A complex maze of trenches, this redoubt included deep dug-outs and was bristling with machine guns which dominated the Granatloch, Hindenburg trench, no man's land and the old British front line.

This part of the Leipzig Salient was the only ground around Thiepval which had been seized and held since 1 July. From H and K Saps the Yorkshiremen had a clear and unobstructed view across the German rear from Mouquet Farm (known to Tommy Atkins as 'Mucky Farm') to Pozières, which was a considerable tactical benefit.

Once again, the orders of 146 Brigade were to hold their positions at all costs. Initially, the 1/5th Battalion occupied the old British front line, from which the 1 July attack had been launched between Oban Avenue and Thiepval Avenue. This stretch had taken a pounding and was in places no more than a series of connected muddy shell holes. In front of them, the 1/7th Battalion held the Granatloch and part of Fort Hindenburg, with the enemy occupying Fort Lemburg.

The Germans launched a continuous and furious attack on the invading occupiers of the Granatloch and sought by any means to drive the BEF back out of the deep mined dug-outs constructed by German sappers in Fort Hindenburg. With two companies in the old front line and two in reserve, the 1/5th Battalion suffered four dead and thirty-six wounded in their first four days there, mostly from artillery fire aimed at the support and reserve positions.

Just as a major assault was launched at the southern end of the battlefield, in the early hours of 14 July, the 1/7th Battalion went over the top, in an attempt to throw the enemy out of Fort Lemberg, but the attack was not a success. The German counter-attack was supported by brutal shelling which hit the 1/5th in support, killing Arthur Boldison from York and wounding Lieutenant Sidney Birbeck. James Elsworth and Walter Andrews, both from Harrogate, suffered shrapnel wounds. Taking the initiative, the Germans attacked again at 4am on 15 July, deploying gas and flame-throwers on British forward positions in Hindenburg Trench.

The enemy intention was to trap those Yorkshiremen in the front line in the path of the spouting fire by shelling heavily the communication trenches behind them. Colonel Bousfield sent forward a platoon and two sections of A Company through the inferno to support the 1/7th and 1/6th Battalions in the front line. Ten men of the 1/5th Battalion were killed. Some lost their lives in the communication trench and some made it into the salient. The fifteen who were wounded during this action included Lieutenant Eric Shillaker, who made it as far as the enemy wire. He was awarded the Military Cross for this action, with the following citation, which suggests he penetrated as far as the enemy parapet:

He volunteered for a dangerous reconnaissance, and on reaching the enemy parapet was wounded in two places by bullets and received about ten shrapnel wounds. He hid for a time in a shell hole, and then coolly completed his reconnaissance alone, bringing back a valuable report.

Originally from Glasgow, Eric was commissioned into the 2/5th battalion on 6 June 1915 and was drafted to the 1/5th in April 1916. He recovered from his wounds and returned to the battalion in November 1916 and served out the war.

The action on 15 July met the approval of General Gough, who considered that the *'defence was firmly and stoutly conducted and that the dispositions were sound'.*

On 16 July it was time for the 1/5th Battalion to take over and consolidate Fort Hindenburg for three days. Captain Tempest characterises the hurried and bad-tempered hand-over ceremony as follows:

'Where the hell have you been all this time?' demands Officer Commanding outgoing Company of the incoming perspiring Subaltern, who has informed him he is 'the relief'. 'Heaven alone knows, ask your damned guide,' says the latter, who has been wandering for hours with his platoons, all over the front.

During this relief, the 1/5th suffered one man killed and five further casualties, putting up defensive belts of barbed wire in the Granatloch. One of these was George Winter, a baker and brother-in-law of Nobby Abrams. Winter was evacuated to hospital in Weymouth; he ultimately recovered to return to the battalion, only to lose his life in the last week of the war.

Hindenburg Trench and the Granatloch
On 20 July, the 1/8th Battalion attempted finally to clear the Hindenburg Trench of the remaining enemy occupiers, with the assistance of 1/5th Battalion bombers. A and B companies of the 1/5th Battalion supported the attack by delivering bombs and clearing communications trenches. In doing so, they suffered six dead and thirty-one wounded, including Second Lieutenant William McCartney.

Edward Iredale, of A Company, wrote home to his mother that this action: *'was the greatest honour I have been permitted to take part in, to stand in a trench which we ourselves captured*

William McCartney. [YA. Killed in the Leipzig Salie

from the Prussian Guards and to see the wounded Germans laid about with our chaps bandaging them, dead Germans blown to bits with our bombs and the remainder on the retreat.'

After one week's rest, baths and training, the 1/5th Battalion returned to the Granatloch, this time improving and deepening the trenches across the old no man's land under fierce artillery and machine-gun fire. The BEF was so impressed with the deep mined dug-outs they had found behind German lines that the Royal Engineers sought to replicate them, using the same techniques. Lieutenant Goodwill and twenty-seven other ranks began work on such a dug-out in a communication trench across no man's land, with the help of a quarryman, and stayed to finish the job after the rest of the battalion had retired into support lines. During this five-day relief, the 1/5th battalion lost three killed and nineteen wounded.

The proximity of the front lines in the Leipzig Salient is demonstrated by a number of 'friendly fire' incidents. On 7 August, the 1/5th Battalion re-entered Hindenburg trench just before a British shell landed on K Sap, 40 yards short of Lemberg trench. Two Yorkshiremen were killed and four wounded in the blast.

Trench improvement continued in and around Granatloch and in front of Hindenburg Trench to foil any further counter-attack. Smoke was poured into no man's land on occasion to 'panic' the enemy, which usually resulted in minenwerfer retaliation. Artillery, trench mortar and bombing duels continued for the next fortnight, each side battering the other's infantry, with neither side gaining the upper hand. Roy Holmes from Harrogate, was in a dug-out which collapsed under artillery fire on 11 August, and died from his wounds four days later. An electrical engineer, he had been enlisted by the Harrogate Defence League on the outbreak of war.

The 1/5th Battalion was finally relieved in the Leipzig Salient on 15 August, and retired to rest at Acheux Wood. Their work in holding back the enemy in July and August 1916 allowed creeping advances to be made by other units in September 1916, culminating in the seizure of the Wundt-Werk on 17 September. In turn, these advances as far as Thiepval Chateau formed the foundation for the successful attack on Thiepval at the end of September and ultimately the capture of the Schwaben Redoubt. Therefore, the 1/5th Battalion would reap the benefit at the Battle of Thiepval a month later, but the price was heavy. By 8 August its fighting strength stood at only 594 all ranks, reduced from 940 on 26 June; a casualty rate of 37 per cent in just over six weeks.

On 24 August 1916, General Haig wrote: *'I do not think that any troops could have fought better than the 49th (West Riding) division has always fought, and I am proud to have you under my command.'*

His words, though, ring hollow in light of the criticism he was to level at the Yorkshiremen after events on 3 September.

Casualties of the Leipzig Salient

On 15 August the battalion war diary mentions for the first time two soldiers suffering from 'shock'. The following day two men are said to have be wounded, also suffering from 'shell shock'. It is significant that such an ailment is attributed to other ranks, when Colonel Wood had been described as 'sick' when almost certainly suffering from the same condition on 2 July. Divisional Orders on 19 June 1917 outlawed the use of the phrase 'shell shock'.

Overall, twenty-seven officers and men of the 1/5th Battalion were killed in and around the Leipzig Salient. York man Bertram Sandbrook was killed within hours of his arrival at Authuille. On 9 July Charles Chapelow from Durham and Joseph Cutler were also killed. The next day John Loftus from Selby lost his life.

On 15 July, Wallace Rennie was killed in the Leipzig Salient, helping resist the enemy assault that day. According to the *Yorkshire Herald*:

Mrs Rennie of 11 Hope Street, York, has received official notification that her husband, Private Wallace Stanley Rennie was killed in action on 15th July. He had been married three years and leaves two children. The deceased man was 24 years old and the eldest son of Mr and Mrs Rennie, of Bishopthorpe Road, York. He was in the employment of the Midland Railway Company at York as a fitter and had served six years in the local Territorial Battalion of the West Yorkshire Regiment. On the outbreak of war he re-enlisted in his old unit and went on active service in the spring of 1915. Early in November last he was removed to a London hospital suffering from shell shock; after recovery, was on leave during January, and returned to the front again early in February.

The same day, Harry Walker of Pateley Bridge was killed. The *Harrogate Advertiser* reported on 5 August that he was one of the first to enlist, having worked for Mr Pudsey before joining the army. Around the same time William Sharp was wounded and died from his wounds on 21 August in hospital in France. He had joined the 5th Battalion in May 1914 and was a joiner with Mr Usher of Lawrence Street, York.

George Hick was with Rowntree's, employed in the starch room. He was captain of the Britannia Rovers rugby club. Wounded on 3 August, he died the same day at the dressing station in Martinsart, as described by a chaplain:

The poor boy was wounded in several places, and an arm was broken, and he was insensible when he was brought to the medical dressing station where he died ten minutes afterwards. You will feel, therefore, that death came as a release: he seemed to have fallen asleep. I took his funeral on September 5th at a British military cemetery, outside a village, some way behind the line, so that his grave will be known and marked, and every care taken of it. The Colonel and his company commander attended the service.

The proximity of the trench line, as at Turco Farm, made snipers a constant threat. Peter Wilson reports a German sniper's bullet finding the tiny loophole through which he was pointing his own rifle and striking its rear sight. On 16 August Nathan Graham, from Darley, was shot by a sniper. The next day the battalion bombing officer, William Prest was picked out by a sniper and shot dead. Prest was originally from Hull, but was educated in York at St Martin's College, under the guardianship of his aunt, who lived in Coney Street. Like Peter Wilson, he had joined Beckett's Bank on leaving school and then enlisted into the 2/5th Battalion in October 1914. Commissioned in May 1915, Prest transferred to the 1/5th Battalion, arriving on 16 January.

Second Lieutenant James Armistead was seriously wounded when shrapnel pierced his helmet and tore out a piece of his skull on 13 July. He was a 24-year-old Yorkshireman from Bingley who had studied Law at Cambridge and at the Inner Temple. Like Prest, Armistead was commissioned in the 2/5th Battalion in October 1914, then transferred to the 1/5th Battalion at Ypres in late 1915.

James Armistead. [YAM]
Seriously wounded in the Leipzig Salient.

Also among the wounded was Second Lieutenant Bernard E. Brown from Harrogate who was admitted to hospital in Le Touquet on 5 July 1916 with a severe gunshot wound in the back. This was his third wound. Second Lieutenant George Ellison, from Clifton Green, York, was the victim of a Minenwerfer explosion on 13 August. Twenty-one years old, he had only just arrived and was so badly wounded that he did not return. His elder brother by three years, Charles Ellison, who had been an electrical engineer with the North East Railway, was an old soldier by now and served with the 1/5th until he was wounded in August 1917.

On 21 July 1916 Private H. Gledhill was wounded again, and George Mackridge was killed, the day after his nineteenth birthday. Then, on 29 July, Horace Rymer succumbed to his wounds in Wimereux, having taken a piece of shrapnel below the knee. He was originally from the Isle of Man and a fine club cricketer. He was one of the best batsmen at Harrogate and played for Yorkshire 2nd XI, a sign of rare talent in those days. He was 17 when war was declared, the son of a retired school teacher who had turned his hand to running a hotel, The Dirleton on Ripon Road.

Bernard Brown. [Ackrill]
Wounded three times.

Horace was the subject of a letter which is astonishing and moving in its candour, relative to the censored words of well-meaning but sometimes stilted sympathy which were commonly penned by young officers. It was written by Sister Florence M. Reid to Rymer's parents:

Your son was conscious up to 45 minutes before his death, and talking about his cricket, and kept asking me why I was doing the numerous treatments for him, and when I said, "it is just to buck you up", he replied, "I am alright Sister,

I don't want bucking up", and again when he had the brandy he said "I don't like this but I will take it if you think it will do me good." He was looking forward to going to England, and he had written to you to say so. The doctor was devoted to him, and spent some time each day by his bed side.

We have every treatment that is known to try and stimulate the boys here, but evidently the germs that had entered his system were far too strong for us to battle with, and the dear lad's heart just gave out. Sister Robertson (day Sister) and myself send our deepest sympathy with you all in your great sorrow. I cannot tell you how the death of these fine, strong young lads upset us. This war is too terrible for words, and we feel so helpless when we have these awful germs to combat; all we can do is to make the poor men comfortable, and try and battle against the dreadful things, sometimes with success, and again not, as in your dear boy's case, which makes us feel so useless.

Reporting the War

The publication of this letter in the *Harrogate Advertiser* characterises a subtle shift in the approach of the local press to the war. There was now an acceptance in this part of Yorkshire that the war represented a brutal and savage burden, rather than a noble quest and opportunity for glory. As a result, the story of the 1/5th Battalion necessarily becomes less personal and more of a military history. Just as one of its commanders was said to have become angry when asked for details after the war, other men refused point blank to discuss their experience. Many medals went unclaimed at the end of the war. A silence fell on the scene and, as a result, the personal stories of many of those who served with the 1/5th from this point onward are lost forever.

Chapter 8

The Schwaben Redoubt
(September 1916)

'It was a wonder any of us escaped alive.'

New Officers

In August 1916 the 1/5th was reinforced by fourteen officers, some new and some returning. One of these was Peter Wilson. He had gone back to England in November 1915, the proud recipient of a field commission, with all the privilege and responsibility which went with that. Fortunately, it also diverted him from the horror of phosgene at Turco Farm, and the opening exchanges of the Battle of the Somme.

After a period of home leave in Haxby, Peter was posted to the 3/5th Battalion, which was based at Clipstone Camp, near Mansfield, to train with other newcomers to the officer corps. After Christmas 1915 he was sent to Scarborough for officer training and in May 1916 he attended a Northern Command signals training course at Otley, where he did well.

Peter Wilson. [Ackrill]

In late June 1916 he was detailed to return to the 1/5th Battalion, but only made it as far as Rouen, a day or two after the start of the Somme offensive. Caught up in the flow of wounded men bound for England, Wilson was ordered to turn around and escort a group of them to London. Having completed this unexpected mission, he reported back to Clipstone for further orders.

After further home leave, Peter returned again to France via Southampton and Le Havre. He arrived at Martinsart Wood, eight miles behind the front, on 7 August with other new subalterns, including Dudley Wallace, a magistrate's son from Colchester. At Martinsart, they were allowed a meal and allocated their kit, including a steel helmet and Webley revolver. They were also assigned a batman and Wilson was granted the services of Walter Bradbury, from Pateley Bridge. From Martinsart the new officers were taken by mule-drawn limbers to Authuille, south of Thiepval Wood, where they alighted amidst a furious artillery bombardment which lit up the night sky.

Wilson was allotted to D Company, commanded by Captain Pierce Mandeville.

Pierce Mandeville.
School teacher and pre-war Terrier.

Pierce Mandeville's Medals.
Left to right: 1914-1915 Star, British War Medal 1914-1920, Allied Victory Medal.

Mandeville was an imposing Irishman with an MA from Trinity College Dublin and was a professional schoolmaster. He had been commissioned into the 5th Battalion in March 1909, then resigned to move away for his new role as a prep school headmaster in Liverpool. In 1913 29-year-old Mandeville moved again to Wolverhampton and the same year married his American sweetheart; their first and only child was born in 1914. Mandeville was mobilised as a National Reservist on the outbreak of war.

As soon as Peter Wilson arrived in the Leipzig Salient, Captain Mandeville put him through his paces, with the four-hour duty shift from 4am. Mandeville followed Wilson round the trenches and saw him wake a sentry who had fallen asleep, exhausted, at his post, 100 yards from the German lines. This was probably in K Sap, which had been bombed twenty-four hours earlier. Later, quietly, Mandeville admonished Wilson for failing in his duty to enforce discipline, even on tired, miserable troops.

Preparing for Battle
On 18 August the 1/5th Battalion moved out of the hellish Leipzig Salient and into Acheux Wood for rest, reorganisation and to check clothing and kit indents. Here 146 Brigade was preparing itself for an attack on the section of enemy front line known as the Triangle (adjacent to the Pope's Nose). This amounted to a full frontal assault on the Schwaben Redoubt from the wood, over the same ground where so many Ulstermen of the 36th Division had fallen on 1 July. A short burst of fire on the enemy front line would precede the attack, and the barrage would move forward (or 'lift') to the next enemy line, with the infantry following close behind. The tactical objective was to render useless the machine guns at the Schwaben Redoubt, which would otherwise enfilade the British attack on Flers-Courcellette, planned for the middle of September.

The attack was originally planned for 31 August, but was postponed until 3 September due to heavy rain. In Acheux Wood there was rudimentary training with bayonets and extended order drill, with the 1/6th and 1/8th Battalions having limited

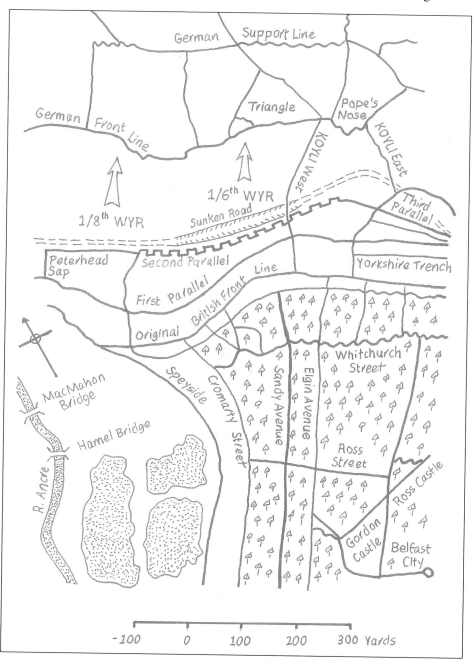

146 Brigade Attack on 3 September 1916. [Sketch Map 11]
Showing British support trenches in Thiepval Wood, the newly dug parallels and the planned line of attack..

time to practise their role as spearhead for the attack. Once they had secured the German front and support lines, the plan was for the 1/5th and 1/7th Battalions to leap-frog them the following day, pushing the advance beyond the Strassburg line.

All battalions of 146 Brigade were now greatly reduced in strength. In addition to the casualties of 1 July and the Leipzig Salient, which were only marginally offset by a draft of thirty-two other ranks from the 1/6th Battalion on 25 August, the 1/5th had suffered other losses in recent days. Men identified by their company commanders as unfit were shed to the labour battalion. Others were sent to a composite 146 Brigade Company set up under Captain Charles Foulds to provide labour for the Royal Engineers. By the date of the attack the battalion numbered only 360, all ranks, about one-third strength.

After a week in the rear, the 1/5th Battalion, severely weakened as it was, moved back into Thiepval Wood on 26 August in preparation for the attack. Initially, they occupied the front line facing Thiepval, where they were heavily shelled. Two days later they moved to the left, to take up the position they would hold immediately before the attack at the northern edge of the wood, from Sandy Avenue (roughly) to the River Ancre, a stretch which included KOYLI West Sap.

That day Captain Foulds, a former bank employee and hockey player from Wetherby, was wounded. Also on 26 August, No.4 Section machine gun was destroyed by artillery fire at Hamel. Machine Gunner Robert Barrett from Harrogate was killed in the blast. Lieutenant J.R. Bellerby wrote an earnest letter of sympathy to Robert's mother, confirming that he owed a debt of gratitude to her son, as a loyal NCO, and that: *'He had the cause and his duty at heart, and he never once flinched from carrying it out, no matter how trying the circumstances were....'*

At this point the role of the 1/5th and 1/7th Battalions was to clear and repair the new 'parallels' which had been dug into no man's land since the disaster of 1 July, as the jumping off point for the 1/6th and 1/8th to go over the top.

Charles Foulds and Henry Scott. [YAM]
Relaxing at a post war camp, probably Scarborough in 1921.

The parallels had been dug in a hurry, to bring the British lines within 100 yards of the Pope's Nose and the Triangle. They were deep and narrow with no dug-outs or other comforts. In the week preceding the attack on the Schwaben Redoubt they were shelled mercilessly. Clearing them was therefore a continuous and burdensome job and 146 Brigade worked day and night to achieve this and to bring the necessary supplies and ammunition forward to Speyside Trench from the dumps in Aveluy Wood and Paisley Avenue.

Officers and men were all utterly exhausted by the end of August, suffering in some cases from extreme symptoms of sleep deprivation. Captain Tempest reports a sergeant (reluctantly) kicking a man awake, after spending all night on fatigues under shell fire and gas attack. The mood was grim in all ranks, made worse by the fear that the attack was doomed to failure. If the Ulstermen had been unable to take and hold this ground after months of training and preparation, including a week-long barrage, how was the 49th Division to achieve it when exhausted and under-prepared?

The men were also sceptical about the new artillery tactics, and rumours spread that they were intended to advance under their own shell fire rather than behind it. Having witnessed the charnel house of 1 July, it was no great leap of imagination to envisage the staff using such a suicidal tactic.

The atmosphere was not improved by the constant attrition caused by enemy artillery searching Thiepval Wood. On 29 August Peter Wilson was washing his feet in a steel helmet, when a shell landed right in front of him. The blast blew him into the air but he survived, shaken up. Seven other men were wounded and one killed. The dead man was 19-year-old Acting CSM Edward Iredale, from Tadcaster, who was struck in the chest by a flying splinter of shell casing which killed him instantly. He was just returning to Speyside from the parallels where A Company was situated and was about 100 yards from the blast. Edward was very young, even then, to bear the responsibility of sergeant major and Pierce Mandeville spoke of him in glowing terms, in a letter to his mother.

Over the next three days the 1/5th Battalion clung on to its position on the edge of the wood in the face of further heavy artillery fire, establishing a bombing post in West KOYLI Sap, yards from the enemy front line.

In what had become the traditional prelude to an assault of this sort, the British artillery now started firing shrapnel into the German wire, attempting to cut it and forge a path for the attacking Yorkshiremen. This was too close for comfort for the companies in the parallels, who were ordered to withdraw to the old front line.

The Attack on the 'Triangle'

On the night of 2/3 September the 1/5th returned to the parallels. At 4am, shortly before dawn, eight patrols from C Company climbed ladders and crawled over the slimy parapet and into no man's land. Their job was to lie in the sunken road just beyond the second parallel and the shell holes and long grass, to cover and protect the attacking troops of the 1/6th and 1/8th Battalions as they moved forward into the parallels. One hour later the 1/5th patrols withdrew to Gordon Castle as dawn broke over Thiepval and, following a three minute 'hurricane' of the enemy front line, the attack began. As feared, it was a disaster.

The first wave of the 1/6th Battalion made it to the German wire relatively unscathed, and some penetrated into the enemy front line where they were mauled by its occupiers, who were reinforced by troops arriving from the Schwaben Redoubt. There is no evidence of any counter-battery fire to prevent the German guns laying down a curtain of shrapnel and high explosive in no man's land, which decimated the second wave, and left the first wave isolated. Peter Wilson, now acting as a signalling officer, describes the advance from his viewpoint in the trenches and the signals dugout, probably behind Peterhead Sap, which became Battalion HQ when Gordon Castle was blown in by a shell:

We had moved forward and we got right up to the German saps, almost under the German wire, but we simply couldn't move. The shelling was so furious and our casualties were so enormous! Most of the Company Commanders were killed – there was no-one to lead the men and the number of shells that fell was absolutely fantastic. We were simply blown to blazes and we couldn't do a thing. We were waiting for signals but of course no word came back. It was a misty morning, so we could see nothing and no runner could have got through that shelling. It was quite frightful. It was a wonder any of us escaped alive.

As the first wave were fighting hand to hand in the German front line trench, the machine gun in the Pope's Nose started up and was able to fire along the German wire, enfilading the second wave as it arrived in front of the Triangle and throttling its advance. As on 1 July, no man's land became a killing zone. Survivors of the second wave were forced back into the sunken road, which had already been renamed 'bloody road' by the Ulstermen on 1 July, where they were piled up, dead and wounded. Many of those who had retreated from the enemy wire later claimed to have been ordered to retire. When it was later disputed that a British officer ever gave such an order, some men claimed that this must have been a German soldier impersonating a British officer at the enemy wire. Captain Tempest viewed such claims with suspicion. He clearly thought that some troops had taken it upon themselves to turn back in the face of overwhelming odds.

The reaction of the brigadier to the disaster was to renew the attack by pressing the 1/5th and 1/7th Battalions into action twenty-four hours ahead of schedule. Twice, the 1/5th was ordered forward from its supporting position in Thiepval Wood to take up the attack. This would have been a vain throw of the dice given the battalion's weakened state, depleted further during the day by the heavy shelling of Gordon Castle and Speyside.

At 8.10am the 1/5th Battalion was ordered into the first parallel, but the attack was cancelled half an hour later. At 3.45pm the battalion was ordered back into the British front line with orders to take the German front and support lines. Completely unrealistic, this attack was cancelled at 6.30pm. Finally, at 7pm, the order was given for 146 Brigade to be relieved by the 148th. From midnight until the relief arrived at

View from The Pope's Nose.
Looking from a German observation post to towards the third parallel and Thiepval Wood beyond.

5.30am, the 1/5th Battalion occupied the British front line, forced to hear the cries and wails coming from the sunken road and the newly abandoned parallels.

Scapegoats

This was an apparent disaster for the 49th Division as a whole, as it was squarely and unfairly blamed by the generals for their failure to take and consolidate the German front and support lines beyond the Triangle that day. Lieutenant General Claud Jacob blamed failure on the lack of 'martial qualities' of the men. General Gough pointed to a lack of 'discipline and motivation', as well as 'ignorance' on the part of commanding officers and 'poor spirit' in the ranks.

General Haig recorded in his diary that:

> *The units did not really attack, and some men did not follow their officers. The total losses for this division were under a thousand! It is a Territorial Division from the West Riding of Yorkshire. I had occasion a fortnight ago to call the attention of the Army and Corps Commanders (Gough and Jacob) to the slackness of one of its Battalions in saluting when I was motoring through the village where I was billeted. I expressed my opinion that such men were too sleepy to fight well, etc! It was due to the 49th Division that the 39th (which did well, and got all their objectives) had to fall back.*

Captain Tempest and Peter Wilson, who were both present at the scene, record a lack of enthusiasm for the fight, but at least they were able to place this into proper context. After eight months on the Somme, having lived through the initial attacks, the hell of the Leipzig Salient and seen their friends and comrades from back home killed, wounded, or left for dead in no man's land, Tempest and Wilson were not surprised that the exhausted men of 146 Brigade were generally down-hearted and lacking confidence in their ability to succeed where others had failed.

Even then, the level of leadership, commitment, and military discipline far exceeded that expressed by the generals in their disparaging comments. Derek Clayton reminds us that the 49th Division suffered 70 per cent casualties among its officers that day. There were 1,728 casualties (not the 'under a thousand' recorded by General Haig) in total which amounted to about 30 per cent overall, with about 10 per cent killed. Captain Tempest reports that the 1/6th Battalion suffered two-thirds casualties and, according to Captain Bales, the 1/4th Duke of Wellington's suffered more than 50 per cent casualties. Without even leaving the parallels, or entering no man's land after 5am, we know that the 1/5th Battalion itself suffered more than 30 per cent casualties (six officers and 103 other ranks) for the day. Of these, forty-eight men lost their lives, including two officers. The weight of the available evidence therefore points to the Yorkshiremen following their orders until it became impossible to achieve their objective (mainly because their officers had been incapacitated) and paying with their lives for the flawed planning of the staff.

The main reason for failure was insufficient artillery preparation including a lack of counter-battery fire. This led to a high casualty rate among officers and the inability of such reserves as were available to support the first wave. The exhaustion of the troops may have been a factor, but without sufficient artillery preparation they were doomed to fail as they advanced into a wall of shrapnel and machine-gun fire. Any lack of military discipline had no bearing on the outcome.

It could be argued that in laying the fault directly at the door of the Yorkshire Territorials, the senior generals actively sought to draw a veil across their own tactical failure. At best, they misunderstood what actually happened. For example, General Haig was given to understand that casualties were half the real figure. He also asserts that 39th Division would have been successful but for the failure of the 49th Division, when in fact the inability of the 39th to seize the machine guns in the Ancre Valley exposed 146 Brigade to deadly enfilade fire from the left, as well as the Pope's Nose on the right. For an officer trained in the ways of the Victorian army, it was natural for Haig to draw adverse conclusions from an incident of apparent indiscipline behind the lines, and also from a relatively light casualty rate of 15 per cent, but his picture was further skewed by the information and opinion provided by his army, corps and divisional commanders, all of whom had an interest in blaming a formation of the Territorial Force, beleaguered and criticised since its inception in 1908.

If this is an example of what is now known as confirmation bias (the tendency to interpret new evidence as confirmation of one's existing beliefs or theories) it explains why it took so long for some lessons to be learnt, particularly on the importance of heavy artillery and creeping barrage. As such it also goes some way to explaining why the 1/5th Battalion was doomed on 3 September to relive the horrors of 1 July.

The 1/5th on 3 September
It is impossible to piece together a precise and comprehensive picture of what happened

to the 1/5th on 3 September, or to identify when each of the casualties met his fate. However four incidents are well recorded. The first was the collapse of an assembly trench under shell fire, probably Speyside, soon after the first attack. Nineteen-year-old Lance Corporal James Barron was buried alive, as reported to his mother by his platoon sergeant Fred Terry, and then by Lance Corporal (probably Herbert) Cousins:

> *We were doing our duty as usual in the trenches, and your son was in the best of spirits through the night. Just after dawn a shell burst, knocking in part of the trench, and your son and one or two of his comrades were buried in the debris. We all, including his company officer, worked very hard but it was all in vain.*

James had been a pre-war Terrier, and drummer boy in the 5th Battalion before being called up on the outbreak of war. He was a church chorister and chocolate worker at Rowntree's.

Peter Wilson describes a second incident involving the tragic death of a signaller, probably 23-year-old Gilbert Crowe from York, who had enlisted on the first day of the war (although it could have been Daniel DeMersey, from Starbeck near Harrogate, who was also killed that day). The signal line from Battalion HQ at Gordon Castle to the parallels was cut by an explosion at around 10am, necessitating the use of heliographs (solar reflectors) to transmit incoming reports from the forward positions and outgoing orders from Battalion HQ. Wilson describes the scene as follows:

James Barron.
[Yorkshire Herald]
Pre-War Terrier and drummer boy with the 5th Battalion. Killed by a collapsing dugout in 3 September 1916.

> *After a long search for the broken line, he finally discovers the "break" and under heavy shell fire he mends the cable. With his "tapping in" wire he joyfully establishes communication with his unit, and the troops in the advanced post are again in direct contact with the artillery behind. Suddenly, a screech tears the desolated village and shrapnel finds its mark. Stricken in death he falls...*

'West Yorks Signaller'
[Michael Wilson]
Sketch by Peter Wilson. The signaller is probably Gilbert Crowe but may have been Daniel DeMersy.

Second Lieutenant Pallister, battalion signalling officer, wrote to Gilbert Crowe's mother to say:

> *He behaved with great gallantry during a very heavy bombardment by going out and mending cables. His death was instantaneous. He was much liked by all his comrades, and his spirit was much to be admired.*

A joint letter from privates Ernest Cotterill and Stanley Collings was more detailed on the nature of Gilbert's passing:

Daniel DeMersy. [Ackrill] Killed in action (missing), 3 September 1916.

> *It was during the attack on the 3rd. A heavy shell burst near him, a piece of which entered his stomach. He passed away almost instantly. He held out his hand to shake, but said nothing...We have known him ever since he joined the Army and miss him very much. With our united sympathy...*

In the third recorded incident, 24-year-old Lance Corporal William Crust was killed by shell blast while leading his machine gun section. In the Lewis gun team, the lance corporal was usually the spotter, instructing the gunner where to fire. A keen cricketer and rugby player, Crust had been employed by Hummerston in Harrogate and was said by Corporal Haines to be 'extremely brave' and to have 'stuck to his gun to the last'.

The fourth incident, at the end of the day, was the shell blast which killed Captain Alfred Watson. He was badly wounded around midnight while the 1/5th were holding the parallels awaiting relief by 148 Brigade. Accounts differ as to whether he died at the scene of the blast or was still alive when he arrived at the dressing station. As ever, the letters to the widow from former comrades are solicitous. Colonel Bousfield, Second Lieutenant Hardwick and Watson's own batman, Private J. Christie, all wrote to say that her husband had not suffered at all. Colonel Bousfield wrote:

William Crust. [Ackrill] Killed at Thiepval on 3 September 1916

> *On the Friday before he was killed, walking around the piece of line we were holding, I heard he had come out. I soon found him and we had a long talk together. The next day we met again and he and I went all round the trench mortar positions. Afterwards we went into one of my dug-outs and talked for quite an hour of old times. One of the very last things he said to me when I asked him how he was had been: 'I'm alright but I am afraid the wife will be fretting a good deal.' All the same he was so awfully cheery.*

Alfred Watson.
York Cricket Captain
and born leader.

Alfred Watson Grave.
[Imperial War Graves
Commission]
Buried at Lonsdale
No. I Cemetery,
Authuille.

Imperial War
Graves
Commission
Card.

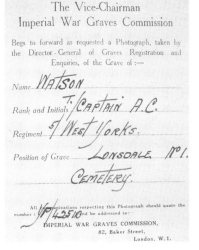

The Vice-Chairman
Imperial War Graves Commission

Begs to forward as requested a Photograph, taken by
the Director - General of Graves Registration and
Enquiries, of the Grave of :—

Name... *WATSON*

Rank and Initials *T. CAPTAIN A.C.*

Regiment *5/ WEST YORKS.*

Position of Grave *LONSDALE Nº I.*
CEMETERY.

All communications respecting this Photograph should quote the
number (*JR/42510* nd be addressed to:—
IMPERIAL WAR GRAVES COMMISSION,
82, Baker Street,
London, W. 1.

The next evening he was killed. There had been a very big attack that day and they could not bring his body just at once; all energy was spent trying to rescue the wounded. It was therefore a great comfort that I was able to do this for him with a small party of his own men. We took him to a small cemetery not far away, and his grave is among so many of those who have died out there. A cross is being made and I will see that it is put on his grave.

Captain Watson joined the 1/5th Battalion in August 1915, was promoted to lieutenant in November, then captain in December 1915, just before the phosgene attack. He was clearly marked

WATSON, ALFRED CHARLES.
Captain, 5th West Yorks. Regt. Aged
35 years. Born at York. Last resided
at 206, Bishopthorpe Road, York.
Killed in action 3rd September, 1916,
near Thiepval Wood, France.

Alfred Watson Mourning Card.

out for command. The *Yorkshire Gazette* commented on 16 September that:

> *The War has exacted a heavy toll on sportsmen and to the sad list of those "who have gone out west" has to be added the name of Capt. Alfred C. Watson of York. He had only been with the army for just over a year, but his ability marked him out for rapid promotion and he became a captain after a few months. He has died a soldier's death in France – bowled out on a more desperate fray than that of his favourite field – the field of cricket.*

Second Lieutenant Cyril Goodwill also died on 3 September. He was 29 and a senior clerk with the North Eastern Railway in York before the war. He had been a 'Saturday Night Soldier' with the (Territorial) Royal Garrison Artillery, before receiving his commission in May 1915. He had trained in Harrogate as a Beechwood boy with the 2/5th before transferring to the 1/5th Battalion; he was newly married.

Willie Spinks, formerly a waiter at the Café Imperial in Harrogate (now Betty's Tea Room), was only 18 when he was killed on 3 September. Wounded three times already, he had recently been awarded his Certificate of Merit by the Divisional Commander, Major General Perceval, for 'distinguished service in the field'. The deaths of Frederick Lickley, printer from Ripon, and Michael Jackson, an old soldier, were also reported in the local press.

Major Cattley was wounded, although this seems to have been missed by the newspapers. They did pick up the wounding of Wetherby men, Privates Maurice Wrigglesworth, Harold Pratt and Sergeant Walter Mellor. Norman Richardson from Harrogate was mortally wounded and died shortly after. Charles Inman from York was reported as having been wounded in the head, but died the same day. Corporal William Beck, who had been wounded in the face at Ypres, was injured again on 3 September, this time in both legs. One of the wounds turned sceptic, forcing amputation.

Charles Inman. [Ackrill] Fatally wounded on 3 September 1916

Sergeant Horace Shields of Ashfield Terrace, Harrogate, was wounded in the back and lower part of the body. He was evacuated to Lord Derby's Hospital in Warrington, where he was said to be 'going on as well as can be expected'. Harry Barber, friend of George Exelby, was wounded and died the next day.

Thirty-four-year-old Thomas Watson, from Bradford, was killed on 4 September, probably just after Captain Watson (no relation) met his end, in the early hours before the 1/5th was relieved in the parallels. A further six men were to die of wounds sustained on 3 September by the end of the month, including 20-year-old Arthur Hudson from Pilgrim Street, York.

To the families of those who died and were wounded, General Haig's suggestion that they lacked commitment would surely have rung hollow.

Training, Drafts and Indents

Between 2am and 5am on 4 September 1916, the 1/5th Battalion marched back through Thiepval Wood, across the Ancre marshes, to Martinsart Wood. There is a sense that they were being sent away in shame, at the point when they should have been forming up to attack the second objective. Numbering 360 all ranks, the battalion had suffered about 128 casualties since 1 September.

Apart from counting the men, assessing their fitness and sending some, like Captain Bland, to hospital for sickness, the next few days were spent indenting for clothing and kit, resting and receiving reinforcements. These included Captain Lansdale and Second Lieutenant Reginald Walker. Four new subalterns arrived on 23 September, one of whom, Second Lieutenant Whittle, was to be wounded in battle only four days later. In the first half of September the battalion more than doubled in size, with 220 other ranks drafted in. They came from the Northumbrian Cyclist Corps, the West Riding Regiment, the KOYLI and the York and Lancaster Regiment. On 12 September they were inspected by the Divisional Commander, Major General Perceval. He must have known it would be no easy job to form them into a fighting unit.

In Divisional Reserve at Forceville from 6 September 1916, the 1/5th started the whole process of training again, with the basics such as gas helmet drill and elementary musketry being taught to the new arrivals. Working parties were formed in the usual way to repair huts and lay lines. From the middle of the month an accelerated programme of battle manoeuvres was rehearsed, including attacks on two lines of trenches. The 49th Division then moved back to Martinsart Wood, where they were shelled and then gassed. From Martinsart, parties were sent daily back into Thiepval Wood to clear 'rubbish' from Paisley Avenue. Private Harold Wray was killed by a shell blast on 20 September. Sergeant A. Watson sent Harry's effects to his mother in High Shaw Mills, with the usual assurance that he had died instantly and without suffering.

Peter Wilson discovered that the life of a young intelligence officer was highly dangerous, as well as exciting. It was intended that the new-fangled 'tanks' would be deployed on the battlefield soon, and Colonel Bousfield needed to understand their interaction with the infantry. So he sent Peter Wilson, on horseback, to observe the machines going into action at the Battle of Flers–Courcelette on 15 September. Wilson was most impressed by the power of the new weapon and reported back accordingly. He explained that the tanks attacked the strongpoints, allowing the infantry to clear the trenches and dugouts.

On his return, Wilson was detailed to lead a party out of Hammerhead Sap and into Thiepval to capture an enemy prisoner for interrogation. To his relief, the plan was aborted at the last minute.

On 19 September he was sent with his batman, Private Bradbury, to an observation post on Jacob's Ladder near Hamel, to sketch the defences of the Schwaben Redoubt, including the Triangle and the Pope's Nose, which were laid out before him. Over four days, sleeping on the floor of the observation post and observing the enemy fortifications, Wilson drew a series of detailed maps which were sent back to Brigade

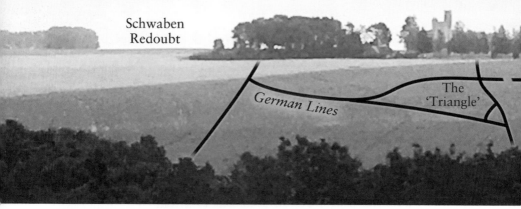

Schwaben Redoubt

German Lines

The 'Triangle'

Part of the Schwaben Redoubt from Jacob's Ladder. [Author]
Showing Schwaben Redoubt, the location of the Triangle, and British lines in Thiepval Wood.

Peter Wilson. [Ackrill]
Recuperating at the 5th Northern General Hospital. Leicester, October 1916.

HQ, in preparation for the forthcoming attack. He saw and recorded dozens of machine-gun posts going back as far as the enemy reserve lines.

Four days into this task, Wilson's observation post was hit by a German shell which blew it to pieces. He received eighteen wounds, the worst which were in his legs. Bradbury looked after him very well, possibly saving his life, and Wilson was

Thiepval Wood

British Lines

2nd Parallel

3/5th Battalion Officers at Clipstone. [Fraser Skirrow YAM]
Taken between 3 March and 3 June 1917.
Back Row: Andrew Clubb (far left), James Armistead (sixth from left), William McCartney (far right),
Middle Row: John Foxton (second from right), Rupert Lansdale (far right)
Front Row: Peter Wilson (second from left) John Banton (far right)

evacuated to hospital in Leicester. He was to play no role in the Battle of Thiepval at the end of the month, but recovered well enough to return to light duties at Clipstone on 3 March 1917, where he joined other convalescing officers of the 1/5th Battalion. They included Second Lieutenants Frederick Saxby, William McCartney and John Banton from Tadcaster. Like Wilson, 22-year-old John Banton was a pre-war Terrier, and lance corporal with the 5th Battalion, and was commissioned on 19 November 1915. He had been a bell-hop at the Metropole and then the Great Northern Hotels in Leeds, before the war. Other old faces at Clipstone included Lieutenant Armistead, Captain Foxton, and Captain Lansdale.

The Battle of Thiepval
The 1/5th Battalion was the only unit of the 49th Division involved in the partial capture of the Schwaben Redoubt. Its role was to participate in the attack on the western tip of

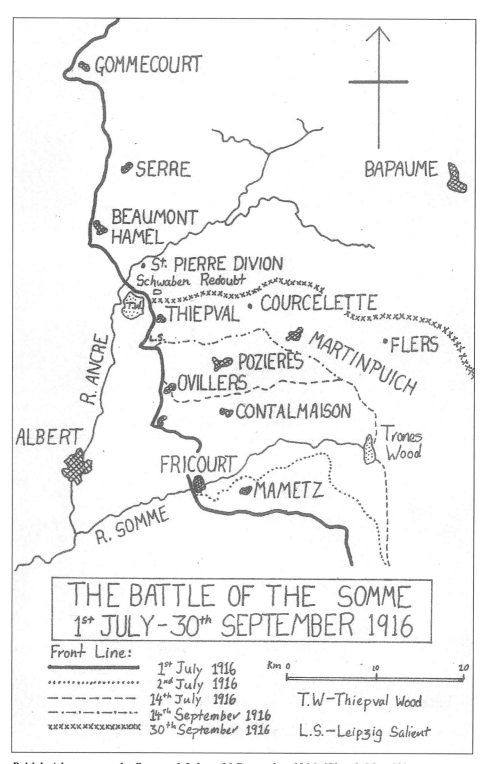

GOMMECOURT

SERRE

BAPAUME

BEAUMONT HAMEL

St. PIERRE DIVION
Schwaben Redoubt

COURCELETTE

THIEPVAL

L.S.

FLERS

MARTINPUICH

POZIÈRES

OVILLERS

CONTALMAISON

ALBERT

Trones Wood

FRICOURT

MAMETZ

R. ANCRE

R. SOMME

THE BATTLE OF THE SOMME
1st JULY – 30th SEPTEMBER 1916

Front Line:
——————— 1st July 1916
·············· 2nd July 1916
— — — — 14th July 1916
—·—·—·— 14th September 1916
xxxxxxxxxxxxxx 30th September 1916

Km 0   10   20

T.W – Thiepval Wood

L.S. – Leipzig Salient

British Advances on the Somme 1 July to 30 September 1916. [Sketch Map 12]
Showing advances from the south resulting in the seizure of the Leipzig Salient, paving the way
for the Battle of Thiepval and, ultimately, the seizure of the Schwaben Redoubt.

the Redoubt on 28 September, while temporarily attached to 53 Brigade, 18th Division. Conducting itself with 'great dash and gallantry', according to the general officer commanding the 18th Division, Major General Ivor Maxse, the 1/5th Battalion helped lay the ground for the complete seizure of the Redoubt in October 1916, and at the same time rehabilitated its own reputation, following the events of 3 September.

Since the failed attacks of the summer, the British line had advanced at Ovillers and Pozières, with the reduction of the defences at Mouquet Farm in the last week of September. This meant that the British front line now pivoted delicately on the Thiepval Sector, and on the Schwaben Redoubt in particular.

It also created better conditions to attack Thiepval itself and the Schwaben Redoubt, as the angle and orientation of British pressure came no longer from Thiepval Wood, which had been the starting point of so many vain attacks in the summer and early autumn, but from the south and the Leipzig Salient which had now been seized, yard by yard, by the British.

26 September

On 25 September the German front line lay on the newly dug, and heavily fortified, Joseph Trench which ran east from the old German front line, 500 yards south of the village.

The attack was fixed for 26 September and was to be carried out by 53 and 54 Brigades of the 18th Division on the left, and the 11th Division on the right. Occupying the old British front line on the eastern edge of Thiepval Wood, 146 Brigade (excluding the 1/5th Battalion) was to hold its ground as the attack advanced along the top of the ridge, from right to left before their eyes. The 1/5th Battalion was to take a more active role, joining the attack as it developed north beyond Thiepval Village. The objectives were Thiepval and ultimately the Schwaben Redoubt.

Following a three-day bombardment, including gas, 53 and 54 Brigades attacked through the wasteland of the Thiepval Chateau Redoubt and beyond through the razed village itself. However, they did not make it to the Schwaben Redoubt at the top of the rise. The 1/5th waited all day in Martinsart Wood without being called forward, as the advance of 54 Brigade stalled at Zollern Trench on the right flank and Schwaben Trench on the left.

The fighting was brutal and foreshadowed the experience of the 1/5th two days later; 54 Brigade diary records that:

The whole area over which the attack was carried out is practically inconceivable without actually seeing it… The numerous craters made the advance slow and once men lost their officers (as they did) the organisation and cohesion of units presented great difficulty. The fight became one of individual bravery, and separate battles between our men and the enemy, in which our men invariably proved themselves superior.

With the help of the tank, C5, 'Crème De Menthe' the front line had now moved forward as far as Zollern Trench, but the enemy still held a rectangle of ground on the left flank, facing Thiepval Wood.

The battalions of 54 Brigade which had carried out the attack on 26 September were utterly exhausted by the experience. It was decided that the attack should continue after a fresh bombardment and that it be carried out by the 7th Battalion, Bedfordshire Regiment, closely supported by the 1/5th West Yorkshires. That night, by way of preparation, the 1/5th was ordered forward into the Leipzig Salient, where it concentrated at the Granatloch and Lemburg Trench, as part of 54 Brigade.

Colonel Bousfield was called to a conference with Colonel Price of the 7th Bedfordshires on the evening of the 26th, where the attack plan was explained. Captain Meares of 54 Brigade staff was then sent to assist the 1/5th in forming up and understanding the ground, as Bousfield and his officers had no real time to reconnoitre for themselves. The plan was that the Bedfords would seize 'the rectangle' at bayonet point that night. This would straighten the front line along the length of Zollern Trench, allowing the forming up tapes and the first wave, to range across it before attacking on the afternoon of the 27 September.

With one company of the 1/5th in close support as 'moppers up' (whose role was to clear dugouts) and the others in reserve, the two battalions would advance north to the line between strongpoints 19 and 86, on the left, and the north-western tip of the Schwaben Redoubt, on the right. Here 53 Brigade would advance on the right. There was to be no preparatory bombardment, but a creeping barrage would start at Zero hour, advancing at 100 yards every three minutes.

About 6am on 27 September, in pitch darkness, A Company of the 1/5th Battalion arrived at Joseph Trench, with Battalion HQ remaining in the Granatloch. Simultaneously, the Bedfords successfully attacked 'the rectangle' at bayonet point in a single rush, straightening the line, as planned. Meanwhile, all four companies of the 1/5th lay down in the trenches and shell holes in the devastated wasteland south of Thiepval Chateau until they were ordered to form up at 4pm for the attack at 5pm. This operation was carried out in broad daylight and in full view of the Schwaben Redoubt, under heavy rifle fire and artillery bombardment. Yet again, at the last minute the attack was postponed until the next day, due to a heavy and unexpected rainstorm. Mercifully, the foul weather gave the 1/5th invaluable cover, allowing it to withdraw back to the quarry and other points of deployment with casualties limited to sixteen men, of whom eight were killed.

These included Joseph Wrather from Harrogate, who left a wife and five children, and 19-year-old William Johnson from Wetherby. Twenty-year-old George 'Fred' Wilson from Hutton Conyers and 19-year-old Edward Tiffney from Thitton Moor, near York, were both reported missing and later assumed to have been killed on the day.

28 September

Following the false start on 27 September, the attack was rescheduled for 1pm the following day. In order to avoid their arrival being spotted by the enemy, the 1/5th returned to the same positions south of the Chateau and in the Leipzig Salient by 6.30am, before dawn. Again, they spent the morning lying down in muddy shell holes

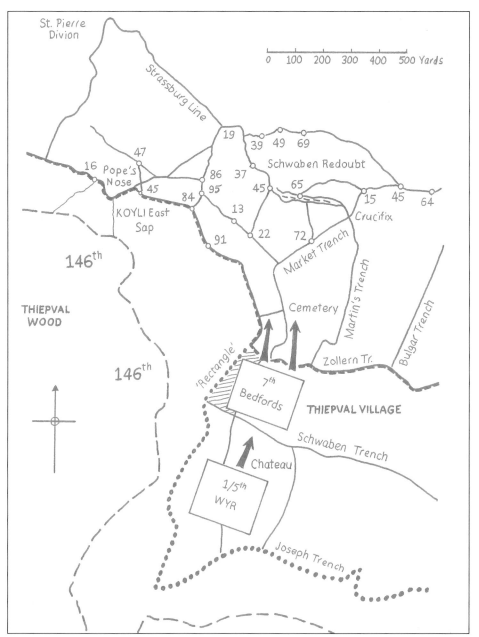

The 54 Brigade Starting Positions at 1pm on 28 September 1916. [Sketch Map 13]
Showing the 7th Bedfords on Thiepval Ridge with the 1/5th West Yorkshires in support, south of the Chateau.

and the slimy remains of destroyed trenches. The only features were the shattered remains of the chateau showing a few inches above ground, and ahead the abandoned hulls of the two tanks which had ditched on 26 September. In his report, Colonel Bousfield later recorded that:

Judging from the entire absence of enemy fire, the battalion got into position without their knowledge. They lay there practically undisturbed until 1pm. I should like to say that in my opinion the successful performance of this delicate operation on the previous evening, and again before the following dawn, is evidence of the fine leadership of the Company Officers, and great steadiness on the part of the men.

At 1pm the battalion formed up for the attack, guided by Captain Meares. The advance was to be by company, each with a frontage of 250 yards, in line of section, with 150 yards between each. To the observer, the battalion was to rise out of the ground in artillery formation and move forward as four waves of men, bayonets fixed.

The creeping barrage started on time and was the signal for the attack to begin. The 1/5th advanced either in columns of platoons or columns of sections in fours. A Company, under Captain Lansdale, was at the front with its right flank on the Chateau and the left on the old German front line. Behind, in reserve to the main assault came C Company (Captain Pierce Mandeville), D Company (Lieutenant Arthur Gaunt), and B Company (Lieutenant Kenneth Mackay), with headquarters in the rear. The brigade report confirms that the 1/5th 'went forward in excellent order'.

Following the Bedfords along the ridge, the distance between companies (and the two battalions) decreased rapidly as they moved through the hail of bullets and shell fire. B Company lay down as reserve when they reached the line of the Chateau and supported the advance by rifle fire, although both the company's Lewis guns had been knocked out by the hostile artillery bombardment. Colonel Bousfield reported that of the other three companies:

A large proportion of the men were diverted towards the left flank of the attack, for there the trenches and the German strength lay, whereas on the right it was an attack over the open. On the left there was much confused fighting in the German front and second line trenches and the communications between them. Became involved in hand to hand scrapping and dug-out clearing, and almost at once the three supporting Coys became part of the main advance.

With progress slower on the left flank, the 1/5th Battalion continued to push up the ridge at a good pace on the centre and right of the advance. As they passed Thiepval Chateau, the leading companies came under heavy machine-gun fire from the Schwaben Redoubt and suffered significant casualties. No.12 Platoon, on the right flank of C Company suffered most heavily from a machine gun located in Market Trench, at about point 72. The Bedfords had slowed down too, and were broken up by the fire pouring down from the Schwaben Redoubt, so that A Company of the 1/5th passed through them at one point to engage in the heavy bayonet fighting and trench clearance around point 91, on the left.

In fact, the whole attack veered to the left, under pressure from 53 Brigade on the right. The Bedfords and West Yorkshires were ordered to maintain the pace and to press through to the Schwaben Redoubt in the centre and on the right, which they attempted to do. By now, though, the formations were breaking up and the chain of command had collapsed in the field, with officers and men separated in the chaos.

As the left flank of A Company was busy clearing the dug-outs at Point 91, two platoons of C Company overlapped over open ground and were themselves drawn to the left as they started to clear the trenches and dugouts at Point 84, further up the ridge. They used their Lewis gun to knock out the enemy machine gun there, allowing the general advance to make progress.

This action helped the remaining platoon and others of C Company, mixed with Bedfords, to reach a location just south of Point 45, on the right. By this time, the frontage of the assault had splayed slightly, now covering 300 yards.

The two platoons of C Company on the left now advanced up the old German front line trench, beyond Point 84. This party was led by Sergeant Kitchen from Wetherby. Simultaneously, the Bedfords advanced in parallel up the support trench, taking points 13, 22 and 95, where the two trenches met and the parties of West Yorkshires and Bedfords were able to join hands. Together, they moved forward to take Point 86, 200 yards short of the final objective.

Meanwhile, about 3pm, the party of West Yorkshires at Point 45 lacked an officer to take command. Coolly noting this, CSM Harold Pattison took charge of the platoon and assaulted the trench on either side of this strongpoint. Joined by troops from A and D companies of the 1/5th, as well as men from the Bedfords, Pattison bombed his way up the trench towards the final objective at Point 19, making a defensive bombing stop, seizing an enemy machine gun, and capturing more than 100 prisoners in dug-outs on the way. For this, Pattison was awarded the *Croix de Guerre*. At Point 19, he linked up with Sergeant Kitchen's party which included bomber Albert Farnhill. Together, Kitchen and Farnhill had bombed their way up on the left, capturing and killing thirty of the enemy on the way.

But, lacking an officer, they could not hold Point 19 and withdrew to Point 86, putting in a further defensive bombing stop. Meanwhile the Bedfords had taken and consolidated the communication trench running between points 45 and 22, and their officers began to take over the mixed groups of Bedfords and West Yorkshires elsewhere. The trench between points 19 and 86 was occupied again, with a stronghold 50 yards to the left. This position was counter-attacked by the Germans, but the assault was driven off.

By now the Bedfords and West Yorkshires were starting to run out of ammunition and Mills bombs, essential for clearing the deep mined dug-outs of the Schwaben Redoubt. In his report, Colonel Price later stated that 'Boche bombs for dug-outs were of immense value', but the dug-outs mined underneath the trench between points 19 and 45 remained uncleared for several hours.

By the time Kitchen and Pattison had arrived at the final objective, only two officers of the 1/5th Battalion were still operational: Arthur Gaunt, commanding D Company, and Second Lieutenant Terence Gilsenan. They were 250 yards behind the leading elements, at Point 84. Gaunt and his party turned left here and bombed down the German front line stretching north between points 84 and 45, extending the seized

167

territory to the eastern edge of the Pope's Nose. Here the trench they were in was stopped by a bombing block erected by the retreating enemy. It is likely that Gaunt was wounded at this point.

In an act of marvellous bravery and initiative, Gilsenan took over, climbing over the block and leading a party beyond. He seized the Pope's Nose in its entirety, capturing twenty-seven prisoners on the way. In doing so, Gilsenan destroyed one of the machine-gun posts which had slaughtered the second wave of the 1/6th Battalion's attack on 3 September. At Point 16 he then constructed his own bombing block, to make it defensible against counter-attack from the north. One hundred yards in front, the Bedfords held the support trench between points 86-47.

By now the enemy was in headlong retreat towards St Pierre Divion, presenting a good target for the Lewis guns. Two platoons of Lancashire Fusiliers were able to cross no man's land with impunity from KOYLI East Sap into the Pope's Nose, to reinforce the bombing block at Point 16. By late afternoon, the situation appeared to have stabilised somewhat and Colonel Bousfield moved 1/5th Battalion HQ forward from the Chateau. Initially he headed for the right flank, on the western tip of the Schwaben Redoubt. On arrival, he found it to be 'in the air' and vulnerable to counter-attack from the east. It was precarious because 53 Brigade had failed to make equivalent ground on the right and had yet to reach Point 65. This left the trench and dug-outs between points 65 and 45 occupied by the enemy.

Bousfield called forward Lieutenant Kenneth Mackay and B Company from its reserve positions to reinforce here, and eventually join hands with the left flank of 53 Brigade which arrived much later that evening. Mackay arrived about 7pm with bombs and ammunition which enabled Sergeant Pattison's party, now commanded by the dynamic Lieutenant Keep of the 7th Bedfords, finally to clear the dug-outs between points 19 and 45. Together, they put in a bombing block at point 39 to secure their position. Here they fought off a series of counter-attacks until men of D Company were called forward to reinforce at midnight. In order to keep the exhausted troops awake in the early hours, officers of the Bedfords carried out continuous patrols of the newly occupied trenches until the West Kents arrived at 6am to relieve them.

Most of the 7th Bedfords and 1/5th West Yorkshires were able to leave the captured trenches by dawn. However, the 1/5th Battalion Bombing Officer and a party of sixty-two bombers stayed in the Redoubt until long after sunrise, when at last they were able to withdraw safely due to the early morning fog. These men had fought for thirty hours continuously, without sleep, food or water.

By then the western tip of the Redoubt and the old German front line as far as the Pope's Nose was in British hands. It was not until mid-October that the Schwaben Redoubt was finally consolidated and secured, but the actions of the 1/5th Battalion and the 7th Bedfords on 28 September were critical in allowing this to happen.

Colonel Bousfield later summed up events by noting that:

The accounts I have received all show that the men of my Battalion were possessed with one intention only, to get to the top of the hill as soon as possible, and the only men who stopped were those who were involved on the intermediate fighting in the trenches on the left, and in the collection of the men surrendering.

One can read clearly between the lines a defensive assertion that the officers and men of the battalion had demonstrated all the qualities which General Haig had accused the 49th Division of lacking on 3 September. Colonel Price commented that the battalions had demonstrated 'great dash and bravery'. The report from 54 Brigade states that the 1/5th Battalion was out to prove itself, and there can be no doubt that its conduct on 28 September was under close scrutiny. They passed the test. In his report, the views of Brigadier General Shoubridge, commanding 54 Brigade, were reported as follows:

The fighting the brigade was engaged in during the capture of Thiepval was particularly severe, and he feels certain that when fuller details can be extracted, it will be found that the gallantry displayed by all ranks, in the severe hand to hand fighting that took place from the very outset of the battle, has practically been unrivalled in the annals of the current campaign,

The 54th Infantry Brigade will never forget the advance of the 1/5th West Yorkshire Regiment on that day.

General Gough also sent congratulations on the performance of the 18th Division.

Honours
The bravery of the men of the 1/5th Battalion was recognised, too, by the award of numerous honours. In some cases the citations illustrate the story with vignettes which cannot be accurately placed in the narrative.

The citation for Lance Corporal N. Pascoe's DCM recorded that:

He patrolled alone in a shrapnel barrage and reported that dug-outs were full of the enemy. He immediately took a party of three men onto the top of the trench in question and dropped in before the barrage lifted doing great execution to the enemy.

Sergeant Kitchen's gallantry was marked not only by the award of the DCM, but also by Wetherby Parish Council, chaired by Councillor John Thomas Allan, who presented him with a mantel clock on 5 February 1918, accompanied by the following words:

It has been the wish of the Council from the earliest days of the War to take a special interest in the Wetherby men who have nobly gone forth to do battle for the right.

The difficulty of taking any definite action would be apparent when it is realised that in a War of several years duration no procedure can be arranged which would pay a tribute of admiration on an equal degree to all our young men in service.

They are scattered through the various units fighting in Flanders and Eastern Europe, in Asia and in Africa.

Only a small proportion can come home on leave to receive an acclaim which they richly deserve but which must be left until the final home coming.

When that time comes no effort will be spared to prepare a welcome for our returned heroes and to give expression to the public feeling of enthusiasm and profound gratitude only turned towards all those – many of whom will never return – who have so nobly defended our homes against a powerful & inhuman foe.

We do however wish to mark the occasion of your receiving special honour for valiant service at the hands of the Army Chiefs & to congratulate you most heartily in the name of the Town of Wetherby on achieving a distinction for bravery & other soldierly qualities.

You have received honour for noble deeds and the honour is reflected on your family & on the town in which you live.

We devotedly hope that you may survive the horrors of War and may be fortunate enough to return in good health to your friends and neighbours who are all proud of you and of the distinction which has been conferred on you.

The clock is inscribed:

Mantel Clock. [Chris Noble Presented to Sergeant G. Kitchen by Wetherby Parish Council.

Presented by the TOWNSPEOPLE of WETHERBY to Sergt. G. KITCHEN. D.C.M. 1/5th West Yorks. Regt. as a token of esteem for GALLANTRY at THIEPVAL during the Great European War November 1916

The Military Cross was awarded to five officers of the 1/5th Battalion for various acts of gallantry. Second Lieutenant Terence Gilsenan received his for bravery at the Pope's Nose and in capturing twenty more prisoners later in the day. For the same act he was further awarded the *Croix de Guerre* on 30 May 1917: *'for gallantry and leadership on the 28th September 1916, in reorganising his men and leading them over a bombing block which had temporarily held them up, and capturing 47 prisoners'.*

Captain John 'Jack' Peters was awarded the Military Cross for his daring command of the 49th Divisional Trench Mortar Battery in Thiepval Wood from 20 June to 30 September 1916. He had commanded E Company in Harrogate before the war and been attached to the 146th Trench Mortar Battery in November 1915.

Bernard Ablitt: *'organised a party to shoot down a party of the enemy, who were firing into the backs of our advance. He also sent in valuable reports, of the situation. Later he assumed command of the right flank, displaying great courage and ability.'*

Frederick Saxby: *'led two platoons with great courage and determination. Later, although wounded, he remained at his post and sent back most valuable information.'*

Kenneth Mackay: *'led his company with great courage and determination, establishing a support line at a critical time. He has on many previous occasions done very fine work.'*

Kenneth was the younger brother of Donald P. Mackay who had been a pre-war Terrier. Educated at Durham School, he followed in the footsteps of his father and brother, and was training to be a solicitor at Messrs Gray & Dodsworth in York when war was declared. He applied for a commission immediately and was gazetted second lieutenant on 9 September 1914. He was promoted to lieutenant five days after the Battle of Aubers Ridge, and to captain after the Battle of Thiepval.

Kenneth Mackay. [Yorkshire Herald]
Decorated for gallantry at Thiepval Ridge, and ultimately to become peace-time commanding officer of the 5th Battalion in the 1920s.

At least thirteen Military Medals were awarded to NCOs and men of the 1/5th Battalion for their gallantry on 28 September 1916. They were:

Private Benjamin Butler
Private John Clarke
Sergeant H. Haynes
Private James Maw
Private B. McAndrew
Lance Sergeant A. Metcalfe
Company Quartermaster Sergeant Richard Render
Private John Shillito
Lance Corporal F. Smith
Private L. Trousdale (Bar)
Private Francis W. Dixon
Private A. Brooks
George Chadwick
Private C. Twineham

Dixon and Brooks *'consistently showed determination and devotion to duty as runners,'* while Smith also ran messages through shell fire as headquarters orderly, and Trousdale *'handled a Lewis Gun with skill and bravery.'*

George Chadwick: *'Took command of a bombing party near Thiepval on 28th September, 1916, and clearing and holding a communication trench.'*

Clifford Twineham: *'Laid and maintained under shell fire a telephone wire from Thiepval to the Leipzig Salient during the attack on the Schwaben Redoubt on the 28th September 1916.'*

Twenty-five-year-old James Maw had enlisted in October 1914, in York. He was a cyclist orderly who was said by the *Yorkshire Herald* to have had *'many exciting experiences at the front'* including a shrapnel wound to the hand in July 1916.

Casualties

On the eve of the Battle of Thiepval, the 1/5th Battalion numbered about 580 officers and men. On 29 September Colonel Bousfield gave the casualty figures for the attack on the Schwaben Redoubt as 17 killed, 94 wounded and 61 missing. In total, as far as Bousfield was aware, the battalion had lost 172 men; a casualty rate of just under 30 per cent. Among the officers, the casualty rate was even higher at 58 per cent, including ten out of the seventeen who proceeded to the Leipzig Salient in the early hours of 26 September.

It is now possible to calculate that in addition to the eight who fell on 27 September, 43 members of the 1/5th Battalion were killed on 28 September, making 51 deaths directly attributable to the attack on the Schwaben Redoubt. The *Illustrated History* puts the total figure at 79, including those who were known to the authors to have died later of wounds. This may well be accurate but it is impossible to verify now, following the loss of official records. In any event, the level of bloodshed and loss of life was such as to underline, once more, the bravery and commitment of the battalion.

A particular tragedy is that some of those who died could have been saved for want of stretcher-bearers. Some men were simply left to die where they fell. Acting Sergeant Harry Beetham Holmes was walking wounded, but does not seem to have found a stretcher-bearer in time. He was not seen again, alive, after the battle. Sergeant Clarke Waite of 14th Platoon, D Company, wrote a heartfelt letter to Harry's sister after the battle:

Acting Sergeant Harry Beetham Holmes

I received your letter quite safe and I am sorry to hear you have not heard anything of Harry. I was not with the Battalion when they went into action last time. I was detailed to go and act as quarter-master for a composite company that had been formed, and when I left them I handed Harry my books concerning the platoon as he was such a good man, and I thought the most likely to take charge of the platoon. After the attack we all assembled, and I am sorry to say Harry was not with the platoon. I made extensive enquiries after him, but I could gain no further information than that he had been wounded in the leg, and that he was going back to the stretcher bearers when last seen. It is hard lines for us and our comrades, but we have orders to keep going forward until we reach our objective, so you can tell we have no chance of staying behind to give any assistance. I sincerely hope we shall see something of Harry, and that it will be for the best, as I can assure you that we all miss him; he was a good friend to all he met.

Miss Holmes had sent cigarettes to Harry and these were distributed among the men of the 14th Platoon. His body was discovered at some point in the following few weeks and months and he now lies in Mill Road Cemetery, on the very site of Point 19.

Those who died on 28 September 1916 included Captain Mandeville, Second Lieutenants William Barraclough from Barnsley and Ernest Lee from Saltburn. Barraclough must have died after he was evacuated to the rear as he was listed as wounded in the battalion diary. Also killed was Lieutenant Edward Gaunt, who was an officer of the 1/5th Battalion attached to 146 Brigade Trench Mortar Battery.

Pierce Mandeville.
[Ackrill]
Killed at the Battle of Thiepval.

Edward Gaunt was originally from Leeds and had served for twelve years in the ranks of the Leeds Rifles, before moving to York and joining the 5th Battalion in 1913; at the time he worked for Messrs Ben Johnson of Micklegate, York. Having attained the rank of sergeant before the battalion embarked in April 1915, he received a field commission in November 1915 at the same time as Peter Wilson and returned home for officer training. Gaunt returned to the front in April 1916 and was killed by a shell burst at the entrance to a first aid dug-out where he was sheltering on 28 September. The Divisional Commander, Major General Perceval, no less, wrote to Mrs Gaunt, offering his condolences.

Not all those who were killed had served with the 5th Battalion exclusively. Six had arrived from the Northern Cyclist Corps, a Territorial battalion formerly part of the Northumberland Fusiliers. Six were transferred from the West Riding Regiment, two from the Durham Light Infantry and one from the York & Lancaster Regiment.

Others were luckier, and may have had their lives saved by Private Charles Boldison, Arthur's brother. According to the citation for his DCM, Charles *'attended to wounded all day with complete disregard of danger'*.

Private F.V. Wilkinson of Albert Road, Harrogate, was wounded in the back, left arm and both legs. He was evacuated to Glasgow and by November 1916 was said to be 'going on fairly well'. He survived his wounds. Willie Hutchinson, from Harrogate was wounded but recovered to receive a commission and serve with the 2/5th Battalion before being killed on 22 November 1917 at the Battle of Cambrai. Drummer Walter Holdsworth, of Kirkgate, Knaresborough, was wounded in the shoulder and hand. Private Ernest Harrison was wounded and transferred to hospital in Kent. Private Willie Hobson, aged 22, of Hookstone Avenue Harrogate, wrote home to his mother, saying:

Just a few lines to let you know I am getting along all right. I am in hospital at a place called Eastleigh, near Southampton. I have got a bullet through my left foot. I got hit as we were going over to see old Fritz near Thiepval. I am not sure of the date – it was either the 28th or 29th of September.

Anyway, it is nice to be in Blighty again. The people are alright here, but there is one drawback – you can't draw money when you are in hospital, and cigs are scarce. I got wounded about five minutes after we went over. We had a thousand yards to go when we set off. Well, after that I got down a dugout while things quietened down a bit, then I worked my way down to the dressing station, where I had my foot dressed. They put me in a motor lorry there and took me to a hospital further back. From this one I got to the Red Cross train. We were on that about 20 hours, and we landed at a hospital at the sea coast. They gave us a blue suit there, and put us to bed. I was there about two days and a half when they put us into a motor ambulance and took us to the boat. It took us about 8 hours to get over, but we managed it all right without being seasick, and landed at Southampton with colours flying. Another little train ride and here we are.

I expect getting moved again on Monday into Yorkshire so don't write while you hear from me again. Don't worry, it is not a bad wound I have got, just enough to get me home. It's grand to get a rest. You know we have been in the big advance since it started. We have been over to see Fritz five times. – With Love to All....

Driver Douglas Morris of the transport section managed to write a letter from hospital in France, having taken three machine gun bullets in his right arm. He told his mother:

We went over the top on the morning of 28th September, and I was getting on fine, when I was knocked over by machine gun bullets catching me on the right arm. There are three wounds, but none of them serious – in fact hardly bad enough to get me to England. However, I will hope for the best. You must excuse scrawl, as it is with difficulty that I use my hand. Don't worry about me as I am well looked after, and get every attention. The hospital overlooks the sea. Yesterday I went on the beach, and listened to the band, so you see, it is a place 'so near yet so far' from home.

He returned to action with the 1/5th but was killed a year later at Passchendaele.

Sergeant Arthur Alderson was badly wounded in the left leg, and was still in St George's Convalescent Hospital in Harrogate in February 1918, eighteen months later. As mentioned, he died of his wounds in 1938.

Second Lieutenant Frederick Saxby, aged 44, who was honoured for his actions on 28 September, was also severely wounded in the face and right arm. He was evacuated two days later to hospital in London, and recuperated sufficiently to return to his battalion in March 1917. Whilst in hospital, he wrote to his mother:

On Friday last an officer visited me at the hospital. He offered me a piece of purple and white ribbon, and congratulated me on winning the Military Cross. You cannot imagine my surprise, as I was unaware of any outstanding conduct to my credit. It seems we happened to do the right thing at the right moment by a bit of luck, and thanks to some good sportsmen in my wake.

Although much older than Peter Wilson and William Prest, Frederick Saxby had also been an employee of Beckett's bank in York, having started work there in 1891. He was a committed churchman and chorister at All Saints in York. Even though he was too old to enlist, he successfully did so as a private in August 1914. He embarked with the 1/5th Battalion in April 1915, and was promoted through the ranks to corporal, receiving his field commission on 16 November 1916. He did his officer training with the 3/5th Battalion at Clipstone and Scarborough, with Peter Wilson and joined the 1/5th Battalion on the Somme in May 1916. He survived the war with the 1/5th, transferring to a labour company in 1919, presumably due to his age.

Frederick Saxby.
[Yorkshire Herald]
Wounded at Thiepval
Ridge.

As we have seen, Lieutenant Arthur Gaunt was wounded, probably in the Pope's Nose. Second Lieutenant Banton was so badly wounded that he did not return to the front until July 1917.

Some men survived the battle, though wounded, only to succumb in the following days, weeks and months. Private Ernest Haigh was a pre-war Territorial, from Boroughbridge. He came home on leave for Christmas 1915 and contracted rheumatism. Returning to the front in August 1916, he too, was wounded on 28 September at Thiepval, and was repatriated to a hospital in Kent where he died of his wounds. The son of a local police constable, his body was returned to Boroughbridge where a funeral was held on 14 October 1916, with full military honours. As was customary at the time, the townspeople closed their blinds as the cortege passed by, escorted by men of the Essex Regiment.

Ernest Haigh. [Ackrill]
From Boroughbridge, died
in hospital in Kent, of
wounds sustained at
Thiepval Ridge.

CSM John Exelby, aged 21, was one of those who died much later from wounds sustained at Thiepval. He had joined the 5th Battalion as a drummer boy in 1912 and was at Scarborough when war was declared. On 28 October 1916 he was described in the *Yorkshire Herald* as:

A quiet unassuming youth, respected by everybody with whom he came in contact, he was originally apprenticed a plumber but subsequently found employment on the cake moulding department at Messrs. Rowntrees. He resided with his parents.

Having counted the casualties, the 1/5th Battalion marched off from the scene of the battle on 30 September, never to return. They had no choice but to leave the missing behind.

Via North Bluff, Authuille, they proceeded to Martinsart where they boarded buses for Arquèves. The next day they marched to Halloy and then Warluzel, about 12 miles north west of Thiepval, and six miles behind the front line at Gommecourt.

Chapter 9

Patrol
(October 1916–July 1917)

*"We are all proud of the Battalion which carried out
such a successful enterprise."*

Reinforcements

In the nine months after it departed the Thiepval sector, the 1/5th Battalion received reinforcements of nine officers and 523 other ranks, bringing it to a virtually full establishment of 1,020 officers and men on 8 July 1917. These new men ranged from highly experienced old soldiers to fresh-faced recruits.

More than half were Yorkshiremen, mainly from the traditional recruiting ground of the 5th Battalion. They included a draft of 123 soldiers who had been recruited into the 5th Battalion early in the war, then posted to the Leeds Rifles battalions to fill gaps when they first arrived on the Somme. By returning 'home', they helped maintain the links between the 1/5th Battalion and its West Riding origins at a time when all units were losing their local character.

On Christmas Day 1916 the 1/5th received a further sixty-eight new recruits from the third line of the Leeds Rifles. The 2/5th battalion was no longer seen as a reserve pool for the 1/5th, but as a fighting battalion in its own right as it prepared to embark for the front a few days later.

In June 1917 a draft of forty-three men was drawn from various units of the West Yorkshire Regiment. They included Territorials of the 1/6th and 1/7th Battalions and old reservists of the 4th Battalion. Also among their ranks were Kitchener's men of the 9th and 10th Battalions, the 1st Leeds Pals of the 15th Battalion, as well as the 1st and 2nd Bradford Pals of the 16th and 18th Battalions, West Yorkshire Regiment.

Together with the remaining old sweats, these were the men who would fight the coming patrol war and struggle through the mud of Passchendaele in October 1917.

The Officer Cadre

The core of the 1/5th officer cadre had been destroyed at Thiepval. Few experienced officers remained, with Lieutenant Colonel Wood no longer on active service and Major Thompson killed. This created a structural problem, and a big hole to fill, not only in terms of numbers, but also in experience.

The solution to the experience problem involved the training of long serving officers for higher rank, and many were temporarily promoted. Major Lansdale was sent to a commanding officers' school in England on 13 October 1916, and the majority of existing battalion officers received general training of some type, during this period.

The numbers problem could only be resolved by recruitment. As veteran junior officers stepped up to become company commanders, new subalterns arrived to replace them as platoon commanders. Like Peter Wilson before him, Norrie Beech arrived back at his old Battalion on 9 October, this time with his second lieutenant's pip. Other arrivals were new to the Western Front in late 1916, like 19-year-old Noel H. Treleaven. He was originally from Exeter, educated at Bath, and moved with his family to Kendal in Westmorland, where he was a cadet before receiving his commission on 5 August 1916. He arrived at the front with the 1/5th Battalion on 8 October 1916.

In the first half of 1917 there was a further influx of seventeen newly commissioned second lieutenants, arriving in seven drafts between 5 January and 13 June. Some were to play a key role in the events of 1917 and 1918.

Second Lieutenant John W. Rushforth, from Halifax, arrived in June 1917. He had enlisted in the Harrogate Terriers after the outbreak of war, worked his way up from the ranks, receiving his field commission on 25 April 1917. S.M Claney had been commissioned from the ranks of the Yorkshire Dragoons. James and Beauchamp Northcote were brothers, 21 and 25 years old respectively, from Monkgate in York. Harold Goddard was from Sheffield. Percy Cheesman had been a commercial traveller in drapery and was the father of a young family in Selby. He was destined to play a key role as Battalion Intelligence Officer.

Specialist skills were instilled by intensive training. Second Lieutenants Robert Wycherley from Wakefield and Sydney Dawson from Easington, who had both arrived on 22 September 1916, were now trained in Lewis gunnery and sniping. Second Lieutenants Thomas Harper, John Sayes and Wilfred Howe were given specialist training in the roles of Battalion Transport Officer, Scout Officer and Bombing Officer, respectively.

To deal with the structural problem, officers were transferred for short periods across the brigade to fill short-term gaps. Captain Heselton and Second Lieutenant Scales were brought across from the 1/6th to command A and B Companies respectively in mid-October 1916. On 29 October, Second Lieutenants F. Edwards and William E. Wordsworth also came across from the 1/6th. They replaced Kenneth Mackay, Harry Irish, and second lieutenants Stillwell and Bowles, who were away on courses at the time. These were short-term, temporary measures, and Heselton and Scales returned to their parent battalion later in the year, once the company officers of the 1/5th were sufficiently trained.

With such training came promotion, often temporary, which allowed those with the substantive rank of second lieutenant (or lieutenant) like Kenneth Mackay, Bernard Ablitt, and Charles Ellison, to operate in the rank of captain. With the field experience these men had gained at Ypres and on the Somme, they were better qualified than their predecessors who had disembarked in April 1915 as substantive company commanders. Despite their relative youth, their credentials included wound stripes and gallantry medals. As a result, they had the respect of their men, even if they did not have the easy, familiar relationship between Territorial officers and other ranks which had been a prominent feature of 1/5th Battalion culture in the first full year of the war.

Long-standing officers who had been away on periods of convalescence found a new, more hard-bitten culture when they came back. These included Major Rupert Lansdale, who returned for a short period on 9 January to command C Company. He was ultimately replaced in that role by Barnet Bland, who arrived back on 16 April 1917.

In addition to temporary transfers borne out of short-term necessity, some officers were permanently exchanged between battalions to ensure that the right levels of experience and authority were in the right places. As part of this process Bernard Ablitt was transferred to the 1/6th, and then returned to the 1/5th as temporary captain on New Year's Eve 1916. On 8 December 1916, Second Lieutenants Sydney Dawson, Walter De Groot from Golders Green, and Walter Whittle from Leicester, were posted to the 1/6th Battalion. Later in 1917, Victoria Cross winner Sam Meekosha from Bradford transferred in the opposite direction, serving with the 1/5th Battalion from 20 August 1917.

Sometimes these transfers caused confusion in official records. Only two weeks after his arrival at the front, Noel Treleaven was posted to the 1/6th Battalion and was killed by trench mortar fire, fighting with them on 23 November. The regimental records never caught up with the move, as one of many at the time, and have him listed to this day as a 1/5th Battalion officer when he was killed.

Officers were also exchanged between the arms, and again the movements were not always properly recorded. Second Lieutenant Richard G.R. Allen is listed on the 1/5th Battalion's roll of honour, but in fact he had left the infantry and joined the Royal Flying Corps. He was killed in aerial combat on 16 November 1916.

Fonquevilliers – Hannescamps

By mid-October 1916, the recovery from the Battle of the Somme started in 'good' billets at Warluzel, 15 miles north-west of Thiepval, on the Arras to Doullens Road. The 1/5th stayed here for a fortnight, where they received and incorporated the first draft of reinforcements. The new men were inspected by the battalion medical officer, then Colonel Bousfield, and allocated to companies to receive some basic training in musketry and drill. On 6 October, Bousfield went to England on leave, just as clean clothes arrived for the remaining officers and men. Together they carried out fatigues and trained in bayonet fighting and Lewis gunnery until 18 October, when the battalion moved back towards the Somme, this time to the Fonquevilliers – Hannescamps line, west of Gommecourt.

The intention was for the 49th Division to support the imminent attack on Gommecourt, but this plan was scrapped. The only part played by 146 Brigade at the Battle of the Ancre was a fire demonstration on 13 November, as a feint to the north of the main attack.

The trench system near Hannescamps was famously complicated, with transport

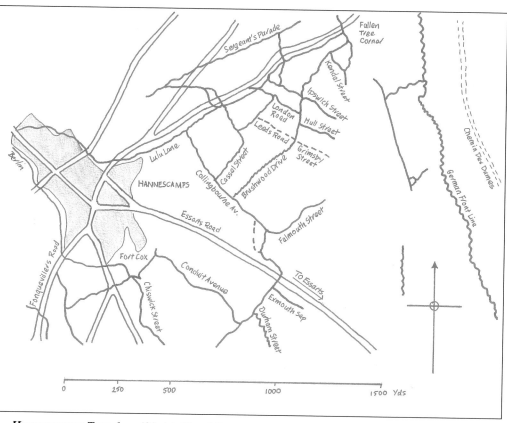

Hannescamps Trenches. [Sketch Map 14]
Showing the site of 1/5th Battalion action at Hull Sap and Exmouth Sap.

officers, scouts and even brigadiers getting hopelessly lost in the old, and sometimes disused, trenches. The three battalions of 146 Brigade held a 3,000-yard front, each with three companies in the front line and one in support.

It was a quiet sector, with the occasional exchange of shell fire. On 5 November 1916 an enemy shell landed in the line held by B Company, with no recorded casualties. The enemy artillery became more active in the middle of November, particularly on the left flank, but with very few casualties partly because the weather had turned damp making shell blasts less destructive.

The winter rains weakened trench structures, which were then collapsed by incessant, nightly, trench mortar bombardments for the rest of the month. Daylight hours were spent in the laborious tasks of gridding, revetting, repairing and draining them. Some trenches were given up to the elements and some, like Ipswich Sap, were filled in and wired to prevent them being of use to the enemy.

There was some action, too. On 6 November at 8.15pm a German patrol approached the wire in front of Hull Sap under cover of darkness. They were trying to ascertain whether the sap was occupied, or whether the 1/5th Battalion had withdrawn to a less exposed position. Hull Sap was occupied by B Company, who challenged the German patrol. The raiders threw two stick grenades into the sap and retreated. One of them was wounded by rifle fire and brought in as a prisoner. He died shortly after, his unit having been identified. Two soldiers of the 1/5th were wounded in the fight.

The following night a German soldier approach Exmouth Sap, held by D Company. Second Lieutenant Wycherley and Sergeant Metcalfe went out into no man's land, disarmed the man and brought him in as a prisoner. He was handed over to Brigade HQ for interrogation.

The 1/5th sent its own nightly reconnaissance patrols out into no man's land and occasionally came into contact with enemy parties which invariably retreated, as they were usually much smaller in number and feared coming off worse in any exchange. Colonel Bousfield recorded in the diary that *'much valuable information'* was acquired.

While in this sector, the 1/5th Battalion alternated with the 1/6th in the front line and was billeted in St Amand and Bienvilliers when in support and reserve. Here they bathed and attended to matters of personal hygiene. During November 1916, trench foot made a reappearance and company by company the battalion had its feet rubbed with whale oil. The 49th divisional orders reveal that a systematic approach was needed to combat lice, too. It was expected that in a two-room billet, an energetic NCO and six men would de-louse a platoon in one hour, as follows:

Hugh Delabere Bousfiel. Officer Commanding 1/5t West Yorkshire Regiment July 1916 to 11 October 1917.

Undressing is done in the empty room in which there is a brazier. As each man undresses, he turns his coat and trousers inside out and hands it to an orderly who takes the articles into the open and shakes them and rapidly brushes along the seams and under the coat collar, and then hands them to an ironing orderly. The hot iron is run along the seams and along the coat collar, special attention being paid to the trousers at the fork. Articles are then passed to orderly at the brushing table who brushes the now roasted eggs from the seams, etc, and passes on to the grease table. Here the finger or a suitable stick grease is rubbed along under the seams and powder is dusted under the collar and along the arm pits. The garments are now ready to wear.

One member of the 1/5th Battalion was killed during the period they held the Fonquevilliers – Hannescamps sector. This was 18–year-old Private Frank Hingley from County Durham, who lost his life 'accidentally' on 26 November, probably in a collapsed dug-out, following heavy shelling. He had been drafted into the 1/5th with his comrades from the Northern Cyclist Corps in the summer. There were some casualties, too, including Second Lieutenant Fred Terry, who was wounded by a machine-gun bullet when commanding a wiring party on 29 November. There was also the mysterious case of Second Lieutenant Tom Wilton, who had arrived back at the front on 14 November, and was accidentally wounded during revolver practice less than a week later, on 20 November 1916.

Christmas Games and New Year Honours

On 8 December 1916, the 1/5th moved to Bouquemaison, eight miles west of Warluzel, and well behind the front line. Here they spent the period around Christmas and the New Year continuing to train and on working parties. This included such bucolic activities as getting in the winter harvest at Croisette, under the supervision of Sergeant Calverley. The scouts were trained hard under Second Lieutenant Sayes, preparing for intensive patrol activity on the front line near Bailleulmont.

Christmas 1916 was quiet, with no work or training on 25 December. Baths were had in the morning and at noon the men had a raucous Christmas lunch, probably served by their NCOs. The officers dined at 8pm. After Christmas, the main diversion was a series of divisional competitions in soldierly skills including drill, musketry and Lewis gunnery. Platoons were selected to represent the four companies at the battalion competition. The winner of each battalion competition would then compete at brigade level, with the brigade champions going forward to the divisional competition. A Company represented the 1/5th Battalion with some success. Its Lewis gun section were divisional champions and No.4 Platoon represented 146 Brigade at the ceremonial drill competition. They scored the highest marks in the 'turn out' and 'arms drill' sections, but finished second overall to 148 Brigade in the divisional competition.

The *London Gazette* announced in the New Year that the Military Cross had been awarded to Captain Walter Freeman and Lieutenant Leonard Birbeck, from Whitby. Captain Armistead was awarded the Military Cross for conduct with the 1/5th Battalion, although he was now serving with the 1/6th Battalion. RSM Fred Raynor was awarded the DCM: *'for conspicuous gallantry and devotion to duty. On several occasions he has displayed great courage and determination in rescuing wounded men and in bringing up rations under intense fire.'*

Captain Douglas Green from Boroughbridge was mentioned in despatches. He was notable for having been ever-present at the front with the 1/5th Battalion since disembarkation and remained so until the Armistice, returning home in April 1919.

Bailleulmont and Ransart

On 6 January 1917, the battalion moved by motor bus, due east, to Bailleulmont, pronounced by the men of 146 Brigade: 'Ballyoolamon'. This was a large straggling village, where they were billeted in dilapidated barns, four miles behind the front line at Ransart. The bitter cold of mid-winter was fought off by wood-cutting in Lucheux

Wood and furious games of football. Captain Tempest records (with some understated glee) that the 1/6th Battalion beat the 1/5th Battalion by eight goals to nil, on a muddy field. He gratefully notes, too, that at this time the war seemed 'hundreds of miles away'.

The next day orders were received for the 1/5th and 1/7th to move forward into the trenches opposite Ransart, occupying 3,000 yards of line between the Bellacourt–Ransart Road, and Renfrew Road Trench. Unusually, behind the front line and in front of the reserve position at Bailleulmont was 3,000 yards of undefended land.

The 1/5th entered the trenches on 8 January and was shelled for the first time in a while, with four members of D Company wounded. The weather was now stormy and much effort was expended draining the trenches. On 9 January, 23-year-old Walter Elton was killed by machine-gun fire over Ridge Road, while returning from a working party in a communication trench. Walter was from Dringhouses in York and had enlisted in the autumn of 1914.

Two days later, the 1/5th Royal Engineers Platoon was shelled, with Second Lieutenant Henry Airey, Wally Franks and Sergeant Ernest Wain killed instantly. The *Harrogate Advertiser* reported that:

Henry W.S. Airey. [Yorkshire Rugby Football Union]
Killed in action on 11 January 191?
Ransart.

Mrs W.S. Franks, of 8, Albany Road, Harrogate, has received official intimation that her husband, Pte. Walter S. Franks, West Yorks, was killed in action on January 11th. Accompanying the message was the King's commands assuring Mrs. Franks of the true sympathy of His Majesty and the Queen in her sorrow. Also the Army Council expressed their sympathy. Previous to joining the Army, two years and six months ago, Pte. Franks was for fifteen years a faithful servant at the Post Office, and gained the esteem of his fellow workers and civilian friends. He also belonged to the Territorials, and on the outbreak of war volunteered for active service. He was afterwards wounded and sent back to England, and was for some time convalescent at Grove House Hospital, Harrogate. He was drafted back again last June, and met his death by shell explosion.

Eleven were wounded in the explosion, including John Black, William Burks and Joseph Dobson, who succumbed to their wounds on the day. Fred Broadbent and George Smillie died the next day.

George Lister and Harold Hood were both killed on 17 January, under a 'light shelling', made all the more dangerous by the frozen ground which shattered and

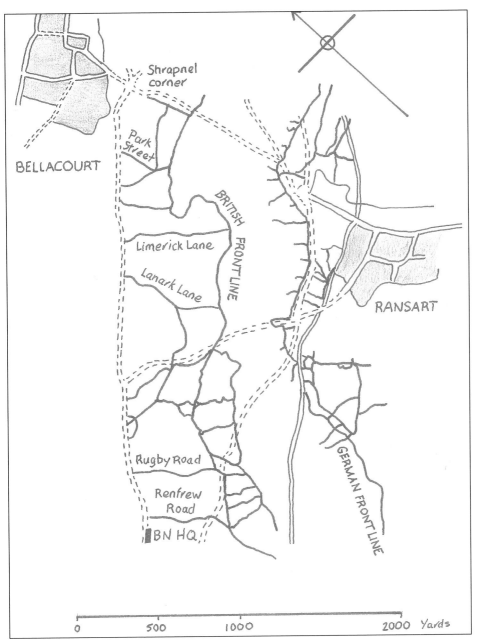

Ransart Trenches. [Sketch Map 15}
Showing the British and German trench lines.

splintered under the explosions. On 29 January Bernard Gilmore was killed while serving with the Divisional Salvage Company in Basseux. The hapless Major Lansdale was injured again on 14 January, when he fell on his shoulder and was sent to hospital, having only arrived back on 9 January.

183

Winter Activity

On 17 January it had started to snow. Defensive patrols were carried out nightly in the frost, with white capes for camouflage, repairing wire and showing a presence in no man's land. Each company in the front line put out up to twenty coils of wire per night. There were many contacts with enemy fixed posts in no man's land and every night there was machine-gun activity too. On occasion, patrols found that the enemy had withdrawn temporarily and left the front line unoccupied. On 2 and 3 February patrols led by Second Lieutenants Hardwick and Wallace heard noises from the German lines; they found the enemy wire to be strengthened, but were able to pass through it virtually to the enemy parapet.

Dudley Whistler Wallace. [Laurie Holmes]
From Colchester, led a daring raid on enemy trenches at Laventie and killed at Passchendaele.

During the day trenches were prepared for the new 'A' frames, which were being adopted along the front as allowing better drainage. This was necessary as the trenches were badly constructed and the walls collapsed easily after rain. General Perceval suffered the indignity of being stuck in the mud in Limerick Lane for half an hour until he was hauled out.

The snow and frost returned with a vengeance in early February 1917, requiring the use of sandbags tied over boots to prevent slipping on the boards. This made work very difficult, until the thaw set in on 17 February, but as usual this only meant collapsing trench walls.

Following the receipt of substantial further reinforcements during January 1917, Colonel Bousfield records at the end of the month a reorganisation of the companies to absorb the new men. They were tested for musketry skills and some were found wanting. Four new Lewis guns were added to the battalion strength, one per company.

On 30 January, three companies practised a new form of attack. On 11 February Colonel Bousfield gave a lecture on this and two days later company commanders observed a demonstration by the Brigade School (although it is nowhere described). There was further practice throughout February, interspersed by work and lightened by a visit to Bailleulmont on 12 February to see The Tykes in concert. The generals visited too. On 26 January, Lieutenant General Mann came to the front line. In February the 1/5th Battalion was visited on several occasions by the brigadier and Major General Perceval.

The line was so quiet that a composite 146th Battalion was created under Major William Oddie, supported by Harry Irish, to hold the firing trench without overcrowding it, allowing the four substantive battalions of the brigade to train and work in the rear. Each company supplied a single platoon for the composite battalion, which was to have the newly arrived Territorials of the 2/2nd London Regiment attached to it for training purposes, one platoon per company.

On 20 February 1917 the experienced men of the 1/5th Battalion were relieved in

Ransart by the 2/7th Londons. The 1/5th moved to La Souich, on their way to Laventie, where they arrived by series of route marches on 2 March 1917. Fourteen months after its arrival at the Somme, the battalion had now left Picardy for ever.

Laventie

When the 1/5th Battalion arrived in the Laventie sector, they were to hold the line at Fauquissart. While only a small proportion of the men would have remembered it from the spring of 1915, the trench lines were unmoved and still consisted of shallow ditches protected by breastworks. This time, however, the sector was truly quiet, as no great battle was in the offing and the enemy was in no mood for violent confrontation. This allowed the 1/5th Battalion to undergo three days of intensive training at the beginning of May.

There was a working assumption that the Germans would seek to withdraw from their current lines at some point in the near future. Frequent patrols were therefore employed to identify any retirement so that the enemy could be pursued and harried. As a result, the period at Laventie was quintessentially characteristic of trench warfare and of patrolling in particular.

The Portuguese Expeditionary Force had arrived in the Laventie sector for familiarisation, with a view to taking over its occupation in the summer. Just as the 1/5th Battalion had been chaperoned in the front line in April 1915, and looked after the Londons earlier in 1917, so it was now required to play the role of 'tutor' to the forces of the newly arrived ally. This was something of a challenge as, according to the Divisional diary: *'Portuguese troops attached to 146th Brigade arrived badly provided with socks and not understanding the method of cleaning the British rifle with which they are armed.'*

When in the front line, the 1/5th occupied the line between Rue Masselot and Bond Street, in Fauquissart Sector II. This sub-sector had been known as the F Lines in 1915, and the 1/5th had supported the attack on Aubers Ridge from here on 9 May. Now they held a line stretching for 2,400 yards, which in 1915 had been occupied by three battalions.

This was possible because the enemy fire trenches were commonly unoccupied and in poor repair. In effect, the Germans had withdrawn to the New Deleval Line, 1,500 yards to the rear of its firing trenches, leaving only lonely observation and firing posts dotted along the front line. In April 1917 1/5th Battalion patrols noted that the enemy front line was flooded, with the Rivière des Layes swollen and lakes forming between the German front and second lines. On occasion, the German artillery peppered its own front line, as well as no man's land, in the expectation that it would be occupied by British patrols rather than German troops.

Patrolling

Patrols were described either as 'reconnoitring patrols' or 'fighting patrols', and went out every night, except when there was too much light from a full moon, or too little light during new moon.

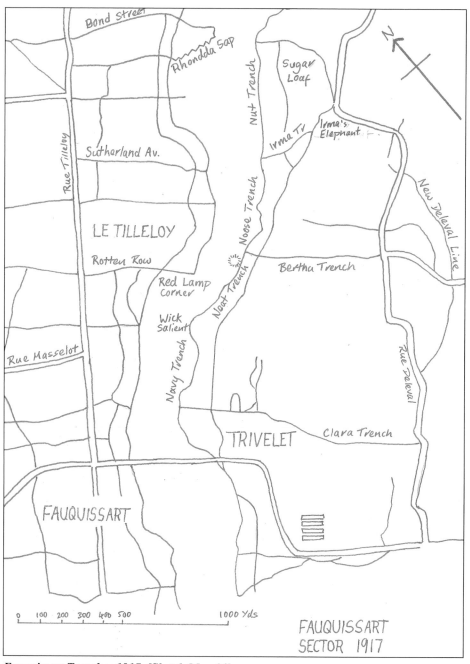

Fauquissart Trenches 1917. [Sketch Map 16]
Showing the British and German trench lines.

Reconnoitring patrols sought to identify which parts of the enemy line were occupied, and to find German observation and firing posts. They focused mainly on the Sugar Loaf, Wick Salient, and the 'deltas' at the heads of Irma Trench and Bertha trench. Commonly they would cross the unoccupied front line trench and penetrate to the support trench. Aside from keeping an eye on the enemy, patrols were used to trick the enemy into thinking that another attack on Aubers Ridge was imminent, drawing German attention from Messines, which was the actual location of the next big attack.

Sometimes patrols had specific intelligence objectives such as the examination of the light railway line (parallel to Nut Trench) in mid-June. A patrol confirmed that the track was unusable. The gauge was measured and a piece of track brought back as evidence.

Such reconnaissance patrols required great courage and discipline. In the middle of the night, for three or four hours, a group of one or two officers with an NCO and a handful of men would feel their way forward across the morass of no man's land, and the remains of German wire, to the enemy front line breastwork. They would slide over the parapet into the (hopefully) unoccupied trench, or over a bridge, then on across the criss-crossing dykes and drainage ditches to the support trench. On occasion German star shells and flares would light the scene, followed by machine guns. If spotted, the patrol had little chance of getting away unharmed. All the while, a covering party lay in no man's land awaiting their return. As the patrol made its way back, often following a white tape, it was again vulnerable to enemy fire, climbing back over the British parapet so that the officer could prepare and deliver his report.

On occasion, patrols encountered enemy working parties behind the German front line. In these cases, the enemy usually withdrew, as the British had established ascendency in this sub-sector. Where fixed enemy posts were found to be occupied, they would be revisited the next night by a fighting patrol to attack it, in the hope of killing or capturing the occupants. This process was known as 'winkling'. Even where a German party was encountered, or seen at a distance, a fighting patrol would be sent out the following night to capture or kill it.

While patrols were a clear cause of danger to the infantryman, casualties had other causes too. On 22 February there had been a spurt of action as concerted enemy artillery fire preceded an attempt by a German patrol to get into the British front line. The attack was aimed at the stretch of trench held by A Company, in the centre of the Fauquissart II sub-sector. Three men were killed and four wounded before the enemy was driven off. In order to prevent a similar occurrence, defensive patrols were sent out into no man's land at Wick Salient to intercept any German attack. None was forthcoming. The dead men were William Dufton, Francis Ward and James Lyon.

Unusually, Donald Mackay, acting adjutant, notes on 24 February that one member of the battalion suffered a self-inflicted wound, without giving further details. This may have ended in court martial, but would certainly have resulted in the victim being sent to a special hospital for such cases.

On 31 March Henry Jervis was shot dead by a sniper and a week later Joseph Crossley was killed by a shell while he was in New Bond Street Trench.

April 1917

During April the 1/5th Battalion carried out three reliefs in the front line. On arrival, on each occasion, Colonel Bousfield sent out night reconnaissance patrols, to assess enemy strength at Irma, Bertha and Wick respectively.

On 4 April two consecutive patrols were sent out, at dead of night, in front of D Company on the left flank. The first passed through the British wire and then worked along it, without drawing the enemy's attention. In order to check whether the enemy front line was occupied, a second, larger patrol of twenty-four other ranks commanded by Second Lieutenant Claney crossed no man's land as far as the enemy parapet. Here they heard a sentry shout, and a machine gun opened up at them. Only two British soldiers were slightly wounded, but the Portuguese contingent suffered badly, with one killed and two wounded. This may well indicate the naivety of the newcomers, relative to the comparatively highly experienced and well-trained men of their hosts.

On 13 April three patrols were sent out under Second Lieutenant Beech, Captain Ablitt and Second Lieutenant Benjamin. They crossed no man's land on parallel courses. Norrie Beech found Bertha Post to be protected by new, impassable wire. Ablitt reported that Wick Salient was covered by an active machine gun which fired on them, and the German front line was protected by a flooded borrow pit. The wire at Irma was penetrable, but again, the enemy front line was well protected by flooded ditches, which also prevented Benjamin from working round it sideways.

On 25 April the enemy front line was held more strongly on the left. Second Lieutenant Claney, with a party of just three other ranks, approached it between Bertha and Irma. They were supported by Second Lieutenant Sayes and a party of twenty men, who followed them out and lay down in no man's land. They had with them a portable bridge to help get over the borrow pit in front of the enemy parapet. As Claney approached the enemy front line, a German sentry sent up a flare and the twenty to thirty occupants of the trench opened a sustained fire on the two patrols. Claney decided to retreat, but left one man behind. Sergeant Thornhill, Corporal John Raftery and two stretcher-bearers immediately went back out to the enemy wire where they found the man and brought him in. The name of the wounded man, as well as his fate, are unknown, but Thornhill was awarded the Military Medal for his bravery, in preventing the enemy from making an identification. Thornhill was presented with his medal ribbon by Colonel Bousfield just over a week later, on 3 May.

In addition to Claney's foray, two other patrols were sent across on 25 April, but were unable to penetrate the enemy front line. One of the parties was fired on by a machine gun, and Leonard Newman, from Pudsey near Leeds, was killed.

On 29 April Harry Irish led a patrol of twenty men towards Irma post, in order to capture a prisoner. It was a risky mission on a moonlit night, but information was needed on the apparent build-up in the enemy front line. The patrol moved through the British wire and, as the men progressed across no man's land, they were spotted and a machine gun opened up on their left. Irish and his men dropped to the ground, but bravely continued moving forward. They made some progress towards the German wire. However, they were now being fired on from the right as well and had no alternative but to withdraw.

May 1917

In early May it appeared that the enemy had weakened its presence in the front line again so that on 9 May, one NCO, Corporal J. Raftery, and six men crossed Nut Trench 50 yards north of Irma Post and penetrated as far as the German support trench which they found to be occupied and heavily protected by wire. They crossed numerous obstacles and were out for two hours. Raftery was later awarded the Military Medal for this and was mentioned in despatches for 'penetrating 500 yards behind German front line'.

The next day three officer patrols were sent out which discovered the enemy front trench to be unoccupied over two thirds of its length. On the left and in the centre, the ground between the German first and second lines was cut up, but suitable for an advance in extended order. On the right, however, there was a lake of water behind Near Trench, in front of Wick Post, which would have prevented an advance on this flank.

Clearly something was going on, though, as a German observation balloon was sent up on 10 May and a sentry post at the head of Bertha Trench kept the British front line at Red Lamp Corner under observation by periscope. At 3.15am the next morning a German patrol sought to pass through the British wire 200 yards to the north of Red Lamp Corner, but was spotted and fired on. They retreated immediately.

On 12 May the 1/5th was relieved by the 1/8th and withdrew to billets in Laventie. Here, the next day, two shells landed on a billet occupied by five platoons of A and B companies. The houses were full of men but, amazingly, just four other ranks were wounded, along with Second Lieutenant Saxby and Major Oddie. Oddie went to hospital for a brief stay and his role as second-in-command was temporarily taken by Donald Mackay.

The battalion returned to the trenches on 18 May, carrying out a series of patrols over two nights which found the ground to be drying, although it was still flooded behind Wick Salient. Sergeant Albert Hewson and Corporal Ernest Radband had noted, on an earlier patrol, the position of the sentry post at the junction of Bertha Trench and Noose Trench, which was still occupied.

A decision was taken to winkle out the troublesome post. Second Lieutenant Dudley Wallace and sixteen men of A Company were given the task of silently neutralising it and capturing a live prisoner if possible. There were to be three parties from A Company involved. The assaulting party was to be led by Wallace, with eight other ranks. It was named A Party. B Party, commanded by Sergeant Thompson with seven other ranks, was to cover them. A further party of Second Lieutenant Sidney W. Birbeck and eight other ranks was to stand ready for an emergency at A Company's advanced HQ and to escort any prisoners to the rear if the raid was successful.

Hewson and Radband went out at 3am on 18 May to reconnoitre the post again and saw that the best way in was on its left side. On hearing this, Wallace used an aeroplane photo to mark out with tapes the layout of the post on some ground behind the British front line, so that the raiding parties could practise their assault during the day. The plan was temporarily scrapped, though, when it was seen through a periscope that the occupants of the sentry post had placed coils of barbed wire onto the inner sides of the parapet wall, preventing a direct silent assault. It is likely that they had noticed night-

B Company at Laventie 1917. [YAM]
Captain Barnet S. Bland (Front Centre) is flanked by Sergeant Harry Westerman (left) and
Second Lieutenant John H. Banton (right). [Identified by Author]

time activity nearby and feared such a raid was likely. At dawn on 19 May, Hewson
and Radband once more crossed no man's land to reconnoitre and find a way past the
new wire. This time they skirted the post and located a new route which led into the
rear. The raid was on again.

By Colonel Bousfield's Operational Order No.6, issued by Captain Walter Freeman
on 19 May, all ranks involved in the fighting patrol were to be in fatigue dress, with
gas masks and soft caps. Faces and hands were to be blackened and all papers, photos,
badges and identity disks left behind. They were to carry rifles, with bayonet fixed and
blackened, and ten rounds of ammunition in the magazine. A further five clips of
ammunition per man were to be carried in one pocket and two Mills bombs in the
other. Chillingly, each man was to carry a cut-throat razor in his breast pocket.

At 2.45am on 20 May, in silence, Sidney Birbeck assembled his emergency
detachment in Rue Tilleloy and waited. Fifteen minutes later Wallace and his party
rolled over the breastwork parapet, 150 yards north-east of Red Lamp Corner. They
passed through the British wire, across no man's land and through the remains of the
enemy wire. Wallace and his men then skirted the sentry post at the top of Bertha

Trench, just as Hewson and Radband had done the night before. B party followed them out across no man's land, lying down on the left of the old crater, 50 yards to the right of the post, underneath the parapet of Near Trench, the enemy front line.

Silently, Wallace moved up to the rear of the sentry post and waited for dawn. As first light appeared in the eastern sky, allowing the nine figures in the enemy post to be seen in outline, he and his men rushed into the trench. They took the occupants entirely by surprise. One called loudly for grenades and was immediately shot by Wallace. Another turned to escape down Bertha trench and was instantly shot dead. Of the remaining seven, six made signs of surrender, by putting their hands up. They were disarmed. The seventh German soldier had tried to make it down Bertha Trench, too, but got stuck in deep water and could not be extricated from the mud. He was shot dead. The six prisoners, relieved to be alive, were led back across no man's land and into the British front line trench at 4.15am. The only retaliation was a few machine gun rounds from well back and some shells which landed on Rotten Row trench, with no casualties.

Wallace was awarded the Military Cross on 10th June: *'for bold initiative and courage in organising and carrying out a silent raid on the enemy's trenches on the night of 20th May 1917 in which 3 Germans were killed and 6 taken prisoners.'*

Hewson, Radband and Thompson were all awarded the Military Medal on 18 July 1917 for their exploits, with the following citation noted in the Divisional HQ diary: *'for gallantry and devotion to duty during a silent raid on 20th May in which 3 Germans were killed and 6 taken prisoner, thus obtaining valuable identification.'*

The raid was sufficiently extraordinary in its success, to come to the attention of Major General W.H. Anderson, the Chief of Staff of First Army. He called it *'a well planned, little affair, skilfully carried out'*. Lieutenant General Haking, commanding XI Corps, passed on his own congratulations. His note said:

'I should be glad if you will direct the G.O.C., 146th Brigade, to express to Lt Col Bousfield, D.S.O. Commanding 5th West Yorkshire Regiment, my appreciation and congratulations on the very successful raid carried out by a party of men of his Battalion last night under 2nd Lt Wallace.

The preparations for the operation, and the determined and skilful manner in which it was carried out, reflect great credit on all concerned, and the Battalion may be rightly proud of

Lieutenant General Haking.
Commended Dudley Wallace's raid on enemy trenches.

capturing a complete hostile post, with the employment of so few men, and bringing in six prisoners, the remainder having been killed.

The absence of any casualties on our side, shows that great care must have been taken in working out the plan.

The Divisional commander, Major General Perceval, stated that he thought this praise well deserved. Perhaps, most tellingly, the scale of the achievement was marked by the words of Lieutenant Colonel R.H Hudson, of the brigade staff who said: *'We are all proud of the Battalion who carried out such a successful enterprise.'*.

June 1917

The pattern of patrols continued through June and early July, with the 1/5th carrying out four reliefs in the front line at Fauquissart II. The enemy front line was only sparsely and infrequently occupied, although sufficient presence was maintained to prevent the 1/5th Battalion advancing. Where German front line posts were found to be occupied, Colonel Bousfield made sure the occupants were made uncomfortable. On 13 June two strong patrols were sent to the Sugar Loaf and Irma Trench respectively. Both were fired on from the second line and returned without any loss of life.

On 24 June the Brigadier General ordered the 1/5th Battalion to:

establish two day sentry-posts tomorrow, 25th instant, in the German front line, leaving our lines at 2.30am and remaining in the enemy front line until dusk.

Object

(1) Daylight reconnaissance of the vicinity and examination of any work done recently there.

(2) Preparation of a plan for inflicting casualties on the enemy's night working parties...

On 25 June Second Lieutenants William Banks from Darlington and Dudley Wallace carried out patrols and set up observation posts opposite Sugar Loaf Post and the Wick Salient, respectively. In effect, they were in the enemy front line. Supplementary to the brigadier's typed order, according to the 146 Brigade war diary, their task was *'to find out enemy's habits ref. posts etc'*.

Banks and his party went across no man's land at 2.45am and lay down under the noses of the sentries in a German day post. Here they stayed all day, prone in the long grass. They made a series of observations of the German front line, identifying a new German machine gun post at 'Irma's Elephant', and confirming that the trench tramway behind Nut Trench was still disused and probably unrepaired. They waited until 10.45pm to return and made their way back into Rhondda Sap to report.

Wallace, accompanied by Second Lieutenant F. Edwards, had an altogether easier time at Wick Salient. They also moved across at 2.45am and at first light found the enemy front line to be unoccupied. They did see smoke rising along the length of New Deleval Trench, probably field cookers, indicating strong occupation. They entered

Navy Trench, and collected items to bring back, including an alarm bell, bombs, a rifle and a periscope. At noon, they returned across no man's land under cover of the dyke.

Enemy Raid

On 5 July A Company held the centre section of the sector, between Rotten Row and Sutherland Avenue. This included seven night sentry posts, each occupied by an NCO and a handful of men. The front line trench was crenellated so that each post was out of visual contact with the next and separated from it by about five bays and traverses in each direction.

Generally, there was one officer in the firing trench, a subaltern, responsible for the company front line. He was relatively isolated from the Company Commander, Major Donald Mackay, who had his advanced Company HQ at Le Tilleloy, 200 yards behind the front line. Battalion HQ was 1,000 yards away, at one of the reserve posts behind Rue Tilleloy.

It was clear from initial intelligence and listening patrols that there was greater activity in the German front line than noted in previous reliefs, as the ground was now drying out. This included a series of Minenwerfer bombardments designed to isolate sections of the British front line trench from its flanks and supporting line, cutting off the defenders and making them vulnerable to a trench raid.

Colonel Bousfield and Major Mackay read the signs, and Mackay suggested a plan for dealing with such an attack. Bousfield agreed that following the start of any Minenwerfer box barrage, the night time sentry posts within the bounds of the barrage would withdraw 50-80 yards to one or two of three support posts, from which they could observe the front line parapet. This would rob the raiders of the element of surprise. By allowing them into the front line trench, unopposed, it would also leave the attackers vulnerable to counter-attack from behind and the risk of being taken prisoner. Mackay and his platoon commanders ensured that C Company practised the scheme, but unfortunately they did not follow it properly on the night of 8-9 July 1917.

It was a very dark night, with the moon obscured by cloud. At three minutes past 1am, a flare was sent up from the New Deleval Line, and a box barrage of minenwerfer bombs was launched against the section of British front line between Red Lamp Corner and Rifleman's Avenue, to a depth of about 300 yards. Two sentry posts were cut off by this action, at Bay 12 and Bay 22. In accordance with the plan, Second Lieutenant F. Edwards, who was responsible for C Company's front line that night, vacated his position and headed back to the pre-arranged reserve position, where Sergeant Lynch took a roll call. Before hearing the outcome of Lynch's checks, Edwards went straight to advanced Company HQ to fetch Mackay.

Completing his register, Sergeant Lynch found that two men had not made it back from the sentry posts, Privates C. McConnell and G. Holdsworth. Private Lax said that he had seen them coming out of a shelter near Bay 22 as he left for the rear and assumed they were following him, but they did not arrive at the support post.

McConnell and Holdsworth were newly drafted into the 1/5th and, although they had experience of the front line; they were not on sentry duty but carrying out orderly

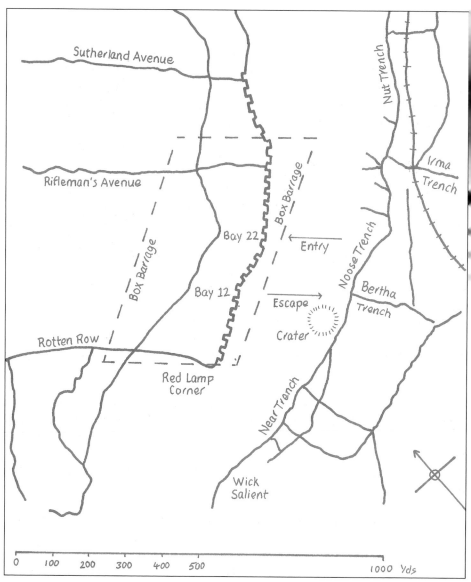

Enemy Trench Raid 9 July 1917. [Sketch Map 17]

Showing the box barrage laid down by German trench mortars as a prelude to the trench raid. The barrage was intended to trap the occupiers of the front line, but they had withdrawn according to Donald Mackay's plan, all except privates C. McConnell and G. Holdsworth, who did not get away and were captured.

functions at the time. They may not have been fully aware of Mackay's scheme. It seems very likely that just as they left the shelter, the raiding party dropped into the trench and attacked them from behind as they chased after Lax – someone had shouted from Bay 22 'they are coming over', about this time. The enemy raiders then took McConnell and Holdsworth back out across no man's land.

194

Not all of the Germans departed, though. Two stayed in the British front line and headed south-west along the now deserted front line trench towards Red Lamp Corner, where they turned a traverse and almost ran into Private Herbert Carr and Sergeant Edwin Tattersfield who were coming the other way.

Edwin Tattersfield. [Ackrill] Tried to save Smith Fryer from drowning in 1915 and helped resist a German trench raid at Laventie in 1917.

Carr and Tattersfield had just re-entered the trench at Red Lamp Corner at the conclusion of a wiring patrol and were heading back to Bay 22 to find out what was going on. Alerted by the barrage, they had bayonets fixed. As the two pairs ran into each other the leading German fired his revolver at Carr, but missed and Carr simultaneously lunged forward, catching his opponent in the arm with the point of his bayonet. The two Germans then fled, but Carr hit one of them with a rifle shot before they disappeared around a traverse. Seconds after the raiders had disappeared, two British sergeants arrived from the direction of Red Lamp Corner and together the four men headed to the reserve line, in accordance with Mackay's plan. With Sergeant Lynch they then returned to the front line, but the raiders had gone, leaving at a point near Bay 12.

Major Mackay then arrived in the front line with Second Lieutenant Edwards and together they worked towards Red Lamp Corner, but were stopped by the continuing barrage before they could get to Bay 12. As they headed back towards Bay 22, a silver flare soared over the German front line, probably intended to indicate that the raiding party had returned to their own front line. As a result, the trench mortar barrage then moved to search the whole front line trench between Bays 12 and 22 for two or three minutes.

Second Lieutenant Edwards immediately ordered the sentries to return to their positions in the front line, which they did. Only then did Edwards discover that two men were missing. Immediately after the bombardment ended the whole party of officers searched the front line trench as far as Red Lamp Corner, but could not find the two missing men. They only came across Second Lieutenant Yates and three other men who had been wounded by the bombardment. Yates and his comrades had probably come from the same wiring party as Carr and Tattersfield.

The incident was over, but the next day a full search was carried out for McConnell and Holdsworth. The only evidence was the blood on the trench wall and at the exit. Also found under the parapet (where the raiders had left) was the dead German soldier fired on by Private Carr, with a bullet in his chest.

Honours

While at Laventie, officers and men of the 1/5th Battalion participated in two medal presentation ceremonies.

On 27 April, at Merville, General Haking presented medal ribbons to officers and men for gallantry on the Somme. Awarded the Military Cross were Captain and Adjutant Walter Freeman, Captain Kenneth Mackay and Second Lieutenant Frederick Saxby. Recipients of the DCM were Regimental Sergeant Major Fred Raynor, Company Sergeant Major H. Pattison and Private Albert W. Farnhill from Bilton near Harrogate. Lance Corporal F. Smith was awarded the Military Medal and Bar. The Military Medal ribbon was awarded to Company Quartermaster Sergeant R. Render, Sergeant A. Metcalfe and Privates T.V. Maw, B. Butler, J.W. Shillito, F.W. Dixon, A. Brooks, J.W. Clark and C. Twineham.

Albert W Farnhill. [Ackrill *From Bilton, Albert was awarded the DCM for clear dugouts at the Battle of Thiepval Ridge.*

On 10 June, Colonel Bousfield presented medal ribbons for the Military Cross to Dudley Wallace; the Military Medal to Sergeant A. Hewson, Lance Sergeant J. Raftery and Corporal E. Radband; the *Medaille Militaire* to C. Sell and Sergeant Pattison. He also presented gallantry cards to Frederick Saxby, Harry Irish and Sergeant R. Thornhill.

It is likely that Irish received his award for an act of bravery in La Gorgue on 23 May. According to the citation in Divisional orders:

A horse attached to a civilian van took fright and bolted. The driver jumped off the seat. The horse was galloping down the narrowest point of the street, when 2nd Lieut. Irish sprang at the animal, caught it by the bridle and held on, although he was dragged for a distance of about 25 yards. No.247508, Private J.D. Wood, West Yorkshire Regiment, then seized the bridle from the opposite side and brought the horse to a standstill.

Private Wood appears not to have been with the 1/5th Battalion.

A month later, the redeemed and regenerated 1/5th Battalion left the relative quiet of Laventie for the Belgian coast, the Ypres Salient and the hell on earth of the Battle of Passchendaele.

Chapter 10

Passchendaele
(July–November 1917)

'..heads down but hearts up...'

Operation Hush

Following the disastrous French offensive at the Chemin des Dames in May 1917, and the spread of mutiny in the ranks of the French Army, a new campaign was needed to relieve the pressure. Field Marshal Sir Douglas Haig had always favoured an attack in Flanders, around Ypres, to break out of the Salient and now Prime Minister David Lloyd George was prepared to give him his head, grudgingly. Lloyd George was not personally in favour of an assault in Belgium and later distanced himself from the horror and carnage of the Third Battle of Ypres, also popularly known as the Battle of Passchendaele, which was launched on 31 July and lasted until 10 November 1917.

The British were buoyed by success at the Battle of Messines of 7–14 June 1917, which drove the front line forward onto the Messines–Wytschaete Ridge, south of Ypres. General Plumer, who commanded the attack, wanted to continue on towards Passchendaele Ridge and the Gheluvelt plain, but Haig did not agree. He was intent on a co-ordinated thrust on a broad front across the Salient and decided to wait until all was ready.

As a prelude to the main attack, Operation Hush was a planned amphibious landing on the Belgian coast north of Nieuwpoort, intended to allow the extension of the existing bridgehead on the north side of the Yser by land-based assault. This bridgehead would be the jumping off point for the attack, the success of which would lend additional impetus to the main attack on the German lines around the Ypres Salient, intended for early August 1917.

In order to check Operation Hush, the German Army made a pre-emptive strike code-named Operation Strandfest, or 'Beach Party'. This was a frontal assault on the Nieuwpoort bridgehead. Launched on 10 July 1917, the bridgehead was driven in, with thousands of British soldiers forced to swim across the Yser to the relative safety of the south bank. By 12 July the land occupied by the BEF on the north bank had shrunk to about one square mile, which rendered it ineffective as a base for Operation Hush, which was abandoned.

Mustard Gas at Nieuwpoort

On its departure from Estaires on 13 July, three days after Beach Party was launched, the 1/5th Battalion headed from Laventie to the Belgian coast, where it was due for a spell of coastal defence. Following the abandonment of Operation Hush, the battalion was to occupy the front line in the St George's Sector, two miles east of Nieuwpoort, with the 1/6th Battalion occupying the relatively quiet, marshy positions on the right. At 3am the 1/5th relieved the 16th Lancashire Fusiliers in the hotly contested left sub-sector opposite the German-held concrete bunker known as 'Rat Post'.

Rat Post was a tall and apparently impregnable concrete bunker, 80 yards from the brigade left. According to the 1/5th Battalion war diary, *'Very little work has been done in the sector – trenches (breastworks) not even bullet-proof.'* The artillery activity was so intense that a thick pall of smoke hung over this part of the front line day and night. The plan was that the 1/5th would rotate with the 1/7th and 1/8th Battalions who started in support and reserve, respectively.

On arrival, the 1/5th was shelled heavily at 3.30am, which wounded five men. One was from C Company on the brigade left, holding Nun Trench, which was badly knocked about. Four were from A Company, in the centre, holding Nice Trench. D Company was deployed in support, and B Company in reserve in Nieuwpoort, itself. This was to be the most dangerous position of all, subsequently described by Captain Tempest as 'an inferno'.

The next night was much quieter though, as the enemy artillery concentrated on the bridges across the Yser and destroyed one of them. Major Mackay took advantage of the relative calm to send out patrols, left and right. On the left, the C Company patrol did not come into contact with the enemy, but was fired on from Rat Post. The A Company patrol on the right made no contact at all.

In the early hours of 21 July, further patrols were pushed out and the A Company party encountered an enemy patrol which retreated swiftly to its own lines. The left patrol made no contact, but lay in front of Rat Post for some time, listening, before returning. At 6am there was a further heavy bombardment of the front line and Nun Trench in particular. Private John Lynch, formerly of the 4th Battalion West Yorkshires and a newly arrived A Company reinforcement, was killed by an explosion. Five other men from A Company were wounded, including Second Lieutenant John Rushforth, but this was a relatively minor incident compared to the events of the following night.

According to the 1/5th Battalion war diary, from 2am on 22 July about 2,000 gas shells, including mustard gas and high explosive, were fired into Nieuwpoort. Captain Tempest observes that this 'was one of the great and terrible experiences of the War'. He reports that a man standing near the impact would be killed instantly and that if his comrades nearby failed to don their box respirators swiftly they would succumb too. The gas was novel and smelt, not unpleasantly, of mustard. Many of those who put their masks on quickly had already breathed some of the gas, as it could not be seen in the darkness. They would gasp in their masks, then become so hot from coughing that they would remove them for some 'fresh air', and breathe in lungfuls of gas. Coughing uncontrollably, they would then sometimes die.

The mustard gas lingered for hours in the craters and cellars of Nieuwpoort, glowing rose pink in the pall hanging over the town as dawn broke. Close up, it was

Nieuwpoort 30 July 1917. [Taylor Library]

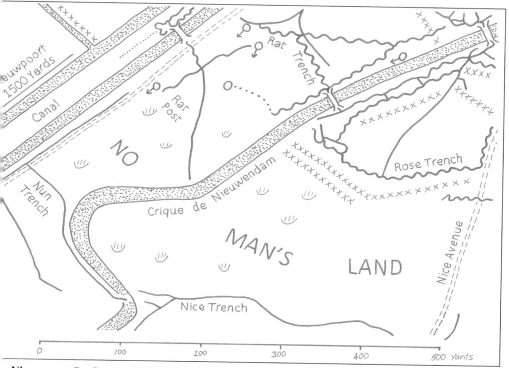

Nieuwpoort St. Georges Trenches, July 1917. [Sketch Map 18]
Showing the location of Rat Post, Nice Trench and Nun Trench relative to the town.

still very dangerous long after it had appeared to have dissipated. Many removed their gas masks prematurely and were blinded. Coughing, hundreds of men left Nieuwpoort to the south towards Oost Dunkirk and fell down at the roadside.

The evening before B Company had moved forward to work in the front line and so missed the worst of the gas in Nieuwpoort, which caused the 1/8th Battalion to suffer more than 400 casualties. In the early hours of the morning, however, the front line came under heavy bombardment, possibly because the enemy discovered it was heavily occupied. With the gas appearing to have lifted, Colonel Bousfield ordered B Company to retire back into the town in small groups, to escape the worst of the shelling. On arrival in Nieuwpoort their services were commandeered by the Royal Army Medical Corps, who ordered them to help recover the wounded and dead from the cellars of the town.

Failing to understand the lingering danger, the officers and men of B Company probably did not use their gas masks properly and the battalion diary records that they were all casualties, with 141 suffering from gas, including Captain Ellison and Second Lieutenants Stephens, Clough and Waugh. Miraculously, only one man died, Private George Hothersall from Bradford.

Sergeant Edward Ledgard, from Haxby, was awarded his DCM for gallantry at Nieuwpoort that night:

Though he was suffering severely from gas and gradually becoming blind he worked with great determination assisting to evacuate badly gassed cases. His endurance was magnificent.

A well-known professional footballer in York, Edward enlisted into the Beechwood Boys in November 1914 and arrived at the front in September 1915. Having recovered from the Nieuwpoort gas, he sustained a 'blighty' wound in September 1917.

After Effects

Over the following week there were further artillery duels, more gas and constant night patrols to identify any build up and predict an assault. On 25 July, 24-year-old Albert Booth was killed, probably in one of the four patrols sent out to Rat Post. He had been drafted across from the 18th Battalion, 2nd Bradford Pals.

Private Stanley Young wrote to the *Harrogate Herald*, to describe events:

I like to read your letter which you insert every week. One can fair imagine being in Harrogate in reality. We are now in a comparative rough part of the line, and artillery "strafes" are an absolute revelation, and some exciting times seem to be in store. Activity is prevalent all along the line, judging by the racket which is going on. Maybe we will have a repetition of the Somme of last year, which acts as a gentle reminder. The Germans have a slight tendency of sniping one with a few batteries occasionally (so unhealthy, you know). Yes, and we send some back so nicely; I like to hear them go "plonk" right over. Then you can hear the boys say – "That's the stuff to give them." Of course, he is playing too, so we have to give a bit and bob down; "heads down, but hearts up". I am writing this letter in the trenches, where we are likely to be for a few days.

In the ensuing days and weeks large numbers of men were sent to hospital as the long-term effects of gas began to show and the gas shells kept dropping. On 30 July, the MO examined the entire battalion and found that five officers and 132 other ranks were suffering from hitherto undiagnosed effects of gas. On 1 August there were a further forty-eight gas casualties and after this men were sent to hospital in twos and threes, daily, until, it was decided that the 1/1st West Riding Field Ambulance would disinfect all kit and clothing, to remove all traces of the poison.

By 13 August the battalion had recovered its fitness, although total gas casualties by this point ran to more than 400, or nearly half the battalion establishment. Of the twenty-three men of the 1/5th Battalion who died in hospital between 12 July and 9 October 1917, most were suffering from the effects of poison gas.

B Company had, in effect, been wiped out in Nieuwpoort, with Harry Irish and Reginald Walker left in charge of only eighteen other ranks. Colonel Bousfield held a conference of his officers and decided to reconstitute the company with drafts of about twenty-five each from the three other companies, as well as new men as they arrived. Lieutenant Ablitt was brought back from the 1/6th, and given command of B Company when he returned from home leave and by 5 August it had swelled to a relatively healthy four officers and 106 other ranks.

The whole battalion then relived the relatively familiar (by now) experience of regeneration. Between 28 June and 28 September, 24 Officers and 584 Other Ranks were drafted in, including a proportion of those who were returning from convalescence. The effective strength increased to 43 officers and 944 Other Ranks on the eve of the Battle of Poelcappelle ten days later. Of these, 608, or 61.6 per cent of the total battalion strength were newly drafted since the end of June.

The battalion therefore needed to be unified once more and put in touch with its heritage. Captain Freeman records on 28 September 1917 that it was the *'anniversary of the capture of the Schwarben* [sic] *Redoubt'*. Though history may not view the events of twelve months earlier in such conclusive terms, they had clearly gone down in battalion history and were marked as such. For the new officers and NCOs there was also a lecture on the history of the regiment, presumably going back to Famars where in 1792 the 14th Regiment of Foot had fought the French Revolutionary Army. On 8 August the General Officer Commanding XI Corps inspected the brigade on the beach and awarded medals to Acting Sergeant Raftery and Acting Corporal Boldison. He also awarded medals to Acting Company Sergeant Major Thompson for his part in Dudley Wallace's silent raid and to Herbert Carr for shooting the German raider on 9 July.

To boost morale, there were divisional sports with the prizes presented by General Perceval. Second Lieutenant Goddard and 14 Platoon (D Company) won the brigade and divisional musketry competition. Second Lieutenant Claney and the battalion scouts won the brigade fighting patrol and observation competition and came second in the brigade reconnaissance patrol competition, which was won by the 1/6th Battalion. The 1/5th showed themselves, perhaps, to be the best trained battalion in the brigade, winning three out of the four competitions. It probably also gave the battalion a lift in morale to acquire the services of a Victoria Cross winner, Second Lieutenant Sam Meekosha, who joined A Company on 20 August 1917.

Cobbled together again, the battalion was up to strength by 8 October, and there is reason to believe that the new men had absorbed the spirit of their forebears and of the West Riding. Bousfield and his officers had done their best to ensure the battalion was sufficiently prepared to deal with the harshest military test they had yet faced, in the mud of Bellevue Spur at the Battle of Poelcappelle, a chapter in the history of the Battle of Passchendaele.

Sam Meekosha VC [YAM] Joined the 1/5th Batta on 15 August 1917

Training for Passchendaele

The weather was good and the billets brick built and comfortable so 146 Brigade spent a relatively pleasant late summer on the coast around Dunkirk. The training area was on the dunes between Rosendael and Bray, where a sweaty day's activity usually ended with 'bathing parade' in the sea. Nearby, the 1/5th Battalion was billeted initially at Coxyde and then Téteghem, moving to Ghyvelde in September 1917.

On the beach, for two months, the battalion underwent extended order drill, close order drill and physical training, including route marches inland. They did large amounts of bayonet training, with a degree of enthusiasm which put one man in hospital with accidental wounds. There was Lewis gun training, as well as musketry on the short and 200 yard ranges. All other aspects of specialist training were provided, including signals and scouting.

Officers received lectures in the latest thinking on patrol formations, and anti-gas tactics from the divisional staff. Colonel Bousfield lectured the junior officers on all matters, and Norrie Beech took charge of machine gunnery, a matter in which he was now truly expert.

At divisional, brigade and battalion level a great deal of thought and rehearsal was put into advance guard and other attack formations, including night attacks. Practice assaults were carried out across the dunes, with the use of flags and tapes, under the observation of staff officers who rode about in imperious fashion, making notes from time to time. Usually there was a mock shell gas attack, but on at least one occasion the enemy obliged by sending across the real thing.

On 10 September Sir Herbert Plumer watched the 1/5th Battalion make a practice attack and discussed it with Bousfield and his officers afterwards. On 13 September brigade practice attacks were carried out in front of Lieutenant General A.J Godley (II Anzac Corps) and again, Plumer, both of whom addressed the officers at the conclusion. They made it clear that the 49th Division was due to take a role in the forthcoming attack on Passchendaele Ridge, as part of Godley's Corps, and that rehearsals had been designed with this in mind.

On 24 September the 1/5th Battalion moved temorarily back to the Ypres Salient with the other battalions of the 49th Division. Via Coudekerque, they marched to Wormhoudt, Noordpeene, then on 27 September to comfortable billets in St Martin, south-west of Poperinghe.

On 29 September they returned to the coast and took part in two days of divisional manoeuvres at St Omer. The two assaulting brigades, consisting of about 4,000 men, were drawn up over frontage of 800 yards, with the support brigade 1,000 yards to the rear. Before the practice attacks, staff officers handed out 'casualty cards' to officers and NCOs, indicating at what part of the attack their men would fall out, as if they were casualties. Captain Tempest records that those ordered to fall out at the jumping off tapes would be noisily cheery about it, happy to be relieved of a morning's manoeuvres.

The nature of defence and attack had changed over the last year. On the Somme, the British artillery bombarded the German front line trench, then moved forward to bombard the enemy support line and then the reserve line. This was the tactic used on 1 July 1916. Since then, the enemy had learned to place machine guns between the lines, which would be missed by the bombardment, remaining free to fire on the attacking troops as they left the trenches. In turn, British tactics now developed to use the 'creeping barrage', as deployed at the Battle of Thiepval, designed to destroy everything in its path.

To combat the changing nature of the fighting, the Germans created defensive lines in great depth, protected by very broad belts of barbed wire. Numerous small concrete bunkers provided shelter; once the barrage passed over, machine-gun crews and soldiers occupied difficult to spot positions, often in shell craters. This made the task of the advancing infantry very difficult.

On the training ground at St Omer, in late September 1917, red flags indicated the locations of German pill boxes and the direction of attack over open ground. The focus was on advancing quickly on the heels of the creeping barrage. Rather than mopping up trenches and dug-outs, the 1/5th now trained to clear pill-boxes. Where the grenade was the weapon of choice for trench-clearing, the rifle was now most useful in picking off retreating enemy soldiers. As the 1/5th Battalion had discovered in 1916, the key was for officers and men to stay together and keep moving in the right direction.

The Third Battle of Ypres

On 18 July 1917 the artillery of the BEF had started an enormous bombardment of enemy positions across the Salient. Twelve infantry divisions (including a French Corps on the right) went over the top at 3.50am on the last day of the month. On 31 July the infantry attack commenced. Broadly speaking it could be considered a success. Especially on the left where the French did particularly well, and at Pilckem Ridge. Then a month of very unseasonal rain set in. The late summer of 1917 was to be exceptionally wet in Flanders and the heavily shelled ground quickly turned into slushy mud. A further push was made on 16 August at the Battle of Langemarck, but gains were very disappointing. Field Marshal Haig reacted by bringing General Plumer's Second Army into the battle, the victor at Messines four months earlier. Plumer was less expansive than Gough, deciding on a series of more narrowly focused attacks with limited objectives. This approach, known as 'bite and hold', combined with the good weather, set the pattern for the remainder of the Battle of Third Ypres. Ground was gained at the successive battles of the Menin Road and Polygon Wood on 20 and 26 September, then at the Battle of Broodseinde on 4 October. The main ridges to the east of Ypres were now in British hands, and the next objective, Passchendaele Ridge, was in sight.

General Plumer planned his next attack for 9 October, using General Godley's II ANZAC Corps, which now included the 49th Division. For the first time in the Great War, the 1/5th Battalion was to form part of the first wave of a major attack. Their objective was Bellevue Spur at the Battle of Poelcappelle.

Getting to the Battleground

On 3 October 146 Brigade began preparing to move up the line for the attack. Three hours' silence was ordered that afternoon, as they squatted in dirty farm billets near Steenvoorde, 25 kilometres west of Ypres. Some men slept, some wrote letters and others fretted. That night they marched to Vlamertinghe near the west bank of the Yser Canal, where they stayed for two nights.

On 5 October it started to rain heavily. At nightfall the 1/5th Battalion marched through the ruined town of Ypres to reserve positions in shell holes at Spree Farm, just a few hundred yards east of Turco Farm. At dawn the next day they moved east again at one hour's notice, leaving a detachment of about 250 men, as the Second Echelon reserve under Major Donald Mackay.

Approaching the battlefield from the west, Colonel Bousfield led his attacking force of 20 officers and 624 Other Ranks into old German reserve trenches near Wieltje. These were 'quite knocked about' according to the battalion diary. The 1/5th was now on recently conquered ground and on 7 October the grey dawn revealed abandoned tanks and tree stumps, as the men descended into dug-outs out of the heavy rain, to get some rest.

Meanwhile, the officers and NCOs squelched forward five miles to Gravenstafel in order to reconnoitre their forming-up positions for the attack near Calgary Grange. They did this from shell holes in broad daylight and in sight of the enemy. Captain Freeman reported it to be a 'most uncomfortable day', as a heavy bombardment was put down only 400 yards away. Luckily, the party escaped without injury and returned that evening to the battalion at Wieltje.

On 8 October the battalion spent the day in dug-outs getting ready for the attack. They dumped unnecessary kit and changed into 'fighting order', with entrenching tool worn 'sporran' fashion. All ranks were to carry two sandbags, one flare, one bomb and an extra bandolier of small arms ammunition (SAA). In the afternoon Second Lieutenant Claney went forward to tape out the jumping off positions with the help of his scout, Frank Clarkson. They put up notice boards showing where each platoon was to form up for the attack the next morning.

The other officers and men of the 1/5th Battalion climbed out of their Wieltje dug-outs at 5pm that afternoon, to follow in the footsteps of Claney and Clarkson. It was still pouring with rain again, worse than ever. They located the duckboards of No.6 Track and struggled the six miles to the assembly position, mostly in pitch dark. This journey, under normal conditions, would have taken three hours, but took eight hours in an environment which made it extremely difficult to move. The stretch from Kansas Cross to Calgary Grange was particularly hard, even though it was gridded with trenches. The last 800 yards was all but impossible, across ground won on 4 October, which was now nothing but a sea of slimy shell holes.

The description of the move up to the front line is best described by a soldier who was there, Captain Tempest:

The billets were shell holes of familiar Flanders mud. The whole area was crowded with troops, and littered with the debris of battle. All trace of roads or houses east of Wieltje had entirely disappeared. Labour battalions were engaged in building a straight plank road across the mud, and thousands of men were making tracks to lead up to gun positions and dumps on either side of the main plank road, which was the only practicable method of communication on a front of nearly two kilometres.

Hundreds of mules carrying ammunition and rations struggled forward on either side of the plank road. Transport wagons and lorries went forward as far as possible on the planks, but every half hour there was some lorry or general service wagon which slipped into the mud, and caused an obstruction. If it was a G.S. wagon which had come to grief, it was lifted again on to the planks. In the case of a loaded motor lorry this could not be done, so the lorry was tipped off the planks into the mud, and the long line of traffic moved on again. On either side of the plank road there were dozens of derelict motor lorries, thousands of shells, hundreds of dead horses and mules, all of them rapidly sinking in the mud. The enemy shelled the road constantly, and every hit – and there were many – resulted in casualties. But the road was quickly repaired and the traffic moved on.

Near Kansas Cross there was a good land-mark, which went by the name of the 'Incinerated man'. A 5.9 shell had struck a lorry carrying petrol, and set it ablaze. The driver had been hit at the wheel, and had then been burnt to death. His skeleton remained, however, still sitting at the driving seat and leaning on the steering wheel of the lorry. The stream of traffic poured down the plank road past this ghastly landmark, and for two or three weeks no one troubled to move it.

At 1.20am on 9 October, exhausted, soaked and freezing cold, the men of the 1/5th Battalion slid into shell holes at the assembly point, to huddle and await the barrage.

Battle Plan

The 1/5th Battalion was to attack on the brigade right, with the 1/7th and 1/8th Leeds Rifles on their left, the 1/6th Battalion in support and 148 Brigade on the right. They were expected to assemble for the attack on the downward slope, about 500 yards north-east of the captured pill box at Calgary Grange. They were to form up for attack on a two company frontage extending for 280 yards. A Company would be on the left and C Company on the right; behind them, B Company would be on the left and D Company on the right. They were to advance behind a creeping barrage at the pace of 100 yards every six minutes.

Aside from the swamp-like nature of the ground, the only natural barrier was the Stroombeek, a stream running across the line of advance, at the bottom of the shallow valley about 250 yards beyond the forming-up point. On either side of the Stroombeek was 100 yards of particularly soggy marsh, with the consistency of porridge. Beyond the Stroombeek, the ground rose gently, rising up towards Passchendaele Ridge, with Bellevue Spur over on the right. The line of advance presented a relatively open field of fire to the enemy machine guns and rifles sited in shell holes and pill boxes ranged across the German lines, apparently strongest on the spur.

Four hundred yards, beyond the Stroombeek, was the first objective: a line running north-west to south-east, beyond the ruined German trenches at Peter Pan: 600 yards further on, lay the second objective. This was protected on rising ground by heavy wire and the remains of organised trenches to a depth of 300 yards. There were at least two (and as many as five) occupied German pill boxes on the spur. Brigade orders were to seize and hold the second objective with sufficient strength, not only to repulse a counter-attack, but to form a base for the next stage of the attack on Passchendaele itself, which sat on top of the ridge.

It was intended that A and C companies would assault the first objective, at Peter Pan, then consolidate it while B and D Companies would leap-frog them at this point and move on to the second objective beyond Wolf Copse.

The whole battalion was to attack in line of section, which meant that every nine yards along the taped line would be a column of fifteen men in the first wave, ready to move forward on the heels of the creeping barrage. Behind them, in identical formation would be the second wave.

The following officers were to lead the attack:

Headquarters:
Lieut-Col. H.D. Bousfield D.S.O. in command
Capt. B.E. Ablitt M.C. Acting Adjutant
2/Lieut. S.M. Claney, Battalion Intelligence Officer
2/Lieut. B.A. King, Battalion Signal Officer

A Company
Capt. D.W. Wallace M.C.
Lieut. S.W. Birbeck
2/Lt. S. Meekosha V.C.
2/Lt. C.R. Firth

B Company
2/Lt. H. Irish
2/Lt. A.P.F. Neesham
2/Lt. A. Barker

C Company
Capt. B.S. Bland
2/Lt. L.C. Tyrell
2/Lt. N.W. Beech, DCM.

D Company
Lieut. T.W. Hardwick
2/Lt. H. Goddard
2/Lt. J.W. Parker

Four other officers went onto the attack as medical, or liaison officers with the flank battalions. Second Lieutenant Harper was transport officer.

The Attack on Bellevue Spur

About 5am on 9 October, in the pre-dawn, platoon sergeants roused their men from holes in the ground at the assembly point and led them to the tapes. This movement was no easy task as the front line was a morass of adjoining shell holes with the consistency of porridge; to move from one place to another involved skirting the craters and slithering on the slimy ridges between them.

The British barrage was punctual, starting at 5.20am precisely, landing about 150 yards ahead of the tapes. However, it was weak because the ground in the rear was too wet for the guns to get near enough to the front line. They were firing at their maximum range and on unstable ground which reduced accuracy. Also, the mud in the gun-pits made it impossible to feed the guns a steady diet of ammunition, even where the nearest railhead was only a few hundred yards away. Therefore, it was hard for the first wave to see exactly where the line of advance was because the barrage was so threadbare. Almost immediately, they lost the pace in the appalling conditions which were officially described as only 'slippery'.

Five minutes after the off, the German artillery opened up, searching the slope between Calgary Grange and the Stroombeek, but casualties were relatively few due to the soft ground. As the sky lightened, A and C Companies entered the marsh on the southern bank of the Stroombeek fairly intact.

They crossed the stream using all manner of means: laying striplings across or using the fallen trees which were already lying there. Some crossed up to their waists in the muddy water. It all took so long that they inevitably lost contact with the barrage. As the first wave crossed the Stroombeek and dragged themselves through the marsh on the north bank they came within full sight and range of the pill boxes at Bellevue. The German rifles and machine guns sited in the shell holes at Yetta Houses and Wolf Copse also fired through the barrage and the advancing troops were forced to throw themselves down onto the slime and crawl forward, bullets landing all around and

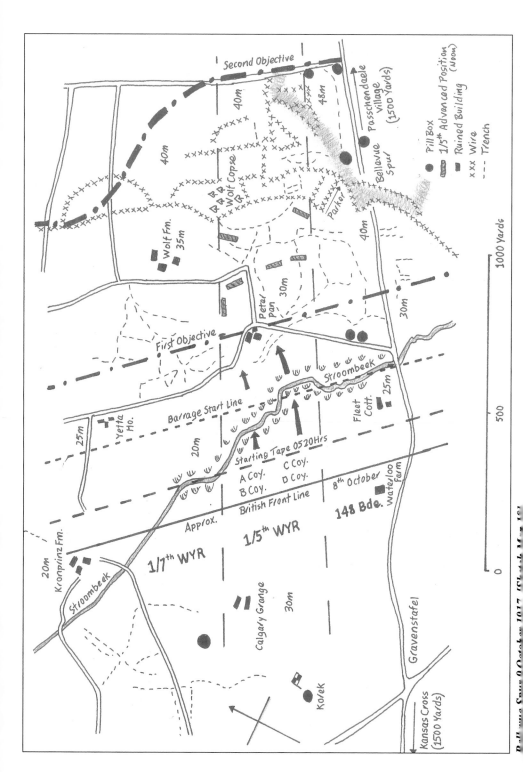

Second Objective

40m

48m

Passchendaele village (1500 Yards)

Bellavue Spur

1/5th Advanced Position (Noon)

● Pill Box
▬ Ruined Building
xxx Wire
--- Trench

40m

Wolf Copse

Parker

Wolf Fm. 35m

40m

30m

First Objective

Petal Pan

30m

Stroombeek

Fleet Cott.

25m

Barrage Start Line

Yetta Ho.

25m

20m

Starting Tape 0520Hrs

A Coy.   C Coy.
B Coy.   D Coy.

British Front Line

Waterloo Farm

8th October

Approx.

148 Bde.

1/5th WYR

1/7th WYR

Kronprinz Fm.

20m

Stroombeek

Calgary Grange

30m

Kolek

Gravenstafel

Kansas Cross (1500 Yards)

1000 Yards

500

0

208

Calgary Grange to Peter Pan. [Author]
Showing the Stroombeek, with Peter Pan on the horizon.

From Peter Pan to the Second Objective. [Author]
Shows the view uphill from the first objective to Bellevue Spur on the right and Wolf Copse on the left.

splashing their faces with liquid mud. The earliest reports say that some men of A and C companies made it to the first objective at about 6.10am, fifty minutes into the attack.

However, the battalion had veered to the left, where they overlapped the right flank of the 1/7th Battalion, causing some confusion. This was probably because the German defensive fire was strongest from the Bellevue Spur ahead and on the right. Naturally, the line thinned on the right and a gap developed on the unprotected flank as the men proceeded up the slope, half an hour or so into the attack.

By 7.05am the first objective was reported as 'completely taken', and some were able to use the ruined barns of Peter Pan for a brief respite. While the first objective does not appear to have been strongly held by the enemy, this was a substantial achievement as the battalion had now caught up with the barrage timetable, although the gap on the right flank had now widened to 500 yards, as 148 Brigade had fallen behind.

Where B and D companies of the 1/5th were intended to leapfrog the first wave, all four companies now became mixed. Elements of the first wave prepared to continue forward to the second objective, which lay 1,250 yards beyond the starting tapes, with their comrades. They moved off together, officers in the lead and NCOs in the rear, as the barrage started creeping forward again at 7.09am, at the slightly slower pace of 100 yards every 8-10 minutes. Seeing the British approach, some enemy posts ahead started to empty and fleeing German soldiers were shot on sight. There was no attempt to take prisoners as there was no way of getting them securely to the rear.

The battle was now raging, with high explosive and shrapnel bursting all around. As the 1/5th Battalion moved towards the main German defences on the western ridge of Bellevue Spur, they met even stiffer resistance and casualties began to mount.

Leonard Tyrell was hit by a machine-gun bullet and died slowly in Barnet Bland's arms. Dudley Wallace was also killed by a sniper's bullet around this time and Sidney Birbeck was shot too, pressing the attack forward. All four of these officers had been in the first wave and were advancing on into the fire, in support of B and D Companies. Unfortunately, the advance stalled on the wire in front of the second objective. No further progress could be made without clearing the machine-gun posts and pill boxes at Bellevue, whose machine guns were able to enfilade the German wire, and create a killing zone in front of the defences. These enemy positions had now been reinforced further with troops from Passchendaele itself.

Responding to the situation, Second Lieutenant John W. Parker of D Company and Corporal Fred A. Tomlinson of C Company gathered a party of men from the 1/5th Battalion and the 1/4th Duke of Wellington's Regiment, which had come forward in support, and attacked the concrete structures. Parker led the assault which, according to Major Foxton, got within 40 yards of the pill boxes when he was held up by wire and a brushwood hedge. He tried to work round the side of the pill boxes but was stopped again by machine-gun fire and was forced to lie down with his small group. Unable to go forward or back, Parker held this position until relieved the next morning, although he was bombed and shelled several times overnight.

Parker was awarded the Military Cross with the following citation, which varies slightly from the diary account:

> When the barrage had got far ahead of the attacking troops on account of the bad state of the ground, he took command of men of different battalions and organised a determined attack on two "pill-boxes" which were holding up the advance. He got within thirty yards in spite of heavy fire. Being then stopped by wire, he consolidated the position, and carried out a valuable reconnaissance.

Fred Tomlinson was awarded a Bar to his Military Medal for his part, which *The Yorkshire Herald* reported as follows: '*He was the only man left of his section, but he rallied others and held onto the position until relieved later.*'

A further view of these events was offered by the Brigade Intelligence Officer, Captain Tempest, who was watching from advanced Brigade HQ at Korek. He refers to some elements of the 1/5th Battalion reaching the hedge 400 yards east of Peter Pan and reports that a few made it to within 200 yards of the Bellevue pill boxes by 9am, when they were stopped by the mud and strong unbroken enemy wire. This was probably Parker's party. Tempest records that half way between the first and second objectives, these men from C and D companies dropped into shell holes, exhausted. Some were picked off by the snipers at Bellevue and Wolf Copse, ahead. Machine-gun fire from Wolf Farm also enfiladed their only route of retreat, trapping them against the enemy wire. It was impossible to get messages back to Battalion HQ at the Calgary Grange pill box, because runners were mown down as soon as they tried to head back. Having advanced further than the battalions on either side, the leading parties of the 1/5th Battalion were now cut-off and exposed to vicious fire from the front and both sides. Battalion HQ at Calgary Grange had very little idea what was going on and the brigade command structure had broken down entirely.

At 8.15am, from his position slightly behind Parker, Lieutenant Hardwick could see what was happening ahead. He was able to get a message back to Colonel Bousfield, saying that help was needed on the right flank. As at Thiepval Ridge a year earlier, the attack was jeopardised by veering to the left. At 7.40am C Company of the 1/6th Battalion had already been sent forward to plug the gap on the right, but was only making slow progress. Captain Tempest records his view from the rear, of brown figures advancing up the slope in the teeth of machine-gun and rifle fire. He states that it was obvious to observers: *'that our second objective could not be reached by the thinning line of exhausted men who were only half way up the Passchendaele slope.'*

In response to Hardwick's message, Colonel Bousfield decided to take his HQ Staff forward in a desperate attempt to support the right flank of the attack and get the advance moving again. He was wounded on the way, probably at the Stroombeek, and Battalion HQ was effectively wiped out, as acting Adjutant Bernard Ablitt reported to the officer commanding the 1/4th Duke of Wellington's about 11am. A message was sent back to Wieltje, where Donald Mackay was waiting in reserve. He set off immediately to replace Bousfield, but it took him many hours to get forward accompanied by Lieutenant John Battersby-Harford. They arrived at Calgary Grange at 3.30pm and within the hour Mackay was also killed. This left Ablitt in command of the battalion.

Further forward, the Royal Flying Corps reported 146 Brigade to be in front of Wolf Farm and Wolf Copse. Some isolated parties of men from the 1/5th Battalion had indeed dug themselves in to a line of posts running from the southern edge of Wolf Farm to the eastern edge of Wolf Copse, on the German wire. They also formed a detached post about 150 yards south-east of the southern corner of Wolf Copse. A support line was established approximately along the line of the first objective, about 200 yards behind the forward posts. The men in these positions managed to hold them until they were relieved, although this involved resisting a series of bombing attacks and heavy shelling overnight and into 10 October, as well as consistently accurate sniping from the pill boxes on Bellevue Spur.

Divisional records note that during the attack, Harry Irish was shot though both eyes but reorganised his platoon and held the ground gained under heavy machine-gun fire. He refused to leave his post when reinforcements came up, saying he had no orders to go from his own battalion. For this he was awarded the Military Cross.

Ultimately, 146 Brigade had failed to reach its second objective, but it had succeeded in advancing further than the brigades on either flank, both of which were stuck at the first objective, where the attack lost impetus all along the line. The second objective was in fact only taken by fresh Canadian troops three weeks later. In the meantime, men were stuck in the mud all over the battlefield.

Relief

In the early hours of 11 October 146 Brigade was relieved by New Zealanders. This was an unusual operation as the men from 146 Brigade were not easy to find in their shell holes. The Anzacs decided to draw a new front line, about where Ablitt had drawn his support line on the night of 9 October, and the advanced parties of the 1/5th Battalion withdrew back through the new front line.

On the night of 11 October, between 6pm and 5.30am, the 1/5th Battalion moved back to the dug-outs in Wieltje, where they had left their kit five days earlier. This journey, part by bus and part by route march, required a herculean effort. Most had not slept for two days and all were exhausted and wet through. Fewer than 400 made it back. Many were walking wounded. They left behind the stretcher cases, the dead and those who were dying in the morass.

About eighty men lay overnight on stretchers around Calgary Grange. Most had crawled, or been brought down from the ridge on 9 October and the number increased slightly during the following day. The enemy artillery had the range of the Calgary Grange pill box, and hits regularly put out its candles. These explosions also served, in Captain Tempest's words, to put some of the stretcher cases *'out of their misery'*. The Battalion medical officer did his best and Captain John Pinder of the Royal Army Medical Corps was awarded the Military Cross on 17 December 1917 for his efforts and bravery with the 1/5th Battalion. The citation reads as follows:

> *For conspicuous gallantry and devotion to duty in attending to wounded under continuous shell-fire. During two days and nights he worked in a shell-hole and sent back a large number of wounded men who would otherwise have died from exposure. He also went forward several times to the front line to attend to wounded men.*

Pinder and his colleagues could not help everyone, though. Private Henry F. Thundercliffe, a tanner's labourer from Hull, was one of those left to die outside a dressing station. He was a member of 13 Platoon, D Company. In the early hours of 10 October his calls from a shell hole were heard by Corporal C. Mitchell, having lain there nearly twenty-four hours. Mitchell's party pulled him out and carried him back 60 yards, but were forced to leave him in another shell hole, 80 yards

Henry Thundercliffe. [Chris Noble]
Died in a shell hole at Bellevue Spur on 9 October 1917.

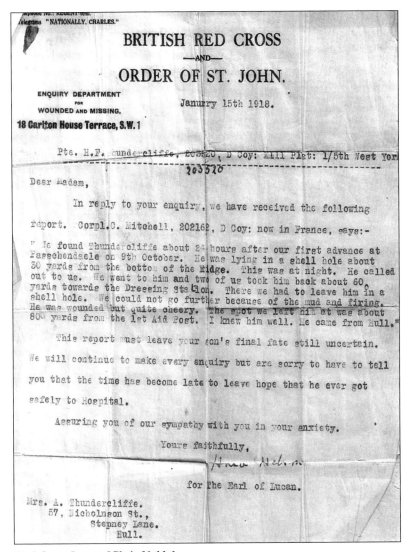

Telephone No.: REGENT 4040.
Telegrams "NATIONALLY, CHARLES."

BRITISH RED CROSS
—AND—
ORDER OF ST. JOHN.

ENQUIRY DEPARTMENT
FOR
WOUNDED AND MISSING,

January 15th 1918.

18 Carlton House Terrace, S.W.1

Pte. H.F. Thundercliffe, 203520, D Coy: XIII Plat: 1/5th West Yor
203520

Dear Madam,

In reply to your enquiry, we have received the following report. Corpl.C. Mitchell, 202162, D Coy: now in France, says:-

" We found Thundercliffe about 2½ hours after our first advance at Passchendaele on 9th October. He was lying in a shell hole about 30 yards from the bottom of the Ridge. This was at night. He called out to us. We went to him and two of us took him back about 60 yards towards the Dressing Station. There we had to leave him in a shell hole. We could not go further because of the mud and firing. He was wounded but quite cheery. The spot we left him at was about 800 yards from the 1st Aid Post. I knew him well. He came from Hull."

This report must leave your son's final fate still uncertain.

We will continue to make every enquiry but are sorry to have to tell you that the time has become late to leave hope that he ever got safely to Hospital.

Assuring you of our sympathy with you in your anxiety.

Yours faithfully,

Anna Nelson

for the Earl of Lucan.

Mrs. A. Thundercliffe.
    57, Nicholnson St.,
        Stepney Lane.
            Hull.

Red Cross Letter. [Chris Noble]
A letter to Mrs Thundercliffe, reporting the last known sighting of her son, Henry.

from the dressing station, as the mud would not let them take him any further. No doubt they were utterly exhausted themselves. Henry died late that day and his body was never recovered.

There were two first aid posts in the rear, near Kansas Cross and Spree Farm, but only those who could take themselves had a realistic chance of making it there, as there were insufficient stretcher-bearers and the ground was impassable for them anyway.

The Cost

Major Foxton's initial report gave the number of battalion casualties as 14 officers and 286 men. Of these, 57 were thought to have been killed, 195 wounded and 52 missing. Overall, this amounted to a 47 per cent casualty rate in less than two days fighting; a relatively heavy price even for the Great War and the 1/5th certainly bore more than its fair share of brigade casualties.

Foxton underestimated the number of fatalities; 103 men (all ranks) are now known to have been killed on 9 and 10 October 1917. At least ten more died of their wounds by the end of the month, and many will have died later from wounds sustained on Passchendaele Ridge.

Officer Casualties

As at Thiepval in 1916, the Battle of Poelcappelle removed men with key roles in the chain of command. Colonel Bousfield had a 5th Battalion pedigree going back to the Boer War, where he served under Cecil Wood and won the campaign medal with four clasps. In July 1916 he had taken on the challenging task of rebuilding and re-moulding the 1/5th Battalion following Wood's departure and the crushing events of the first days of the Battle of the Somme. Already awarded the Distinguished Service Order, he brought the battalion through the horror of the Leipzig Salient and the harsh 'failure' of 3 September 1916, to taste success for the first time in the taking of the Schwaben Redoubt later the same month. In the New Year's Honours list in 1918, he was made a commander of St Michael and St George (CMG) and the following month, awarded the *Croix de Guerre*.

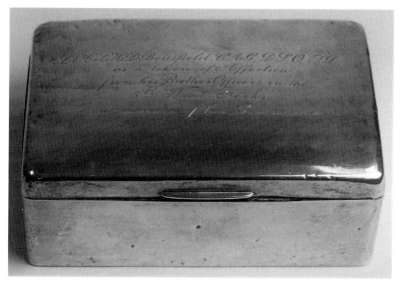

Bousfield Cigarette Case. [Bridgeman Art]
Presented by his brother officers of the 5th Battalion.

Under Bousfield's command the 1/5th had sloughed off its amateurish culture, becoming a hardened professional outfit and earning the respect of senior generals. Bousfield appears to have achieved this, in a period of huge turnover, without losing the battalion's connection with its West Riding and its Territorial heritage. He also earned and retained the personal respect of his junior officers, who presented him with a commemorative cigarette box after the war inscribed *'as a token of affection from his Brother Officers in the 5th West Yorks in memory of his command.'*

By the end of October 1917, Hugh Bousfield was recovering from his wounds at the 1st Eastern General Hospital in Cambridge. He returned to the front on 13 February 1918 with 146 Brigade, only to be taken prisoner whilst serving as a liaison officer with the French Army at the Second Battle of Kemmel on 25 April 1918. He was repatriated from Germany on 28 November 1918 and died in 1951, aged 79.

Donald Paley Mackay.
Long term Terrier and veteran of the 1st VB, killed at Bellevue Spur on 9 October 1917.

The loss of Donald Mackay was also keenly felt. Bousfield's deputy and second-in-command, he was part of the fabric of the battalion, as well as older brother to Kenneth. Mackay had been a central figure in the command structure of the battalion since the outbreak of war, and appears to have played his role as a front-line soldier too, supporting the troops at moments of great danger. Characteristically, he was killed moving forward from a reserve position to take command in the field.

Overall, the 1/5th Battalion suffered a massive casualty rate among its officers. Of the fifteen who took part in the advance on 9 October 1917, including Donald Mackay, only two walked away unscathed: Second Lieutenants John Harford and Charles Firth.

The vacuum at the top was soon filled, again by officers from what we now know as North Yorkshire. Having stepped into the breach on 9 October, Bernard Ablitt, from Pocklington, remained in temporary command of the battalion until 13 October when Major Isacke was seconded from 49th Divisional HQ to take over for a week. Ablitt relinquished the role of adjutant, too, when Freeman returned from home leave. On 17 October, Major John Foxton, also from Pocklington, returned from leave and took on the role of second-in-command, and temporary commanding officer from 21 October 1917.

A month later William Oddie, solicitor from Pateley Bridge, returned to take full command of the battalion until it returned to Yorkshire in 1919. He was gazetted lieutenant colonel in due course, which was reported to the battalion on 30 December 1917.

Of the other officers, Sidney Birbeck and Leonard Tyrell were both known to have been killed on 9 October. Birbeck had arrived on 5 January 1917. He was from Whitby and had swiftly made his mark in the patrol war. Tyrell was from Clapham in south London and arrived in November 1916. Arthur Barker was also killed.

The number of missing was a cause for concern, leading to a divisional court of enquiry looking into the matter on 20 October, chaired by Captain Ablitt. Harold Goddard and Norrie Beech were only thought to be missing at first, but later discovered to have been killed. Harold, a 23-year-old painter and decorator from Woodseats in Sheffield, had only been at the front with the 1/5th Battalion since February 1917.

Norrie Beech was the all-action hero from Harrogate. His body was found in a shell hole by a member of the 2nd Wellington New Zealand Regiment in the days following the battle, although his parents and W.H. Breare of the *Harrogate Herald* were still seeking confirmation of his fate at the end of October. Eventually, his death was reported by the *Harrogate Advertiser* on 3 November 1917, in a letter from Colonel Bousfield:

My dear Mr. and Mrs. Beech, I am sorrier than I can possibly tell you to hear that there is now no doubt that your poor boy Norman was killed on 9th October. I had hoped against hope that it would turn out that he had been taken out of the battle alive, but apparently it was not to be, and it only remains for me to tender you my heartfelt sympathy in your great sorrow. I was wounded myself early in the day on the 9th, therefore I have no first-hand information of what happened. I know, however, that I have lost one more first-rate officer. I had a very great regard for your boy, and he had made a really first-rate officer, and he had the confidence and affection of his men to a very marked degree, and that is everything.

It was a sad day for the battalion, though it is some consolation to know that the battalion did simply splendidly, and gained a very great deal of praise for the determined way in which they fought against heavy odds. That your boy played his full share I know full well. He was full of pluck and quiet courage, and we in the battalion will all feel his loss very keenly. I hope that the knowledge that his was a particularly fine career, in rising from the ranks and winning his decoration so gallantly, and that he did his duty out there more than well for so many months will prove some small consolation to you in your sorrow. Will you please accept again my most sincere sympathy for yourselves and the rest of your family, and his poor fiancée, Miss Fortune.

Believe me, yours very sincerely, H. D. Bousfield, Lieut.-Col., West Yorks.

P.S. If you would care for me to come and see you I would be very glad.

On 14 November Breare gave substantial space in the *Harrogate Herald* to correspondence concerning Norrie's death and wrote the lead himself:

I am feeling very sad, boys, just this minute, for I have but now received information that Lieutenant Norman Beech was killed on the 9th of October - that date, if you remember, when the 1/5th had such a trying time. The gloom we feel, however, is partially brightened by the intelligence and the wonderful courage of the lad and how deeply he was loved and admired by his comrades, officers and men. You will see in the *Herald* letters from his fellow-officers which you will peruse with the same glow of pride that warms us all. We are so sorry for the parents and family, but try to console ourselves with the fact that he was not the only son, for Norman Beech has a brother in the Army who is likewise an officer.

Norman Beech. [Ackrill]
An all action local hero and war worn soldier, aged only 22 when he was killed at Passchendaele.

Our lamented friend had been out three years and gone through many severe engagements. Instead of taking his leave, which was overdue, he courageously went up the line, only to meet his death. His friends were looking forward to expecting him home any day. If he had come out of that battle he would have had a long leave such as men who have been out a great time are now getting as "war-worn soldiers". It is difficult to imagine a boy of 22 being a war-worn soldier, but, alas! it is so. You who are his comrades will have pride and satisfaction in keeping his name alive. Leaving such a personality and such a record, he will never be forgotten. Lieutenant Beech was engaged to Miss Katie Fortune, second daughter of Riley Fortune. I know that your generous heartfelt sympathies will be with her as well as with the dear parents and friends.

The *Herald* then printed a series of letters from Norman's brother officers, including a vivid note from Barnet Bland, to Norman's sister on 28 October.

Dear Miss Beech,
My mother has just forwarded your letter to me in hospital, and it has left me at a loss as to what I should really say. After much deliberation, I have come to the conclusion that it would only be a kindness to you to tell you now that you must not hope to see Norman again. Your brother was in my company when we went over the top at Passchendaele on the morning of October 9th, together with another subaltern called Tyrell, who was killed at the beginning, and died in my arms. We were operating over a rather large area of ground, and soon after the start we had to spread out a good deal. I saw Norman until we were half-way up the ridge, when we came under a heavy machine-gun cross-fire. Here poor Tyrell was mortally wounded next to me, and by the time I had finished attending to him the whole show had altered. We had lost very heavily, and only a few of us reached our objective.
I never saw Norman again, and did not hear of him until the evening, when

I found one of my sergeants who had been with him, and he told me your brother had been mortally wounded during the advance. I myself was lying for two days in a shell-hole full of water before I got away with about thirty men out of the 150 I took in. The ground we were operating over was so indescribably bad that it was impossible at the time to find men who had been killed and wounded; most of us were up to our waists in mud and water, and had the greatest difficulty in even walking back after we were relieved by the New Zealanders. Our casualties were so heavy and so few of us left at the end that it is most difficult to get any accurate information as to the definite fate of individuals. I feel sure that had your brother pulled through we should have heard before now. This is the most unpleasant duty I have ever had to perform, and I do hope that you will forgive the somewhat cold-blooded way in which I have written.

Norman has been in my company for a long time, and I have always had a great admiration for his wonderful courage and cheerfulness in adverse times. He was always most popular with his men, and they would have gone anywhere with him. The last I saw of him was half-way up the Passchendaele Ridge at the head of his platoon smoking a cigarette.

I feel most deeply for you, as I know he must have been a great favourite with you all by the amount of correspondence he both received and sent. When men have lived out there for long together they cannot help getting to know a good deal about each other's home lives. I also feel most deeply for Miss Fortune, whose name became so familiar to me, and I know he was always thinking of her. Norman showed me her photo before putting it in his pocket the night before we went into action. Even now I can hardly realise that all these splendid fellows have gone and I am left. This is the second time I have come through an attack after losing both my officers. I am afraid I express myself very badly on paper, and I hope I have not unduly upset you. If it would be any comfort to you or your family I would willingly come over and see you, and tell you anything I can as soon as I get out of hospital. At present I am unable to walk, but hope to be about soon. Please convey to your family my deepest sympathies, and forgive my rather rambling letter.

Dudley Wallace was also a special character. One of a minority of officers who were not Yorkshiremen, he had only arrived at the front in August 1916. He had already demonstrated the fine leadership qualities and steely courage which marked him out from the beginning. An Essex boy from Colchester and the son of a well-to-do nurseryman and Justice of the Peace, Dudley was the eldest of four children, born on 24 April 1897.

He was educated at Colchester Royal Grammar School, then at Felsted from the age of 13, where he stayed until he received his commission. It is very likely that he served there with the junior arm of the OTC.

To quote the Felsted School obituary:

There was nothing of the soldier in Wallace in his schooldays. Big-framed, with glasses, he could last in a run, but do little in a game, and friendly rough-and-tumbles in the houseroom were the outlet of his spirits. The son of R W Wallace, who made the Prefects' border resplendent with tulips, he came in Sept 1910, and during his five years at school developed a passion for English literature and a power with his pen. A literary future was opening before him when the War, instead of Cambridge, attracted him. He received a commission in the West Yorks, went to the Front in August 1916, and was constantly in action. His MC in May showed what a capable, thorough and enterprising officer he had become. Courage and skilful leading brought back his men completely successful without a casualty. His head was in his job and he hoped to remain at it: "As you have to try all the time to get the best you can out of your men, you could not have a better job."

When leading his Company under heavy fire on Oct 9th, he fell to a sniper's bullet. "We all miss him very much, as he was always at his best in a hot corner." This is his description of 'No man's land': "It is a quiet place never trod by human foot except after the sun has gone down. At night it exercises a grim fascination; it calls one to explore its dark recesses whence, sudden as light, death may spring. Always it lures like some mocking spirit step by step, ever further into its arms. It is full of creeping; to the tired eyes of the sentries the barbed wire pickets move; they walk and stoop and slip like men. Every bush seems to creep slowly this way or that; then the star-shell flares into the sky and shows only the wires and the bushes, as they were before night fell and as they will be tomorrow again and on many other weary days."

Casualties in the Ranks

Arthur Draper, of Nydd Vale Terrace, Harrogate, had been a half back with Harrogate Wednesday Football club, and enlisted with the 5th Battalion on the outbreak of war. He went to France with the 1/5th in April 1915 and at some point trained as an artillery observer. He was killed spotting for the artillery on Passchendaele Ridge on 10 October 1917 and later mentioned in despatches for his bravery.

Pre-war Terrier, Christopher Topham had served with the 1st Volunteer Battalion since 1904, when he enlisted when a 17-year-old builder's apprentice. He received a glowing obituary in the *Harrogate Advertiser* on 27 October 1917, which printed the letter from 'his officer' to Mrs Topham:

Your son was sent to us as serjeant-major, and he pulled the company together wonderfully, and made a very fine body of men. He is a greater loss to the battalion than any other man who lost his life that day. I had the greatest personal liking for him, and know all the other officers had the same. As far as I can make out he was killed while bravely leading the company, when all its officers were knocked out. I am sure it is the kind of death he would have chosen.

The career of 32-year-old Sergeant Harry Westerman had ebbed and flowed with the fortunes of his 1/5th Battalion. A Wetherby man, he had been a labourer at the Samuel Smith brewery in Tadcaster before the war. He was also a pre-war Saturday Night Soldier, helping recruit Terriers for the 5th Battalion in Wetherby and Tadcaster. As a time expired soldier (and possibly on the National Reserve list) when war was declared, Harry enlisted back into the 5th Battalion on 18 August 1914. A month later, he was promoted to corporal, then lance sergeant immediately after the Battle of Aubers Ridge and sergeant on 2 July 1916, following the heartbreak in front of Thiepval.

Fred Jackson. [Ackrill]
Died of wounds sustained on Bellevue Spur.

On 25 August 1916, he was posted to the 33rd Infantry Base Detail at Étaples, on the coast, where he was attached to No.1 Training Camp as an instructor. In effect, this was a finishing school for new recruits and wounded men returning to the front. The camp contained the notorious 'Bull Ring' where new recruits were drilled by NCOs. Harry returned to the 1/5th Battalion at Laventie in March 1917, in time to take part in a group photo featuring Barnet Bland and John Banton [p.190].

Like so many others of the battalion, Harry Westerman was gassed at Nieuwpoort and received initial treatment at the 91st Field ambulance Station. He was bad enough to be admitted to the No.2 Canadian General Hospital, near Abbeville, on 31 July, but recovered sufficiently to return to the battalion on 28 August. He was allowed some home leave in September before returning to the front again on 5 October 1917. Four days later he led his platoon to Calgary Grange, across the Stroombeek and up the Ridge. At some point he was killed, or fatally wounded. His body was one of the few to be found and later identified. On 19 February 1918, his wife received his possessions, including a pocket book, flash lamp, razor and platoon roll book. In 1921 she claimed his medals.

Douglas Morris. [Ackrill]
Died of wounds sustained on Bellevue Spur.

Douglas Morris, who had been wounded on Thiepval Ridge, and stretcher-bearer Frederick Jackson were also killed. The notice of Fred's death, in the *Yorkshire Herald* read:

Died of wounds overseas on Oct 11th, Private Fred Jackson, West Yorks Regt.,
dearly beloved husband of Nellie Jackson, 49 Dennis Street aged 25, - RIP
  He did his bit
  From his sorrowing wife and children

Sergeant Arthur Calverley received a whole column to himself in the *Harrogate Advertiser*, including a letter from local officer, Second Lieutenant Charles Firth:

As you will, no doubt, have seen in the papers, we Yorkshire boys took a share in the recent "pushing" on the Western Front in the most trying of circumstances and conditions, and it was during that fighting that we lost Sergt. Calverley. He was acting company sergeant-major at the time, and you will probably derive a little comfort from the knowledge that he was killed almost instantaneously and suffered no pain. The whole company – even the whole battalion – deeply deplore his death, particularly we boys who come from Harrogate. He was my platoon sergeant for a time, so I can testify to his efficiency as an N.C.O. and a soldier. All the boys loved him, and I personally feel that I have not only lost my platoon sergeant, but also a friend. Allow me to assure you of our deepest sympathy, one and all of us, in the time of your bereavement. That God will comfort you and give you strength to bear up under this weight of sorrow will be the prayer of, yours in sympathy, Chas. R. Firth, 2nd Lieut. – West. Yorks., Regiment.

Shortly after the battle RSM Fred Raynor was allowed home on leave, and visited Mrs Calverley to give his condolences personally.

Signaller Frank Clarkson, from Harrogate, who had helped Claney tape out the jumping off point, was wounded in the arm during the attack, but still able to make his way down the Ridge towards the dressing station. Unfortunately, he was wounded again before making it to Calgary Grange and was not seen again. It is likely he died where he lay after this, and was found and buried by a Royal Engineers unit two months later. His mother received confirmation of her son's death and a sombre letter from a Yorkshire soldier of the Royal Engineers, in January 1918:

Signaller Frank Clarkson.

I now take the extremely sorrowful duty of writing to tell you of your poor son's burial. I could not tell you exactly when he met his death, but am sending you all the property found on his body the day we buried him. You will find enclosed his watch, also some photographs, and all the money we found on him was a threepenny bit, which you will find enclosed, Well, I am a Yorkshire lad myself, so I think it was only my duty to give him as decent a burial as we could, but I can tell you this – he died facing the enemy. All I ask is for you to send me word whether you get his property, then I shall feel that I have done my duty towards a dead comrade. I must now conclude my short letter, hoping you do not take it hard – Believe me, yours respectfully… Sapper M. Spink

On 7 November, the *Harrogate Herald* recorded the death of Private Fred Fairburn:

Private Frederick Long Fairburn (WY), one of the Beechwood Boys, who joined up in December, 1914, and went to France in April, 1915, was killed in action on October 9th. He was wounded previously in the big push on 1st July last year, and on recovering returned to France in January last. He is the brother of Mrs Wrightson, 46 Park Street, New Park, Harrogate, who has two other brothers serving with the colours, also her husband, and nephew of Mrs S Jackson, Quarry Lane, New Park, Harrogate. Private Charles Fairburn has been in the regular Army eight years, and with the Dragoon Guards in France three years. Sapper H Fairburn is in a searchlight section with the REs, and B Fairburn, another brother, has been twice rejected on account of age. Private T Wrightson joined the Army in September, 1915, and went to France with the Beechwood Boys.

The official notice was accompanied by the King and Queen's message of sympathy. A comrade sympathising with the family says: "he died a hero's death"; and another says: "I always found him cheerful and happy under the most adverse circumstances. He cheered me and other comrades up when perhaps we felt the depressing effects of the continuous hardships and dangers. I am sure I am not saying too much when I say he was like a father to me while out in France."

The writer expresses his own and his parents' sympathy with the bereaved family, and says he feels sure the officers and men of the battalion would like to join him in that expression. Deceased was employed for a number of years by the Harrogate Brickworks Company.

Clifford Gamble. [Ackrill]
Wounded on 9 October but survived.

On 22 December the *Yorkshire Herald* reported the death of Harry Lee, from Strensall. He had only been married a few months.

Two rare records of men who were wounded and survived appear in respect of Private William Hargreaves of Bilton and Corporal Clifford Gamble, Harrogate. William was wounded on 9 October by shrapnel in the arm, shoulder and back, and was evacuated to No.2 Military Hospital in Canterbury. Clifford was wounded in both legs and was evacuated to the Ontario Military Hospital in Kent.

Honours
In addition to the three Military Crosses referred to above, at least five men were awarded Military Medals for gallantry on 9–10 October 1917. They were W. Benson from Bilton near Harrogate, R. Bland from Selby, L. Lockwood from Leeds, Albert Long from Harrogate and C.H. Mitchell from Lincoln.

Tyne Cot CWGC Cemetery. [Author]

Following the meagre gains made at the Battle of Poelcappelle, mainly due to the conditions, Major General Perceval was 'de-gummed' and replaced by Major General N.J.G Cameron as officer commanding the 49th Division. Haig pressed on in spite of the weather, although there was sense in seeking to obtain mastery of the Passchendaele ridge for the winter. From the line occupied by the New Zealanders on 11 October, General Plumer's Fifth Army therefore attacked again on 12 October, and on three subsequent occasions later in the month, in worsening weather and appalling conditions, eventually seizing the village of Passchendaele on 6 November 1917. Pride, honour and a tactical advantage were apparently satisfied by this achievement, despite the failure to achieve the goals set in the summer, and Sir Douglas Haig called an end to the Third Battle of Ypres.

Chapter 11

Broodseinde and Wytschaete
(October 1917–September 1918)

"...there are not too many of the old crowd left..."

Winter 1917

Having withdrawn to Wieltje on 12 October 1917, the 1/5th Battalion moved the next day to Winnizeele, two miles north of Steenvoorde, about 10 miles behind the lines. They started training again on 15 October, once more going back to basics. The weather remained terrible and the 1/5th was shelled from time to time. Private Fred Edwards kept a diary from mid-October to December 1917 and he recorded that on a number of occasions the new German Gotha heavy bomber flew over and dropped bombs which did some damage. At the end of October the battalion had 27 officers and 663 other ranks, and over the next six months it went through the regeneration process again, increasing to 47 officers and 998 men by the end of March 1918, in time for the Second Battle of Kemmel on 25 April.

Following a month in training, on 11 November 1917 the 1/5th was inserted into the front line once more, this time in a purely defensive capacity, on the east face of Broodseinde Ridge. This ground had been seized on 4 October 1917 during the Battle of Passchendaele, and was sited roughly 3,000 yards south of Bellevue.

They were to hold a 500-yard stretch, running north to south, 200 yards east of Broodseinde village. The front line positions were 400 yards from the crest of the ridge. In front and below were China Wood and Anvil Wood, with the Heulebeek stream at the bottom of the valley. Beyond was the lower ridge crested by the Keiberg Spur, 2,000 yards distant, where the Germans were dug in. The enemy had little inclination to come down into the valley at this point in the winter.

Battalion HQ and the two supporting companies held the crest of Broodseinde Ridge and were the constant target of enemy shell fire, including mustard gas. During their occupation of this position, Major Oddie sent out frequent night patrols. Often commanded by Second Lieutenants Sayes and Roberts, these parties went forward into and around China Wood. Some patrols penetrated 900 yards along the Broodseinde to Moorslede Road, until first contact was often had with the enemy adjacent to Table Wood.

Captain Tempest reports that conditions here were as bad as they had been at Turco Farm in 1915. The two-company front line consisted of no more than twelve holes in the slushy ground, converted into rifle pits, with three forward listening post holes in

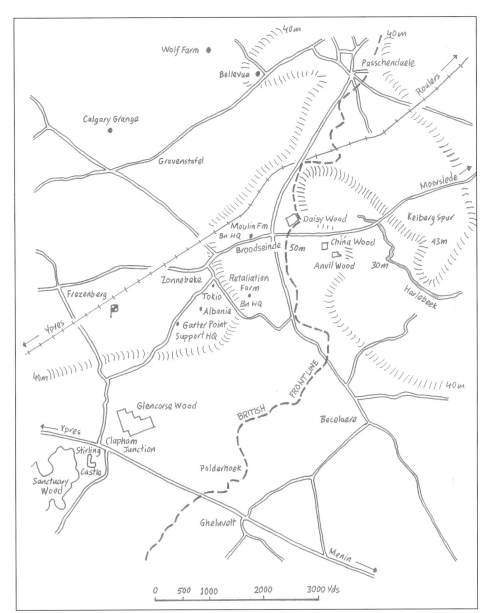

Broodseinde and the Menin Road (Winter 1917-1918). [Sketch Map 20]
Showing positions occupied by the 1/5th Battalion on Broodseinde Ridge and then astride the Menin Road during the withdrawal in April 1918.

no man's land. It was impossible to move about except at night, as the enemy had a clear view of the British positions from the Keiberg Spur. Tempest wrote that:

> *It was pointless digging the holes deeper, as they filled with water. If one tried to make them larger, they attracted the attention of the enemy. Almost every*

Shell holes at Broodseinde January 1918. Note the signs of a bunker in the course of construction. [Taylor Library]

attempt at digging resulted in the disturbance of dead bodies, in every stage of decomposition. No fires could be lit; no hot food brought up from behind; water was very scarce owing to the extraordinary difficulties of the carrying parties in such a sea of mud, and the only chance of a hot drink depended on the inhabitants of the shell hole being in possession of Tommies' cookers.

Alternating in the front line with the 1/6th Battalion, the 1/5th were put to work when in support. Shelters were built to fortify the line and large parties of officers, NCOs and men were lent to the divisional salvage officer, whose business was to reclaim, where possible, the detritus of the battlefield.

They were in brigade support from 23 December at Dragoon Camp and were given a half-day holiday on Christmas Day. A lunch of roast beef and plum pudding was enjoyed, but in light of the discipline problems suffered by the French Army after three years of war and the events of Christmas Day 1914, orders had been given by the divisional commander on 17 December to prevent fraternisation of any sort with the enemy. The effect of these commands was reinforced by a heavy enemy bombardment of the whole Passchendaele sector from 5pm. A proper Christmas dinner was only allowed five days later, once the battalion was well behind the lines at Halifax Camp, near Vlamertinghe, in Brigade Reserve.

The 1/5th returned again to the front line between Broodseinde and Passchendaele on 4 January 1918, and they were in full occupation of the rifle pits and listening posts by 7pm. D Company was on the left and B Company on the right. The listening post just in front of Daisy Wood had been placed there to prevent a surprise attack on the front line which was screened by the wood.

This post was occupied by three men and an NCO, when at 9.30pm it was 'rushed' by a German patrol of about fifteen soldiers. A struggle took place, during which one of the occupiers escaped, but the NCO and two men were taken prisoner. Lieutenant Battersby-Harford immediately took out a party of twelve men to find out what had happened but there was no sign of the German patrol or the captured men. Two further patrols were sent out in front of D Company and B Company lines, but they did not find the enemy patrol, either. The following night two patrols were pushed out into no man's land and lay down in wait, but again, there was no sign of enemy activity.

On 13 January 146 Brigade embussed for the Staple area, to rest. This meant 'recreational training' at Bavinchove, near Cassel, including three days on the rifle range at Moulle. There were brigade competitions, with the 1/5th Battalion victorious in the 'observer' and 'fighting patrol' competitions. They also won a rugby match against the 1/6th Battalion which Captain Tempest omits to mention, presumably for reasons of loyalty.

While at Cassel, the 1/5th Battalion also reaped the benefit of a reorganisation of the BEF, as infantry brigades were generally reduced from four to three battalions. One battalion in each brigade was disbanded, with the majority of its officers and men redistributed among the remaining three. In the case of 146 Brigade, the 1/8th Battalion (Leeds Rifles) was disbanded on 31 January 1918, with ninety-two of its other ranks transferred into the 1/5th Battalion. Five 1/8th Battalion officers, including Major Isacke were also transferred to the 1/5th. This followed a draft of seven new officers in early January, including Major T. Clarke, who immediately took up the role of second-in-command to Colonel Oddie.

Also returning from home leave was Lieutenant Andrew Clubb. He had received his commission on 27 September 1915, six months after his younger brother, Philip. Both had originally joined the 2/5th Battalion, where Philip stayed. Andrew was drafted to the 1/5th on the Somme in February 1916, and was wounded quite badly in the hand and shoulder on 1st July. It took him eighteen months to recuperate, before returning to action with the 1/5th on 17 January 1918.

In the early weeks of 1918, the 1/5th was brought up to establishment strength. In addition to the drafts from the defunct 1/8th Battalion, reinforcements included 117 new men on 6 January and a further 75 on 6 February.

On 11 February the 1/5th moved to Devonshire Camp, near Ouderdom, south-west of Ypres, noted by Captain Tempest to have been condemned for occupation by troops, but still in use due to the lack of alternative accommodation in the Salient. Here, officers and NCOs received lectures on carrier pigeons and large working parties were sent out to develop and reinforce the rear defences. Daily, they made their way by combination of route march and railway to the Corps Line at Anzac Ridge, two miles east of Ypres, to do four hours work, and then returned to camp for the night, exhausted.

For five weeks from 23 February, they swung between the Broodseinde Lines and Brigade Reserve at Hussar Camp, near Politje. At Broodseinde they patrolled most nights, rarely making contact with the enemy, at least until the end of March when enemy activity increased, in concert with the start of the German Spring Offensive further south.

Andrew Clubb. [Ackrill]
Wounded at Thiepval on 1 July 19
then posted back to the 1/5th
Battalion on 17 January 1918.

In support, with posts at the Garter Point, Cemetery, Moulin Farm, Retaliation Farm, Tokio and Albania, the 1/5th was shelled and gassed. In reserve at Hussar Camp they worked, digging more deep dugouts at the Corps Line, to help defend against the major attack which was expected in Flanders.

The Bigger Picture

On 21 March 1918, the German Army attacked on the Somme and at Arras, driving the British and French troops back some considerable distance, and regaining in the process ground lost in 1916. The Beechwood Boys of the 2/5th Battalion, West Yorkshire Regiment were engaged at Bucquoy, and acquitted themselves well. In fact, enemy activity increased all along the line as the 1918 campaigning season began, but the German Spring Offensive failed to score a decisive breakthrough in Picardy.

Now that the Flanders mud was starting to dry out and enemy resources were dwindling, the German High Command initiated the Battle of the Lys by launching an attack aimed at the Hazebrouck railway hub and the Channel ports. If successful, this would cut the BEF supply lines and potentially knock the British out of the war before the Americans arrived.

On 9 April 1918 four enemy divisions smashed their way through the Portuguese Corps which had taken over at Laventie from the 49th Division in July 1917. The following day, the German Fourth Army attacked in Flanders, towards Messines, aiming at Mount Kemmel and the Channel ports beyond. The 49th (West Riding)

Division was rapidly moved to the south of Ypres to help hold the line. This was the eventuality for which the reserve positions at the Corps Line had been prepared in January and February.

Unfortunately, German advances to the south now threatened the viability of the Salient, newly enlarged at the Battle of Passchendaele in 1917, and forced Sir Douglas Haig to accept that withdrawal was unavoidable. On 13 April the bridges across the Steenbeek were prepared for demolition; two days later the BEF vacated the Passchendaele Ridge and retreated towards new lines on Pilkem Ridge. Further south, a parallel tactical withdrawal was made along the Menin Road. Between 15 April and 25 April 1918 the Salient was reduced to its 1915 proportions.

On 17 April the German Army attacked again, with designs on Mount Kemmel. The Allies successfully resisted in the First Battle of Kemmel, but on 25 April, three French divisions were overpowered by seven German divisions, and the enemy seized the 200m high hill, which dominated the surrounding ground for miles around. The 1/5th Battalion was to be caught up in this battle, known as the Second Battle of Kemmel, at Wytschaete.

1/5th on the Menin Road

Having been virtually undetectable during January and February, in March 1918 enemy infantry started to assert itself again in the broad band of no man's land around Broodseinde. They reoccupied abandoned pillboxes to rake the British lines with machine-gun bullets while the German artillery battered the British front lines. On the night of 17 March, Colonel Oddie sent out a fighting patrol of three officers and sixty other ranks to look for the enemy but no contact was made. The following night, on the brigadier's orders, Major Clark sent three platoons into no man's land with the objective of identifying the enemy unit, but the patrol was instantly scattered by an inferno of high explosive and mustard gas, causing twenty-one casualties.

On 27 March the 1/5th Battalion was temporarily attached to 148 Brigade and moved four kilometres south, to the line in front of Glencorse Wood. Here, they were to guard the northern side of the Menin Road and were much closer to the heavy fighting of the Battle of the Lys. They stayed until 15 April, when General Plumer started to reduce the size of the Salient, according to Haig's plan.

During these days the battalion held the front line at Polderhoek with a single company; the other three were on a line between Glencorse Wood and the Menin Road at Clapham Junction. In the prelude to the first battle of Kemmel Ridge, there was a marked increase in enemy machine-gun and artillery activity, with gas shells mixed in. On the night of 6 April, Intelligence Officer, Second Lieutenant Percy Cheesman, Second Lieutenant James Wilde from Oldham and two other ranks left the line to reconnoitre a ruined pillbox. When only 40 yards short of the concrete emplacement, a machine gun opened up and fired ten rounds at them. The patrol returned unscathed.

Over the next four nights there was regular hostile contact in no man's land and on two occasions enemy raiding parties were driven off by rifle fire. Things quietened down slightly after that, until 15 April when the order was received for the 1/5th Battalion to move to Ouderdom, as part of Haig's strategic withdrawal from the Salient. Perhaps it was a strange honour, though, for B and C companies under Major Foxton, to act as rearguard for the retreat along the Menin Road. They were to hold the line astride the road between Glencorse Wood and Stirling Castle for three days until 18 April. Foxton's orders, from the brigadier, were: *'It must be clearly understood that there is no question of the Corps Line troops withdrawing from that line.'*

They must stand, fight, and if necessary, die to hold it. According to the *Illustrated History:*

> *They remained in Corps Line Posts, seven in number, and during the morning of 16th dummy carrying parties were marched about the trenches to show that the front line was still held. At 3.30pm the enemy approached along the whole Brigade area and Lewis Gun, machine gun and rifle fire was opened at once on the Germans, who suffered heavy casualties. The night of 16th – 17th was quiet. On the 17th, the posts north of Menin road were heavily trench mortared and those south of the road were shelled with 'whizz bangs,' but again the advancing enemy lost heavily. Similar actions took place on the 18th and on the night of the 18th-19th the 1/5th battalion was relieved.*

John Foxton and his two companies rejoined the battalion at Ouderdom. Hearts must have been heavy, as Captain Tempest regarded the partial withdrawal from the Salient as being *'almost an act of treachery towards comrades who had given their lives in capturing it in October and November 1917.'*

Within a week they would find themselves directly in the line of German advance at the Second Battle of Kemmel.

Casualties

In the relatively quiet period between 12 October 1917 and 18 April 1918, when the 1/5th Battalion arrived at Wytschaete, forty-six men lost their lives. The balance of the battalion was clearly shifting as only eight were from its original heartland around Harrogate and York. In total, thirty-six were from the north of England, including twenty-eight from Yorkshire. The other ten were from further afield, including Alexander Smith, who enlisted in Argyll, and Lionel McGuckin from South London. Two men, Lescombe Harrison and George Higgins, had been born abroad, in South Africa and Belgium respectively.

Two of the York-based soldiers were pre-war Terriers, whose service records partially survive.

Lance Corporal James R. Harrison was killed on Broodseinde Ridge, probably by a shell, on 17 November 1917. He was originally from Fulford and was an errand boy in 1911. By 1913 he was a 'chocolate hand', most likely at Terry's, and on 23 January, aged 17, he enlisted in the 5th Battalion, A Company, for a four-year term, having been examined by Surgeon Major Stoddart and attested before Captain Sydney Wilkinson.

In August of that year he was present at the annual camp at Aberystwyth. Then, on 14 September 1914, he volunteered for Imperial Service.

Early on, James had something of a minor disciplinary record, mainly concerning elicit activity during route marches. On 28 August 1914 in York he was caught smoking a cigarette 'on the march' by Captain Percy Williamson, and was 'Confined to Barracks' (C.B.) for three days. Shortly after the Battle of Aubers Ridge, Donald Mackay inflicted a punishment of two days C.B. for elicit consumption of emergency rations and on 6 July 1915 James received the same punishment from Sergeant Calder for drinking from his water bottle on the march.

James appears to have redeemed himself over the following year or so and in April 1916 was attached to 146 Brigade HQ. He was promoted lance corporal on 28 July 1916, and on Christmas Eve he was awarded 'Efficiency Pay Class II'. He came to the attention of the medical authorities only twice, for scabies on Christmas Day 1916 and a foot-related ailment in June 1917. He was granted ten days home leave on 7 October which saved him from the Battle of Poelcapelle, but was killed one month after his return to the front.

Private Philip Bean was a chocolate coverer by trade. He had enlisted for a term of four years with the 5th Battalion in December 1909, aged 17, and was discharged in 1913. He re-enlisted on 28 August 1914 and embarked with the 1/5th in April 1915. He was 'lightly gassed' at Turco Farm and again at Thiepval on the first day of the Battle of the Somme. Treated at Le Havre, he returned to the 1/5th via Étaples. Philip was killed on 14 April 1918, probably on patrol in no man's land with Robert Frankland from Tadcaster, John Gratton from Sheffield, and Arthur Regan from Leeds. Their officer was 20-year-old Second Lieutenant William B. Row from Newcastle, who was also killed.

One of the other fatalities is particularly worthy of mention as it was apparently accidental. Private John W. Mallorie was born in Starbeck, near Harrogate, and lived in Spofforth. By trade he was an upholsterer. He was killed on 4 December 1917 when a rifle was discharged near his bed as he slept.

Kemmel Ridge

At the First Battle of Kemmel, on 17–19 April 1918, the German Army had severely dented the southern end of the Ypres Salient. They had evicted the BEF from Wytschaete and left it clinging to the northern edge of the ridge, 300 yards outside the town. Behind the new British front line, to the north-west across the 2,000 yards of the Wytschaetebeek Valley was the Vierstraat Ridge, the last major natural obstacle guarding the plains leading to the Channel ports.

Two miles to the west lay Mount Kemmel, now home to the 49th Division's trench mortars. Six hundred feet high, it dominated the ground to the south of Ypres and was clearly visible from the Wytschaetebeek Valley. Mount Kemmel was a major prize for the Germans and was now protected to the south by a shield of three French divisions.

Field Marshal Haig knew that a German attack on Mount Kemmel would necessarily include on its right flank an advance from Wytschaete, across the

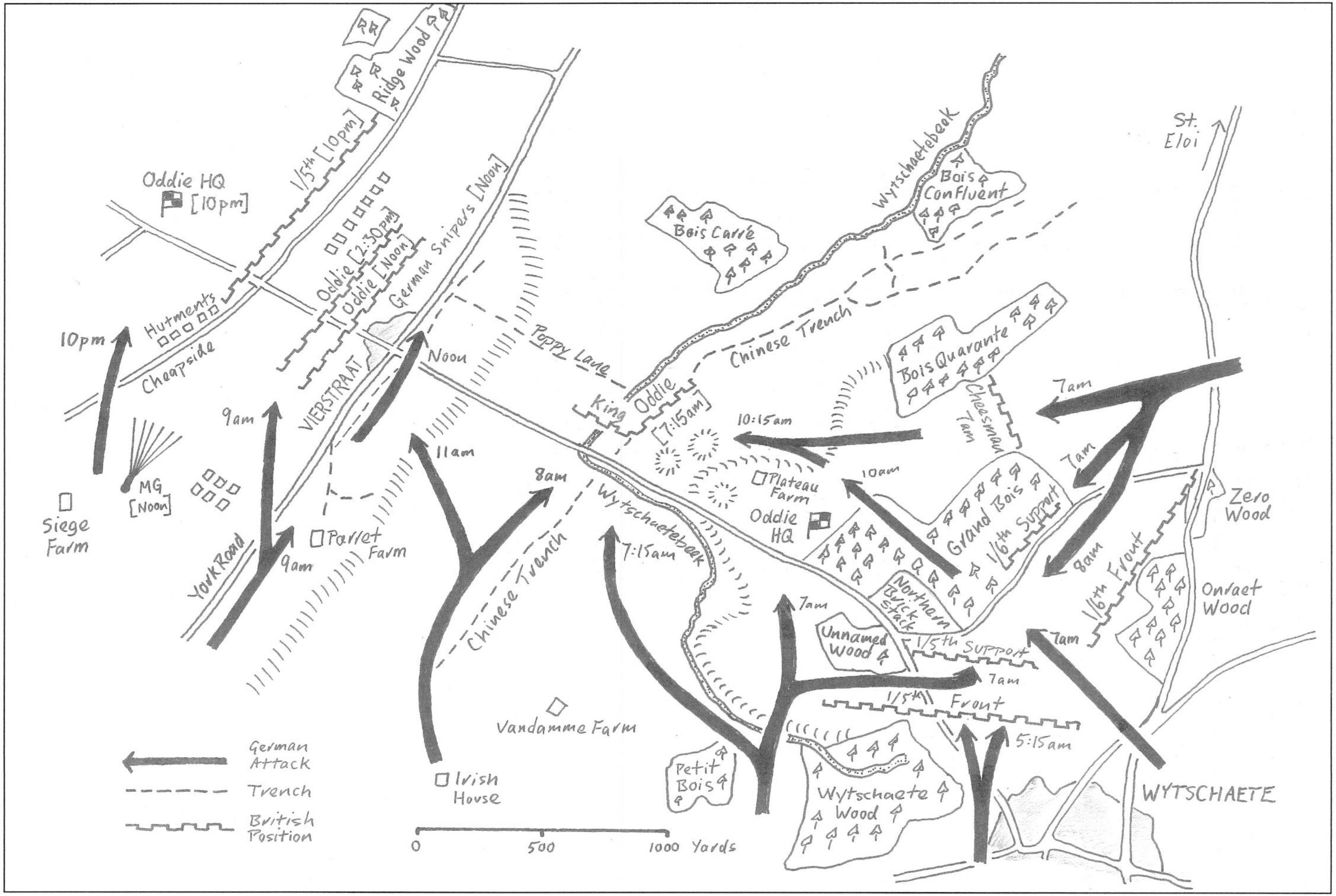

WYTSCHAETE

St. Eloi

Zero Wood

Onraet Wood

1/6th Front

7am

7am

8am

Cheesman Farm

Bois Quavante

Bois Confluent

Wytschaetebeek

10am

Fields

1/6th Supp's

Grand Bois

Northern Brick Stack

1/5th Support

1/5th Front

5:15am

7am

7am

5:15am

Chinese Trench

10:15am

Plateau Farm

Oddie HQ

Unnamed Wood

Wytschaete Wood

Bois Carré

7:15am

Oddie

King

Wytschaetebeek

7:15am

Petit Bois

1000 Yards

Poppy Lane

Noon

8am

Chinese Trench

11am

500

Vandamme Farm

Irish House

VIERSTRAAT

German Snipers [Noon]

Oddie [2:30pm]

Oddie [Noon]

Parret Farm

9am

0

Ridge Wood

York Road

9am

9am

1/5th [10pm]

Huttenberst

Cheapside

MG [Noon]

Oddie HQ [10pm]

10pm

Siege Farm

German Attack

Trench

British Position

Dug-out (Exterior) in Unnamed Wood. [Chris Noble]
This concrete dug-out could well have been A Company HQ.

Dug-out (Interior) in Unnamed Wood. [Chris Noble]

Wytschaetebeek valley to seize the Vierstraat Ridge, which was an objective in its own right. He therefore knew the positions of the BEF, on the north-western outskirts of Wytschaete, to be critical in checking the German plan to advance through Flanders to the Channel, and that an attack was inevitable and imminent. On 11 April, he issued his famous 'backs to the wall' message to the troops:

> *There is no other course open to us but to fight it out. Every position must be held to the last man: there must be no retirement. With our backs to the wall and believing in the justice of our cause each one of us must fight on to the end. The safety of our homes and the Freedom of mankind alike depend upon the conduct of each one of us at this critical moment.'*

The Tactical Position

The German attacks in early 1918 had ended the stalemate of trench warfare and now required every brigade in the BEF to engage in actively defending the line, rather than

Unnamed Wood today. [Chris Noble]

simply occupying trenches. Following the losses at Passchendaele and the necessary reorganisation of the infantry, the brigades were less formidable than they had been, varying considerably in strength and experience. Adaptability and fortitude was the key.

At this point 146 Brigade was down to about two thirds strength and battalions were getting used to lending platoons and companies to each other. For example, in early April the 1/6th Battalion borrowed one platoon from the 1/5th, under Second Lieutenant Rowley. Major Foxton's force of B and C companies had been hived off to fight on the Menin Road as a detached force in its own right, before re-joining the 1/5th. The same need for flexibility now saw the 49th Division divided up, with the 1/5th and 1/6th Battalions temporarily attached to 64 Brigade (9th Infantry Division) and 146 Brigade was left with only the battered and denuded 1/7th Battalion which had fought with distinction at the First Battle of Kemmel on 17 April 1918.

Into the Line
On 19 April 1918 the 1/5th Battalion marched from Scottish Camp at Ouderdom

Labels in image: Grand Bois, Unnamed Wood, Wytschaete Wood, Oddie HQ, Plateau Farm, Wytschaetebeek, Chinese Trench

The Wytchaetebeek Valley. [Author]
Taken from Vierstraat at the junction of Wytschaete Road and York Road,

towards the front line at Wytschaete. They spent the nights of 19 and 20 April at Siege Farm 1,500 yards south-west of Vierstraat, in Divisional Reserve. Before dawn on 21 April they headed north-east into the Brigade Reserve line north of Vierstraat and that evening they moved south-east to join the Grand Bois garrison, occupying a 1,000-yard stretch of the front line opposite Wytschaete. This was not an organised trench but a series of ditches, shell holes, dug-outs and ruined trenches extending between Black Cot on the right and North House on the left, bisected by the Wytschaete to Vierstraat road.

On the (lower) right flank, which ran down to the Wytschaetebeek, A Company of the 1/5th had the stumps of Wytschaete Wood in front and Unnamed Wood behind. In the centre and on the exposed (higher) left flank, D, B, and C companies were on the outskirts of the town, with the ground falling away behind to Grand Bois and Onraet Wood. The front line was held by ten platoons in total and Colonel Oddie put four platoons in close support. Company headquarters were sited in disused cellars, gun-pits and pill boxes.

On the left of the 1/5th Battalion were the 1st East Yorkshires and the 15th Durham Light Infantry (DLI), who were guarding the south-eastern outskirts of Grand Bois, in line extending 1,000 yards to Onraet Wood and Zero Wood. The DLI would be relieved by the 1/6th West Yorkshires around midnight on 24/25 April, amid a gas bombardment, putting the two West Yorkshire battalions side by side just in time for the German attack.

The 1/5th Battalion HQ was in a concrete dug-out on the plateau, on the north-western edge of Grand Bois, 100 yards north of the Wytschaete to Vierstraat road.

Colonel Oddie kept two platoons from D Company close at hand in Reserve, 600 yards behind the battalion right flank at Black Cot. The Battalion HQs of the 1/6th West Yorkshires and the 1st East Yorkshires were adjacent, in order to aid communication and a co-ordinated defence.

Thus, there was little by way of a defensive line between the 1/5th Battalion front line and the Vierstraat Ridge, should the Battalion's Reserve be deployed. The Wytschaetebeek was insignificant as an obstacle, according to Captain Tempest, 1,500 yards behind (and parallel to) the front line. One hundred yards in front of the Wytschaetebeek was the only trench line fit for defensive duty in the sector, named Chinese Trench after the indented men of the Chinese Labour Corps who had recently dug it. From 24 April it was garrisoned by two platoons of the 1/6th Battalion.

Further back, the Vierstraat Ridge was held by the remnants of the exhausted 1/7th Battalion, numbering about 200 men, with the 9th KOYLI behind them. If the enemy could break through the arrowhead of the 1/5th and 1/6th lines in front of Grande Bois, there would be very little to stop them sweeping across the Wytschaetebeek Valley, up onto the Vierstraat Ridge, and beyond towards Mount Scherpenberg.

George Baxter. [Ackrill]
From Denmark Street Harroga
George was killed in action on
April 1918 at Wytschaete

The Battle Begins

Immediately on arrival at Wytschaete, 1/5th Battalion casualties started to mount at a rate unknown since Passchendaele. The troops were harassed by artillery and trench mortars intended to soften up the British for the attack, with four other ranks wounded on 19 April. The next day, Second Lieutenant F.G. Baker and a further four other ranks were killed, with Lieutenant Benjamin Cussons and twenty-three other ranks wounded by artillery fire. On 23 April four other ranks were killed and seventeen wounded. Then, on 24 April, the eve of the battle, Second Lieutenant J. Hudson and a further three other ranks were wounded.

Following increased noise levels from German lines, indicating intensive preparations, at 2.45am on 25 April, the enemy artillery opened out along the front line and support positions in front of Kemmel and Wytschaete, firing huge amounts of high explosive mixed with phosgene and smoke. Despite the bright moonlight, visibility was soon reduced to nil at the front line and in the Wytschaetebeek Valley. All three Yorkshire battalions weathered this initial bombardment well, under minimal cover, the forward troops of the 1/5th notifying Colonel Oddie at 4.50am that the gas was clearing and they were able to remove their gas masks.

However, ten minutes later a second, terrific bombardment started, lighting up the sky and setting the local farms ablaze. Machine guns clattered too, intent on preventing any movement or reorganisation in the British front line or behind and of cutting communications. In this last objective the bombardment was very effective, as the officers commanding the 1/6th West Yorkshires and the 1st East Yorkshires, Colonel Wistance and Major Cole, lost contact entirely with their front line troops on the other side of Grand Bois.

Colonel Oddie also lost telephone contact with his forward companies, although Signals Officer Second Lieutenant Byron King, managed to set up a communications relay to keep messages coming through, for a period. Twice he ran through heavy artillery fire, between the relay post and Oddie's HQ, to pass messages back personally.

The precise timing and sequence of events in the front line is very hard to determine but it is clear that the enemy infantry appeared out of the thick smoke and fog to launch a full frontal attack on the 1/5th line between 5am and 6am. At 5.15am, we know that one of the front line companies sent up an S.O.S. flare.

The German attackers brought up small field guns to fire directly into the defenders' lines and at least one enemy aircraft flew low, up and down the line strafing the occupants of the trenches and shell holes. The men remained steady and acquitted themselves well, repulsing the assault with machine-gun and rifle fire. At 7am Byron King got messages to Colonel Oddie from B and C companies, saying that the enemy had been beaten off.

Casualties in the front line appear to have been relatively few at this point, but these messages were probably an hour out of date and they masked the grim reality that the enemy had succeeded in piercing both flanks of the battalion front. By the time Colonel Oddie received the messages, which were the last from the front line, he could see German parties at the northern brickstacks, which was directly behind the 1/5th support line. This could only mean that the battalion right flank had been turned and that the enemy was in behind A and D companies. It was now impossible for Byron King to keep communication going and he gave this up, and spent the rest of the day at Battalion HQ, making himself very useful.

It is likely that all four companies were encircled by this point in the battle and were fighting desperately to escape: this was certainly Oddie's conclusion. He thought they must have fought to the finish, although it is more likely they fought until their ammunition ran out later in the day. Practically all were casualties, with about one third killed and the others taken prisoner, many of whom were wounded.

After the war reports came in from repatriated prisoners of war that elements of the British had fought the enemy attackers until 1pm on the south-eastern face of Grand Bois and there is some evidence that pockets of resistance remained until 7pm. From the sparse lists available, it is clear that all fourteen platoons of the 1/5th Battalion fought hard, as fatalities were spread evenly between them. Each of the four companies had about thirty men taken prisoner.

Sadly, this is the extent of our knowledge of events in the front line. The main story which survives is that of Colonel Oddie's HQ detachment.

A Fighting Withdrawal

By 7.15am on the right, the enemy was sighted marching in close order from the south west, approaching the Wytschaete to Vierstraat road, adjacent to Battalion HQ. The Germans had come from the valley between Petit Bois and Wytschaete Wood and were following the route of the Wytschaetebeek towards the lower ground north-west of Plateau Farm. This was particularly alarming as it put the three Battalion HQs (on the south-western slope of Grand Bois) at risk of being cut off in the rear.

Colonel Oddie was ill-equipped to defend his position, as twenty minutes earlier he had sent his two reserve platoons forward in support of C Company of the 1/6th Battalion, which was reported to have been fighting a rearguard action at Zero Wood; the enemy was pushing them back towards the gap between Grand Bois and Bois Quarante and ultimately threatening Plateau Farm from the north-east. Responding to a direct appeal from Colonel Wistance, Oddie ordered his Intelligence Officer, Second Lieutenant Percy Cheesman, to lead his reserve into the gap and to plug it.

Having lost contact with his forward companies, and now without his reserve, Colonel Oddie consulted further with Colonel Wistance and Major Cole. The three commanders appear to have settled on a plan to prevent encirclement and form a defensive line. Oddie's part was to evacuate his HQ dug-out on the edge of Grand Bois and withdraw 750 yards over open ground to Chinese Trench, just in front of the Wytschaetebeek. This would prevent immediate encirclement and allow his HQ staff to engage the German troops now filtering down the Wytschaetebeek valley.

On arrival at Chinese Trench, about 7.15am, Oddie sent his adjutant, Captain Freeman back to Vierstraat to make contact with 64 Brigade HQ, as all communications to the rear had now been cut. Freeman achieved this, resisting a series of flank attacks on the way.

Colonel Oddie put the newly unemployed Byron King in command of the 100 men of the 1/6th Reserve waiting in Chinese Trench. He wanted them to form a defensive flank on the right, stretching 300 yards north-west from Chinese Trench, parallel to the Wytschaete to Vierstraat road and straddling the Wytschaetebeek. By creating this 'arrow head', pointing south, Oddie's dual intention appears to have been to prevent the German parties getting behind his HQ and the Vierstraat Ridge, and to cover the HQ of the 1/6th and 1st East Yorkshire Battalion HQs, which had now moved back to the shell craters below the plateau.

Protected from the rear by Colonel Oddie's action, and shielded on the left by Cheesman's Force, Colonel Wistance and Major Cole took their HQs forward again to the rise in Grand Bois, to form a defensive line 100 yards east of their original positions. Here they stayed for about an hour, sniping enemy infantry through Grand Bois and, as they appeared in ever greater force from the sunken road on the right, from the direction of the northern brickstacks. Colonel Wistance therefore sent a runner back to Chinese Trench asking Colonel Oddie for support on his right. Dutifully, Oddie ordered a sergeant forward with a small party, who encountered a second, wounded runner coming from Grand Bois at about 9.50am. The runner carried news that the 1/6th HQ had already withdrawn. In fact, Wistance, his RSM and other members of his HQ detachment had been killed in a brave last stand, overwhelmed by German attackers flooding through Grand Bois and from the south.

Oddie knew that withdrawal was now inevitable, given that enemy machine guns had been established around Plateau Farm for at least an hour. Grand Bois appeared to be lost and it was certain that the greater part of all three battalions had been put out of action.

Twenty minutes later, the remnants of the HQ detachments of the 1/6th Battalion and the 1st East Yorkshires arrived back at Chinese Trench, with the enemy hot on their heels, having broken through Cheesman's Force and the now undefended north-western edge of Grand Bois. German machine guns were now advanced in the craters beneath the plateau, only 300 yards in front of Chinese Trench.

Two miles away the German Army had driven through the French defences in front of Kemmel and taken the hill about 9am. They were now beginning to appear in force around Irish House and Vandamme Farm, heading for Vierstraat and threatening to turn Oddie's right flank. Their machine guns raked the valley between Grand Bois and Vierstraat from the south-west and the area around Vandamme Farm. About 10.15am Oddie decided to carry out a fighting withdrawal to Vierstraat. Around the same time Lieutenant Cheesman arrived back at Chinese Trench, wounded, with the remains of his force which had fought hard to slow down the enemy advance from the direction of Zero Wood.

At this point, the weak forces at Colonel Oddie's immediate disposal included his Battalion HQ detachment, together with the 1/6th reserve and the remnants of Cheesman's Force which had made it back to Chinese Trench. Once it was clear that HQ detachments of the 1/6th and East Yorkshires had escaped or could not be saved, Oddie led his party back along Poppy Lane to the Vierstraat Line, arriving just before noon. Thankfully, Vierstraat was still in British hands, although German snipers had already infiltrated as far as the ruined buildings on the north-eastern edge of the village and stronger enemy forces were approaching from the direction of Kemmel, to the south-west.

The Defence of Vierstraat

Vierstraat was not going to be easy to defend. New trench lines had been dug in front of the village and a switch trench had been prepared 500 yards to the south as a defensive precaution. However, there were clumps of hutments and hedges on the edge of the village which gave the attackers cover when close in. As Captain Tempest points out, it seems that only the stiff defence of Grand Bois early in the day had drawn the sting out of the German advance and prevented the enemy sweeping over these meagre defences on 25 April.

On arrival at the Vierstaat line in front of York Road, Colonel Oddie came across a small party of the 1/7th Battalion to supplement his force. He started to prepare a defensive line 200 yards behind (and parallel to) York Road, but this was never established, as the enemy soon appeared to the south of the village, threatening Oddie's right flank, which was in the air. Captain Tempest later explained that the position at Cheapside was 'very tense' at this point as the enemy was able to enfilade the Ridge with machine-gun fire from the south-west.

Therefore Oddie instructed Byron King to set up a defensive flank facing south-west towards the enemy, running along Vierstraat as far as its junction with Cheapside. This allowed King to join hands with a small detachment of the 12th Scottish Rifles on his right (western) flank, and Oddie set up an outpost line 100 yards behind King, should the enemy break through. They held these positions for about four hours under shelling and continuous machine-gun fire. They knew the Germans were close at hand, but had no real idea when and where the main attack would happen.

About 5pm, 146 Brigade's Intelligence Officer, Lieutenant Tempest, appeared. He arranged for a detachment of the King's Royal Rifles Corps (KRRC) to come forward and support Oddie in the positions he had resolved to hold until more information was forthcoming. Then, about half an hour later, the enemy attacked, but Oddie and his twenty or so men (including a few KRRCs) held them up until relief arrived shortly after 10pm. In doing so, he bought sufficient time for the completion of a second line of defence 1,000 yards behind and parallel to Cheapside, which extended from Vierstraat Road as far as Ridge Wood to the north. When Oddie was later relieved in the front line by a Canadian battalion, he withdrew his HQ to a mined dug-out behind the new second line, accompanied by Captain Freeman, Captain King and twenty-one other ranks.

In front, the second line was now occupied by sixty or so men, including one officer and about twenty men from each of the 1/5th, 1/6th and 1/7th battalions. Between 9.30pm and 10pm the Germans swept up the Vierstraat Ridge from the south-west and they appear to have outflanked and broken through the Canadians who had relieved Oddie in the front line and contact was lost. The enemy also pierced the second line in places, cutting off the 1/5th contingent under Captain Ablitt, which held the left flank at Ridge Wood.

As night fell it was very unclear where the front line lay, although Captain Tempest suggests it was about 300 yards south and west of the Cheapside junction, which means that the German attack halted before completely smashing the British second line. It was so dark that a rations party sent up to Oddie's HQ went straight past it and almost blundered into the enemy.

That night it was decided to withdraw the remains of the 1/5th, 1/6th and 1/7th West Yorkshires to Ouderdom, and messengers were sent out to find them, as they were scattered all over the battlefield between Vierstraat and Voormezeele. In dribs and drabs they pulled out and headed north-west to rejoin 146 Brigade. At some point on 26 April, Colonel Oddie and the remnants of his battalion joined them.

Relief
On arrival at Ouderdom the Second Echelon was waiting. Bernard Ablitt also arrived the next day with his party. The total remaining strength of the 1/5th Battalion appears

to have been twelve officers and seventy-eight men at this point; less than 10 per cent of its wartime establishment.

The three battalions of 146 Brigade were now reunited, but had been reduced to about 600 men in total. To convert these remnants into a useful fighting force, at a time when further enemy advances were feared, the second echelons of the 1/5th, 1/6th and 1/7th battalions each provided one company for a composite battalion. This '146th Battalion' was commanded by Major R. Clough and remained at Ouderdom when the exhausted veterans of the fighting at Kemmel marched off to camp at Hoograf. William Oddie took nine officers and sixty-six men to Hoograf, leaving three officers and twelve other ranks with Major Clough.

The Composite Battalion remained in reserve to 147 Brigade during the enemy attack on Scherpenberg Ridge on 29 April, but the French line held and the 146th Battalion was not called into action. It moved back to Vierstraat on 2 May and was then disbanded three days later, with the companies returned to their parent battalions.

Field Marshal Haig showed his appreciation of the gallantry exhibited by the 49th (West Riding) Division, and on 30 April, Major General Cameron (now commanding the division) addressed the 1/5th Battalion:

> We shall shortly, we hope be filling up with new men. Let every old hand put his shoulder to the wheel in the task of instilling into our new blood the spirit of courage, determination and efficiency which has carried you through your recent trial so successfully.

On 2 May he wrote to the brigade commanders, saying that the 1/5th and 1/6th battalions had:

> added great lustre to the record earned by your brigade and the 49th: West Riding Division in the recent fighting. It is a wonderful achievement that these two Battalions stood their ground on the WYTSCHAETE RIDGE on 25th April without a single unwounded man coming back. My great hope now is that you will find that you have sufficient old hands remaining to carry on the great spirit which has animated the 146th Brigade and infuse it into the new drafts which I hope to see joining you soon, in order that the name of the 146th Brigade shall live forever. Please let your Battalions know that I feel deeply proud of them.

Honours

Colonel Oddie was awarded a Bar to his DSO for his fighting withdrawal on 25 April 1918. Walter Freeman, Maurice Wilson, Byron King and Robert Wycherley were awarded the Military Cross for their gallantry. Bernard Ablitt was awarded a Bar to his MC. Captain Wycherley showed 'great pluck and initiative', according to his citation, rallying men who had been driven out of forward posts. Second Lieutenant Maurice Wilson, from Bradford, who had arrived with the battalion after

Passchendaele, held: *'a post in advance of the line under very heavy shell and machine-gun fire on both flanks after the machine guns covering his flanks had been withdrawn. It was largely owing to his pluck and determination in holding this post that the enemy attack was held up.'*

Thirteen Military Medals and one Bar were awarded on 13 September 1918, of which all but two were for bravery at Wytschaete. All the recipients were Yorkshiremen, with three from Harrogate: Thomas Kitson, Albert Long (Bar) and Norman Rogers. Joseph Blanchard was from York, Arthur Ingleby from Ripon, and Rowland Light from Pateley Bridge.

Rowland Light. [Ackrill]
Awarded the Military Meda
gallantry at Wytschaete on
April 1918.

Dead, Wounded and Missing

The 1/5th Battalion was virtually wiped out on 25 April 1918: 131 officers and men were killed on the day, and by the end of July a further 45 men (out of the 83 thought by Oddie to have been wounded) had died, making a total of 176 dead. It appears now that more than 122 men were taken prisoner (they are listed in Appendix 5), which means that the total actual casualties for the day were at least 336 and probably more than 400, as the numbers of prisoners and wounded cannot be precisely calculated.

The manner and circumstances of most casualties are shrouded in mystery, as very few soldiers from the front line returned until after the war, and were usually disinclined to recount their experiences. We do know, however, that as at 1 October 1918, 197 soldiers of the 1/5th Battalion were still regarded as missing, four months after the battle. Their families retained hope that they had been taken prisoner of war, but 89 were eventually confirmed as killed. In the meantime, there was the agony of uncertainty as to the whereabouts of sons, brothers, friends and comrades. William Wilkinson, from Denmark Street, Harrogate, was reported missing after the battle. His wife, Annie, and their three children were officially notified in June

William Wilkinson. [Chris Noble]
Reported Missing, 25 April 19

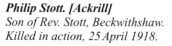

Philip Stott. [Ackrill]
Son of Rev. Stott, Beckwithshaw.
Killed in action, 25 April 1918.

1919, fourteen months later, that he was presumed to have been killed on 25 April 1918.

The few remaining officers and NCOS had their work cut out in writing to the families of the missing. The Reverend H.R. Stott received a letter from William Oddie:

I am exceedingly sorry to have to inform you that your son, Lt. P. H. Stott, has had to be reported as missing. The Battalion was involved in a great struggle on the 25th April, and put up a magnificent fight. Your son was with his company on the front line, but as not a man reported to the battalion after the fight, I have no information to work upon, and can only hope that he is wounded and in the hands of the Germans. Your son had not been very long with us, but quite long enough to appreciate his value: he was a most reliable officer, and his loss is a serious matter to the battalion. Sympathising with you in the terrible uncertainty about his fate, and hoping you may have good news, of him before long...

Unfortunately, Philip Stott had been killed. He was from the village of Beckwithshaw, just outside Harrogate. The vicar's son, he was educated at St Bee's school in Cumberland, where he was head boy, and Merton College Cambridge. He was commissioned in February 1917 and went to the front with the 4th Battalion the following month. He transferred to the 1/5th after Passchendaele.

The other officers killed were 32-year-old Captain Frederick Phillips from Pateley Bridge, who joined the 1/5th in November 1916; Lieutenant Reginald Walker from York who had arrived at the front with Claude Bulmer on 1 August 1915; Captain Charles Blackburn from Harrogate; Second Lieutenant Cyril Kiddle on temporary attachment from the 4th Battalion and Captain Morris Clough, who was probably on temporary attachment from the 18th Battalion, Bradford Pals.

While the numbers of pre-war Terriers and men recruited by the Harrogate Defence League had reduced substantially over the previous year or so, William Wilkinson was not the only one to be killed defending the line at Wytschaete. George Herd, from Otley Road, was with D Company, and probably died fighting with Percy Cheesman in the rearguard action between Grand Bois and Bois Quarante.

Fred Barton and Jesse Adkin had been 'Saturday Night Soldiers' in Wetherby, and both fell on 25 April 1918. Fred was a gardener when he attested before Captain Cross in April 1913, aged 17, in time for the Aberystwyth annual camp. Fred became a specialist bomber. He was shot in the shoulder at Thiepval on 1 or 2 July 1916, and was repatriated on the 3rd. Arriving back at the front in January 1917 he survived Passchendaele and was granted a week's home leave on Christmas Day, returning to the 1/5th on 8 January 1918. Fred was killed with B Company on 25th April 1918.

Jesse Adkin from Wetherby was a plumber by trade. He enlisted in May 1913, aged 17, his front line service only interrupted by a dose of impetigo in March 1916, and then by a bayonet wound to his hand suffered at the Battle of Poelcapelle, which put him in hospital for nine weeks.

Stanley Young, from Harrogate, also fell on 25 April. Unfortunately the initial telegram to his parents went to the wrong address. Richard Wegg of C Company, who was one of the Harrogate Wesleyans, was also missing, although his death was confirmed later.

The most resounding loss for the battalion was that of Regimental Sergeant Major Fred Raynor. He was wounded in the face, although reports differ on the gravity of the injury. Fred died of his wounds at hospital in Sidcup, Kent on 1 May 1918. Sergeant William Salisbury (who survived the war) wrote to Mrs Raynor on 16 April:

Stanley Young. [Ackrill]
Killed in action 25 April 191

I feel we have lost a very dear friend, whose place will not be easily filled by anyone else. He was held in the highest esteem by all ranks, because he had all the characteristics of a true Britisher. He was unfailingly devoted to duty, whilst his genial and kindly nature endeared him to all those who came under his authority .... In the action during which he was wounded he set an example to his men which maintained the highest traditions. Please accept this message of sincere sympathy from one who voices the sentiments of every man in the Battalion.

Colonel Oddie added his own condolences:

I saw him and had a word with him on his way back from the aid post, and having heard that he had got to England. I thought the worst was over, particularly as the doctor did not consider the wounds as very dangerous.

We have lost a regimental sergeant-major second to none: your husband did a lot towards making the battalion what it is, and he was always so enthusiastic in anything connected with the 1-5th.

There are not many of the old crowd left, but all of them – officers and men – join me in sympathising with your loss.

Fred Raynor's gravestone. [Author]
Grove Road Cemetery, Harrogate.

244

Military Funeral At Harrogate. [Ackrill]
Fred Raynor was buried with full military honours on 4 May 1918.

Fred's body was brought to Harrogate for a funeral with full military honours on Saturday, 4 May. His coffin, draped in the Union Jack and 'his accoutrements', was borne on a gun carriage to Grove Road Cemetery, and the cortege was headed by a detachment of the 15th West Riding Volunteers. The funeral was attended by Colonel Wood, Major Cattley, Sergeant Sim, Regimental Quartermaster Sergeant Milner, Band Master Helps, and a party of wounded and discharged

As would be expected, now that the 1/5th Battalion was more broadly based following Poelcappele, many of those who died on 25 April 1918 did not hail from Harrogate or York. However, the vast majority were still from the north of England and Yorkshire in particular. Many had been drafted to the 1/5th from other regiments, but these still tended to be relatively local. They included for example, men from the King's Own Yorkshire Light Infantry, The Duke of Wellington's (West Riding) Regiment, the East Yorkshire Regiment, the Durham Light Infantry, the Green Howards and the Northumberland Fusiliers. Only a dozen or so (or about 10 per cent) of those killed at Wytschaete with the 1/5th came from outside Yorkshire.

Prisoners

Eight officers of the 1/5th Battalion were taken prisoner on 25 April 1918. On 18 May 1918 the *Harrogate Advertiser* reported that:

> *Second-Lieut. B. Archer, whose parents now reside at York ... was taken prisoner on 25th April 1918. He joined the West Yorks on the outbreak of war, and went to France in April 1915, with the battalion, and being promoted on the field to the rank of sergeant, he was granted a commission with the West Yorks last year and proceeded to France again this year and has been engaged in much of the fighting.*

The following week it reported that Second Lieutenant Charles Firth, who had been reported missing, was slightly wounded and a prisoner in Germany. The six others were Andrew Clubb from Harrogate, 33-year-old Percy Cheesman from Selby, 21-year-old Richard Blacker from York, 22-year-old John Dunnington from York, 37-year-old John Hatton from Leeds, 19-year-old Stanley Mardon from Hertfordshire and John Sayes.

All officer prisoners (except Hatton) were taken to a camp in Karlsruhe and then to a fortified camp in Mainz, near Frankfurt. They were not treated terribly well and there was very little to eat. Many attempted to escape but none succeeded. The only instances of direct physical abuse appear to have been reserved for failed escapers. Those who survived the experience were repatriated at the end of the year. For example, John Hatton was released on 11 December 1918.

Charles Firth. [Ackrill]
*Died as a prisoner of war a[t]
Mainz in Germany.*

Some did not survive. Charles Firth died in captivity at Mainz, two days before the Armistice. He had recovered from the fractured leg he suffered in the fighting on 25 April, but died of pneumonia. Colonel Bousfield, who had also been a prisoner at Mainz, wrote to Firth's parents on 5 December 1918 to say that he: *'had devoted his whole energies to the first duty of a prisoner of war, that of escaping, and extremely clever and ingenious he was in the appliances he improvised.'*

Bousfield said that if Firth had survived, he would have escaped. However, while making keys for the prison gates and doors he went down with 'grippe' which killed him. He was probably a victim of the flu epidemic which swept Europe in 1918. He was buried in the prison cemetery.

By mid-summer 1918, news of some men taken prisoner started to trickle in. On 3 August the *Harrogate Advertiser* reported that Mrs Thos. Rhodes had received a letter from her son Albert, missing since 25 April. He had been a Terrier since 1911 and was wounded twice at the front.

On 23 November the *Advertiser* reported that Percy Lawty was also captive in Germany.

The other ranks who were taken prisoner, including those captured at Wytschaete on 25 April 1918, were treated worse than the officers, required to work under harsh conditions. They were constantly moved from camp to camp, so that mail and parcels rarely caught up with them. Herbert Timmins (the younger brother of George Timmins) had been captured a year earlier at Laventie, probably while out on patrol. On 8 January 1919 he was interviewed by the *Harrogate Herald* about his time in captivity:

After capture he was four months behind the lines and then broke down with dysentery. He was sent to hospital at Halle, near Brussels. He was hardly able to crawl about, and the patients were doped with a kind of opium which sent them to sleep for about 24 hours, to wake up worse than ever. Their treatment whilst at work was similar to many others, the men being butted with rifles and sticks for the most trivial affairs.

An incident that occurred whilst Timmins and Lince were together shows the dreadful condition they were in. About 20 of them were ordered to parade at 5.30 in the morning. One dropped down dead and another completely collapsed. So weak were the rest that they could hardly walk the 20 or 30 yards they had to go. Everything possible was done, said Timmins, to make the English suffer.

Private Timmins next went to a place near Douai, where there was a camp with 3,000 prisoners. Here he saw Ellis who was formerly employed at Mr J.R. Ogden's. They were nearly starved to death there, having only 1/8th of a loaf, about the size of a 2½d brown loaf in England, morning and night, and thin barley water at noon. From this place they were sent to Baden and then to work in a wood yard at Freiburg, where again he collapsed through weakness. At the hospital there the Englishmen were picked out and received the worst treatment. He saw a Russian prisoner brought in having something the matter with his hand, and four fingers were taken off without any anaesthetic, and his shrieks were heartrending. Timmins and a chum were condemned to the cells for five days for some trifling offence, but the former escaped by falling sick. By way of punishment they were sent to a camp where the Germans were treating sick horses from the firing lines and Russia. Then they were transferred to Metz to do work on the borders of Lorraine.

Here they heard of the signing of the armistice, when they were set free and were fortunate to get a good meal. Later, 50 were sent by rail to Bavaria to work unloading food trains, the German soldiers receiving their rations therefrom. After a week's work they were liberated again, and after being sent so far by train they were dropped and left to fend for themselves. They walked about 30 kilometres, and then obtained their first square meal during their captivity at Metz. From there they travelled in a hospital train to Nancy and Calais, crossing to Dover. Timmins reached home on December 9th. He was very weak from his privations, but now is beginning to feel better.

Although several parcels were sent from home he never got one.'

Doberitz Prison of War Camp. [YAM]
Shows men of the West Yorkshire Regiment dreaming of the prisoner exchange.

It is quite likely that some ended up at Doberitz camp with other comrades from the West Yorkshire Regiment.

Others did not make it to Germany. Charles Metcalfe, who had enlisted in July 1915 and joined the 1/5th at the front in early 1916, was wounded when taken prisoner at Wytschaete and never recovered. He died in captivity on 5 May at Harlebeke in Belgium, behind German lines. His parents received notification three months later.

Joseph Henderson was unwounded when he was captured. However, he died on 4 October 1918 in Hautmont. He had enlisted with the 5th Battalion on the outbreak of war, was wounded twice and gassed. He seems to have had a heart condition which took his life in a German hospital. Five months later his wife was notified of his death.

Summer's Rest and Reinforcement

Throughout May 1918, the flood of 'new blood' promised by General Cameron poured into the 1/5th battalion, with 17 officers and 592 other ranks joining. In June, July and August a further 9 officers and 326 Other Ranks arrived.

While the reinforcement drafts received after the Somme and then Passchendaele had largely come from Yorkshire and northern England, in the summer of 1918 the 1/5th Battalion was brought up to fighting strength by an influx of recruits from all over Great Britain. Many were very young volunteers and conscripted men aged 18 and 19 who had been sent out hurriedly to replace the losses of the German Spring Offensive.

As Major General Cameron had hinted, the integration of so many barely trained men would be a challenge. Therefore, most of May and June was spent training in everything from basic musketry, with three days on the range at St Omer, to brigade attack schemes. Training was interspersed with the usual fatigues, as parties were sent out to help beef up the defensive fortifications between Poperinghe and Ypres. There was also an opportunity for rest and leisure activity as the usual impromptu and organised football matches started up on the beach.

One of the new men was Private Ernest Law, from Deptford in south-east London, who was interviewed by the Imperial War Museum in 1989. Ernest recalled that he had left his job as a grocer's boy to enlist in the autumn of 1917 and was transferred straight into the 97th Training Reserve at Aldershot. Basic training took six weeks and included musketry, route marching and gas training. He was taught how to count to five before throwing the Mills bomb and how to use a bayonet.

Basic training complete, Ernest transferred into the 51st (Graduated) Battalion, which was based in Colchester, and from February 1918 in Cromer on the Norfolk coast. He was kitted out for war in Colchester and had a 'rough' Channel crossing to France, probably in March 1918. Having disembarked at Calais, he and his four mates (all from London) marched to No.1 Training Camp at Étaples, where Harry Westerman had been an instructor in late 1917.

From Étaples, Ernest and his comrades travelled to the front in cattle trucks, taking a day to get there. They were bound for the 1/5th Battalion, West Yorkshire Regiment, B Company, which was at the time stationed in the line east of Ypres. Ernest was aware that the 1/5th had been 'wiped out' and that he and his friends were to 'make them up'. He says that the 1/5th Battalion was in the front line when he arrived and that it was 'chaos'. He recalls a trench collapsing and hiding in shell holes. It must have been a shock for him, but in truth this was a very quiet period.

The divisional front line between Potijze on the left and Zillebeke on the right was about 2,000 yards east of Ypres, but the enemy opposite was generally not interested in disputing superiority in no man's land and casualties were minimal. The battalion patrolled at night to keep the enemy trenches occupied and were fired on from time to time with only a few casualties.

Albert White from Leeds and Harry Herman from Northumberland were killed on 17 and 20 June respectively. Harry took a bullet when attacking an enemy post 500 yards east of Hellfire Corner on the Menin Road. Six other men were wounded and four missing in this failed attempt to get an identification and take some prisoners. The following night a small party went out to collect Harry's body but only saw signs of him having been dragged into the enemy post.

Further fighting patrols were pushed out on subsequent nights in June 1918, sometimes with artillery support, to deal with enemy strongpoints, including that to the north-east of Dilly Farm. These patrols were not successful in engaging the elusive enemy, but at least casualties were limited to wounds.

Having spent June in the line north of the Menin Road, in July the 1/5th moved south, to the area between Hellfire Corner and Zillebeke Lake. Here, it was even quieter with occasional shelling and patrols only occasionally challenged by distant machine-gun fire. George Dudley from Harrogate received his 'blighty' wound and was repatriated to hospital in Eastleigh. Benjamin Thorpe from Knaresborough injured himself lifting a girder in the trenches.

American troops had now arrived in the front line for familiarisation, with one American platoon per company of the BEF. Ernest Law described them as 'boastful' but not unpleasant. After all, they had chocolates and chewing gum which they were prepared to share with their British comrades.

On 30 July Major General Cameron presented medal ribbons for gallantry at Wytschaete and the battalion marched past, before spending a week in reserve. On 8 August they returned to positions east of Ypres, north of the Ypres–Roulers railway. This part of the line was exceptionally quiet.

However, night patrols were still dangerous and on 11 August Second Lieutenant Lewis Mitchell was killed by a sniper's bullet in the head, as he skirted the enemy wire. His body was recovered the following night by special patrol. General Cameron sent his condolences to Mitchell's brother and Colonel Oddie wrote that: *'He was a fine character: so reliable, absolutely fearless, and yet so unassuming. He was a great favourite with all ranks…'*

In mid-August the 49th Division left the Salient for good; 146 Brigade headed for the coast near Calais for a fortnight's further training and practice attacks in the dunes. Meanwhile, the Allied forces attacked the exhausted German Army, whose Lys Offensive had run into the sand at the end of April 1918. The static trenches were now a distant memory as the war became one of movement, with infantry sometimes shielded by advancing tanks. By the end of August, the enemy had been pushed back to the Hindenburg Line, which utilised the Canal Du Nord as a natural barrier. A salient was held for a few weeks around Arras, but this was driven in by the Canadians on 28 August, as the Allied armies advanced eastward.

The same day, the 1/5th Battalion left the coast for Arras, arriving at Foufflin Ricametz, 10 miles west of Arras, at 5.20am the next morning. On 2 September they embussed for Lancaster Camp, three miles north-west of Arras, where the battalion trained and laboured in reserve for the best part of three weeks. On 20 September, they moved forward again to relieve the 1/6th between Roeux and Plouvain, occupying the new front line seized by the 51st Division on 28 August. They were shelled in earnest by the desperate enemy, with five men killed and two wounded on 23 September.

Three days later the battalion moved back to spend a fortnight in barracks in Arras as the BEF prepared to push on and drive the enemy out of France. It seemed as if the whole BEF was on the move as the night sky was lit by flashes along the whole, fragmented front line. The 1/5th trained for their part in the big attack and studied maps of Valenciennes, as the streets of Arras thronged with troops and war machinery passed through, heading east for the front.

In mid-August, the 2/5th Battalion was disbanded, allowing the 1/5th Battalion to revert to its original name: the 5th Battalion, West Yorkshire Regiment. As such it would play a key role in the final advance.

Chapter 12

The Last Battles
(October–November 1918)

'...a magnificent example of leadership and courage...'

Cambrai

On 7 October 1918, 146 Brigade left Arras, heading south-west towards the front at Cambrai on buses. Half way, they bivouacked for two nights at Hendecourt. On 9 October, they crossed the old Hindenburg Line at Sains-lès Marquion, on the Canal Du Nord, singing 'Tipperary', and bivouacked again on the north-western outskirts of Cambrai. The next day they could hear the sound of the Canadian 4th Brigade attacking nearby at the Second Battle of Cambrai. The Canadians eventually ran out of steam on 10 October, at Iwuy, three miles east of Cambrai, and the 49th Division was called forward at 2.30pm to take over the attack the following morning.

Here 146 Brigade was to attack on a 400-yard frontage. Their jumping off point was the sunken road from Iwuy to Rieux, with the axis of attack north-east onto the ridge facing them, and then beyond towards Avesnes-le-Sec, three miles away. The first objective was the railway station in the cutting south of Avesnes and the second was the village of Haspres, on the east bank of the River Selle.

Overnight, Major Foxton guided the 5th Battalion along congested roads, across the River Escaut at Escaudoeuvres, to its starting positions just north of Naves. They arrived before dawn and were heavily shelled. Foxton then returned to the transport lines, leaving Captain Ablitt as second-in-command to Colonel Oddie. A Company was commanded by Captain Headley Heaton, who had served as adjutant to Colonel Bottomley in the 2/5th Battalion in Harrogate, and then throughout its service on the Western Front. He had been transferred to the 5th Battalion on 4 September 1918, following the disbanding of the 2/5th's B Company, including Ernest Law and his mates, which was commanded by Second Lieutenant S.L. Jones. Captain W.H. Bird commanded C Company and Captain Wycherley, D Company.

At this point the 5th was the weakest battalion in the brigade, with a strength of 573 all told, and its role was to support the attack. Colonel Oddie ordered that artillery formation was to be used with D and B companies in front and C and A companies behind. Two thousand yards ahead, the 1/6th and 1/7th Battalions were to spearhead the attack and they arrived at the sunken road between Iwuy and Rieux in time for the creeping barrage to start at 9am. They were to attack uphill and could see the crest of

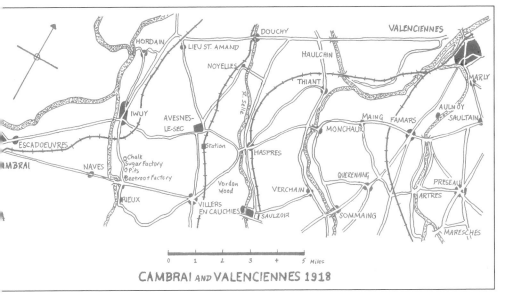

Cambrai and Valenciennes 1918. [Sketch Map 22]
Showing the path of 146 Brigade's advance from Iwuy to Marly.

the ridge running across their path, 1,000 yards to the east.

The barrage was magnificent, starting at the top of the ridge which was heavily occupied by enemy machine-gun posts. It lingered on the ridge for half an hour before moving forward at 100 yards every three minutes towards the Avesnes–Villers Road. Just as the 1/5th had supported the Bedfords at Thiepval on 28 September 1916, at 9.30am they moved forward through the mist and mustard gas fumes in support of the 1/6th and 1/7th Battalions. Iwuy was still in enemy hands and D Company drew machine-gun fire from an isolated post 500 yards distant, on the left. This was probably situated on the railway embankment skirting Iwuy to the south, giving a commanding view of the troops advancing from the direction of Naves. Colonel Oddie ordered the flank platoon of D Company to extend and fire back with its Lewis gun, putting the enemy team out of action and allowing the advance to continue through the enemy artillery barrage as far as the Iwuy–Avesnes road. For

William Oddie. [Ackrill]
Commanding Officer of 1/5th
West Yorkshire Battalion.

this swift action, Robert Wycherley was later awarded a Bar to his Military Cross.

By 10am the 1/6th and 1/7th Battalions had mounted the ridge and seized its summit, probably at bayonet point. They moved across the plateau and down the reverse slope then on to the outskirts of Avesnes, taking more than 400 prisoners and two field batteries on the way. So far this amounted to an advance of nearly four kilometres.

The line of advance. [Author]
Taken from near the site of the German machine gun post cleared by D Company.

Then, ominously, at least four German tanks appeared from the other side of the railway line that lay across the attackers' path. The lumbering machines approached the West Yorkshires through the dip between the higher ground at each end of the Avesnes–Villers road.

The men of 146 Brigade had never seen German tanks before. The British artillery was not yet close enough to engage them and the machines rumbled forward up the reverse slope, firing into the ranks of the West Yorkshires with their machine guns and 6-pounders causing a mild degree of panic in the ranks of the 1/6th and 1/7th Battalions. A German artillery barrage also searched the ground around them as many of the attackers retreated fast towards the crest of the ridge they had taken only an hour or so before. They were also raked by machine guns sited on the high ground south-west of Avesnes and suffered heavy casualties as a result.

Not all retreated, though; some lay down in the long grass as the tanks rolled past. The tanks lacked any infantry support which allowed these isolated parties of West Yorkshires to remain in their forward positions until dusk.

Meanwhile, the 5th Battalion had arrived at the sunken road at 10.30am and when the tanks entered the battle Colonel Oddie was ordered by Brigadier General Rennie to move up to the crest of the ridge and dig in. Seeing Oddie's men approaching up the western slope of the ridge, the 1/6th and 1/7th Battalions gathered themselves and turned to fight with their comrades. Having reached the crest, and seeing the West Yorkshires rally, the tanks fought viciously for a while, but then retreated and the counter-attack waned about 11.30am. The tanks patrolled in front of Avesnes for a further hour and then disappeared.

All three battalions of 146 Brigade then moved back into the attack and advanced over the crest of the ridge. They did this in the face of a heavy artillery bombardment which continued to pound both the men on the ridge and their comrades in advanced posts near Avesnes, preventing any further movement that day.

As the position stabilised, the officers and men of the 5th Battalion were ordered to disentangle themselves and pull back to the Iwuy–Rieux road. There was no possibility of renewing the attack as the Canadians on the left had failed to take Iwuy and any movement forward would have left the brigade's left flank in the air. As it was, the 5th Battalion had lent half a company to the Canadians and these men had suffered heavy casualties by the time they were recalled towards dusk.

254

The Ridge. [Author]
Looking up the ridge from the Iwuy-Rieux road.

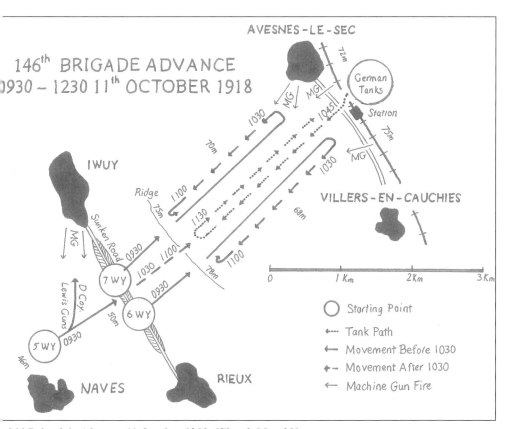

146 Brigade's Advance 11 October 1918. [Sketch Map 23]
Showing how the 1/5th Battalion helped the 1/7th and 1/8th Battalions repulse the tank attack on the morning of the 11th.

The enemy continued to shell the ridge during the afternoon. The 1/6th and 1/7th Battalions took further heavy casualties there and were allowed to withdraw to the sunken road at 4pm. General Rennie then ordered the 5th forward to hold the ridge until morning which they did successfully, despite very heavy artillery bombardment all night long and the bitter cold. D Company held the left and A Company held the right. C Company stayed in the sunken road with B Company just in front.

The BEF was on the move all along the line and momentum needed to be maintained. Overnight the Canadians on the left were relieved by the 51st Division; artillery was brought up to deal with the tanks, and the 5th was ordered to lead the attack the next day. Rennie held a hurried conference of his battalion commanders and Zero hour was fixed for noon. Colonel Oddie's HQ was in a red brick house, 500 yards from the sugar factory on the Iwuy to Rieux road, which became the hub of activity overnight.

However, plans changed suddenly shortly before 9am on 12 October, as it became clear that the enemy had withdrawn beyond the Avesnes–Villers road overnight. Both 146 and 147 West Riding Infantry Brigades were therefore ordered to advance as soon as possible and to take the Avesnes to Villers railway line without waiting for a barrage.

The 5th Battalion was already on the ridge and so naturally formed the first wave of the advance, with the remains of the 1/6th in support and the 1/7th in reserve. They moved forward quickly about 11am, on a two-company frontage of 1,200 yards, with D Company on the left and A Company on the right. The initial advance met no resistance and there was no sign of enemy infantry until they started to descend towards the Avesnes–Villers road. At this point, an hour or so into the advance, they came in view of a machine gun sited on the higher ground around Avesnes-le-Sec. The gun opened up from the town, causing the front two companies to extend and fire back. B Company moved up to make it a three-company front line and after five minutes the advance continued, with the machine gun put out of action. At 12.45pm the railway line was secured and all four companies dug in to hold it against counter-attack which was threatened, but never materialised.

Colonel Oddie set up his HQ in a house near the railway station, just as the German artillery opened up on Avesnes, converting it into rubble. However, there was no sign of the enemy wanting to retake the lost ground and in the afternoon Colonel Oddie pushed out patrols to the east onto the high ground overlooking the valley of the River Selle. Advanced posts were set up by two platoons per company, in a line extending east from the eastern edge of Avesnes. Later, the line was pushed a further 1,000 yards east of Avesnes; 147 Brigade conformed on the right, but Oddie was forced to throw out a defensive flank, using D Company on the left, because the 51st Division had failed to make sufficient ground to cover him there.

From this base the battalion was ordered to 'trickle' forward, right up to the River Selle, in the hope of securing points on the west bank for building bridges. Bridging equipment was requested and two platoons under Second Lieutenant Henry Berghoff and Sergeant Kavanagh tried to get to the west bank, which was occupied along its length by the enemy. Berghoff was pinned down by machine-gun fire, artillery and

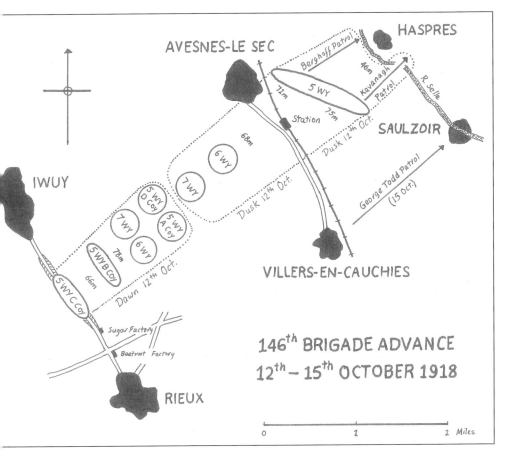

146 Brigade's Advance 12–15 October 1918. [Sketch Map 24]
Showing the advance of the 1/5th Battalion to the River Selle.

gas shells, just short of the bank, west of Haspres. He tried to make it to the water's edge twice but was beaten back each time. He was awarded the Military Cross for these attempts.

Sergeant Kavanagh was more successful to the south of Haspres. He got across the footbridge and remained all day, according to the brigade diary: *'inflicting numerous casualties on the enemy'* and only withdrew after dark. Originally a Leeds rifleman with the 1/7th Battalion, Kavanagh was awarded the DCM with the following citation:

> He was in command of a platoon, and in spite of the fact that both banks of the river were held by the enemy, he succeeded in obtaining possession of the bridge, and establishing posts there, successfully driving off all counter attacks. Throughout the subsequent fighting he showed a magnificent example of leadership and courage.

Sergeant John McQuade, aged 23, from Heslington Road in York, was also awarded the DCM when acting as a platoon commander:

When advancing, his left flank became exposed, but he made his dispositions in the most successful manner, and sent messages to his company commander, which were of the greatest assistance in clearing up the situation. His courage and initiative were most marked.

On 12 October, Major General Cameron, commanding the 49th Division, sent a note to the brigade's commander:

Warmly congratulate you and your Battalions on the very fine advance you made yesterday. I think that it materially helped the situation even though some of the ground won could not be held. Please communicate to all ranks and explain that enemy retreat today largely due to your efforts yesterday.

The 5th held its positions just short of the Selle until 6pm on 13 October when the whole brigade moved back to the beetroot factory on the Iwuy–Rieux road, and went into Divisional Reserve, leaving 148 Brigade holding the front line.

The following day Colonel Oddie moved his HQ to the gas-soaked village of Villers-en-Cauchies and on 15 October he sent his new Intelligence Officer, Second Lieutenant George Todd, forward into the village of Saulzoir, still partially occupied by the enemy, to see the state of the bridges over the Selle. Todd left Villers-en-Cauchies at 7am and returned thirteen hours later with the critical information that the bridges were all down. The citation for his Military Cross describes how he carried out this *'daring reconnaissance in the face of machine gun fire, and despite shell gas.'*

Nineteen-year-old George Leslie Todd was one of the keen young Harrogate men who enlisted as soon as war was declared. His father had died young, leaving George's mother, Annie, to run a boarding house for young women and to bring up three children single-handed. This may partly explain why George jumped at the chance to enlist with the 5th Battalion on 6 August 1914, aged only 16. He embarked with the 1/5th on 15 April 1915, shortly after his seventeenth birthday and was wounded in June 1916, just before the Battle of the Somme. By February 1917 he was a corporal and less than six months later acting company sergeant major, at the age of only 18. George then responded to the call for volunteers from the ranks to train as officers and joined an officer cadet unit, returning to the 1/5th Battalion on 20 September 1917, his commission following six days later. He survived the war, returning to England from occupied Germany on 2 February 1919.

On 16 October 1918 146 Brigade withdrew to Divisional Reserve at Escaudoeuvres to re-group once more, before what turned out to be the final push. They were billeted in comfortable conditions in Iwuy and a week later reinforcements arrived from the Divisional Reception Camp.

Casualties

The Adjutant, Captain Freeman, calculated that in the fighting around Cambrai from 11 to 16 October the 5th Battalion suffered 26 killed (we now know that 43 lost their lives), 163 wounded and 11 missing. Either way this amounted to a 34 per cent casualty rate, with the battalion reduced to 384, all ranks.

Thirty-five–year-old Colour Sergeant Albert Pook had seen it all by the time he died from his wounds at the Casualty Clearing Station on 12 October. He enlisted in the 1st Volunteer Battalion in 1899 for four years, re-enlisting for a further term in 1904. He attested into the 5th Battalion the day after its creation, on 2 April 1908, for one year's service, then re-enlisted annually until 1914, having been promoted to sergeant in April 1910. Albert was embodied on 5 August 1914 and signed Imperial Service papers on 12 September, before Colonel Wood at Strensall. This kept him in the Army until March 1916, when he once more consented to continue serving, this time for four years or for the duration of the war, which he so nearly survived.

Albert was never wounded, but had two serious bouts of sickness which saw him in hospital at Rouen during the Battle of Thiepval Ridge and again in the summer of 1918. Apart from one month's home leave in April 1916, his wife Ada had seen very little of him for four years when he was killed. He had been a clerk in the Town Clerk's office in York before the war.

Charles Plowes had also served with the 1st Volunteer Battalion before joining the 5th Battalion in 1912 at Selby. Embodied and having signed up for Imperial Service, he was transferred into the 2/5th Battalion, serving with them until posted to the 5th Battalion on 31 July 1918, following his recovery from a wound. He was killed on 12 October at Cambrai.

Thirty-eight-year-old Edwin Stead, from Heaton in Bradford, was killed while fighting with A Company, on the battalion right. It seems likely that he volunteered in late 1915 and served with the 1/5th for about two years before being killed. He lies buried at Niagara Cemetery on the Iwuy–Rieux Road.

Grave of Edwin P. Stead. [Author]
Killed in the advance on 11 October 1918.

Niagara Cemetery. [Author]
At the foot of the ridge, on the Iwuy-Rieux Road. Containing the graves of Edwin Stead and William. Sanger, both killed on 11 October 1918.

Six officers were wounded, including Lieutenant Stanley Bennett who had arrived on 15th September, and 21-year-old Leonard Joseph Quarrington from Finsbury Park in North London. He had been a corporal with the Bedfordshire Regiment, commissioned into the West Yorkshires in January 1918.

Honours
In his letter of condolence to Edwin Stead's widow, Hedley Heaton described the advance as a 'great victory'.

In addition to the DCMs awarded to Kavanagh and McQuade, Heaton was himself awarded the DCM for gallantry at Avesnes-le-Sec from 11 to 16 October:

> *'When his courage, coolness and initiative were a fine asset to his company, which was in the front line throughout the attack, and performed excellent service. Despite heavy shelling of the advanced posts, machine gun fire, and an extraordinary amount of shell gas, he, by his personal example and devotion to duty maintained a splendid spirit amongst his men.'*

Robert Wycherley was awarded a Bar to his DCM.

> *Throughout the operations he rose to all the demands on his skill and courage, and during the attack his promptness in dealing with a critical situation avoided a possible catastrophe, and his splendid example inspired his company to resist all attacks after advance posts had been established.*

On 18 October, Sergeant Joseph Henderson from Harrogate was awarded the DCM for his energy, leadership and devotion to duty.

Return to Famars

As the month of October rolled on, the 51st Division heaved the front line further forward towards the Belgian border, to within two miles of Valenciennes, in the early hours of 29 October, when the 49th Division relieved them once more. Ernest Law recalled the Germans being *'on the run'* by this point and that the British *'couldn't catch 'em'*.

With the enemy in full flight, the battle lines were now changing hourly as unit commanders made independent tactical decisions in order to exploit opportunities as they arose. The stalemate of trench warfare had been fully replaced by a war of movement and relative chaos. The 146 Brigade diary records that the front line was 'obscure', and that the relief was 'impossible to arrange' in detail. Battalion and company commanders simply did their best, improvising as they went.

The 5th Battalion was to hold the brigade front line, running 1,000 yards to the east of Famars. This was the scene of the battle in 1793 where the 14th Regiment of Foot had fought the French Revolutionary Army, and the coincidence was not lost on the Adjutant, Bernard Ablitt. He added in the margin of the battalion war diary, underlining 'Famars': *'Remarkable as the place where the Regiment won the right to have the "Ça Ira" as the Regimental Quickstep in 1793.'*

Despite three and a half years of fighting on the Western Front, and the huge turnover in men, the 5th Battalion still cherished its regimental roots.

The Battle of Valenciennes

On 27 October the 5th Battalion moved forward from Iwuy to Douchy, about six miles west of Valenciennes, and on the night of 28/29 they relieved the 6th Battalion, Seaforth Highlanders in the front line. C and B companies formed a defensive 'V' Shape, or arrow head, skirting the eastern edge of Famars, pointing at the River Rhonelle. B Company was to the east of the village facing east towards Preseau and C Company was to the north of the village, facing north towards Valenciennes. A and D companies were 100 yards behind.

The initial plan was to attack in the early hours of 30 October, but this was put back to 1 November. In the meantime, Colonel Oddie was offered relief in the front line but decided to remain there, despite the heavy 'counter-preparation' shell fire on his trenches, particularly in the late afternoon of 30 October when three men were killed and five wounded. Meanwhile the civilian occupants of Famars were gassed heavily and led out to relative safety by the British.

The attack would pass through Aulnoy-les-Valenciennes, on the brigade left, with the left flank following the River Rhonelle as far as Marly. The right flank would follow the Famars to La Villette road. The objective was the railway line south of Marly and the northern section of the sunken road between Marly and Preseau which represented a planned advance of about 4,000 yards. Overall, this attack formed part of Field Marshal Haig's intention to straighten the line immediately to the south of Valenciennes in preparation for a great set-piece attack on the River Sambre.

On the eve of the attack, the 14 officers and 404 men of the 5th Battalion moved into their assembly positions; a straight line on the eastern outskirts of Famars, facing east-north-east. The battalion was to attack in two lines, with B Company on the left, supported by A Company and C Company on the right, supported by D Company. Each company was to attack in two lines, with two platoons in front and two in support. The left front-line platoon and the left support platoon of B Company were detailed to mop up that part of Aulnoy which lay on the right bank of the River Rhonelle, under the command of Second Lieutenant Rushforth.

The 5th Battalion was to lead the attack, with the 1/6th and 1/7th Battalions in support and in reserve, respectively. A very heavy creeping barrage was arranged with the main natural obstacle being the Rhonelle, where it crossed the path of the attack south of Aulnoy, about 750 yards beyond the assembly trenches. The river was on average 6ft wide and 2ft deep.

The attack was due to start at 5.15am, well before dawn, to give the element of surprise and allow the Rhonelle to be crossed in darkness, using seven 20ft temporary bridges carried by the front line platoons. The barrage was to move forward at 100 yards every three minutes, halt for twenty minutes to allow the river to be crossed, and then continue at 100 yards every four minutes, slowing again as it passed Aulnoy.

The Attack

The bombardment started at Zero hour and was again magnificent by comparison with the weak effort seen at Passchendaele a year earlier. It included sixteen machine guns on 'barrage work', to keep the heads of defenders down and prevent them moving forward.

Ernest Law describes the officers standing looking at their watches by the trench ladders and blowing their whistles at precisely the right moment. The officers were the first to go over the top, shouting 'away we go', followed by the men, with the NCOs behind to make sure that everyone was out of the trench.

Shortly after leaving the trenches, one of the seven bridges was destroyed by artillery fire as it was being carried forward. The three officers of C Company were all wounded, probably in the same incident. They were Lieutenant G.A. Barnes and Second Lieutenants James Wilde and E.C. Thornton. Observing from Brigade HQ, Captain Tempest describes the attack as being more a promenade than a battle, but he underestimated the effect of withering enemy artillery fire opening out between Famars and the River Rhonelle, where many other casualties were suffered.

Nonetheless, by 6.15am, troops of the 5th were seen from the rear to be approaching the Rhonelle. There was a good deal of confusion at the river, due to the darkness and the loss of one of the bridges, but fifteen minutes later, and on time, a lamp was seen signalling from the east bank on the battalion's right, meaning that the river had been crossed by C and D companies.

John Rushforth's Military Cross citation helps tell the story on the left:

At an early stage in the attack he led his men across the Rhonelle River, wading waist high, threw the first bridge across, and remained in the water supporting it under heavy fire while the first wave passed over.

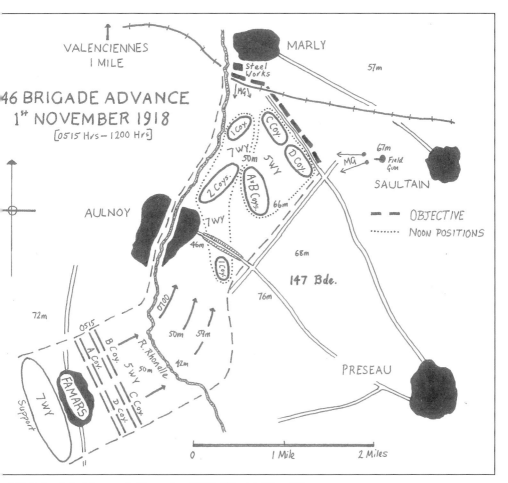

MARLY

Steel
Works

57m

I Coy.

C. Coy.

7 WY
50m

D Coy.

A+B Coys.

2 Coys

7 WY

66m

67m

MG

Field
Gun

SAULTAIN

OBJECTIVE

NOON POSITIONS

AULNOY

7 WY

46m

I Coy.

68m

76m

147 Bde.

72m

0515

0700

50m 59m

42m

A Coy.

B Coy.

R. Rhonelle

5 WY
50m

C Coy.

D Coy.

FAMARS

7 WY
Support

PRESEAU

0   I Mile   2 Miles

146 Brigade's Advance 1 November 1918. [Sketch Map 25]
Showing the advance of the 1/5th Battalion from Famars to the outskirts of Valenciennes.

On the east bank, once the whole attacking force had crossed, the twenty-minute halt was used to reorganise and Second Lieutenant Herbert Straker was transferred over from D Company and placed in command of C Company, to even things out. He was from Barnsley and had served in the ranks with the London Regiment until September 1917. He was commissioned into the 1/6th Battalion, arriving at the front on July 1918 and was then posted to the 1/5th.

On the left, John Rushforth's force then spent about four hours clearing Aulnoy, capturing a German regimental commander as well as three officers. More than 600 prisoners surrendered and were sent back. Rushforth's MC citation continues:

> *He mopped up in Aulnoy capturing three guns and their crews. His initiative and organisation of patrols and mopping up parties were admirable.*

263

In the centre and on the right, there was much less resistance as the sunken road to the east of the Rhonelle was crossed and a German machine gun was put out of action with the crew bolting. By 8.30am D Company (commanded by Captain Wycherley) had advanced up the rise and reached the Marly to Preseau Road, where they dug in.

Things were much less straightforward on the battalion's left. With Rushforth's force held up at Aulnoy until 11am, the right hand platoons of B and C companies found it hard to stay in touch with the River Rhonelle as they advanced towards Marly. They were relatively weak now and came under head-on attack from machine guns sited in the steel works, beyond the railway line. As a result, the remains of both companies veered to the right and tucked in behind C and D companies, leaving the left flank vacant until elements of the 7th Battalion (A Company) arrived to shore it up. Even then, the 7th could not get close to the railway line on the left flank of the brigade objective due to the machine guns in the steel works.

By noon, Captain Tempest describes the situation on the brigade's front as being 'rather serious', as there were no reports from the left flank, due to the steel works machine guns, and on the right both D and C companies had come under heavy fire from machine guns and a field gun in front of Saultain. By 12.50, Second Lieutenant Straker had been wounded, leaving Wycherley in command of both forward companies and he sent up an S.O.S. rocket requesting urgent support. Unable to hold the Marly to Preseau road under such intense fire, and with both flanks in the air, Wycherley decided to withdraw 500 yards and dig in. He held this line all day in the face of fierce defensive machine-gun fire from the front and both flanks. By 3pm his force was joined at last by a detachment from the 1/6th Battalion, which formed a defensive flank on the right, pending the arrival of 147 Brigade which had been held up on the Aulnoy to Preseau Road.

At 4pm the Germans counter-attacked on the right flank but were beaten off by Lewis gun fire and they finally retreated to Marly Aerodrome. By 8.30pm, the battlefield was relatively quiet and orders were received to advance to the final objective, as the Duke of Wellington's were catching up on the right. The final objective was seized straight away and occupied as an outpost line.

The 5th Battalion was relieved without fuss at 4.30am on the morning of 2 November and moved out of the firing line for the final time.

Casualties

During the battle, Second Lieutenant James Wilde and 32 other ranks were killed, including 21-year-old John W. Smith, who had enlisted in York at the beginning of the war.

Albert Bailes, a 35-year-old Harrogate Terrier died from a head wound sustained at the Battle of Valenciennes. He had been a nurseryman before he was recruited by Fred Kelley on 25 November 1914. He had already been wounded in the head and arm on 23 February 1916, probably in a Minenwerfer explosion.

John McQuade had been awarded the DCM for bravery at Cambrai nineteen days earlier. An insurance clerk before the war, he had enlisted with his cousin, Gerald, on the outbreak of war and served as a Beechwood Boy before embarking in October 1915 to join the 5th Battalion at Ypres. The other thirty hailed from as far afield as Carlisle and Cornwall.

One of those killed was Lawrence Shepherd, from Leeds. Ernest Law remembers that he was hit in the stomach by a 'dum-dum' bullet (altered to shatter on impact). He cried out for water but the sergeant told the men not to give him any as this was known to aggravate abdominal wounds.

Lieutenant Barnes, Second Lieutenants Straker and Thornton and 121 other ranks were wounded. Herbert Straker died of his wounds on 9 November 1918. George Winter, brother-in-law of Nobby Abrams, was shot in the stomach. He underwent an operation and appeared to be recovering when he declined and died on 3 December. George's father, a munitions worker, had recently died of TNT poisoning in Armley Hospital, Leeds.

In addition, 20 men were missing.

William Wood. [Ackrill]
Died of gas poisoning at Valenciennes on 1 November 1918. He lived at Duncan Street Harrogate.

Honours

In addition to the DCMs mentioned above, eleven Military Medals were awarded for gallantry at Cambrai and Valenciennes, to men born all over the UK, from King's Cross to Exminster, with only four from Yorkshire. They were W. Rastrick, S.G. Avery, E. Marriott, J.T. Holford, H. Dickens, J. Miller, H.H. Wellington, H. Butterfield, A.E. Payne, A.J. Chandler, and W. Watson.

On 29 December 1918, as acting commanding officer of 146 Brigade William Oddie had the pleasure of announcing in brigade orders the award of the Military Cross to Headley Heaton, George Todd and Henry Berghoff, and the Bar to Robert Wycherley. It is worthy of note that he also announced the award of the DSO to the sometime Brigade Intelligence Officer and future author of the History of the 1/6th Battalion, Lieutenant E.V. Tempest.

George Winter. [Ackrill]
Died on 3 November 1918 of stomach wounds suffered at Valenciennes on 1 November 1918. He lived at Dixon Terrace Harrogate.

Chapter 13

The Peace
(October–November 1918)

'...it seemed part of a pleasant dream.'

Ceasefire

As a fighting unit, the 5th Battalion had done its job. The last man of the 1/5th to be killed in action was 27-year-old Samuel Smith who was caught in a shell blast on 4 November. He lived in Harrogate and had been a brewery worker in Tadcaster.

Over the following days the front line was pushed mercilessly towards the Franco–German border at the Battle of the Sambre. The German Army was still on the run and its national economy collapsing.

On 7 November Colonel Oddie acted on behalf of the Brigadier General, in receiving formally the thanks of the mayor and municipal council of Valenciennes for the liberation of the town. The 5th Battalion was represented at the ceremony by Captain Wycherley and twelve other ranks.

Over the following days rumours of imminent peace circulated at the front and at 10pm on 10 November, news of the planned ceasefire was received at 146 Brigade HQ by Kenneth Mackay:

> *For some hours the intelligence was barely creditable; it seemed part of a pleasant dream, and the men were afraid of waking up to the bitter reality of continued war! But on the morning of the 11th, all parades were cancelled, men gathered together in groups in the billets and in the village streets, and discussed the great event with madame in the farm kitchen.*

On 11 November 1918 the Great War ended at 11am. Ernest Law recalls that though he was glad it was over, there were no celebrations. At 1.30pm Colonel Oddie commanded a brigade parade, where the general gave a speech, followed by a thanksgiving service. The band of the 5th Battalion played the Marseillaise and the 1/6th band played God Save the King.

Last Days in France

Following the ceasefire there was little for the 5th Battalion to do. Colonel Oddie held a battalion sports day on 15 November at Evin. In mid-December the battalion was

Liberation of Valenciennes [IWM]
Colonel Oddie received the thanks of the Mayor of Valenciennes.

pressed into action as an armed guard for the rations trains passing through Douai Station, but otherwise, time was taken up with education and training. Captain Tempest lectured to groups of fifty men on 'Art', and lessons were given on world affairs, including the 'evils' of Bolshevism and the 'benefits' of the British Empire. Officers and NCOs with any knowledge of academic and practical subjects including mathematics, science and gardening, were also asked to give lectures to the other ranks.

Colonel Oddie frequently stood in for the brigade commander, with Walter Freeman taking command of the 5th Battalion. Major John Foxton was promoted to the rank of lieutenant colonel and placed in command of the 1/7th Battalion.

At the end of 1918 the prisoners who had survived captivity were repatriated. Christmas appears to have been quiet and in the New Year demobilisation started in earnest, with a trickle of six officers and sixteen men de-mobbed while on home leave.

On 20 January 1919 the 5th Battalion was reunited with its colours, as Lieutenant Edwards, Second Lieutenant Todd and CSM Atkinson brought them out to France from the Colliergate Drill Hall in York.

The 1/5th Battalion in Cologne.
8th Platoon, 'B' Company, including private H. Drake, on 20 May 1919.

Army of Occupation

On 2 March 1919 the 5th Battalion left France for the Army of Occupation in Cologne, Germany, as part of the 2nd Northern Infantry Brigade. Over the following eight months they did little but train and look after their equipment.

Ernest Law recalls that fraternising with German people was strictly forbidden, at least for the first six months of the occupation. He thought that the Germans outside the city centre were 'scared to death and heard we were going to kill them all'. They appeared to live behind drawn curtains. Gradually this changed as civilians got used to their new occupiers, and a degree of normality returned.

Demobilisation

On arrival in Germany the 5th Battalion started to take substantial cross-postings from other units, as they were removed from the order of battle. The battalion grew to 1,500 all ranks in April, then shrank, as groups of men were demobilised on home leave. By the summer its strength was about 1,000 men, then by the early autumn about 500.

On 31 October 1919, ninety-two other ranks of the 5th Battalion were cross-posted to the 1/6th Battalion, leaving a small cadre of unknown size. Lieutenant Colonel Oddie led this last party of 5th Battalion officers and men out of Germany on 8 November 1919. The German civilians all flocked around to wave them off.

The 5th Battalion arrived at the Colliergate Drill Hall on 12 November and in his final return, recorded in the battalion war diary, Colonel Oddie reported that the cadre finally dispersed on 13 November 1919.

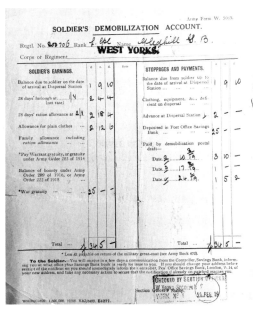

George Gledhill's Demob Account.

Army Form Z21.
Following demobilisation George B Gledhill was disembodied as a territorial on 3 March 1919.

'Ca Ira'

According to William Oddie's final return, 8,084 men had passed through the ranks of the 5th Battalion, West Yorkshire Regiment, during its time on the Western Front. Of these he recorded that, 3,263 were wounded and 824 were killed or died of their wounds. Including the missing, many of whom were taken prisoner, the 5th Battalion suffered an overall casualty rate of 47 per cent.

The Colliergate War Memorial. [Fraser Skirrow]
At Colliergate Drill Hall, York.

The 1/5th Cross. [Harrogate Herald].
Originally at Thiepval, then moved to York.

In other words, any man joining the battalion had only an even chance of coming out unscathed. More than one in ten would not survive at all. Those joining at the end of the war, like Ernest Law, faced better odds, but the original 'Saturday Night Soldiers' and Harrogate 'Pals' recruited by Fred Kelley stood very little chance.

The last to lose his life, according to the regimental lists, was Benjamin Butler who died from his wounds on 18 February 1919 in Ripon, where he had lived before enlisting at York on the outbreak of war.

In 1919 Ernest Law returned home to a 'Land Fit for Heroes', where unemployment and poverty were the common reward. He was demobilised on 29 November 1919, at Crystal Palace. With a new lice-ridden suit and £29 in cash, he returned home to his mother who was now living in Greenwich.

Widows received a pension and families restructured themselves to survive without the main breadwinner. Annie Wilkinson, wife of William Wilkinson, moved from Harrogate to Wetherby when she heard he had been killed at Wytschaete. She and her three children moved in with her mother and brother, who was the landlord of the Fox Inn.

Servicemen were entitled to campaign medals and these were often collected by the family where the soldier had not survived; many of the receipts are date stamped 1920, 1921, and 1922.

Great War Memorials were constructed and dedicated across the British Empire, and Lord Halifax dedicated the Harrogate Cenotaph in 1923. Its brass plaques contain the names of the local men who died with the 1/5th West Yorkshires. The names of the others are listed on memorials across Yorkshire and Great Britain. The missing are remembered on the great memorials at the Menin Gate, Thiepval and the graves of those whose bodies were recovered can be visited.

Most survived, though, and some old soldiers maintained their links with the battalion. Harry Fearn spent much of his post-war spare time running the bar in the Colliergate Drill Hall. He died a modest, but well respected, man in 1953. Annual reunion dinners were held for those who had experienced the trenches, as the 5th Battalion reverted to its peacetime role, training part-time soldiers to defend the realm.

A few individual stories can easily be traced after the war. For example, Jack Peters emigrated to the USA, Charles Whitworth was elected Mayor of Harrogate in the 1930s and Maurice Wilson was killed in his attempt to climb Mount Everest in 1934. Peter Wilson (no relation) went up to Brasenose College Oxford where he studied to be a doctor and then went into practice as a GP until his retirement in 1969. Kenneth McKay became commanding officer of the 5th Battalion after William Oddie's retirement.

Letter to Mrs F.C. Thompson.
From the Adjutant General dated 22 June 1921.

Major F.C. Thompson's Medals.

Armistice celebrations in Harrogate.

Harry Waddington. [Tim Waddington]
Photographed near Wetherby after the War.

5th Battalion Officers at Scarborough 1921.
Left to Right back row: Lt. S.M. Claney, Lt. Sabine, Lt. Oddie, Lt. Barnes, Lt. Cochrane, Lt. Swann, Lt Burridge, Lt. Col W.A. White (Rtd.), Capt. Riley M.C., Lt Swain, Lt Brookes, Capt. Plackett, Capt. Procter, Capt. Harper.
Middle row: Maj. Rupert R. Lansdale, Capt. Charles E. Foulds, Capt. Walter H. Freeman, Capt. Adj. T.H.S. Swanton, Lt. Col. William Oddie, D.S.O., Capt Arthur Gaunt, Capt. Henry I. Shaftoe.
Front row: Lt. Barnes, Lt A.P. Ward.

Thirty-year-old Benjamin Dickinson from 9 Tower Street, Harrogate, had enlisted on the outbreak of war and served for the duration without being wounded. On demobilisation in 1919 he returned home to his wife Minnie, and son Ernest. Benjamin died in 1962, aged 73.

Dr Alexander Stoddart returned to York at Christmas 1918, and according to his 1923 obituary in the British Medical Journal: *'It was evident that the War had left its mark upon him, and he suffered from ill health up to the time of his death.'*

The families of all those mentioned in these pages will know much more of their individual post war stories. Without doubt, all were affected deeply for the rest of their lives by their experience on the Western Front.

Many veterans, perhaps the great majority, preferred not to speak about their memories of the Great War. Some became angry when asked. Harry Waddington declined to tell anyone what had happened in great detail, as it was all too painful. He kept his uniform, though.

Benjamin Dickinson c.1915. [Tom Cruikshanks]

Benjamin Dickinson with his wife Minnie and son Ernest. [Tom Cruikshanks]

Sources and Bibliography

UNPUBLISHED MANUSCRIPT SOURCES
York Army Museum
5th Battalion West Yorkshire Regiment, Orders 1911-1914
1/5th Battalion West Yorkshire Regiment, War Diary 1915-1919
1/5th Battalion West Yorkshire Regiment, Nominal Roll (other ranks) February 1917
1/5th Battalion West Yorkshire Regiment, Nominal Roll of Officers who served in
    France, including Italy, between 5 August 1914 and 30 November 1918
2/5th Battalion West Yorkshire Regiment, War Diary 1915-1918
Fred Edwards, manuscript diary
Don Jackson, Prince of Wales's Own West Yorkshire Regiment complete list of
    awards and medals 1914-1919
Charles W. Whitworth, manuscript diary
Cecil E. Wood, letters 1909
Cecil E. Wood, manuscript diary
Cecil E. Wood, commission 1901

University of Leeds, Brotherton Library, Liddle Collection
A.E. Green, letters
Arthur G. Wilson, manuscript diaries
Arthur G. Wilson, transcript of interview with Dr Peter Liddle 1978

York Minster Library
The King's Book of York Heroes

PUBLISHED ORAL SOURCES
Imperial War Museum, Sound Archive
Tom E. Adlam, interview 1974
Ernest Law, interview 1989

ON-LINE RESOURCES
1. Prisoners of the First World War ICRC Historical Records
2. Soldiers Died in the Great War
3. Commonwealth War Graves Commission
4. Harrogate People and Places
5. Wetherby War Memorial
6. York and the Great War
7. The Yorkshire Indexers
8. National Archives:
Medal Roll index cards

Unit War Diaries:

Battalion:
1st Battalion East Yorks Regiment
1/7th Battalion West Yorkshire Regiment
1/8th Battalion West Yorkshire Regiment
7th Battalion Bedfordshire Regiment
12th Battalion Royal Scots Regiment

Brigade:
54 Brigade
64 Brigade
109 Brigade
146 Brigade
146 Machine Gun Company

Division:
49th Division (Adjutant and Quartermaster)
1st West Riding Field Ambulance

PUBLISHED PRINTED SOURCES
Lists and Directories
Ackrill's Harrogate War Souvenir 1914 (Harrogate: R. Ackrill, 1914)
Ackrill's Harrogate War Souvenir 1915 (Harrogate: R. Ackrill, 1915)
Ackrill's Harrogate War Souvenir 1916 (Harrogate: R. Ackrill, 1916)
Ackrill's Harrogate War Souvenir 1917 (Harrogate: R. Ackrill, 1917)
Ackrill's Harrogate War Souvenir 1918 (Harrogate: R. Ackrill, 1918)
Craven In The Great War (Skipton)
Enquiry List No.14, 1917. Wounded and Missing (London: British Red Cross and
   Order of St. John 1917)
Kelly's Directory, North & East Riding 1905, 1912, 1913
London Gazette
Edinburgh Gazette
The Army List
Medal Records Index Cards

Newspapers consulted 1896-1938
Claro Times
Harrogate Advertiser
Harrogate Herald
Malton Gazette & Herald
Rothwell Courier and Times
Sheffield Independent

Yorkshire Evening Post
Yorkshire Herald

Unit Histories
Anon, *The Fifth West Yorks: Illustrated Historical Sketch of the 1/5th and 2/5th Battalions during the Great War* (Harrogate: R. Ackrill, 1933)
Anon, *The 49th Division in France and Flanders (*London: 1921)
Bales, Captain P.G. *The History of the 1/4th Battalion Duke of Wellington's Regiment 1914-1919* (Halifax: Edward Mortimer Ltd., 1920)
Magnus, Laurie. *The West Riding Territorials in the Great War* (London: Kegan Paul, Trench, Trubner & Co., 1920)
Tempest, Capt. E.V. *History of the Sixth Battalion west Yorkshire Regiment – Volume I – The 1/6th Battalion (Bradford: Percy Lund, Humphries & Co., 1921)*
Wyrall, Everard. *The West Yorkshire Regiment in the War 1914-1918* (Volumes I and II – London: John Lane The Bodley Head, 1924-1927)

Articles and Lectures
Palmer, Peter J. (Lecture by Clayton, Derek) *From Disaster to Triumph – The 49th (West Riding) Division in The Great War (WFA 24 March 2011)*
Tattersfield, David. *Attacking the Pope's Nose (Military History Monthly 15 July 2013)*

General Histories
Burnham, Karyn. *York in the Great War* (Barnsley: Pen & Sword Military, 2014)
Cave, Nigel. *Passchendaele The Fight For The Village* (Barnsley: Pen & Sword Military, 1997)
Dennis, Peter. *The Territorial Army 1906–1940* (London: Royal Historical Society, 1987)
Fletcher, J.S. *Harrogate and Knaresborough* (London: SPCK, 1920)
Gilbert, Martin. *The Somme* (London: John Murray, 2006)
Hancock, Edward. *The Battle of Aubers Ridge* (Barnsley: Pen & Sword Military, 2005)
Hart, Peter. *1918 A Very British Victory* (London: Weidenfeld & Nicholson 2008)
Hart, Peter. *Voices From The Front – An Oral History of The Great War* (London: Profile Books, 2015)
Major and Mrs Holt. *Ypres Salient and Passchendaele* (Barnsley: Pen & Sword Military, 2011)
Jennings, Bernard. *History of Harrogate and Knaresborough* (Harrogate: the Advertiser press, 1970)
Kearsley, Lieutenant Colonel A. *1915 Campaign in France (Naval & Military Press)*
MacDonald, Andrew. *First day of the Somme* (Auckland: Harper Collins, 2016)
MacDonald, Lyn. *Somme* (London: Penguin 2013)
MacDonald, Lyn. *1914 The Days of Hope* (London: Michael Joseph 1987)
MacDonald, Lyn. *1915 Death of Innocence* (London: Hodder Headline 1993)

MacDonald, Lyn. *They called it Passchendaele* (London: Michael Joseph 1978)

Middlebrook, Martin. *The First Day on the Somme* (London: Allen Lane, 1971)

McGreal, Stephen. *Boesinghe* (Barnsley: Pen & Sword Military, 2010)

Peacock, Alf. *York in the Great War*

Philpott, William, *Bloody Victory, The Sacrifice on the Somme (London: Little, Brown 2009)*

Pickup, Dixon. *West York Rifle Volunteers* (Leicester: KD Pickup)

Prior, Robin and Wilson, Trevor. *Passchendaele The Untold Story (Yale UP 1996)*

Prior, Robin and Wilson, Trevor. *Command on the Western Front The Military Career of Sir Henry Rawlinson 1914-1918* (London: Blackwell 1992)

Prior, Robin and Wilson, Trevor. The Somme *(Yale UP, 2006)*

Raw, David. *Bradford Pals* (Barnsley: Pen & Sword Military 2005)

Sheffield, Gary (Ed.) and Todman, Dan (Ed.) *Command and Control on the Western Front: The British Army's Experience 1914-18* (London: History Press Ltd, 2008)

Sheffield, Gary: *The Chief: Douglas Haig and the British Army* (London: Aurum Press 2011)

Sheffield, Gary: *Forgotten Victory* (London: Headline, 2001)

Sheldon, Jack. *The Germans at Thiepval* (Barnsley: Pen & Sword Military 2006)

Skirrow, Fraser. *Massacre on the Marne The Life and Death of the 2/5th Battalion West Yorkshire Regiment in the Great War* (Barnsley: Pen & Sword Military 2007)

Stedman, Michael. *Manchester Pals* (Barnsley: Leo Cooper, 1994)

Stedman, Michael. *Thiepval* (Barnsley: Pen & Sword Military 1995)

Steel, Nigel and Hart, Peter. *Passchendaele: The Sacrificial Ground* (London: Weidenfeld & Nicholson 2015)

Stevenson, David. *1914-1918 The History of the First World War* (London: Penguin, 2012)

Strohn, Matthias (Ed.). *World War 1 Companion* (London: Osprey Publishing 2013)

Swinden, Mark and Jeremy. *E.E. Iredale – The Great War Diary of a Tadcaster Man* (York: Quacks Books, 2016)

Todman, Dan *The Great War: Myth and Reality* (London: Bloomsbury, 2005)

Van Emden, Richard. *The Somme* (Barnsley: Pen & Sword Military, 2016)

Volans, Andy. *Two Yorkshire Soldiers – Family Heroes 1914-18 (Scarborough: Farthings Publishing, 2014)*

Waugh, Alec. *The Prisoners of Mainz (London: Chapman and Hall Ltd, 1919)*

Westlake, Ray. *Tracing the Rifle Volunteers 1859-1908* (Barnsley: Pen & Sword Books Ltd, 2010

Wilkinson, Roni. *Pals on the Somme 1916* (Barnsley: Pen & Sword Military, 2008)

Wilson, Arthur G. *Peter – A Life* (Michael Wilson, 1993)

Wilson, Michael. *From Trench to Sky: Letters Home 1915-1918* (Durham: Roundtuit Publishing, 2008)

Winter, Dennis. *Death's Men – Soldiers of the Great War* (London: Allen Lane, 1978)

Appendix 1

Officers Known to Have Served

Of the 264 officers who served with the 1/5th Battalion overseas between 15 April 1915 and 8 November 1919, 227 have been identified by the author. This nominal roll from 1919 records dates of active service at the front with the 1/5th Battalion, the reason for their return and rank. Names in **bold** cross refer to the Roll of Honour in Appendix 3.

At.	*Attached*
D	*Demobilised*
DD	*Divisional Duty*
DGCM	*Dismissed – General Court Martial*
DW	*Died of Wounds*
I	*Injured*
K	*Killed*
KOSB	*King's Own Scottish Borderers*
M	*Missing*
MGC	*Machine Gun Corps*
NK	*Not Known*
P	*Posted*
PoW	*Prisoner of War*
RC	*Relinquished Commission*
RE	*Royal Engineers*
RFC	*Royal Flying Corps*
S	*Sick*
SS	*Still Serving*
TMB	*Trench Mortar Battery*
UK	*UK Duty*
W	*Wounded*

Name	Rank	Dates served at the front
Ablitt, Bernard E.	Capt	21/09/15 – 04/7/16 (W)
		29/12/16 – Still Serving
Airey, Henry W.S.	**2/Lt**	**25/11/16 – 11/01/07 (K)**
Allen, R.E.R.	2/Lt	15/04/15 – 02/10/15 (S)
		30/11/15 – 08/06/16 (P – RFC)
Allen, Nicholas C.	2/Lt	07/07/15 – 20/09/15 (UK)
Anderson, W.A.	2/Lt	13/01/16 – 28/01/16 (P – 146 MGC)
Andrew, James	Lt	06/01/18 – 29/01/19

Armistead, James H.	Lt	08/07/15 – 03/08/16 (W)
Armitage, S.	2/Lt	01/01/16 – 28/01/16 (P – 146 MGC)
Bailey, E.T.	NK	29/01/18 – 09/02/18 (S)
Baines, G.H.	2/Lt	25/08/16 – 12/09/16 (W)
Baker, F.G.	**NK**	**04/02/18 – 17/04/18 (K)**
Banks, William A.	2/Lt	29/06/16 – 01/07/16 (P – 49 Division TMB)
Banton, John H.	2/Lt	25/08/16 – 30/10/16 (W)
Barker, A.	**NK**	**25/08/17 – 09/10/17 (W)**
Barnes, G.A.	Lt	07/08/16 – 07/10/16 (W)
		11/10/16 – 05/12/18 (W)
Barraclough, W.J.	**2/Lt**	**07/08/16 – 28/09/16 (K)**
Battersby-Harford, J.V.	Lt	02/06/16 – 16/07/16 (W)
		14/11/16 – 28/02/17
		13/08/17 – 25/04/18 (M)
Beall, Cyril	2/Lt	16/11/18 – 16/2/19
		D
Beech, Norman	**2/Lt**	**05/10/16 – 09/10/17 (M)**
Bell, J.V.	2/Lt	03/06/16 – 04/10/18
Benjamin, Rudolph	Lt	22/02/17 – 01/09/17
Bennett, S.	NK	30/12/17 – 15/05/18 (UK)
		09/09/18 – 14/09/18 (W)
Berghoff, Henry		
Billington, R.F.	2/Lt	18/11/18 – 17/12/18 (S)
Birbeck, Leonard S.	2/Lt	25/05/16 – 20/08/16 (W)
Birbeck, Sidney W.	**Lt**	**08/01/17 – 09/10/17 (K)**
Blackburn, Charles J.C.	**Capt**	**26/09/16 – 25/04/18 (W)**
Blacker, R.	2/Lt	16/11/17 – 25/04/18 (M)
Bland, Barnet S.	Capt	15/04/15 – 17/08/15 (S)
		11/03/16 – 06/09/16 (S)
		16/04/17 – 14/10/17 (W)
Bodimead, E.J.	2/Lt	18/11/18 – (SS)
Bousfield, Hugh D.	2/Lt	03/07/16 – 11/10/17 (W)
Bowles, E.	2/Lt	26/09/16 – 27/04/18 (S)
Brodie, Henry	2/Lt	01/05/17 – 09/07/17 (W)
Brown, Bernard E.	Lt	14/04/15 – 13/10/15 (W)
		13/03/16 – 04/08/16 (W)
Buck, N.W.	Lt	15/04/15 – 09/10/17 (W)
Burrows, John	Lt	01/08/16 – 01/09/16 (NK)
Carter, Edmund G.	2/Lt	31/07/18 – 25/02/19 (S)
Casebourne, Rowland	**Lt**	**Post – 02/07/16 (K)**
Cattley, Robert	Major	15/04/15 – 27/06/15 (W)
		24/07/16 – 13/09/16 (W)
Claney, S.M.	Lt	03/02/17 – 29/11/17 (W)

Charlton, R.	2/Lt	23/08/18 – 07/10/18
Cheesman, Percy	Lt	08/01/17 – 31/03/17 (S)
		21/11/17 – 25/04/18 (W)
Clough, W	Lt	15/04/15 – 05/07/15 (S)
		28/05/16 – 28/07/16 (S)
		08/05/17 – 02/08/17 (W)
Clough, Morris	**Capt**	**04/02/18 – 25/04/18 (M)**
Clubb, Andrew W.	2/Lt	14/02/16 – 08/07/16 (W)
		15/01/18 – 25/04/18 (M)
Cooklow, G.C.	Lt	08/01/17 – 25/10/18 (P – RE)
Cope, N.H.	Lt	15/04/15 – 23/08/15 (S)
		11/04/16 – 04/05/16 (S)
Cork, S.	2/Lt	Post – 14/09/18 (W)
Cussons, Benjamin J.	Lt	04/11/17 – (SS)
Dawson, Sydney T.	Lt	26/09/16 – 12/06/18 (NK)
De Groot, Walter	Lt	08/09/16 – 08/12/18 (NK)
Demaine, Charles F.	Lt	22/09/18 – 21/03/19 (NK)
Dent, Albert E.	Capt	28/05/16 – 19/06/16
		04/01/17 – 18/03/17 (NK)
Deuchar, Albert G.	2/Lt	15/04/15 – 13/08/15 (S)
Dodsworth, Benjamin	Lt	19/04/16 – 18/04/18 (NK)
		19/04/18 – 13/12/18 (NK)
Dresser, W.	Lt	Post – 05/07/16 (W)
Dunnington, John W.	2/Lt	16/11/17 – 25/04/18 (M)
Edwards, F.	Lt	28/10/16 – 08/03/18 (UK)
Elliott, George N.	2/Lt	04/01/17 – 21/01/18 (NK)
		18/11/18 – 01/03/19 (P)
Ellison, Charles C.	Capt	15/04/15 – 23/12/15 (S)
		04/03/16 – 03/08/17 (W)
Ellison, George G.	2/Lt	07/08/16 – 25/08/16 (W)
Everist, H.U.	2/Lt	18/11/18 – 13/02/19 (D)
Firth, Charles R.	**Lt**	**15/08/17 – 25/04/18 (M)**
Firth, Bernard	Lt	25/04/15 – 01/01/16 (NK)
Fotherby, Richard	Lt	18/04/18 – 18/10/19 (NK)
Foulds, Charles E.	Lt	15/04/15 – 12/08/15 (S)
		17/06/16 – 19/09/16 (S)
Foxton, John A.	Major	15/04/15 – 27/02/16
		03/06/17 – 17/10/18 (P – 1/7th)
Frankland, Alfred	2/Lt	22/11/18 – (SS)
Freeman, Walter H.	Major	15/04/15 – (SS)
Frost, Robert	Lt	05/01/17 – 03/05/17 (NK)
		20/11/18 – 01/05/19 (NK)
Gaunt, Arthur	Capt	15/04/15 – 16/10/15 (S)
		24/12/15 – 12/10/16 (S)
Gaunt, Edward	**2/Lt**	**30/04/16 – 27/09/16 (DW)**

George, T.S.	2/Lt	28/07/18 – 16/10/18 (S)
Gill, James	2/Lt	29/07/18 – 13/10/19 (NK)
Gilsenan, Terence D.C.	Lt	21/08/16 – 05/10/18 (W)
Goddard, Harold	**Lt**	**26/02/17 – 09/10/17 (W)**
Goodwill, Cyril	**2/Lt**	**10/07/16 – 03/09/16 (K)**
Gordon, George S.	Capt	05/01/17 – 05/05/17 (NK)
Goulding, Walter H.	Lt	04/10/18 – 02/07/19 (NK)
Green, Douglas	Capt	14/04/15 – 04/03/17 (P – 146 Bde Staff)
Green, Robert	Capt	04/01/17 – 28/01/18 (NK)
		20/05/18 – 28/01/19 (NK)
Griffiths, O.	Lt	Post – 03/01/16 (W)
Grimshaw, Job	2/Lt	31/05/18 – 06/01/19 (NK)
Hanson, J.A.	NK	20/11/17 – 14/04/18 (K)
Hardaker, E.C.H.	Lt	06/07/18 – 05/11/18 (P – RE)
Hardwick, Thomas W.	2/Lt	07/08/16 – 15/10/17 (W)
Harley, R.W.H.	NK	13/08/17 – 12/10/17 (W)
Harper, Thomas	Lt	14/04/15 – (SS)
Harrap, Tom	NK	25/08/17 – 31/10/17 (I)
Hartley, Richard W.H.	Lt	12/08/17 – 09/10/17 (NK)
Hatton, John G.	Lt	11/01/18 – 25/04/18 (PoW)
Hearn, Bernard J.	2/Lt	06/10/18 – (NK)
Heaton, Hedley F.	Capt	04/09/18 – 09/11/18 (S)
Hellewell, A.S.	2/Lt	01/11/18 – 14/02/19 (D)
Henderson, Andrew	2/Lt	10/10/18 – 19/03/19 (NK)
Hepworth, Reuben S.	Lt	18/11/16 – 30/12/16 (NK)
Herring, M.O.L.	2/Lt	21/09/15 – 28/12/15 (S)
Hodson, Fred	2/Lt	08/01/18 – 01/08/18 (NK)
Holdich, William J.	2/Lt	21/08/16 – 08/09/16 (W)
Hopper, Robert E.	2/Lt	15/04/15 – 12/07/16 (W)
Howe, William T.	Capt	25/11/16 – 10/09/17 (S)
Howe, Wilfred	Lt	22/09/16 – (SS)
Hoyle, Clement	2/Lt	19/11/17 – 01/07/18 (S)
Hudson, J.	NK	02/03/08 – 28/04/18 (W)
Hudson, Robert C.	2/Lt	31/05/18 – 30/12/18 (UK)
Ingram, H.A.	2/Lt	18/11/18 – 01/03/19 (P)
Irish, Edward	**2/Lt**	**15/04/15 – 20/06/15 (K)**
Irish, Harry	2/Lt	28/08/16 – (P – 1/7th Bn)
Isacke, R.	Major	29/01/18 – 02/02/18 (DD)
Jackson, Harold K.	2/Lt	15/04/15 – 25/07/15 (W)
James, W.L.	Lt	22/04/18 – 15/10/18 (W)
Jameson, James L.	**Lt**	**15/04/15 – 02/07/16 (K)**
Jones, Godfrey	Lt	25/11/16 – 20/04/17 (W)
Kennedy, J.B.	2/Lt	23/11/18 – (SS)
Kidd, Edward J.C.	2/Lt	22/02/17 – 11/12/17 (P – RFC)
Kiddle, Cyril F.	**2/Lt**	**04/02/18 – 25/04/18 (K)**

King, Byron A.	Lt	08/01/17 – (SS)
Kitching, W.C.S.	NK	02/03/18 – 23/03/18 (W)
Lane, William I.	2/Lt	23/03/16 – 27/10/16 (P –146 TMB)
Lansdale, Rupert R.	Capt	15/04/15 – 07/06/15 (W)
		29/11/15 – 04/12/15 (W)
		28/07/16 – 12/10/16
Lee, Arthur B.	**2/Lt**	**08/07/15 – 30/09/15 (W)**
		17/01/16 – 02/07/16 (K)
Lee, Ernest W.	**2/Lt**	**28/05/16 – 28/09/16 (K)**
Lyne-Stephens, S.E.	2/Lt	17/08/18 – 04/10/18 (P)
Macaulay, W.J.	Lt	14/07/16 – 26/07/16 (W)
		18/09/18 – (SS)
Mackay, Donald P.	**Major**	**15/04/15 – 09/08/16 (S)**
		09/02/17 – 09/10/17 (K)
Mackay, Kenneth	Capt	15/04/15 – 07/11/15 (S)
		10/02/16 – 24/01/19 (D)
Mandeville, Pierce	**Capt**	**15/04/15 – 28/09/16 (K)**
Marshall, H.C.	2/Lt	21/04/18 – 20/07/18 (P)
Mason, Lancelot W.H.	2/Lt	08/10/16 – 14/04/17 (K)
Maufe, C.G.	Lt	08/01/17 – 02/02/19 (D)
McCartney, William	Capt	01/06/16 – 01/08/16 (P – 1/6th)
Meekosha VC, Samuel	2/Lt	15/08/17 – 19/12/17 (S)
Mellor, Walter	2/Lt	06/10/17 – 28/01/18 (NK)
Mitchell, J.G.	2/Lt	14/05/17 – 20/08/17 (W)
Mitchell, Lewis M.	**2/Lt**	**28/05/18 – 11/08/18 (K)**
Monkman, Thomas	Capt	15/04/15 – 01/03/18 (UK)
		25/10/18 – 01/03/18 (D)
Morris, William ST.	NK	20/11/17 – (SS)
Neesham, Arthur P.F.	Lt	15/08/17 – 01/11/18 (W)
		01/05/18 – 01/08/19 (SS)
Newton, George H.	2/Lt	18/10/15 – 24/02/16 (S)
North, Edwin	2/Lt	21/04/18 – 28/01/19 (NK)
North, Alfred E.	2/Lt	23/11/18 – 03/02/19 (D)
Northcote, James F.G.	2/Lt	08/01/17 – 09/10/17 (M)
Northcote, Benjamin	Lt	22/02/17 – 01/08/17 (W)
		05/04/18 – 20/04/18 (W)
Oddie, William	Lt Col	15/04/15 – 16/04/16 (S)
		01/08/16 – 24/05/17 (W)
		21/11/17 – (SS)
Pallister, W.J.	2/Lt	02/06/16 – 08/11/16 (P – RFC)
Parker, John W.	**NK**	**25/08/17 – 13/11/17 (NK)**
Pearson, Harold E.	Capt	01/01/16 – 12/03/16 (NK)
Penlith, C.	2/Lt	Post – 14/01/19 (D)
Peters, John C.	Capt	14/04/15 – 05/11/15 (P –146 TMB)
Petty, W.	2/Lt	23/04/18 – 05/07/18 (P – KOSB)

Phillips, Frederick G.	**Capt**	**09/11/16 – 25/04/18 (K)**
Pollard, Ernest A.	Capt	01/07/16 – 01/12/16 (NK)
Prest, William C.S.	**2/Lt**	**13/01/16 – 17/08/16 (K)**
Quarrington, Leonard J.	2/Lt	23/04/18 – 29/10/18 (W)
Quitzow,	Capt	21/04/18 – 23/11/18 (S)
Renny, W.	NK	12/02/18 – 27/02/18 (DGCM)
Reynolds, E.A.	2/Lt	16/06/16 – 06/09/16 (W)
Rhodes, Cecil	Lt	14/03/18 – 21/03/18 (NK)
Roberts, A.M.	2/Lt	08/01/17 – 20/2/18 (S)
Robinson, C.	2/Lt	13/01/16 – 02/03/16 (S)
		25/05/16 – 27/05/16 (S)
Row, William B	**2/Lt.**	
Rushforth, John W.	Lt	23/06/17 – 5/08/17 (W)
		09/10/18 – 23/10/18
Samuel, Horace	Lt	01/05/18 – 01/09/18 (NK)
		01/01/19 – 01/08/19 (NK)
Sanders VC, George	Lt	25/08/17 – 26/12/18 (NK)
Saxby, Frederick	2/Lt	25/05/26 – 30/09/16 (W)
		01/04/17 – 08/10/17
Sayes, John	Lt	10/02/16 – 25/04/18 (M)
Scales, W.A.	2/Lt	26/09/16 – 29/12/16 (P – 1/6th)
Scarlett, S.P.	2/Lt	23/04/18 – 20/07/18 (P – MGC Grantham)
Scoby, H.H.	Capt	10/07/15 – 11/03/16 (P – 2nd Bn)
Scott, Henry C.	Capt	13/04/15 – 23/05/16 (NK)
Shaftoe, Henry I.	Lt	02/03/18 – 07/11/19 (NK)
Shillaker, Eric C.H.	Lt	20/04/16 – 17/07/16 (W)
		02/11/16 – 17/01/18
		21/07/18 – (SS)
Smith, Percy R.	Lt	26/09/16 – 03/04/17 (P – RFC)
Smith, L.E.	2/Lt	22/04/18 – 22/01/19 (D)
Smith, John L.W.	Lt	01/01/17 – 01/05/17 (NK)
Smith, Pigott E.G.H.	Lt	04/07/18 – 08/08/18 (P – 15/17 Bn)
Southeraw, C.R.	2/Lt	18/11/18 – (SS)
Sowerby, Geoffrey	Capt	15/04/15 – 06/10/16 (P – Corps Staff)
Spamkis, D.W.	2/Lt	18/11/18 – 01/03/19 (P)
Stephens, F.O.	2/Lt	26/09/16 – 03/8/17 (W)
Stillwell,	2/Lt	
Stoddart, Alexander	Surgeon	15/04/15 – 15/08/15
Stott, Philip H.	**2/Lt**	**04/02/18 – 25/04/18 (M)**
Straker, Herbert	**2/Lt**	**30/07/18 – 09/11/18 (W)**
Terry, Fred A.	2/Lt	
Terry, N.G.	Lt	19/08/16 – 23/12/16 (W)
Tetley, W.G.	Lt	25/11/16 – 29/12/16 (P –1/6th Bn)
Thacker, H.H.	Lt	18/10/15 – 13/05/16 (S)
Thompson, Fredk C.	**Major**	**15/04/15 – 01/07/16 (M)**

Name	Rank	Dates
Thompson, Roland	Lt	10/02/17 – 02/02/19 (NK)
Thornton, C.A.F.	Lt	4/02/18 – 24/03/18 (UK Duty)
Thornton, A.S.	2/Lt	17/10/18 – 9/11/18 (W)
Thornton, Albert	2/Lt	01/10/18 – 01/11/18 (NK)
Todd, George T.	2/Lt	20/09/17 – 02/02/19 (NK)
Treleaven, Noel H.	2/Lt	08/10/16 – Posted (K)
Trevor, S.F.	2/Lt	22/04/18 – 20/07/18 (P – MGC Grantham)
Tucker, F.	Capt	15/04/18 – 16/11/15 (UK)
Tyrell, Leonard C.	**Lt**	**18/09/16 – 09/10/17 (K)**
Veal, Frank	Lt QM	15/04/15 – (SS)
Wacker, R.F.	2/Lt	07/08/16 – 25/04/18 (M)
Walker, John C.	**2/Lt**	**15/04/15 – 19/12/15 (K)**
Walker, Reginald	**Lt**	**01/08/15 – 25/04/18 (K)**
Wallace, Dudley W.	**Lt**	**07/08/16 – 09/10/17 (K)**
Ward, L.	2/Lt	16/11/17 – 04/12/17 (S)
Ward, R.W.	2/Lt	18/11/18 – (SS)
Watson, Alfred C.	**Lt**	**07/08/16 – 03/09/16 (K)**
Waugh, E.R.	2/Lt	08/01/17 – 01/08/17 (W)
Wells, W.R.	NK	25/08/17 – 27/11/17 (S)
White, R.F.	2/Lt	09/03/16 – 30/09/16 (W)
Whitworth, Chas W.	Capt	10/04/15 – 04/02/16 (P – 3/6th Bn)
Whittle	2/Lt	
Wilde, James G.S.	**2/Lt**	**06/01/18 – 01/11/18 (K)**
Wilkinson, Sidney J.	Capt	15/04/15 – 04/11/15 (UK)
Williamson, Percy G.	Capt	15/04/15 – 22/10/15 (S)
		10/02/16 – 21/02/16 (RC)
Willow, T	2/Lt	13/04/15 – 20/11/15 (W)
		29/05/16 – 04/12/16 (W)
		10/10/17 – (SS)
Wilson, Maurice	Lt	28/11/17 – 12/08/18 (NK)
Wilson, Arthur G.	2/Lt	07/08/16 – 28/09/16 (W)
Wilton, Vincent R.	2/Lt	14/11/16 – 31/03/17 (S)
Wilton, Tom	Lt	25/05/16 – (SS)
Wood, Cecil E.	Lt Col	14/05/15 – 20/08/15 (S)
		25/09/15 – 07/07/16 (S)
Wood, Ronald M.	Lt	15/04/15 – 26/12/15 (S)
		15/03/16 – 15/11/16 (S)
Wordsworth, W.S.	2/Lt	28/10/16 – 15/10/17 (S)
Wordsworth, Wm E.	2/Lt	22/09/16 – 15/10/17 (NK)
Wycherley, Robert B.	Capt	26/09/16 – 01/02/19 (D)
Yates, H.	2/Lt	18/06/17 – 12/10/17 (W)

Appendix 2

Other Ranks known to have served with the 1/5th Battalion

Of the 7,823 Other Ranks who served with the 1/5th Battalion overseas between 15 April 1915 and 8 November 1919, the following have been identified by the author. Names in bold cross refer to the Roll of Honour. With their last known rank, they were:

Abbott, Joseph E.	Cpl	200598		Anthony, Thomas H.		202349
Abbott, Thomas Luke	L/Cpl	200605		Appleton, Marmaduke	Pte.	200418
Abbott, James	**Pte.**	**54306**		**Appleyard, John W.**	**Pte.**	**40248**
Abrams, Ernest	**Pte.**	**1159**		Archer Benjamin	Sgt	200633
Adams, Alfred	Pte	205071		**Archer, Wilfred**	**Pte.**	**62864**
Adams, G.	RQMS	203951		**Armitage, Frank**	**Pte.**	**202992**
Adamson, Robert	Cpl	200577		**Armitage, Harry**	**Pte.**	**201582**
Adamson, E.	Pte.			Armstrong, Thomas R.	Pte.	200574
Addy, Edgar	**Pte.**	**18/289**		Arnot, Albert R.	Pte.	201503
Adkin, Jesse	**L/Cpl**	**200171**		**Ashby, Alfred**	**Pte.**	**235615**
Ainley, William	Pte.	201629		Ashby, John	Cpl	200159
Akers, John	Sgt	200350		Ashton, William		21826
Akers, Fred	Pte.	200770		Askham, Arthur	Pte.	201433
Alcock, William	**Pte.**	**202889**		Aston, Bernard		200544
Alden, Thomas	**Pte.**	**265883**		Atkinson, Henry	C/Sgt	200086
Alderson, Arthur H.	L/Sgt.	200546		Atkinson, Edward	Sgt	200205
Alderson, George	Pte.	200547		Atkinson, Percy	A/Sgt	200253
Alderson, Roland	Sgt	200548		Atkinson, Frederick G.	Pte.	200532
Aldis, Harry	Pte.	201315		Atkinson, Charles	Cpl	200747
Aldous, James	Pte.	200748		Atkinson, Sidney	Pte.	200821
Alexander, Thomas R.	Cpl	200673		Atkinson, Arthur	Pte.	200849
Allan, William S.	Sgt	200369		Atkinson, J.	L/Cpl	1488
Allen, Matthew	**Pte.**	**54577**		**Atkinson, James**	**Sgt**	**288**
Allen, A.J.	Pte.	1817		Atkinson, R.	Pte	204445
Almond, Ernest	Sgt	201573		**Atkinson, Robert**	**Pte.**	**50445**
Altoft, Fred	**Pte.**	**307380**		Austin, Charles E.	Pte.	200122
Ambler Robert	Pte	54889		Austin, Robert	L/Cpl	200236
Ambrose William	Sgt	200130		Austwick, T.	Pte	42812
Anderson, Robert W.	**CSM**	**1846**		Avery, S.G.	Pte.	62512
Anderson Thomas H.	**Pte.**	**5914**		Ayers, William A.	Pte.	200391
Anderson, W.	Pte.			Aylott, E.	Pte	67452
Andrews, William	Pte.	200277		**Backhouse, Alfred**	**Cpl**	**200338**
Andrews, Walter	L/Cpl	200971		**Bailes, Albert**	**L/Sgt.**	**2794**
Andrews, John M.	**L/Cpl**	**5903**		Bailes, T.		
Anfield, Reginald T.	Cpl	200779		**Baines, Albert**	**Pte.**	**2582/**

		200817	Beech, N.W.	Pte.	2158
Baines, Benjamin	**Pte.**	**2123**	Beilby, John	Pte.	201595
Baines, Percy Oswald	**L/Cpl**	**1722/**	**Belcher, Richard**	**Pte.**	**40770**
		200324	**Bell, Jonathan W.**	**Pte.**	**235619**
Baker, Edward A	**Cpl**	**2301**	Bell, T.W.	Pte	57751
Baker, Frederick	**Pte.**	**20723**	**Benn, Tom**	**Pte.**	**202725**
Baker, James	Pte.	200139	Bennett, C.E.L.	Pte	
Bairstow, James Louis	Pte.	200294	**Bennett, Harry**	**Pte.**	**205314**
Balmforth, J.	**L/Cpl**	**202927**	**Bennett, Henry**	**Pte.**	**202226**
Balmforth, Joseph S.	Cpl	200636	Bennion, J.H.	Pte	205072
Balmforth, S.			Benson, Charles	Pte.	200386
Bamford, John M.	**Pte.**	**203144**	Benson, George	Pte.	200107
Barber, Henry	**L/Cpl**	**2167**	Benson, Harry	Pte.	200181
Barker, A.	Pte		Benson, W.	L/Cpl	7733
Barker. Edward	**Pte.**	**201509**	**Benson, William J.**	**Pte.**	**52753**
Barlow, Frank	**Pte.**	**202804**	**Bent, James C.**	**Pte.**	**325189**
Barlow, Sydney	Pte	5825	**Bentley, Wilfred**	**Pte.**	**5943**
Barnes, C.W.			**Bickerdike, George**	**Pte.**	**5053**
Barnes, Fred	**Pte.**	**22684**	**Binks, George**	**Pte.**	**202202**
Barnie, Peter	Pte.	200734	Binns, Albert	L/Cpl	201293
Barratt, William G.	Pte.	201360	Binns, Gordon	Pte.	202178
Barrett, Robert	**Cpl**	**2253**	Binns, John	Pte.	200582
Barrett, Thomas	**Pte.**	**51811**	Birbeck, J.	Pte.	9547
Barron, James W.	**L/Cpl**	**1198**	Birmingham,William	L/Cpl	200128
Barron, Wilfred	**L/Cpl**	**58948**	**Bishop, Charles**	**Pte.**	**2576**
Barton, Fred	**L/Cpl**	**200183**	**Black, John**	**L/Cpl**	**5938**
Barton, Fred	L/Cpl	1451/	**Blackburn, Frank H.**	**L/Cpl**	**1653/**
		200077			**200280**
Barton, William H.	Pte.	200244	**Blackwell, Griffith A.**	**Pte.**	**54324**
Barwood, Edward C.	**Pte.**	**235624**	Blackstone, Edward	Pte.	
Baser, Albert George	Pte.	200803	Blades, Charles W.	Pte.	202173
Baslington, James	**Pte.**	**203050**	Blagden, J.	Pte	58984
Bassingthwaite, Reginald	Pte.	200941	Blakey, Harry Stanley	Pte.	200780
Bates, Harry	**L/Sgt.**	**236184**	Blanchard, Joseph	Pte.	200670
Bates Walter	Pte	58988	Bland, Robert	Pte.	200946
Bates, William	**Pte.**	**19774**	**Blanshard, Herbert S.**	**Pte.**	**2278/**
Bateson, James T.	**Pte.**	**305014**			**200623**
Batters, Sydney H.	**L/Sgt.**	**1099**	Blythe ,William	Pte.	200056
Battle, Daniel	Sgt	200053	Boehrer, William D.	A/Cpl	200602
Baxter, George W.	**Pte.**	**201366**	**Boldison, Arthur**	**L/Sgt.**	**540**
Bays, James B.	Cpl	200640	Boldison, Charles	Sgt	
Bean, Fred	**Pte.**	**2359**	Bolton, George	Sgt	200223
Bean, Philip	**Pte.**	**200390**	Bolton, Robert S.	Pte.	200406
Bean, Thomas A.	Pte.	200490	**Bonnett, Harry**	**Pte.**	**4770**
Beard, Arthur	Pte	40321	Bonney, William	L/Cpl	200616
Beattie, J.W.	L/Cpl	248	**Booth, Albert**	**Pte.**	**18/1050**
Beck, Cecil	Pte.	200604	Booth, Edward	Pte.	200659
Beck, William	Cpl	200137	**Booth, William**	**Pte.**	**201394**
Beckett, Russell	Pte	20906	**Bootham, William**	**Pte.**	**3880**
Bedell Ernest L	**Cpl**	**372**	**Boothman, Albert**	**Pte.**	**19520**

Borrows, John R.	Pte.	203632		Brown, Webster	Pte	205349
Boston, John Frederick	L/Cpl	201586		Brown, William	Pte.	200113
Bowen, Edward	Pte.	59047		Brown, William	Pte.	200133
Bowman, Arthur	Pte.	267498		Brownbridge, Geo. A.	Pte.	200264
Bowman, Henry Dixon	Sgt	200580		Buck, George William	Pte.	201375
Bowman, John	Pte.	200445		Buck, William	Pte.	62580
Bowman, Robert	Pte.	307277		Buck, William Francis	Pte.	200199
Boyes, George	Pte.	200611		Buckborrough, Edwin	Pte.	2565
Boyes, William	A/Cpl	200692		Buckle, Harold	Pte.	200212
Boynton, Fred				Buckle, Leonard	L/Cpl	2819
Boynton, John E.	Pte.	241509		Buckle, Thomas H.	Pte.	2109
Bracewell, Leonard L.	Pte.	1467		Buckley, Fielding	Sgt	200408
Bradbrook, William J.	Pte.	203399		Buckroyd, J.	L/Sgt	26205
Bradbury, Walter	L/Cpl	200329		Buller, William	Pte.	21870
Bradley, George A	Pte.	4900		Bullock, Herbert	Pte.	203635
Bradley, Horace FB	Pte.	456		Bulmer, G.W.	L/Cpl	203145
Bradley, Sidney	Pte.	22780		Bulmer, William R.	Pte.	200147
Bradley, William	Pte.	201098		Burks, William	Pte.	4887
Braithwaite, George				Burnett, Reginald	Pte.	200863
Braithwaite, James E.	Pte.	4697		Burnley, Ernest	Sgt	200518
Brandon, Henry	Pte.	200019		Burrows, Oates	Pte.	202738
Brannan, J.	Pte	66513		Burton, Alfred	Pte.	59048
Brier, Edwin Greaves	Pte.	201574		Burton, Harry	Pte.	200323
Briggs, Horace W.	L/Sgt.	200762		Burton, William	Pte.	200186
Brimacombe, James E.	Pte.	66453		Butcher, Frederick	Pte.	62455
Broadbank, Thomas	Pte.	200217		Butler, Benjamin	Pte.	2518
Broadbent, Fred	Pte.	6049		Butler, Robert	L/Cpl	200003
Broadbent, Hugh	Pte.	1769		Butterfield, Horace	L/Cpl	16/1553
Broader, Robert K	Pte.	3267		Butterick, Thomas W.	Pte.	41693
Broadhurst, William E	Pte.	265889		Bycroft, Arthur	Pte.	200752
Brodrick, Anthony	Pte.	59045		Caddick, William	Pte.	205224
Brogden, John Wm	Pte.	22476		Cahill, James	Pte.	2608
Brook, Arthur	Pte.	201618		Cahill, Joseph	Cpl	1066
Brook, Arthur	Pte.	205092		Cairns, E.	Cpl	304042
Brook, James	Pte.	21/712		Calder, George	CSM.	200025
Brook, Leonard	Pte.	21/674		Callaghan, George F	Pte.	201599
Brooks, A.	Pte.	3928		Calpin, James	Pte.	201510
Brookes, William H.	Pte.	58986		Calverley, Arthur	Sgt	203553
Broomfield, Harold	Pte.	202996		Calvert ,Ben	Pte.	200334
Brough, William Dennis	Pte.	200457		Calvert, Herbert	Pte.	2701
Broughton, W.	Sgt.	1643		Calvert, Raymund	Pte.	3499/
Brown, Bernard	Pte.	5829				201401
Brown, Dudley	Sgt	200191		Calvert, Robert	Pte.	200745
Brown, Ernest	Pte.	3939		Cameron, Alex	L/Cpl	200738
Brown, Frederick	Pte.	200290		Cannon, William F.	Pte.	201282
Brown, Frederick	Pte.	201439		Capps, Robert	Pte.	2441
Brown, John	Pte.	2187		Carney, Thomas	Pte.	6428
Brown, John F.	L/Cpl	2648		Carr, Herbert	Pte.	36959
Brown, Thomas Henry	Pte.	200700		Carr, William	Pte.	4251
Brown, Thomas J.	Sgt	202838		Carrack, Herbert	Pte.	200078

Carrick, John William	Pte.	200705
Carrick, George		
Carroll, W.	Pte	58932
Carslake, George	**Pte.**	**20110**
Carter, Albert N.	**Pte.**	**205113**
Carter, Arthur	**Pte.**	**41810**
Carter, Charles Henry	Pte.	201096
Carter, Joseph	L/Cpl	200845
Carter, Joseph	**Pte.**	**202976**
Cartmel, George M.	**Pte.**	**2170**
Carver, Robert W.	**Pte.**	**203623**
Casey, Ernest	Pte.	201339
Cassells, Andrew	**Pte.**	**38073**
Castle, John G.	**Pte.**	**2375**
Cattle, John	Pte.	201239
Cawood, Clarence W	Pte.	200275
Chadwick, George H.	**Cpl**	**5512/ 203147**
Chadwick, William	**Pte.**	**4/9063**
Chamberlin, Charles R.	CSM.	200045
Chandler, A.J.	Pte.	62513
Chapelow, Charles H.	**Pte.**	**23052**
Chapman, Amos	**Pte.**	**205365**
Chapman, Arthur	CSM.	200112
Chapman, Arthur Ernest	Pte.	200666
Chapman, Herbert	Pte.	201412
Chapman, James B	Pte.	200699
Chappell, Herbert T.	**Pte.**	**54091**
Charles, W.D.	Pte	
Chatten, F.		
Childs, Arthur G.	**Pte.**	**54092**
Childs, Percival Ernest	L/Sgt.	200906
Christon, Norman	**Pte.**	**54339**
Christopherson, John T.	**Pte.**	**205366**
Clark, Alfred	**Pte.**	**2687**
Clark, Arthur Stanley	A/L/Cp	200289
Clark, Charles	Pte.	200907
Clark, Henry	**Pte.**	**27227**
Clark, Henry Leopold	Pte.	201491
Clark, John William	Pte.	1289/ 200104
Clark, Richard Henry	Sgt	201446
Clark, Thomas A.	**Pte.**	**307372**
Clark, W.P		268550
Clarke, Archibald T.	**Pte.**	**15/200**
Clarke, Ernest	**Pte.**	**21180**
Clarke, Fred	**Pte.**	**202308**
Clarke, Gilbert	Pte.	201123
Clarke, Victor J.	**Pte.**	**46512**
Clarkson, Frank	**Pte.**	**2103/**

		200520
Clayton, Edward	Pte.	200722
Clayton, George	Pte.	200178
Cleghorn, Ernest	**Pte.**	**202846**
Clements, D.	CSM	203277
Clemishaw, Dennis	L/Cpl	200732
Cleveland, Harry	L/Cpl	201519
Clinton, Frank	Pte	52754
Clithero, George W.	Pte.	200719
Cloak, Henry	Pte	203534
Coates, James	**Pte.**	**62556**
Coates, Joseph	**Pte.**	**307499**
Cobbold, Fred	Pte.	201297
Cockerline, Ernest	**Pte.**	**57231**
Codd, William	**Pte.**	**203067**
Coe, Frederick W.	**Pte.**	**54097**
Coghill, Herbert	**Pte.**	**20738**
Cole, Arthur		200985
Cole, Harry	Pte.	202158
Coleman, Thomas	**Pte.**	**2290**
Coleman, William Jess	Pte.	200189
Coles, Maurice	**L/Cpl**	**201150**
Collings, Stanley	Pte.	200519
Collins, William	**Pte.**	**58931**
Coltman, Robert	**Pte.**	**59049**
Connell, Ernest	Sgt	200138
Connell, Gilbert	**Pte.**	**2387**
Conning, Fred	Pte.	201237
Cook, William H.	**Pte.**	**235631**
Cooke, A.W.	Pte.	1790
Cooper, Harold	**L/Cpl**	**66497**
Cordingly, Harry	**Pte.**	**268895**
Corry, Walter	Pte.	203732
Cosgrove, Frank	Pte.	200676
Cotterill, Ernest	L/Cpl	200341
Cottingham, Edmund	Pte.	202156
Cotton, George	**Pte.**	**241986**
Coupland, Stanley	Pte.	200797
Cousins, Herbert	Sgt	200190
Cousins, Robert	**Pte.**	**1821**
Cowl, Arthur	L/Cpl	200153
Cox, Herbert	**Pte.**	**307140**
Crabtree, Allan	**Pte.**	**54909**
Craven, Arthur	**Pte.**	**203535**
Crawford, William	**Pte.**	**305859**
Crofts, Alfred	**Pte.**	**3860**
Crosby, Tom	**Pte.**	**202719**
Crossland, Samuel	**Pte.**	**26183**
Crossley, Joseph	**Pte.**	**203248**
Crosthwaite, Alfred	Pte.	201242

Name	Rank	Number
Crow, Herbert S.	Pte.	202236
Crowe, Cyril D.	Pte.	5727
Crowe, Gilbert B.	Pte.	1693
Crowehurst, Arthur	Pte.	66481
Crowther, Russell E.	Pte.	205211
Crust, William	L/Cpl	2143
Cullen, Charlie	Cpl	201634
Cundall, J.	Pte	293
Cundall, Noah	Sgt	200036
Cunningham, Herbert	Pte.	59415
Currell, James	Pte.	2588
Curtis, William	Pte.	307500
Cussins, Cecil	Pte.	3557
Cust, Richard	Pte	14076
Cutler, Joseph	Pte.	23112
Cutts, William	Pte.	201410
Dack, William	Pte.	20808
Dalby, Alfred	Pte.	2987
Dalby, John	Pte.	49029
Dale, Albert	Pte.	54358
Daniel, Albert	Pte.	200355
Daniel, Robert	Pte.	1850
Darbyshire, P.		
Darnbrough, John	Pte.	205076
Davey, P.	Pte	203967
Davidson, Fred	Pte.	201579
Davies, Edward	Pte.	202294
Davies, Owen P.	Pte.	54362
Dawes, Frederick	Pte.	1310
Dawson, Fred	L/Cpl	5584
Dawson George	Cpl	200758
Dawson, Walter	Pte.	2235
Day, Arnold E.	L/Cpl	2088
Day, Ernest	Pte.	201605
Dealtry, Edgar	Pte.	201597
Dean, Arnold Piercey	Cpl	200262
Dean, Leonard	Pte.	266782
Deans, Harold	Pte.	2127
Deighton, Robert Arthur		
Delaney, Thomas	Pte.	240446
DeMersy, Daniel	Pte.	201553
Denison, H.		
Denning, Albert	Pte.	54101
Denton, Harry	Pte.	21346
Dewhirst, George F.	Pte.	307442
Dickens, Bernard	Pte	40744
Dickens, H.	Pte.	58951
Dickenson, George M.	Cpl	200514
Dickinson, Benjamin	Pte.	200727
Dickinson, Bernard	Pte.	40744
Dickinson, Ernest	Pte	78
Dickinson, John W.	L/Cpl	201333
Dinsdale	Pte.	
Dixon, Albert	Pte.	203070
Dixon, Edward	Pte.	202856
Dixon, F.W.	Pte.	2552/ 200796
Dixon, Nicholas	Pte.	242873
Dobson, John	Sgt	200679
Dobson, John William	Pte.	201328
Dobson, Joseph	Pte.	3335
Docherty, George	Sgt	203043
Doherty, Arnold	Pte.	1836/ 200394
Dormand, Alfred	L/Cpl	5909
Doughty, Frederick	Sgt	200197
Downey, Albert	Pte.	54355
Drake, H.	Pte.	
Drake, K.	Pte.	48523
Drake, William H.	Pte.	58951
Draper, Arthur	Pte.	2155/ 200552
Driver, Alan	Pte.	200327
Drury, Frederick	Pte.	37847
Drury, James	Pte.	1374
Dryden, William	Cpl	202853
Dudley, George	Cpl	200721
Duffett, Harry	Pte.	28322
Dufton, William	Pte.	4669
Duncanson, Tom	Pte.	201492
Dundas, William	Pte.	201247
Dungate,	Pte.	
Dunn, Frank	Pte.	2423
Duxfield, Ferrie	Pte.	235635
Dykes, George	Pte.	201712
Dyson, Harry	L/Cpl	202794
Dyson, Patrick P.B.	A/CSM	200527
Dyson, Rufus A.	Pte.	205279
Eastwood, George A.	Sgt	266478
Eastwood, Robert		
Eccles, Percy	Pte	235629
Eden, Charles	Pte	200437
Edwards, Fred	Pte.	
Edwards, Walter Henry	Pte.	200529
Edwards, William	Pte.	200317
Ellerby, Harold	L/Sgt.	200146
Ellerker, Bernard	L/Cpl	200896
Elliot, Harold	Pte.	200787
Ellis, Edwin	Pte.	20837
Ellis, J.	Drm	

Ellis, Thomas	Pte	250100	Foster, Robert Joseph	C/Sgt	200311
Elsworth, Fred	**Cpl**	**202447**	Fox, John James	Pte.	200975
Elsworth, George	**Cpl**	**1986**	**Fox, Walter**	**Pte.**	**200976**
Elsworth, James			**Francis, Frank H.**	**Pte.**	**20818**
Elsworth, Samuel	**Pte.**	**202306**	**Francis, Thomas**	**Pte.**	**7898**
Elsworth, Seth	**Pte.**	**54882**	Frankland, Owen	Pte.	201311
Elton, Walter	**Pte.**	**2746**	**Frankland, Robert**	**Pte.**	**37950**
Emanuel, Albert	**Pte.**	**42609**	**Franks, Walter F.**	**Pte.**	**1612**
Emerson, J.	Sgt	6494	**Fraser, John T.**	**Pte.**	**2164**
Evans, George H.C.	**Pte.**	**54374**	**Freeman, Walter**	**Pte.**	**202155**
Evans, Ronald	**Pte.**	**54376**	**French, Charles**	**Pte.**	**52855**
Evans, William	Sgt	200479	**Frith, William**	**Pte.**	**202745**
Exelby, George Albert	Sgt	200370	Fry, Gilbert Harry	Cpl	200829
Exelby, George H.	**Pte.**	**2236**	**Fryer, Smith**	**Pte.**	**2200**
Exelby, John H.	**CSM**	**1204**	Gains, Ernest Frank	Pte.	201266
Eyeington, David	L/Cpl	200665	Galtress, Frank M.	Pte.	201100
Fairbairn	Pte.		Gamble, Clifford	Cpl	200562
Fairburn, Fred	**Pte.**	**201021**	Gamble, Frank	Sgt	200032
Fairburn, Wilfred	**Pte.**	**5503**	**Gardner, Clifford**	**Rfl**	**305266**
Fannon, Thomas	Pte.	200486	Garland, William Henry	Pte.	200031
Fareham, Frank	**Pte.**	**202954**	**Garnett, Arthur E.**	**Pte.**	**201116**
Faricy, John	Pte	35409	Garniss, Harry		40272
Farmery, Frederick E.	**Pte.**	**3237**	Garside, Alfred	Cpl	200709
Farmery, Harold	Sgt	200093	Gatenby, W.A.	Pte.	2485/
Farnhill, Albert	Cpl	201347			200751
Farrar, George William	Pte.	200126	**Gawthorpe, George**	**Pte.**	**202248**
Fawbert, Edward		200413	Gaynor, Joseph	Pte.	200461
Fawcett, George	Pte.	200887	Gibson, Leonard	Pte	58996
Fawcett, H.	Pte.	235031	**Gibson, Ronald**	**Pte.**	**3814**
Fear, Edmond A.	**Pte.**	**66476**	Gibson, William	Pte.	200366
Fearn, William Henry	Sgt	200010	**Gilbertson, Ralph**	**Pte.**	**203670**
Featherstone, Harry	Sgt	200696	**Gill, Austin**	**Pte.**	**202977**
Fee, James	**Pte.**	**63651**	Gill, James Pickersgill	Sgt	200401
Fenton, John W.	**Pte.**	**3194**	**Gilmore, Bernard**	**Pte.**	**6371**
Ferguson, William	**Cpl**	**1870**	**Gilyard, Thomas A.**	**Pte.**	**205098**
Field, Harold	**Pte.**	**1306**	**Glasgow, Norman**	**Pte.**	**202866**
Fieldhouse, Fred	Pte	54846	**Gledhill, Frances E.**	**Pte.**	**54883**
Fieldhouse, James	L/Sgt.	200389	Gledhill, George B.	L/Cpl	200706
Firth, Edward John	Pte.	200687	Gledhill, H.		
Firth, William	Cpl	201178	Gledhill, Jonas		
Fisher, George M.	**Pte.**	**235653**	Glenton, Nicholas G.	Cpl	201362
Fitzpatrick, Reginald	CSM	200016	**Glover, Harry**	**Pte.**	**235643**
Fletcher, Howard	**L/Cpl**	**241813**	Glover, Henry	Pte.	201598
Flint, James	**Pte.**	**202166**	Glover, William H.	Sgt	200344
Flynn, Robert	**Pte.**	**63006**	**Goatcher, Walter**	**Pte.**	**235645**
Forster, John	**Pte.**	**42758**	**Goddard, Joseph**	**Pte.**	**54329**
Foster, Alfred	Pte.	200114	Goldthorpe, A.	Pte	205352
Foster, Arthur	**Pte.**	**202221**	**Gomersall, Ernest H.**	**Pte.**	**2190**
Foster, Arthur	**Pte.**	**58933**	**Goodison, Arthur**	**Pte.**	**325045**
Foster, Charles E.	**Pte.**	**63646**	**Goodman, Morris**	**Cpl**	**203150**

Goodwin, Eric B.	Pte.	202259		Hanson, John E.	Pte.	59057
Goodwin, George F.	Pte.	200639		Hanson, Louis	Pte.	205169
Gouch, Norman	Pte.	5970		Harding, C.E.		
Grace, Joseph Benjamin	Cpl	201583		Hardisty, John	Pte.	200533
Grafton, James	Pte.	203183		Hardwick, Frank	Pte.	1812
Graham, Nathan	Pte.	202524		Hardwick, Harry	Pte.	203179
Grasby, George W.	Pte.	267199		Hardwick Joseph	Pte.	205079
Gratton, John W.	Sgt	202957		Hardwick, William		
Graves, Charles R.	Pte.	4647		Harling, James	Pte.	203562
Graves, Harold J.	Pte.	54123		Harper, Thomas		
Gray, Charles	Pte.	201425		Harris, Harry John	Pte.	59033
Gray, Mark	Pte.	57405		Harris, James	Pte.	201387
Gray, Richard	Pte.	6441		Harrison, Charles	Pte.	200165
Grayson, John	L/Cpl	201434		Harrison, Ernest	Pte.	2754/ 201009
Green, E.J.	Pte.	62503				
Green, Harry	Pte.	200102		Harrison, Frank	Cpl	201591
Green, Robert	Sgt	202217		Harrison, Frederick	L/Cpl	202798
Greening, Arthur	Pte.	54390		Harrison, Henry	Pte.	200082
Greenwood, Charles	Pte	963		Harrison, James R.	L/Cpl	200143
Greenwood, Norris	Pte	18/421		Harrison, Lescombe T.	Rfl.	20468
Gregg, Percy	L/Cpl	200554		Harrison, W.	Pte.	63020
Grice, E.W.	Cpl	1540		Harrison, William	Sgt	1283
Grindell, Tom	Pte.	201399		Harvey, Edward	Pte.	6450
Grundy, Fred J.	Pte.	58955		Hastings, R.T.,	Sgt	
Gubbings, Alfred E.	L/Cpl	6507		Hatter, John	Pte.	28525
Gurden, Charles Robert	Pte.	201235		Hattersley, George	L/Sgt.	200549
Hackett, James	L/Cpl	23048		Hawksby, Albert E.	Pte.	200245
Haddick, George R.	Cpl	202869		Haxby, William	Pte.	200061
Hadfield, James	Pte.	62884		Haynes, H.	Sgt	2379
Haigh, Ernest	Pte.	1411		Hayton, Phineas	Pte.	200811
Haigh, George	Pte.	54873		Headley, Fred	Pte.	200987
Hainsworth, Cecil J.	Pte.	200358		Heath, Philip	Pte.	57426
Hainsworth, Harold	Pte.	201332		Heaton, J.	Pte	430
Hainsworth, James	Pte.	200419		Heavisides, John	Pte.	1723
Haley, William A.	Pte.	2194		Hebditch, Edwin	Pte.	201071
Hall, Arthur	Cpl	200860		Heeley, Sidney	Pte.	200064
Hall, Arthur H.	Pte.	3316		Heeley, Harold	Cpl	200710
Hall, Fred	Pte	203011		Heley, John Edwin	Pte.	200309
Hall, Fred	Pte.	203336		Helliwell, Albert	Sgt	240687
Hal,l George	Pte.	203080		Helliwell, William	Pte.	200694
Hall, George Henry	Pte.	201380		Helps, Arthur	Sgt	200011
Hall, John W.	Pte.	203937		Henderson, Francis J.	Pte.	2296
Hall, Joseph	L/Cpl	24522		Henderson, Joseph	Sgt	200510
Hall, Joseph D.	Pte.	202872		Hendy, Alfred William	Sgt	200198
Hall, William	CSM	200438		Hepworth, Harrison	Pte.	201603
Hambleton, Walter E.	Pte.	200537		Herbert, Owen	Pte.	200614
Hammond, Ernest	Sgt	200357		Herd, George	Sgt	2637/ 200847
Hampshire, Richard	Pte.	202988				
Handley				Herman, Harry	Pte.	204260
Haney, John	Cpl	6509		Heseltine, William	Pte.	200601

Heslop, George	Pte.	42449	Horne, James M.	Sgt	203240
Heslop, Henry	Pte.	5511	Horner, C.F.		
Hesseldon, Arthur	Pte.	5845	Horner, H.		
Hewson, Albert	Sgt	200630	Horner, Reginald	Pte.	200116
Hewson, Frank	Pte.	202341	Horner, Wilfrid	Pte.	201485
Hick, George	Pte.	2507	Horner, William	Pte.	1718/
Hickman, Benjamin J.	Pte.	54861			200321
Hicks, William Edward	Pte.	200027	Hornsea, Thomas E.	Pte.	200912
Higginbottom, Walter	L/Cpl	201631	Horsefield, Percy	Cpl	200142
Higgins, George	Pte.	40545	Horseman, Lawrence	Cpl	200898
Higgins, Peter	Pte.	202934	Horsfield, Harold	Pte.	1356
Hilbeck, Thomas	Pte.	236443	Horsfield, Sidney	Pte.	242950
Hill, George	Pte.	58959	Horsfield, Percy		
Hill, James Bernard	Pte.	200977	Hothersall, George	Pte.	202315
Hill, Joseph	Pte.	200584	House, Arthur	Pte.	42787
Hinchcliffe, Louis	Pte.	41529	House, Frederick	Pte.	66499
Hindle, William	Pte.	202923	Howard, Henry	Pte.	201011
Hingley, Frank	Pte.	5978	Howard, Percy	Pte.	3895
Hinton, Jack D.	Pte.	325159	Howarth, H.	Pte.	18/411
Hobbs, William	Sgt	203153	Howden, Edward	Sgt	201659
Hobday, Harry	Pte.	201437	Hudson, Amos	Pte.	200037
Hobson, William	Pte.	200301	Hudson, Arthur	Pte.	1288
Hodgson, Arthur W.	Sgt	200360	Hudson, George Herbert	Sgt	200545
Holbrey, J.W.	Sgt	203239	Hudson, John Henry	Pte.	201455
Holden, Samuel	Pte.	202222	Hudson, Norman	Pte.	201345
Holdsworth, Walter	Pte.	201310	Hudson, Thomas	Pte.	201238
Holford, J.T.	Pte.	54131	Hull, Sydney	Pte.	201131
Holgate, Edward	Pte.	202574	Hulme, Samuel	Pte.	202215
Holgate, William	Pte.	200581	Hunt, Daniel	Pte.	200099
Holland James A.	Pte.	200157	Hunter, Charles F.	Pte.	325068
Holland Leonard	Pte.	2523	Hunter, Herbert	CSM	200634
Holliday, William	Pte.	14631/	Husband, Robert	Pte.	200768
		200953	Hutchinson, William	Pte.	200742
Holmes, Harry B.	Cpl	200603	Hutchinson, William A.	Pte.	200767
Holmes, James	Pte.	2	Hutchinson, William H.	Pte.	200652
Holmes, John	Pte.	2336	Hutton, Frank	Cpl	200594
Holmes, John H.	Pte.	3871	Hutton, John G.	L/Cpl	203152
Holmes Mark H.	Pte.	54815	Hyde, Joseph	Pte.	203489
Holmes, Norman	L/Cpl	200135	Ibbetson, J.	Pte	
Holmes, Sydney R.	Pte.	2181	Illingworth, Hamer	Pte.	20/9
Holroyd, Norman	Pte.	203748	Illingworth, James	Pte.	59035
Holt, Edwin	Pte.	5491	Illingworth, Joseph	Pte.	205111
Homer, John W.	Pte.	202807	Illingworth, William	Cpl	16/1917
Hood, Harold	Pte.	14231	Imeson, Thomas	Sgt	200468
Hopkin, Horace	Pte	202959	Ingham, Charles	Pte.	53676
Hopkins, Arthur	Pte.	202334	Ingleby, Arthur	Sgt	201114
Hopkins, Harold Leslie	C/Sgt	200628	Inman, Charles	Pte.	1476
Hopkins, John H.	Pte.	1021	Inman, Thomas	Cpl	200714
Hopkinson, Frederick	Pte.	200716	Iredale, Edward E.	CSM	1588
Hopper, Percy	Sgt	200644	Ireson, Edward W.	Pte.	57780

Jackson, Albert E.	Pte.	**202893**
Jackson, Arthur	L/Cpl	200573
Jackson, Charles	**Pte.**	**307725**
Jackson, Frederick	**Pte.**	**1176/ 200063**
Jackson, John	**Pte.**	**58961**
Jackson, John Edgar	L/Cpl	200395
Jackson, John Thomas	Pte.	201024
Jackson, Michael	**L/Cpl**	**6508**
Jackson, Robert	Pte.	200161
Jackson, Sydney	Pte.	200551
Jackson, Wilfred	A/L/Cpl	200753
Jackson, Wilfred	**Pte.**	**203092**
Jackson, William	**Pte.**	**203091**
Jackson, Wilson	Pte.	202588
Jacobs, Herbert	**Pte.**	**27644**
James, Wilmott	Pte	681
Jarvis, Harry	**Pte.**	**52751**
Jenkinson, Arthur	L/Cpl	200607
Jenkinson, F.	Sgt	
Jennings, Francis O.	Pte.	200951
Jennings, William	**Pte.**	**2665**
Jervis, Henry	**Pte.**	**202880**
Johnson, Arnell	**Pte.**	**2757**
Johnson, Gilbert	**Pte.**	**1700**
Johnson, Hugh	**Pte.**	**63032**
Johnson, John E.	**Pte.**	**16/1718**
Johnson, John J.	**Pte.**	**63030**
Johnson, Robert	**Pte.**	**42854**
Johnson, Thomas	**Pte.**	**307335**
Johnson, Walter	Sgt	200039
Johnson, William	**Pte.**	**1630**
Johnstone, Frederick	Pte.	201424
Johnstone, Stewart	**Pte.**	**9736**
Jones, Herbert	Pte.	200054
Jones, Thomas Edward	Pte.	200062
Jones, William	**L/Cpl**	**203093**
Jordan, Reuben R.	**Pte.**	**5527**
Jowett, W.H.	Pte.	21/983
Kane, Joseph	Pte.	200316
Kavanagh, P.	Sgt	
Kay, William	Pte.	200320
Keen, E.H.	Pte	235650
Keenan, James	Pte	235520
Keighley, Leonard	**Pte.**	**203829**
Kell, John	Pte.	200192
Kelly, Fred	**Cpl**	**2012**
Kemp, Clarence	**Pte.**	**63036**
Kemp Thomas Henry	Pte.	201013
Kenah, Thomas Webb	**Pte.**	**202881**
Kendall, Charles J.L.	**Pte.**	**2365**
Kendall, John	Pte.	200567
Kennedy, John	Pte.	200868
Kennett, Herbert Henry	L/Cpl	200688
Kenny, T.	Sgt.	
Kettlewell, Gathorne	L/Cpl	200911
Kidd, William George	Pte.	201243
Kilingback, Willim H.	**Pte.**	**54147**
Kilvington, Charles E.	**Pte.**	**2729**
Kingswood, Walter	**Pte.**	**63652**
Kipling, Edward	Pte.	200423
Kirk, George Henry	Pte.	200115
Kirk, Walter F.	**Pte.**	**201010**
Kirkbright, Thomas	A/Sgt	200365
Kitchen, G.	Sgt	900/ 200040
Kitching, Albert	Pte.	200166
Kitching, Joseph	**Pte.**	**205100**
Kitson, Frank P.	**Pte.**	**2288**
Kitson, Thomas Ralph	Cpl	200703
Knowles, Edwin	**Pte.**	**205082**
Knowles, Fred	**Pte.**	**6001**
Knowles, John H.	**Pte.**	**2313**
Lamb, Frederick S.	**L/Cpl**	**54153**
Lamb, Harold	Pte.	200184
Lamb, William	**L/Cpl**	**15/1364**
Lambert, Herbert	**Pte.**	**235110**
Lamplugh, Tom Alfred	Pte.	200381
Langhan, Joseph	Pte.	200203
Large, George	**Cpl**	**1378/ 200151**
Law, Ernest	Pte	
Law, Melton A.	**Pte.**	**40908**
Lawrence, Frank	Pte.	201280
Lawson, Allen	**Pte.**	**4924**
Lawson, Arthur	**Pte.**	**204280**
Lawson, George G.	Pte.	200861
Lawson, Reginald	**Pte.**	**29623**
Lawty, Percy Humphrey	Pte.	200571
Lax	Pte.	
Lazenby, Herbert	Pte.	200194
Lea, Walter	**L/Cpl**	**988**
Leach, Frank	**Pte.**	**302729**
Leadley, William	**Pte.**	**1631**
Leak, Edwin	Pte	33397
Leaning, Fanthorpe	**Pte.**	**202332**
Leck, Horace	Pte.	347
Ledgard, Edward	Sgt	200875
Ledgeway, Joseph	Pte.	200942
Lee, Fred	**Pte.**	**202310**

Lee, Harry	L/Cpl	1674	Lund, Henry W.	Pte.	2480
Lee, Harry	Pte.	55332	Lund, W.		
Lee, John	Pte.	200306	Lunn, Herbert		
Lee, Joe	Pte.	200458	Lupton, Selwyn	Pte.	1380
Lee, Reginald Jeferson	Cpl	200575	Lusby, Thomas Millner	Pte.	201878
Leeson, William Ernest	L/Cpl	201471	Lynch, John	Sgt	4/6203
Leigh, A.	Pte	1063	Lyons, James	Pte.	203157
Levi, Edward	Pte.	202279	Lyth, Stanley	Pte.	201248
Levitt, Harold	Pte.	202757	MacDonald, Paul	Pte	307306
Leyland, John H	Pte.	2590	Macey, George	Drm	1517
Lickley, Frederick S	Pte.	3330	Mackay, Hector	Pte.	200352
Lickley, George	L/Cpl	201371	Mackridge, George I.	Pte.	2461
Lickley, Henry George	L/Cpl	201371	Mahon, Joseph	Pte	66512
Lickley, James	Pte.	2304	Mainprize, George	Pte.	200117
Liddle, John	Pte.	202882	Malensey, W.	Pte	235665
Light, Rowland	Sgt	200221	Mallinder, James	Pte.	202966
Linton, Fred	Pte.	25019	Mallorie, John W	Pte.	201358
Lister, Charles Percy	Pte.	200057	Malmslie, William	Pte.	235655
Lister, George	Pte.	6054	Maltby, Harold	Sgt	200322
Little, Edwin	L/Cpl	25453	Malthouse, Walter	Pte.	1363
Little, Miles	Cpl	202758	Marks, Ernest	Pte.	27958
Littlefair, William	Cpl	200615	Marr, Albert	Pte.	201452
Littlewood, Albert	Pte.	40909	Marriott, E.	Cpl	241408
Littlewood, Harry	Pte.	200293	Marrison, George	Pte.	201623
Lloyd, Felix	Pte.	54150	Marsden, Lawrence	Pte.	202760
Loadman, John Cecil	Sgt	200672	Marsden, Thornton	Pte.	305525
Locke, Frank	Cpl	201636	Marsh, Albert	Pte.	20593
Lockwood, Joseph	L/Cpl	307569	Marshall, George Henry	Pte.	200206
Lockwood, L.	Pte.	202759	Marshall, James	Pte.	242910
Lodge, Edward James	Cpl	201460	Marshall, Ronald	L/Cpl	2094
Lodge, James	Pte.	200492	Marshall, Tom Reginald	Sgt	200693
Lofthouse, Archer C.	Cpl	200956	Marshall, William	Pte.	59790
Loftus, John	Pte.	5496	Marston, John	Pte.	33389
Loftus, John	Pte.	200760	Martin, Joseph	Pte.	57785
Long, A.	Pte.	202759	Martin, Percy	Pte.	43035
Long, Albert	Sgt	201063	Martlew, Frederick	Pte.	2250/
Long, Edward	Pte.	2388			200606
Long, Frederick	Pte.	1290	Mascall, Charles	Pte.	54163
Long, J.			Mason, Arthur	Pte.	203187
Longfield, Walter	Pte.	201018	Mason, F.W.	Pte	59511
Loughran, John	Pte.	200590	Mason, James	Pte.	202227
Lovatt, William	Pte.	63041	Mason, Percy	Pte.	2435
Lowe, Edward	Pte.	202231	Mason, Walter	Pte.	200910
Lowery, Leonard	Pte.	27650	Maud, William Henry	Pte.	201166
Lucas, Arthur	CSM	200048	Maw, James Valentine	L/Cpl	200818
Lucas, Walter	Pte.	202229	Mawer, Ernest	Pte.	200962
Lumley, George	Pte.	201544	Mayall, Tom	Pte.	63048
Lumley, Thomas	Pte.	200579	McAndrew, B.	Pte.	2220
Lund, Gordon	CSM	200435	McConnell, C.	Pte.	
Lund, Harry	Pte.	200922	McGregor, Donald	Pte.	203099

Name	Rank	Number
McGuckin, Lionel	**Pte.**	**40807**
McNally, John Robert	Cpl	200657
McNichol, Daniel	**Pte.**	**1572**
McNicholas, James		
McQuade, Gerald	Pte.	200786
McQuade, John C.	**Sgt**	**200788**
McTiernan, James	**Pte.**	**2926**
Mee, F.T.	Pte	57910
Meekin, James Patrick	Pte.	201628
Mellor, Walter	Sgt	200472
Melody, James	L/Sgt.	200303
Melvin, John	**Pte.**	**5515**
Mennell, Harry	Pte.	200148
Merrifield, Ernest	**Pte.**	**57871**
Metcalfe, A	L/Sgt	1780
Metcalfe, Arthur	Pte.	201548
Metcalfe, Charles N.	**Pte.**	**201413**
Metcalfe, Harold Linsey	Pte.	201137
Metcalfe, John	Pte.	201568
Metcalfe, O.		
Metcalfe, William H.	Pte.	200340
Micklethwaite, Arthur	**Pte.**	**203565**
Middleton, Harold	Pte.	200886
Middleton, John	**Pte.**	**43297**
Middleton, Orlando	**Pte.**	**235657**
Midgeley, Harold	**Pte.**	**200992**
Midgley, Ronald	**L/Cpl**	**57445**
Milburn, Stanley	**Pte.**	**62563**
Milins, John Thomas	Pte.	201624
Miller, Harry	**Pte.**	**54164**
Miller, Herbert	**Pte.**	**6380**
Miller, J.	Pte.	54901
Millins, John T.	**Pte.**	**201624**
Mills, Alfred	**L/Cpl**	**18313**
Mills, George	**Pte.**	**54162**
Mills, J.L.	Cpl	
Milner James W.	**Drm**	**677**
Mitchell, C.H.	Pte.	202162
Mitchell, Edward N.	Pte.	200599
Mitchell, Henry	**Pte.**	**40793**
Mitchell, John	**Pte.**	**1436**
Mitchell, William	**Sgt**	**203368**
Moffatt, Herbert	Pte.	201171
Molloy, J.	Pte	59064
Moore, Sydney Burgess	Pte.	200737
Moore, Thomas	Pte.	200646
Moore, Vincent	**Pte.**	**202671**
Moran, John	L/Cpl	200827
Morgan, George	**Pte.**	**202965**
Morley, George Alfred	Pte.	200525
Morrell, John	Pte.	242382
Morris, Douglas	**L/Cpl**	**2151/ 200550**
Morrison, Albert	**Pte.**	**63047**
Morton, Albert Edward	Pte.	200180
Morton, Charles	**Pte.**	**57697**
Morton, Matthew C.	CSM	1470/ 200187
Mosby, Fred	**Pte.**	**48748**
Mosley, John	**Pte.**	**203788**
Mosley, Thomas	**L/Cpl**	**5542**
Moss, Herbert	**Sgt**	**305383**
Mounsey, Fred	**Pte.**	**270201**
Moxon, Victor	**Pte.**	**5539**
Moyser, Hubert H.	**Pte.**	**2320**
Mudd, Fred	Pte.	201834
Mulrooney, Martin	Pte.	201400
Mulry, Victor	**Pte.**	**40817**
Mumford, Bert	Pte.	1206/ 200072
Mumford, William	**Pte.**	**1562**
Munday, Herbert	**Pte.**	**2332**
Murray, George	Pte	52433
Murthwaite, Sydney	**Pte.**	**325168**
Naylor, Arthur	**Rmn**	**4011**
Neal, Thomas	Pte.	201627
Neal, Thomas	**Pte.**	**268260**
Needham, Ernest	**Pte.**	**18320**
Nelson, Albert	**Pte.**	**27509**
Nelson Ernest	**Pte.**	**51326**
Nelson, George	Pte.	200163
Nendick, Robert	**Pte.**	**235938**
Nettleton, Edward	Cpl	200285
Newby, Arthur	**Pte.**	**43415**
Newman, Leonard	**Pte.**	**202764**
Newsome, Charles	Pte.	200591
Newstead, K.	Sgt	
Newton, James		
Newton, Thomas	**Pte.**	**5487**
Nichols, Fred	**Pte.**	**171471**
Nichols, William	**Pte.**	**54884**
Nicholson, Arthur	**RSM**	**16/696**
Nicholson, Harry	Pte.	200750
Nicholson, John G.	CSM	2210/ 200583
Noble, Frank	**Pte.**	**306314**
Nolan, Gerald	**Pte.**	**51425**
Nolan, Rutherford	**L/Cpl**	**4/6643**
Norris, Fred	**Pte.**	**21521**
North, Edwin	Pte.	200155

Northrop, Herbert	Pte.	240697		Pickles, John William	L/Sgt.	200530
Norton, Harry	L/Cpl	202907		Pickles, Joseph	Sgt	1304
Oakes, Fred	Pte.	40285		Pickles, Joseph L.	Pte.	202769
Oddy, James Edwin	L/Cpl	200814		Pierce, John Hugh	Pte.	80114
Oddy, Joseph	Pte.	242199		Pinchen, John	L/Cpl	202816
Ogden, Halstead	Pte.	203390		Pinder, Harold	Pte	37617
Ogden, James				Pink, George	Pte.	1573
Ogden, John	Pte.	201590		Pintches, David	Pte.	52454
Oliver, John T.	Pte.	3537		Pipes, William	Pte.	200279
Oliver, Thomas P.	Pte.	200782		Plant, Albert Edward	Sgt	200075
Osbaldeston, Walter	Pte.	203960		Platt, Archibald T.	Pte.	54173
O'Shaughnessy, Amos	Pte	20734		Plows, Charles	Pte.	1252/
Otter, Frank	Pte.	57874				200089
Owen, Herbert	Pte.	2263/		Poe, W.A.	Pte.	24415
		200614		Polikoff, Isaac	Pte.	52456
Oxlade, Mathias W.	Sgt	200339		Pollitt, A.	Pte	59038
Paget, H.	Pte.	202967		Pook, Albert	Clr Sgt	137/
Park, Harry	Pte	57113				200009
Park, John	Pte	242802		Poppletonc, Frank	L/Cpl	201611
Parker, Edward	Pte	325210		Porter, Frank	L/Cpl	21953
Parker, Henry	Pte.	2338		Potter, Fred	Cpl	62500
Parker, James	Sgt	202348		Potts, Charles Norman	L/Cpl	200948
Parker, Richard	Pte.	267478		Potts, Leonard	Pte.	40076
Parker, S.	Pte	307536		Pound, Harold	Pte.	42806
Partridge, Herbert	Cpl	200708		Pounder, Alfred	L/Cpl	1707
Pascoe, N.	L/Cpl	5968		Pounder, George	Cpl	2205
Pattison, Harold	CSM	2226/		Powell, Fred	Pte.	200351
		200593		Pratt, Harold	Pte.	200228
Paylor, Luke	Pte.	200471		Pratt, John William	Pte.	210353
Payne, Fred	Pte	48805		Pratt, William	Pte.	200193
Payne, H	Pte.	54171		Precious, Percy Wilson	Pte.	200949
Peacock, Alec	Pte.	3259		Prendergast, Thomas	Pte.	54821
Peacock, Francis W.	Pte.	1477		Prest, John	Pte.	54488
Peake, Richard	Sgt	200618		Preston, Frederick V.	Sgt	200704
Pearson, John William	Pte.	201551		Price, Henry	Pte.	204338
Pearson, Dick	Pte.	202321		Priestley, William	Pte.	26132
Peet, George	Pte.	4621		Prout, Edward	Pte.	32619
Pennington, Frank	Pte.	1125/		Pryor, Harold	Pte.	3930
		200555		Pulleyn, William Peel	C/Sgt	200535
Penrose, Samuel	Pte.	1218		Purchase, Roy		
Petty, Ellis				Pybus, William H.	Pte.	1785
Pexton, James	L/Cpl	200749		Race, William	L/Cpl	15/1737
Pheasey, Ernest	Pte.	2340		Radband, Ernest T.	Cpl	201125
Pickard, Sidney	Pte.	41282		Radford, John	Pte.	200608
Pickard, Victor	Pte.	2780		Raftery, John	Sgt	2543/
Pickard,	W.					200789
Pickering, John Prince	Sgt	200021		Raine, Thomas	Pte.	200990
Pickles, George	Sgt	1320/		Ralston, Robert Allan	Pte.	200177
		200120		Ramsden, James F.	Pte.	5536
Pickles, Harry	Pte.	18/1288		Ramsey, Edward	Pte.	2431

Rands, Charles	**Pte.**	**202228**	**Robinson, James**	**Pte.**	**2458**
Rastrick, W.	Sgt	21/394	**Robinson, John Cheer**	**Pte.**	**1797**
Rathmell, Charles	Pte.	200364	**Robinson, Richard**	**Pte.**	**2330**
Raw, George	**L/Cpl**	**1154**	Robinson, William	Pte.	200831
Rawson, William W.	Pte.	201954	Robson, Arthur	Pte	235664
Rayner, Fred	**RSM**	**4713**	Robson, Castle	L/Cpl	200850
Rayner, W	Pte	13674	**Robson, John**	**Pte.**	**41095**
Reading, W	Pte	48805	**Rodgers, Stephen**	**Pte.**	**1763**
Reddin, William	**Pte.**	**265261**	**Rodgson, John**	**L/Cpl**	**240274**
Reddish, John Robert	Pte.	202320	Rodwell, Edgar Arthur	Pte.	201614
Reed, Harry	Pte.	200214	Rogers, Norman	L/Cpl	200726
Reed, John	**Pte.**	**235667**	**Ronksley, William**	**Pte.**	**79824**
Reed, Richard	Pte.	200988	**Rose, Samuel**	**Pte.**	**203030**
Regan, Arthur	**Pte.**	**266707**	Rothwell, Harry	Sgt	200123
Render, Harold	Pte.	200969	Rowland, Albert	Pte.	201609
Render, Richard	CQMS	816/	Rowling, Willie	Pte.	200816
		200033	**Royce, Stephen**	**Pte.**	**2145**
Rennie, Wallace S.	**L/Cpl**	**1777**	Ruddick, Frederick	L/Cpl	200388
Rennison, Fred	Pte.	201309	**Rumboldt, Charley**	**Pte.**	**203543**
Renshaw, Charles A.	Pte.	201085	Rushforth, John William	Pte.	200701
Reynard, Joseph	**Pte.**	**40312**	**Rushton, George**	**Pte.**	**201622**
Rhodes, Albert	Pte.	200091	**Rushworth, Albert**	**Pte.**	**21/22**
Rhodes, Henry	Sgt	200307	**Russell, Joseph**	**Pte.**	**200481**
Rhodes, Kenneth	**Pte.**	**26001**	Rutherford, Stanley	Pte.	200622
Richards, Albert	**Pte.**	**235665**	Ryde, Arthur	Pte.	200739
Richardson, Arthur H.	Sgt	200880	**Rymer, Horace**	**Pte.**	**2154**
Richardson, George R.	Sgt	200662	**Sabine, William E.**	**Pte.**	**32449**
Richardson, J.	Cpl	1441	Salisbury, William	Sgt	200085
Richardson, Jack	Pte.	201300	**Sandbrook, Bertram**	**Pte.**	**2095**
Richardson, James	Sgt	200179	Sands, Thomas A.	Pte	
Richardson, John	Pte.	200480	**Sanger, William**	**Pte.**	**66463**
Richardson, Norman	**Pte.**	**2930**	Sanofski, Israel	Pte.	202186
Richardson, Percy	Pte.	200728	**Sawbridge, George C.**	**L/Sgt.**	**33139**
Richardson, Roger	L/Cpl	200136	**Saynor, John**	**Pte.**	**41650**
Richmond, E.	Pte.		**Scaife, William**	**Pte.**	**200376**
Richmond, George	**Pte.**	**205286**	**Scaum, John H.**	**Pte.**	**201543**
Richmond, W.	Pte.		**Schofield, James**	**Pte.**	**201619**
Ridsdale, Frank	**Pte.**	**306273**	**Schofield, Walter B.**	**Pte.**	**235243**
Roberts, Walter	**Pte.**	**59068**	**Scott, Charles**	**Pte.**	**307394**
Roberts, William	Pte	265261	Scott, Ernest	Sgt	200017
Roberts, William B.	**Pte.**	**305484**	Scott, Ernest	Pte.	200068
Robertshaw, Fred	Pte.	202466	Scott, J.A.	Pte	54866
Robins, Joseph	**Pte.**	**205377**	Scott, Jesse	Sgt	200096
Robinson, Albert	Pte.	202773	**Scott, Thomas**	**Pte.**	**205238**
Robinson, Alfred	Pte.	200167	Scott, William Henry	Cpl	200642
Robinson ,Arthur	A/Sgt	200568	**Scurrah, Edgar**	**Pte.**	**28590**
Robinson, Charles	Pte.	200379	**Seal, Albert**	**Pte.**	**1838**
Robinson, Edward A.	**Pte.**	**2415**	**Secker, Wilfred**	**Pte.**	**202900**
Robinson, Ernest	**Pte.**	**6471**	**Sedgwick, Fred**	**L/Cpl**	**21/372**
Robinson, Harold	**Pte.**	**50578**			

Name	Rank	Number
Sefton, William	Pte.	1250/ 200088
Senior, Amos	Pte.	54899
Sergeant, John H.	L/Cpl	235669
Shann, Horace	Pte.	202149
Sharp, A.A.	Pte	230
Sharp, William	Pte.	1598
Sharpe, Alfred	Pte.	307735
Shaw, Fred	Pte.	203163
Shaw, Fred	Pte.	58972
Shaw, William Henry	Pte.	200235
Shepherd, Fred	Pte.	201355
Shepherd, Lawrence	Pte.	37681
Shepherd, W.	Pte.	202152
Shields, Horace	Sgt	200246
Shields, Percy	Pte.	200247
Shillito, Alfred	Pte.	37290
Shillito, Johnson W.	Pte.	200877
Sigsworth, Alfred	Sgt	200023
Sim, John Thomas	CSM	200014
Simmons, Hugh	Pte.	200826
Simmons, Sydney	Sgt	200076
Simpson, Arthur	Sgt	201051
Simpson, Charles	L/Cpl	2335
Simpson, Ernest	Pte.	200095
Simpson, George		
Simpson, Harold Guy	Pte.	200308
Simpson, Joseph S.	Pte.	200071
Skelton, Harry		
Skinner, George H.	Pte.	201090
Slack, Percy	Pte.	202778
Slee, Harold	Pte	
Smailes, John R.	Pte.	59071
Smallwood, Joseph	Pte.	200400
Smillie, Joseph	Pte.	6053
Smith, Alexander	Pte.	202822
Smith, C.	Pte.	3506
Smith, Ernest	Pte	300062
Smith, Frank	L/Cpl	200918
Smith, Harold	Pte.	42795
Smith, Harry	Pte.	201632
Smith, Harry	Pte.	205087
Smith, James	Cpl	200052
Smith, John W.	Sgt	2584
Smith, John William	Sgt	200819
Smith, Joseph		48235
Smith, Joseph R.G.	Pte.	48747
Smith, Leonard	Pte.	203180
Smith, Malcolm	L/Cpl	200333
Smith, Percy	Pte.	3829
Smith, Samuel	Pte.	201053
Smith, Thomas	L/Cpl	236444
Smith, William	L/Cpl	1599
Smith, W.J.	Pte	59072
Smithers, Gilbert	L/Cpl	200038
Smithson, Herbert	Pte.	36476
Smithson, Thomas E	Pte.	201302
Snow, Fred	Pte.	18/24
Snowden, James		
Snowden, Robert		
Souter, Joseph	Pte.	58978
Southwell, Edward	Pte.	20813
Sowden, Leonard	Pte.	58973
Sowden, Tom	L/Cpl	306388
Sowerby, Charles B.	Pte.	66478
Spendley, Fred	Pte.	201052
Spinks, William	Pte.	2677
Squires, George Donald	Pte.	200890
Squires, Mark	Cpl	200653
Stacey, John Henry	Pte.	201536
Stafford, Willie	Pte.	201596
Stairmand, Ernest W.	Pte.	20666
Stamp, R.M.	Pte	
Stead, Edwin P	Pte.	40296
Stead, Frank	Pte.	2261
Stead, Leonard	Pte.	1726/ 200326
Stead, Thomas	Pte.	21/279
Steel, George		
Steel, Harry		
Steer, Joseph	Pte	47179
Stembridge, Eli	A/Sgt	200292
Stephenson, George	Pte.	59073
Stevens, Sidney Henry	L/Sgt.	200724
Stewart, Charles	Pte.	201407
Stewart, Charles	Pte.	305211
Stewart, J.		
Stimpson, Walter	L/Sgt.	201489
Stockdale, Norman	Pte.	200784
Stockell, James	Pte.	59018
Stokes, Martin	Pte.	5873
Stone, Charles	Pte.	201545
Stones, Herbert	Cpl	211751
Storey, Harry	Sgt	200331
Storey, J	Pte	
Storey, T.H.		
Stott, Louis Alexander	Pte.	200553
Stout, John W.	Sgt	235609
Street, Arthur	Pte.	3810
Strudwick, Harry J.	Sgt	6503

Stubbs	Pte			**Thirkell, Alfred**	Pte.	**202555**
Sturdy				**Thomas, Joseph W.**	Pte.	**203555**
Sunderland, Wilfred	Pte.	200812		Thompson, Edwin	Pte.	200291
Sunley, James	**Pte.**	**3704**		Thompson, George	Pte.	200168
Surbuts, Ernest	**Pte.**	**203259**		**Thompson, George R.**	**L/Cpl**	**1239**
Sutcliffe, Thomas	**Pte.**	**202486**		Thompson, Harry	Pte.	200150
Sutcliffe, William	Cpl	201378		**Thompson, Harry**	**Pte.**	**201260**
Suter, Walter	Cpl	200542		**Thompson, Herbert**	**Pte.**	**17/669**
Swaine, Mellin	**Pte.**	**21/715**		Thompson, John W.	Sgt	200049
Swaine, Willie	Pte	240394		**Thompson, Leonard**	**Pte.**	**42808**
Swale, Charles L.	**Pte.**	**202281**		**Thompson, Thomas W.**	**Pte.**	**202335**
Swales, John	**Pte.**	**1800/**		Thompson, William	Pte.	201253
		200424		Thompson, William	L/Cpl	200119
Swales, Leonard	**Pte.**	**3638**		**Thompson, William H.**	**Pte.**	**12872**
Swales, Thomas	Pte.	200592		**Thomson, Peter**	**Pte.**	**13971**
Swallow, Frederick	Pte.	201267		Thornhill, R.	Sgt	203143
Swan, H.F.	Pte			**Thornton, Alfred H.**	**Pte.**	**2693**
Swann, Charles Robert	Pte.	200149		**Thornton, William**	**Pte.**	**202304**
Swires, Edwin	**Pte.**	**1735/**		Thorpe, Benjamin	Pte.	200632
		200332		**Thundercliffe, Henry F.**	**Pte.**	**203120**
Sykes, Clifford	Pte.	201621		**Tiffney, Edwin**	**Pte.**	**201031**
Sykes, Harold	**Pte.**	**25889**		**Timmins, George**	**Pte.**	**1336**
Sykes, J.W.	Pte	58976		Timmins, Herbert		
Sykes, Thomas	A/CSM	200668		Tindill, Parr	L/Cpl	201637
Talbot, Wilfred V.	**Pte.**	**62581**		**Tindle, John W.**	**Pte.**	**203367**
Tasker, Harry	Sgt	200240		Tinsdeall, C.	Pte	59020
Tate, Dennis	**Pte.**	**2285**		Tipling, Joseph	A/L/Sgt	200698
Tattersfield, Edwin C.	Sgt	200678		Toas, Syd Charles	Cpl	200674
Tattershall, Albert	Sgt	200664		Todd, George Leslie	Cpl	200560
Tattershall, Robert	Pte.	200641		Todd, James	Pte.	200790
Tatterton, Alfred	Cpl	200383		**Todd, William S.**	**Pte.**	**53601**
Taylor, Albert	**Pte.**	**49038**		Toft, Arthur	Pte.	201209
Taylor, Charles Harold	Pte.	200173		Toft, Uriah Johnson	Pte.	201530
Taylor, Daniel	**Pte.**	**52756**		Tolley, G.	Sgt	1161
Taylor, Ernest	**L/Cpl**	**265400**		**Tolley, William H.**	**L/Cpl**	**202916**
Taylor, Harold	**Pte.**	**37136**		**Tolmie, George**	**Pte.**	**20/248**
Taylor, John James	Cpl	201890		Tomes, Richard	Pte.	200658
Taylor, Joseph	**Pte.**	**3253**		Tomlinson, F.	ACPL	238024/
Taylor, J.T.	Pte	307237				130953
Taylor, Kenneth	**Pte.**	**60550**		**Topham, Christopher**	**CSM**	**1388/**
Taylor, Richard N.	Pte.	200101				**200156**
Taylor, Robert	Pte.	200222		Topham, Lawrence	Pte.	200160
Taylor, Samuel	**Pte.**	**202780**		**Townend, Albert**	**Pte.**	**2403**
Taylor, Stephen	**Pte.**	**58936**		Towse, A.		
Taylor, Tom Angus	Pte.	200913		Triffitt, Norman	Pte.	201459
Teale, Frank	Pte.	200638		**Triffitt, Thomas**	**Pte.**	**2469**
Terry, Frederick	**Sgt**	**2503**		Trousdale, L.	Pte.	1709
Tetley, Thomas	**Pte.**	**205359**		Trowsdale, Leslie	Pte.	200315
Thackery, Thomas H.	Pte.	200328		**Trumble, Bernard F.**	**L/Cpl**	**66489**
Thackwray, Joe	Pte.	200182		Tuley, Edwin	Sgt	200766

Tunnicliffe, Ernest	Pte.	19844	Walshaw, Seth H.	L/Cpl	16/1722
Tuppen, Alexander D.	Cpl	1284	Ward, Francis E.	Cpl	3482
Turner, Harry G.	L/Cpl	203121	Wardle, Joseph H.	Pte.	201571
Tute, Richard	Pte.	1252	Wargent, Frank	Pte.	200741
Twineham, C.	Pte.	3201/	Warhurst, Ernest	Pte.	16/186
		201221	Waring, Harry	Pte.	1740
Tyson, Arthur	Pte.	202175	Watsham, Edmund	Pte.	200213
Urquhart, Thomas	L/Cpl	202813	Watson, Allan W.	Pte.	307246
Usher, H.	Pte.	2168	Watson, John R.	Sgt	202431
Uttley, A.E.A.	Pte.	202714	Watson, Thomas	Pte.	2645
Varey, Norman	CSM	200558	Watson, W.	Pte.	240888
Varley, George	Pte.	200588	Watt, John Francis	L/Cpl	200663
Vast, Charles	Pte.	203549	Watts, Isaac	Pte.	203431/
Vause, Charles	L/Cpl	201476			203129
Veal, Leo	CSM	200715	Watts, William	Pte.	42783
Vear, Thomas	Pte.	200513	Waudby, John Thomas	Pte.	200620
Vickerman, John S.	Pte.	58937	Waugh, Adam W.	Pte.	27459
Waddington, Harry	Sgt	200359	Weatherhead, Arthur	L/Cpl	200516
Waddington, Harold	Pte.	201160	Weatherill, Gilbert	Sgt	200765
Waddington, Norman H	A/Sgt	200185	Webster, Frank	Pte.	2141
Wailes, Gilbert	Pte.	5877	Webster, George	Pte.	59700
Wain, Ernest	Sgt	1302	Wegg, Richard	Pte.	32230
Waind, William F.	Pte.	200271	Welch, Luke Herbert	C/Sgt	200276
Wain, John R.	Pte.	1662	Wellington, H.H.	Cpl	66507
Wainman, George W.	Pte.	200420	Wells, Charles W.	Pte.	1842
Wainwright, Ernest	L/Cpl	200111	West, Edmund	Pte	202943
Waite, Clarke	Sgt	200152	West, Harry	Pte.	1611
Waite, Wilson	L/Cpl	5540	West, Thomas	Pte.	202151
Walder, Peter	Pte.	200396	Westerman, Alfred	L/Cpl	200169
Walker, Alan	Cpl	2252	Westerman, Harry	Sgt	1816/
Walker, Ernest	Pte.	1490			200384
Walker, Frederick	Pte.	201849	Wetherill, Henry	L/Cpl	2489
Walker, Frederick G.	Cpl	864	Wetherill, John	Pte.	1854
Walker, Frederick W.	Pte.	201365	Wharton, Fred	Pte.	201454
Walker, George	A/C/Sgt	200744	Wharton, Fred Percy	L/Cpl	11623
Walker, Henry	Pte.	1737	Wheeldon, Joseph	Pte.	21/92119
Walker, Herbert	Pte.	202915	Wheeler, H.T.	Pte.	203877
Walker, Herbert	L/Cpl	202915	Whelan, John	Pte.	42810
Walker, Herbert Scott	Pte.	201600	Whincup, Thomas	Pte.	201289
Walker, John Robert	Pte.	201092	Whinn, Joseph Daniel P.	C/Sgt	200065
Walker, John William	Pte.	200176	White, Albert	Pte.	48043
Walker, Leonard	Pte.	202971	White,Charles	Pte.	201097
Walker, Lister W.	Sgt	203609	White, James A.	Pte.	1242
Walker, Percy	Pte.	205107	White, Wilfred	Pte.	42593
Walker, Thomas	Pte.	2360	Whitehead, Tom	Pte.	22965
Walker Thomas G.	Pte.	33038	Whiteley, Joseph	L/Cpl	306521
Walker, Wilfred	Pte	202972	Whitfield, Albert E.	Pte.	1608
Walker, Willie	Cpl	200566	Whitlam, Christopher J.	Sgt	200561
Walls, Percy	Sgt	200110	Whittaker, Thomas	L/Cpl	235611
Walsh, William	Pte.	21/790	Whittington, Percy	Pte.	201576

Name	Rank	Number
Whittle, Walter		
Whitwell, Ernest Alfred	A/Cpl	201502
Wilcock, Henry	**Pte.**	**2355**
Wilcockson, William	Pte.	200697
Wilde, Arthur H.	**Pte.**	**2424**
Wildgoose, Alfred	**Pte.**	**57120**
Wilkins, William	Pte.	201331
Wilkinson, Guy	Cpl	
Wilkinson, Leonard	Pte	307684
Wilkinson, William	**Cpl**	**200170**
Wilkinson, William H.	**Pte.**	**39638**
Williams, Evan P.	**Pte.**	**203037**
Williamson, Frank	Pte.	200677
Willis, Arthur	Sgt	200610
Wills, Ira	Pte.	200735
Wilmot, Robert	**Pte.**	**1330**
Wilson, Albert	Pte.	4923
Wilson, Albert	**Pte.**	**202292**
Wilson, Alexander M.	Pte.	200348
Wilson, Frank	Cpl	201251
Wilson, George Andrew	Pte.	200925
Wilson, George F.	**Pte.**	**3332**
Wilson, H.	L/Cpl	201172
Wilson, Harold	Pte.	201172
Wilson, Henry B.	**Pte.**	**266499**
Wilson, James	**Pte.**	**18994**
Wilson, John	Pte.	201642
Wilson, JW	Pte.	203134
Wilson, Richard	**Pte.**	**2466**
Wilson, Robert	**Sgt**	**5537**
Wilson Samuel	**L/Cpl**	**201602**
Wilson, T.	Sgt	202817
Wilson, William Henry	Pte.	201254
Wilson, William N.	**Pte.**	**202693**
Wilson, William W.	**Pte.**	**5892**
Wilton, Charles	Pte.	200164
Windass, Eric William	Pte.	200572
Winter, George W.	**Sgt**	**200576**
Winter, Joseph	**Pte.**	**205155**
Winterbottom, Austin	**Pte.**	**201420**
Winterburn, Charles	L/Cpl	200172
Wisbey		
Withers, Samuel	**L/Cpl**	**27672**
Witty, Frederick	Pte.	201026
Wood, Harry	Pte.	200174
Wood, James Robert	**Pte.**	**2664**
Wood, Joseph	**Pte.**	**240796**
Wood, Joseph Norman	Pte.	200637
Wood, Robert	Pte.	200862
Wood, William	**CSM**	**31871**
Wood, William Ewart	L/Cpl	200626
Woodhead, John	Pte.	201577
Wooler, Ernest	Pte	202904
Worth, Harold	**Pte.**	**3857**
Wrather, Joseph	**Pte.**	**200843**
Wray, Harold	**Pte.**	**2967**
Wray, John James	Pte.	200769
Wrigglesworth, Maurice	Pte.	200227
Wright, Arthur	**Pte.**	**267847**
Wright, Ernest	**Pte.**	**205117**
Wright, F.	Cpl.	305504
Wright, George	Sgt	200387
Wright, Harold	**Pte.**	**202285**
Wright, Henry	Sgt	201257
Wright, Percy	**Pte.**	**21/470**
Wright, Robert	**Pte.**	**307653**
Wright, Tom	Cpl	200792
Wye, George W.	**Pte.**	**59687**
Yates, Francis C.	**Pte.**	**2093**
Yeadon, John A.	L/Cpl	200087
Yeldham, Edgar C.	**Pte.**	**20948**
Yeoward, D.	L/Cpl	240494
Young, Henry	A/Sgt	200884
Young, Stanley	**Pte.**	**201007**

Appendix 3

Combined Roll of Honour

The following 831 officers and men of the 1/5th Battalion West Yorkshire Regiment lost their lives on active service 1915-1919:

Abbott, James	Pte.	13/11/17	Lijssenthoek Military Cemetery
Abrams, Ernest	Pte.	05/09/15	Essex Farm Cemetery
Addy, Edgar	Pte.	13/10/18	Niederzwehren Cemetery, Kassel
Adkin, Jesse	L/Cpl	25/04/18	Tyne Cot Memorial
Airey, Henry W.S.	2/Lt	11/01/17	De Cusine Ravine British Cemetery, Basseux
Alcock, William	Pte.	29/07/18	Sissonne British Cemetery
Alden, Thomas	Pte.	13/10/18	York Cemetery, Haspres
Allen, Matthew	Pte.	30/10/18	Valenciennes (St Roch) Communal Cemetery
Altoft, Fred	Pte.	27/06/18	Berlin South-Western Cemetery
Anderson, Robert W.	CSM	18/10/16	Puchevillers British Cemetery
Anderson, Thomas H.	Pte.	28/09/16	Thiepval Memorial
Andrews, John M.	L/Cpl	28/09/16	Thiepval Memorial
Appleyard, John Wm	Pte.	18/07/18	Hamburg Cemetery
Archer, Wilfred	Pte.	01/11/18	Auberchicourt British Cemetery
Armitage, Frank	Pte.	28/09/16	Connaught Cemetery, Thiepval
Armitage, Harry	Pte.	09/10/17	Tyne Cot Memorial
Ashby, Alfred	Pte.	05/11/18	Berlin South-Western Cemetery
Atkinson, James	Sgt	18/11/15	Essex Farm Cemetery
Atkinson, Robert	Pte.	25/04/18	Tyne Cot Memorial
Backhouse, Alfred	Cpl	09/10/17	Tyne Cot Memorial
Bailes, Albert	L/ Sgt	01/11/17	Aulnoy Communal Cemetery
Baines, Albert	Pte.	10/10/17	Tyne Cot Memorial
Baines, Benjamin	Pte.	27/12/15	Lijssenthoek Military Cemetery
Baines, Percy	L/Cpl	09/10/17	Tyne Cot Memorial
Baker, Edward A	Cpl	05/08/15	Ypres (Menin Gate) Memorial
Baker, Frederick	Pte.	11/10/18	Vis-en-Artois Memorial
Balmforth, J.	L/Cpl	26/07/17	Coxyde Military Cemetery
Bamford, John M.	Pte.	28/09/16	Thiepval Memorial
Barber, Henry	L/Cpl	04/09/16	Contay British Cemetery, Contay
Barker, Edward	Pte.	03/09/16	Thiepval Memorial

Barlow, Frank	Pte.	04/07/17	Estaires Communal Cemetery and Extension
Barnes, Fred	Pte.	28/07/16	Blighty Valley Cemetery, Authuille Wood
Barraclough, William	2/Lt	28/09/16	Mill Road Cemetery, Thiepval
Barrett, Robert	Cpl	28/08/16	Hamel Military Cemetery, Beaumont-Hamel
Barrett, Thomas	Pte.	11/12/18	Hautmont Communal Cemetery
Barron, James W.	L/Cpl	03/09/16	Thiepval Memorial
Barron, Wilfred	L/Cpl	22/04/18	Tyne Cot Memorial
Barton, Fred	L/Cpl	25/04/18	Tyne Cot Memorial
Barwood, Edward C.	Pte.	13/04/18	Tyne Cot Memorial
Baslington, James	Pte.	25/04/18	Tyne Cot Memorial
Bates, Harry	L/ Sgt	25/04/18	Sanctuary Wood Cemetery
Bates, William	Pte.	25/04/18	Tyne Cot Memorial
Bateson, James T.	Pte.	25/04/18	Tyne Cot Memorial
Batters, Sydney H	L/ Sgt	09/05/15	Fauquissart Military Cemetery, Laventie
Baxter, George W	Pte.	21/04/18	Reninghelst New Military Cemetery
Bean, Fred	Pte.	31/07/15	Lijssenthoek Military Cemetery
Bean, Philip	Pte.	14/04/18	Bailleul Communal Cemetery Extension, Nord
Bedell, Ernest	L/Cpl	18/12/15	Wimereux Communal Cemetery
Beech, Norman W.	2/Lt	09/10/17	Tyne Cot Memorial
Belcher, Richard	Pte.	22/04/18	Wytschaete Military Cemetery
Bell, Jonathan W.	Pte.	09/10/17	Tyne Cot Memorial
Benn, Tom	Pte.	28/07/17	Coxyde Military Cemetery
Bennett Harry	Pte.	18/09/17	Canada Farm Cemetery
Bennett, Henry	Pte.	03/09/16	Thiepval Memorial
Benson, William J.	Pte.	04/11/18	Dewsbury Cemetery
Bent James C.	Pte.	22/04/18	Tyne Cot Memorial
Bentley, Wilfred	Pte.	29/09/16	Puchevillers British Cemetery
Bickerdike, George	Pte.	28/09/16	Thiepval Memorial
Binks, George	Pte.	09/10/17	Tyne Cot Memorial
Birkbeck, Sidney W.	2/Lt	09/10/17	Tyne Cot Memorial
Bishop, Charles	Pte.	13/07/15	Ypres (Menin Gate) Memorial
Black, John	L/Cpl	11/01/17	Warlincourt Halte British Cemetery, Saulty
Blackburn, Frank H.	L/Cpl	05/12/18	York Cemetery, Yorkshire
Blackwell, Griffith A.	Pte.	10/10/17	Tyne Cot Memorial
Blanshard, Herbert S.	Pte.	13/05/18	Larch Wood (Railway Cutting) Cemetery

Boldison, Arthur	L/Sgt	14/07/16	Authuille Military Cemetery
Bonnett, Harry	Pte.	03/09/16	Thiepval Memorial
Booth, Albert	Pte.	24/07/17	Coxyde Military Cemetery
Booth, William	Pte.	14/04/18	Boulogne Eastern Cemetery
Boothman, Albert	Pte.	15/07/16	Authuille Military Cemetery
Bootham, William	Pte.	28/09/16	Mill Road Cemetery, Thiepval
Borrows, John R.	Pte.	01/07/16	Thiepval Memorial
Bowen, Edward	Pte.	25/04/18	Tyne Cot Memorial
Bowman, Arthur	Pte.	25/04/18	Tyne Cot Memorial
Bowman, Robert	Pte.	25/04/18	Tyne Cot Memorial
Boynton, John E.	Pte.	30/07/17	Mont Huon Military Cemetery, Le Treport
Bracewell, Leonard L.	Pte.	29/12/15	Ypres (Menin Gate) Memorial
Bradbroo,k William J.	Pte.	16/10/18	Ramillies British Cemetery
Bradley, George A.	Pte.	03/09/16	Mill Road Cemetery, Thiepval
Bradley, Horace F.B.	Pte.	21/07/15	Ypres (Menin Gate) Memorial
Bradley, Sidney	Pte.	05/07/16	Warley-Baillon Communal Cemetery Extension
Braithwaite, James E.	Pte.	04/10/16	Wimereux Communal Cemetery
Brimacombe, James E.	Pte.	01/11/18	Famars Communal Cemetery Extension
Broadbent, Fred	Pte.	12/01/17	Warlincourt Halte British Cemetery, Saulty
Broadbent, Hugh	Pte.	14/11/15	Essex Farm Cemetery
Broader, Robert K.	Pte.	15/07/16	Authuille Military Cemetery
Broadhurst, William E.	Pte.	23/02/18	Tyne Cot Memorial
Brodrick, Anthony	Pte.	25/04/18	Tyne Cot Memorial
Brogden, John Wm	Pte.	01/11/18	Auberchicourt British Cemetery
Brook, Arthur	Pte.	25/04/18	La Laiterie Military Cemetery
Brook, Arthur	Pte.	09/10/17	Tyne Cot Memorial
Brook, James	Pte.	23/09/18	Vis-en-Artois Memorial
Brook, Leonard	Pte.	17/04/18	Tyne Cot Memorial
Brookes, William H.	Pte.	16/09/18	Poznan Old Garrison Cemetery
Broomfield, Harold	Pte.	09/10/17	Tyne Cot Memorial
Brown, Bernard	Pte	27/09/16	Thiepval Memorial
Brown, Ernest	Pte.	28/08/16	Thiepval Memorial
Brown, John	Pte.	10/07/15	Ypres (Menin Gate) Memorial
Brown, John F.	L/Cpl	18/11/17	Lijssenthoek Military Cemetery
Brown, Thomas J.	Sgt	14/10/17	Nine Elms British Cemetery
Brownbridge George A.	Pte.	28/07/17	Mont Huon Military Cemetery, Le Tréport
Buck, William	Pte.	01/11/18	Auberchicourt British Cemetery
Buckborrough, Edwin	Pte.	20/12/15	Lijssenthoek Military Cemetery

Buckle, Leonard	L/Cpl	03/09/16	Connaught Cemetery, Thiepval
Buckle, Thomas H.	Pte.	06/12/15	Selby Cemetery
Burks, William	Pte.	11/01/17	De Cusine Ravine British Cemetery, Basseux
Buller, William	Pte.	15/07/16	Thiepval Memorial
Bullock, Herbert	Pte.	01/07/16	Connaught Cemetery, Thiepval
Burrows, Oates	Pte.	31/05/17	Laventie Military Cemetery, La Gorgue
Burton, Alfred	Pte.	25/04/18	Tyne Cot Memorial
Butcher, Frederick	Pte.	13/10/18	York Cemetery, Haspres
Butler, Benjamin	Pte.	18/02/19	Ripon Cemetery
Butterfield, Horace	L/Cpl	02/11/18	Thiant Communal Cemetery
Butterick, Thomas W.	Pte.	31/07/18	Terlincthun British Cemetery, Wimille
Caddick, William	Pte.	24/05/18	Ghent City Cemetery
Cahill, James	Pte.	19/12/15	Essex Farm Cemetery
Cahill, Joseph	Cpl	18/06/15	Le Trou Aid Post Cemetery, Fleurbaix
Calpin, James	Pte.	28/09/16	Thiepval Memorial
Calverley, Arthur	Sgt	09/10/17	Tyne Cot Memorial
Calvert, Herbert	Pte.	02/08/15	Ypres (Menin Gate) Memorial
Calvert, Raymond	Pte.	25/04/18	Sanctuary Wood Cemetery
Cannon, William F.	Pte.	26/07/17	Mont Huon Military Cemetery, Le Tréport
Capps, Robert	Pte.	03/05/17	Loos Memorial
Carney, Thomas	Pte.	05/09/16	Forceville Communal Cemetery and Extension
Carr, William	Pte.	25/04/18	Tyne Cot Memorial
Carrack, Herbert	Pte.	28/09/16	Mill Road Cemetery, Thiepval
Carslake, George	Pte.	15/07/16	Authuille Military Cemetery
Carter, Albert N.	Pte.	09/10/17	Poelcapelle British Cemetery
Carter, Arthur	Pte.	13/11/10/18	Vis-en-Artois Memorial
Carter, Joseph	Pte.	28/09/16	Connaught Cemetery, Thiepval
Cartmel, George M.	Pte.	24/12/15	Essex Farm Cemetery
Carver, Robert W.	Pte.	03/07/16	Mill Road Cemetery, Thiepval
Cassells, Andrew	Pte.	09/10/17	Tyne Cot Memorial
Castle, John G.	Pte.	21/07/15	Ypres (Menin Gate) Memorial
Chadwick, George H.	Cpl	09/10/17	Tyne Cot Memorial
Chadwick, William	Pte.	25/04/18	Tyne Cot Memorial
Chapelow, Charles H.	Pte.	09/07/16	Thiepval Memorial
Chapman, Amos	Pte.	30/04/18	Pont-du-Hem Military Cemetery, La Gorgue
Chappell, Herbert T.	Pte.	13/10/18	Vis-en-Artois Memorial

Childs, Arthur G.	Pte.	01/11/18	Auberchicourt British Cemetery
Christon, Norman	Pte.	09/10/17	Dochy Farm New British Cemetery
Christopherson, John T.	Pte.	01/11/18	Aulnoy Communal Cemetery
Clark, Alfred	Pte.	27/01/16	Étaples Military Cemetery
Clark, Henry	Pte.	15/07/16	Authuille Military Cemetery
Clark, Thomas A.	Pte.	24/11/17	Yeadon Cemetery
Clarke, Archibald T.	Pte.	23/04/18	Mendinghem Military Cemetery
Clarke, Ernest	Pte.	16/07/18	Tourcoing (Pont-Neuville) Communal Cemetery
Clarke, Fred	Pte.	09/10/17	Poelcapelle British Cemetery
Clarke, Victor J.	Pte.	25/04/18	Tyne Cot Memorial
Clarkson, Frank	Pte.	09/10/17	Tyne Cot Memorial
Cleghorn, Ernest	Pte.	30/07/17	Longuenesse (St Omer) Souvenir Cemetery
Coates, James	Pte.	04/11/18	Cambrai East Military Cemetery
Coate, Joseph	Pte.	25/04/18	Tyne Cot Memorial
Cockerline, Ernest	Pte.	11/10/18	Vis-en-Artois Memorial
Codd, William	Pte.	10/07/17	Laventie Military Cemetery, La Gorgue
Coe, Frederick W.	Pte.	12/10/18	Naves Communal Cemetery Extension
Coghill, Herbert	Pte.	31/10/18	Étaples Military Cemetery
Coleman, Thomas	Pte.	22/06/15	Sailly-sur-la-Lys Canadian Cemetery
Coles, Maurice	L/Cpl	26/07/17	Coxyde Military Cemetery
Collins, William	Pte.	27/04/18	Harlebeke New British Cemetery
Coltman, Robert	Pte.	28/04/18	Birtley (St John's) Churchyard
Connell, Gilbert	Pte.	21/07/15	Ypres (Menin Gate) Memorial
Cook, William H.	Pte.	09/10/17	Tyne Cot Memorial
Cooper, Harold	L/Cpl	24/10/18	Étaples Military Cemetery
Cordingly, Harry	Pte.	01/11/18	Vis-en-Artois Memorial
Cotton, George	Pte.	13/10/18	Naves Communal Cemetery Extension
Cousins, Robert	Pte.	20/12/15	Hospital Farm Cemetery
Cox, Herbert	Pte.	25/04/18	Tyne Cot Memorial
Crabtree, Allan	Pte.	28/04/18	Pont-du-Hem Military Cemetery, La Gorgue
Craven, Arthur	Pte.	07/07/17	Mont Huon Military Cemetery, Le Tréport
Crawford, William	Pte.	25/04/18	Tyne Cot Memorial
Crofts, Alfred	Pte.	20/07/16	Thiepval Memorial
Crosby, Tom	Pte.	15/04/17	Laventie Military Cemetery, La Gorgue

Crossland, Samuel	Pte.	09/10/17	Tyne Cot Memorial
Crossley, Joseph	Pte.	05/04/17	Laventie Military Cemetery, La Gorgue
Crow, Herbert S.	Pte.	03/09/16	Thiepval Memorial
Crowe, Cyril D.	Pte.	03/01/17	Leeds (Beeston) Cemetery
Crowe, Gilbert B.	Pte.	03/09/16	Connaught Cemetery, Thiepval
Crowehurst, Arthur	Pte.	30/10/18	Valenciennes (St Roch) Communal Cemetery
Crowther, Russell E.	Pte.	25/04/18	Sanctuary Wood Cemetery
Crust, William	L/Cpl	03/09/16	Thiepval Memorial
Cunningham, Herbert	Pte.	23/09/18	Vis-en-Artois Memorial
Currell, James	Pte.	10/07/16	Warloy-Baillon Communal Cemetery Extesion
Curtis, William	Pte.	13/04/18	Tyne Cot Memorial
Cussins, Cecil	Pte.	20/07/16	Thiepval Memorial
Cutler, Joseph	Pte.	09/07/16	Thiepval Memorial
Cutt, William	Pte.	25/04/18	Tyne Cot Memorial
Dack, William	Pte.	19/12/17	Dochy Farm New British Cemetery
Dalby, Alfred	Pte.	20/02/16	Thiepval Memorial
Dalby, John	Pte.	01/11/18	Vis-en-Artois Memorial
Dale, Albert	Pte.	24/11/17	Lijssenthoek Military Cemetery
Daniel, Robert	Pte.	19/12/15	Essex Farm Cemetery
Darnbrough, John	Pte.	25/04/18	Bedford House Cemetery
Davies, Edward	Pte.	03/09/16	Thiepval Memorial
Davies, Owen P.	Pte.	22/04/18	Tyne Cot Memorial
Dawes, Frederick	Pte.	15/07/16	Bouzincourt Communal Cemetery Extension
Dawson, Walter	Pte.	20/12/15	Wimereux Communal Cemetery
Dawson, Fred	L/Cpl	28/09/16	Bray Vale British Cemetery, Bray-Sur-Somme
Day, Arnold E	L/Cpl	13/07/15	Ypres (Menin Gate) Memorial
Dean, Leonard	Pte.	09/10/17	Tyne Cot Memorial
Deans, Harold	Pte.	05/08/15	Ypres (Menin Gate) Memorial
Delaney, Thomas	Pte.	25/04/18	Tyne Cot Memorial
DeMersy, Daniel	Pte.	03/09/16	Thiepval Memorial
Denning, Albert	Pte.	13/10/18	York Cemetery, Haspres
Denton, Harry	Pte.	17/11/17	Tyne Cot Memorial
Dewhirst, George F.	Pte.	23/04/18	Haringhe (Bandaghem) Military Cemetery
Dickinson, Bernard	Pte.	25/04/18	Tyne Cot Memorial
Dixon, Albert	Pte.	09/10/17	Tyne Cot Memorial
Dixon, Edward	Pte.	28/09/16	Connaught Cemetery, Thiepval
Dixon, Nicholas	Pte.	29/10/17	Wimereux Communal Cemetery

Dobson, Joseph	Pte.	11/01/17	Étaples Military Cemetery
Doherty, Arnold	Pte.	24/07/17	Mont Huon Military Cemetery, Le Treport
Dormand, Alfred	L/Cpl	18/09/16	Varennes Military Cemetery
Downey, Albert	Pte.	09/10/17	White House Cemetery, St Jean-Les-Ypres
Drake, William H.	Pte.	27/10/18	St Sever Cemetery Extension, Rouen
Draper, Arthur	Pte.	10/10/17	White House Cemetery, St Jean-Les-Ypres
Drury, Frederick	Pte.	23/09/18	Vis-en-Artois Memorial
Drury, James	Pte.	15/11/15	Essex Farm Cemetery
Dryden, William	Cpl	09/10/17	Tyne Cot Memorial
Duffett, Harry	Pte.	14/05/18	Niederzwehren Cemetery, Kassel
Dufton, William	Pte.	22/03/17	Laventie Military Cemetery, La Gorgue
Dunn, Frank	Pte.	03/09/16	Thiepval Memorial
Duxfield, Ferrie	Pte.	26/07/17	Longuenesse (St Omer) Souvenir Cemetery
Dykes, George	Pte.	01/11/18	Vis-en-Artois Memorial
Dyson, Harry	L/Cpl	25/04/18	Sanctuary Wood Cemetery
Dyson, Rufus A.	Pte.	09/10/17	Tyne Cot Memorial
Eastwood, George A.	Sgt	12/10/18	York Cemetery, Haspres
Ellis, Edwin	Pte.	25/04/18	Tyne Cot Memorial
Elsworth, Fred	Cpl	09/10/17	Tyne Cot Memorial
Elsworth, George	Cpl	20/06/15	Estaires Communal Cemetery and Extension
Elsworth, Samuel	Pte.	03/09/16	Serre Road Cemetery No.2.
Elsworth, Seth	Pte.	17/04/18	Tyne Cot Memorial
Elton, Walter	Pte.	09/01/17	De Cusine Ravine British Cemetery, Basseux
Emanuel, Albert	Pte.	30/09/18	Glageon Communal Cemetery Extension
Evans, George H.C.	Pte.	25/04/18	Tyne Cot Memorial
Evans, Ronald	Pte.	09/10/17	Tyne Cot Memorial
Exelby, George H.	Pte.	19/05/15	Rue-Petillon Military Cemetery, Fleubaix
Exelby, John H.	CSM	01/10/16	Puchevillers British Cemetery
Fairburn, Fred	Pte.	09/10/17	Tyne Cot Memorial
Fairburn, Wilfred	Pte.	15/07/16	Authuille Military Cemetery
Fareham, Frank	Pte.	03/04/18	Menin Road South Military Cemetery
Farmery, Frederick E.	Pte.	15/10/16	Ste. Marie Cemetery, Le Havre

Fear, Edmond A.	Pte.	11/10/18	Vis-en-Artois Memorial
Fee, James	Pte.	30/10/18	Famars Communal Cemetery Extension
Fenton, John W.	Pte.	03/09/16	Thiepval Memorial
Ferguson, William	Cpl	07/01/16	Boulogne Eastern Cemetery
Field, Harold	Pte.	27/05/15	Estaires Communal Cemetery and Extension
Firth, Charles R.	2/Lt	09/11/18	Niederzwehren Cemetery, Kassel
Fisher, George M.	Pte.	26/10/18	Glageon Communal Cemetery Extension
Fletcher, Howard	L/Cpl	25/04/18	Sanctuary Wood Cemetery
Flint, James	Pte.	03/09/16	Thiepval Memorial
Flynn, Robert	Pte.	01/11/18	Auberchicourt British Cemetery
Forster, John	Pte.	12/10/18	York Cemetery, Haspres
Foster, Arthur	Pte.	03/09/16	Mill Road Cemetery, Thiepval
Foster, Arthur	Pte.	12/10/18	Perreuse Chateau Franco British Cemetery
Foster, Charles E.	Pte.	12/10/18	Vis-en-Artois Memorial
Fox, Walter	Pte.	28/09/16	Mill Road Cemetery, Thiepval
Francis, Thomas	Pte.	03/07/16	Thiepval Memorial
Francis, Frank H.	Pte.	19/12/17	Potijze Chateau Grounds Cemetery
Frankland, Robert	Pte.	14/04/18	Bailleul Communal Cemetery Extension, Nord
Franks, Walter F.	Pte.	11/01/17	De Cusine Ravine British Cemetery, Basseux
Fraser, John T.	Pte.	20/07/15	Ypres (Menin Gate) Memorial
Freeman, Walter	Pte.	09/10/17	Tyne Cot Memorial
French, Charles	Pte.	03/05/18	Tyne Cot Memorial
Frith, William	Pte.	25/04/18	Tyne Cot Memorial
Fryer, Smith	Pte.	07/04/15	Hartwith (St Jude) Churchyard
Gardner, Clifford	Rmn	25/04/18	Tyne Cot Memorial
Garnett, Arthur A.	Pte.	25/04/18	Tyne Cot Memorial
Gaunt, Edward	2/Lt	28/09/16	Thiepval Memorial
Gawthorpe, George	Pte.	09/10/17	Tyne Cot Memorial
Gibson, Ronald	Pte.	15/08/16	Authuille Military Cemetery
Gilbertson, Ralph	Pte.	09/10/17	Tyne Cot Memorial
Gill, Austin	Pte.	13/11/17	Tyne Cot Memorial
Gilmore, Bernard	Pte.	28/01/17	De Cusine Ravine British Cemetery, Basseux
Gilyard, Thomas A.	Pte.	15/11/17	Tyne Cot Memorial
Glasgow, Norman	Pte.	30/07/17	Mont Huon Military Cemetery, Le Treport

Gledhill, Frances E.	Pte.	25/04/18	Tyne Cot Memorial
Glover, Harry	Pte.	25/04/18	Tyne Cot Memorial
Goatcher, Walter	Pte.	09/10/17	Tyne Cot Memorial
Goddard, Harold	2/Lt	09/10/17	Tyne Cot Memorial
Goddard, Joseph	Pte.	09/10/17	Tyne Cot Memorial
Gomersall, Ernest H.	Pte.	01/01/16	Boulogne Eastern Cemetery
Goodison, Arthur	Pte.	25/04/18	Tyne Cot Memorial
Goodman, Morris	Cpl	09/10/17	Tyne Cot Memorial
Goodwill, Cyril	2/Lt	03/09/16	Mill Road Cemetery, Thiepval
Goodwin, Eric B.	Pte.	03/09/16	Thiepval Memorial
Gouch, Norman	Pte.	28/09/16	Regina Trench Cemetery, Grandcourt
Grafton, James	Pte.	25/07/17	Mont Huon Military Cemetery, Le Treport
Graham, Nathan	Pte.	16/08/16	Authuille Military Cemetery
Grasby, George W.	Pte.	17/10/18	St Sever Cemetery Extension, Rouen
Gratton, John W.	Sgt	14/04/18	Tyne Cot Memorial
Graves, Charles R.	Pte.	03/09/16	Serre Road Cemetery No.2.
Graves, Harold J.	Pte.	13/10/18	Vis-en-Artois Memorial
Gray, Charles	Pte.	25/07/17	Adinkerke Churchyard Extension
Gray, Mark	Pte.	02/05/18	Ghent City Cemetery
Gray, Richard	Pte.	28/09/16	Mill Road Cemetery, Thiepval
Greening, Arthur	Pte.	11/10/17	Tyne Cot Memorial
Grundy, Fred J	Pte.	25/04/11	Tyne Cot Memorial
Gubbings, Alfred E.	L/Cpl	03/09/16	Thiepval Memorial
Hackett, James	L/Cpl	09/10/17	Tyne Cot Memorial
Haddick, George R.	Cpl	17/04/18	Buttes New British Cemetery, Polygon Wood
Hadfield, James	Pte.	01/11/18	Auberchicourt British Cemetery
Haigh, Ernest	Pte.	11/10/16	Boroughbridge Cemetery
Haigh, George	Pte.	25/04/18	Tyne Cot Memorial
Haley, William A.	Pte.	11/07/15	Ypres (Menin Gate) Memorial
Hall, Arthur H.	Pte.	03/09/16	Thiepval Memorial
Hall, Fred	Pte.	11/05/18	Cologne Southern Cemetery
Hall, George	Pte.	06/10/18	Hamburg Cemetery
Hall, John W.	Pte.	09/10/17	Tyne Cot Cemetery
Hall, Joseph	L/Cpl	25/04/18	Tyne Cot Memorial
Hall, Joseph D.	Pte.	15/10/17	Boulogne Eastern Cemetery
Hampshire, Richard	Pte.	09/10/17	Tyne Cot Memorial
Haney, John	Cpl	28/09/16	Warloy-Baillon Communal Cemetery Extesion
Hanson, John E.	Pte.	27/03/18	Birr Cross Roads Cemetery

Hanson, Louis	Pte.	30/09/18	Glageon Communal Cemetery Extension
Hardwick, Frank	Pte.	27/09/15	Étaples Military Cemetery
Hardwick, Harry	Pte.	28/07/17	Coxyde Military Cemetery
Hardwick, Joseph	Pte.	09/10/17	Tyne Cot Memorial
Harling, James	Pte.	24/07/17	Coxyde Military Cemetery
Harris, Harry John	Pte.	25/04/18	Tyne Cot Memorial
Harris, James	Pte.	03/05/18	Tyne Cot Memorial
Harrison, Ernest	Pte.	26/05/15	Le Trou Aid Post Cemetery, Fleurbaix
Harrison, Frederick	L/Cpl	28/09/16	Thiepval Memorial
Harrison, James R.	L/Cpl	17/11/17	Hooge Crater Cemetery
Harrison, Lescombe T.	Rmn	04/12/17	Rocquigny-Equancourt Road, Manancourt
Harrison, William	Sgt	29/09/16	Thiepval Memorial
Harvey, Edward	Pte.	04/12/16	Étaples Military Cemetery
Hatter, John	Pte.	09/10/17	Tyne Cot Memorial
Heath, Philip	Pte.	11/11/18	St Sever Cemetery Extension, Rouen
Heavisides, John	Pte.	19/12/15	Essex Farm Cemetery
Helliwell, Albert	Sgt	13/10/18	St Aubert British Cemetery
Henderson, Francis J.	Pte.	02/07/16	Thiepval Memorial
Henderson, Joseph	Pte.	04/10/18	Hautmont Communal Cemetery
Herd, George	Sgt	25/04/18	Tyne Cot Memorial
Herman, Harry	Pte.	20/06/18	Tyne Cot Memorial
Heslop, George	Pte.	12/10/18	Vis-en-Artois Memorial
Heslop, Henry	Pte.	02/07/16	Thiepval Memorial
Hesseldon, Arthur	Pte.	27/09/16	Mill Road Cemetery, Thiepval
Hewson, Frank	Pte.	03/09/16	Thiepval Memorial
Hick, George	Pte.	03/08/16	Martinsart British Cemetery
Hickman, Benjamin J.	Pte.	22/04/18	Tyne Cot Memorial
Higgins, George	Pte.	17/04/18	Tyne Cot Memorial
Higgins, Peter	Pte.	28/07/17	Mont Huon Military Cemetery, Le Treport
Hilbeck, Thomas	Pte.	12/10/18	St Aubert British Cemetery
Hill, George	Pte.	25/04/18	Tyne Cot Memorial
Hinchcliffe, Louis	Pte.	09/10/17	Dochy Farm New British Cemetery
Hindle ,William	Pte.	08/04/17	Padiham Cemetery
Hingley, Frank	Pte.	26/11/16	Hannescamps New Military Cemetery
Hinton, Jack D.	Pte.	02/04/18	Tyne Cot Memorial
Hobbs, William	Sgt	30/10/17	Wimereux Communal Cemetery

Holden, Samuel	Pte.	28/09/16	Thiepval Memorial
Holgate, Edward	Pte.	01/07/16	Thiepval Memorial
Holland, Leonard	Pte.	21/12/15	Lijssenthoek Military Cemetery
Holliday, William	Pte.	09/10/17	Tyne Cot Memorial
Holmes, Harry B.	Cpl	28/09/16	Mill Road Cemetery, Thiepval
Holmes, James	Pte.	09/10/17	Tyne Cot Memorial
Holmes, John	Pte.	29/12/15	Ypres (Menin Gate) Memorial
Holmes, John H.	Pte.	09/08/16	Authuille Military Cemetery
Holmes, Mark H.	Pte.	25/04/18	Tyne Cot Memorial
Holmes, Sydney R.	Pte.	15/08/16	Puchevillers British Cemetery
Holroyd, Norman	Pte.	10/08/18	Hamburg Cemetery
Holt, Edwin	Pte.	16/07/18	Puchevillers British Cemetery
Homer, John W.	Pte.	28/09/16	Cayeux Military Cemetery
Hood, Harold	Pte.	17/11/17	Hooge Crater Cemetery
Hopkins, Arthur	Pte.	03/09/16	Thiepval Memorial
Hopkins, John H.	Pte.	02/03/18	Lijssenthoek Military Cemetery
Horne, James M.	Sgt	25/04/18	Tyne Cot Memorial
Horner, William	Pte.	26/04/18	Mendinghem Miitary Cemetery
Horsfield, Harold	Pte.	23/02/16	Thiepval Memorial
Horsfield, Sidney	Pte.	28/10/18	Bradfield (St Nicholas) Churchyard
Hothersall, George	Pte.	22/07/17	Ramscappelle Road Military Cemetery
House, Arthur	Pte.	19/03/18	Tyne Cot Memorial
House, Frederick	Pte.	01/11/18	Famars Communal Cemetery Extension
Howard, Percy	Pte.	03/09/16	Thiepval Memorial
Hudson, Arthur	Pte.	11/09/16	Ste. Marie Cemetery, Le Havre
Hulme, Samuel	Pte.	13/10/17	Lindow (St John) Churchyard
Hunter, Charles F.	Pte.	25/04/18	Tyne Cot Memorial
Hutton, John G.	L/Cpl	09/10/17	Tyne Cot Memorial
Hyde, Joseph	Pte.	28/10/18	Niederzwehren Cemetery, Kassel
Illingworth, Hamer	Pte.	24/07/17	Coxyde Military Cemetery
Illingworth, James	Pte.	25/04/18	Tyne Cot Memorial
Illingworth, Joseph	Pte.	25/04/18	Tyne Cot Memorial
Illingworth, William	Cpl	15/10/18	Bucquoy Road Cemetery, Ficheux
Ingham, Charles	Pte.	12/10/18	Wellington Cemetery, Rieux-En-Cambresis
Inman, Charles	Pte.	03/09/16	Connaught Cemetery, Thiepval
Iredale, Edward E.	CSM	29/08/16	Connaught Cemetery, Thiepval
Ireson, Edward W.	Pte.	01/11/18	Auberchicourt British Cemetery
Irish, Edward	2/Lt	20/06/15	Le Trou Aid Post Cemetery, Fleurbaix

Jackson, Albert E.	Pte.	09/10/17	Tyne Cot Memorial
Jackson, Charles	Pte.	03/05/18	Lijssenthoek Military Cemetery
Jackson, Frederick	Pte.	11/10/17	Nine Elms British Cemetery
Jackson, John	Pte.	10/06/18	Rethel French National Cemetery
Jackson, Michael	L/Cpl	03/09/16	Thiepval Memorial
Jackson, Wilfred	Pte.	13/10/18	Vis-en-Artois Memorial
Jackson, William	Pte.	26/04/18	St Symphorien Military Cemetery
Jacobs, Herbert	Pte.	09/10/17	Tyne Cot Memorial
Jameson, James L.	Lt	02/07/16	Thiepval Memorial
Jarvis, Harry	Pte.	09/05/18	Harlebeke New British Cemetery
Jennings, William	Pte.	25/07/15	Ypres (Menin Gate) Memorial
Jervis, Henry	Pte.	31/03/17	Laventie Military Cemetery, La Gorgue
Johnson, Arnell	Pte.	25/05/15	Le Trou Aid Post Cemetery, Fleurbaix
Johnson, Gilbert	Pte.	28/09/15	Essex Farm Cemetery
Johnson William	Pte.	27/09/16	Thiepval Memorial
Johnson, Hugh	Pte.	01/11/18	Auberchicourt British Cemetery
Johnson, John E.	Pte.	25/04/18	Tyne Cot Memorial
Johnson, John J.	Pte.	13/10/18	York Cemetery, Haspres
Johnson, Robert	Pte.	25/04/18	Tyne Cot Memorial
Johnson, Thomas	Pte.	10/10/18	Niederzwehren Cemetery, Kassel
Johnstone, Stewart	Pte.	05/11/18	St Sever Cemetery Extension, Rouen
Jones, William	L/Cpl	09/10/17	Tyne Cot Memorial
Jordan, Reuben R.	Pte.	20/07/16	Thiepval Memorial
Keighley, Leonard	Pte.	25/04/18	Tyne Cot Memorial
Kelly, Fred	Cpl	15/07/15	Boulogne Eastern Cemetery
Kemp, Clarence	Pte.	03/11/18	Cambrai East Military Cemetery
Kenah, Thomas Webb	Pte.	25/04/18	Tyne Cot Memorial
Kendall, Charles J.L.	Pte.	25/09/16	Varennes Military Cemetery
Kilingback, Willim H.	Pte.	01/11/18	Famars Communal Cemetery Extension
Kilvington, Charles E.	Pte.	19/12/15	New Irish Farm Cemetery
Kingswood, Walter	Pte.	12/10/18	Auberchicourt British Cemetery
Kirk, Walter F.	Pte.	30/07/17	Nieuport Memorial
Kitching, Joseph	Pte.	09/10/17	Tyne Cot Memorial
Kitson, Frank P.	Pte.	02/08/15	Ypres (Menin Gate) Memorial
Knowles, Edwin	Pte.	09/10/17	Tyne Cot Cemetery
Knowles, Fred	Pte.	21/01/17	Warlincourt Halte British Ceetery, Saulty
Knowles, John H.	Pte.	23/11/15	Lijssenthoek Military Cemetery

Lamb, Frederick S.	L/Cpl	01/11/18	Vis-en-Artois Memorial
Lamb, William	L/Cpl	25/04/18	Tyne Cot Memorial
Lambert, Herbert	Pte.	09/10/17	Tyne Cot Memorial
Large, George	Cpl	28/09/16	Mill Road Cemetery, Thiepval
Law, Melton A.	Pte.	09/10/17	Tyne Cot cemetery
Lawson, Allen	Pte.	03/09/16	Mill Road Cemetery, Thiepval
Lawson, Arthur	Pte.	01/11/18	Aulnoy Communal Cemetery
Lawson, Reginald	Pte.	19/10/18	Étaples Military Cemetery
Lea, Walter	L/Cpl	11/07/15	Ypres (Menin Gate) Memorial
Leach, Frank	Pte.	07/08/17	Mont Huon Military Cemetery, Le Treport
Leadley, William	Pte.	26/02/17	St Pierre Cemetery, Amiens
Leaning, Fanthorpe	Pte.	03/09/16	Serre Road Cemetery No.1.
Lee, Arthur B.	2/Lt	02/07/16	Thiepval Memorial
Lee, Ernest W.	2/Lt	28/09/16	Mill Road Cemetery, Thiepval
Lee, Fred	Pte.	03/09/16	Thiepval Memorial
Lee, Harry	L/Cpl	09/10/17	Tyne Cot Memorial
Lee, Harry	Pte.	12/10/18	St Aubert British Cemetery
Levi, Edward	Pte.	09/10/17	Tyne Cot Memorial
Levitt, Harold	Pte.	28/09/16	Thiepval Memorial
Leyland, John H	.Pte.	20/12/15	Lijssenthoek Military Cemetery
Lickley, Frederick S.	Pte.	03/09/16	Thiepval Memorial
Lickley, George	L/Cpl	01/07/16	Thiepval Memorial
Lickley, James	Pte.	30/05/15	Le Trou Aid Post Cemetery, Fleurbaix
Liddle, John	Pte.	28/09/16	Thiepval Memorial
Linton Fred	Pte.	09/10/18	Niederzwehren Cemetery, Kassel
Lister, George	Pte.	17/01/17	De Cusine Ravine British Cemetery, Basseux
Little, Edwin	L/Cpl	09/10/19	Tyne Cot Memorial
Little, Miles	Cpl	13/10/18	Naves Communal Cemetery Extension
Littlewood, Albert	Pte.	25/04/18	Tyne Cot Memorial
Lloyd, Felix	Pte.	16/10/18	Bucquoy Road Cemetery, Ficheux
Locke, Frank	Cpl	09/10/17	Tyne Cot Memorial
Lockwood, Joseph	L/Cpl	12/10/18	St Aubert British Cemetery
Lodge, Edward James	Cpl	09/10/17	Tyne Cot Memorial
Loftus, John	Pte.	10/07/16	Authuille Military Cemetery
Loftus, John	Pte.	24/04/18	Mendinghem Miitary Cemetery
Long, Edward	Pte.	13/08/15	Essex Farm Cemetery
Long, Frederick	Pte.	23/06/15	Le Trou Aid Post Cemetery, Fleurbaix

Loughran John	Pte.	26/07/17	Ramscappelle Road Military Cemetery
Lovatt, William	Pte.	13/10/18	Bucquoy Road Cemetery, Ficheux
Lowe, Edward	Pte.	03/09/16	Thiepval Memorial
Lowery, Leonard	Pte.	09/10/17	Tyne Cot Memorial
Lucas, Walter	Pte.	03/09/16	Thiepval Memorial
Lund, Gordon	CSM	01/07/16	Serre Road Cemetery No.2.
Lund, Henry W.	Pte.	11/07/15	Ypres (Menin Gate) Memorial
Lupton, Selwyn	Pte.	10/01/16	Harrogate (Harlow Hill) Cemetery
Lynch, John	Sgt	21/07/17	Ramscappelle Road Military Cemetery
Lyons, James	Pte.	22/03/17	La Gorgue Communal Cemetery
Macey, George	Dr	11/07/15	Ypres (Menin Gate) Memorial
Mackay, Donald P.	Major	09/10/17	Tyne Cot Memorial
Mackridge, George I.	Pte.	20/07/16	Thiepval Memorial
Mallinder, James	Pte.	09/10/17	Tyne Cot Memorial
Mallorie, John W.	Pte.	10/12/17	Reninghelst New Military Cemetery
Malmslie, William	Pte.	25/04/18	Tyne Cot Memorial
Malthouse, Walter	Pte.	09/05/15	Fauquissart Military Cemetery, Laventie
Mandeville, Pierce	Capt	28/09/16	Mill Road Cemetery, Thiepval
Marks, Ernest	Pte.	25/04/18	Tyne Cot Memorial
Marsden, Lawrence	Pte.	09/10/17	Tyne Cot Memorial
Marsden, Thornton	Pte.	01/05/18	Tyne Cot Memorial
Marsh, Albert	Pte.	25/04/18	Voormezeele Enclosure No. 3.
Marshall, James	Pte.	30/04/18	Kortrijk (St Jan) Communal Cemetery
Marshall, Ronald	L/Cpl	20/12/15	Essex Farm Cemetery
Marshall, William	Pte.	25/04/18	Tyne Cot Memorial
Marston, John	Pte.	01/05/18	Pont-du-Hem Military Cemetery, La Gorgue
Martin, Joseph	Pte.	25/04/18	Tyne Cot Memorial
Martin, Percy	Pte.	03/05/18	Lijssenthoek Military Cemetery
Martlew, Frederick	Pte.	21/10/17	Étaples Military Cemetery
Mascall, Charles	Pte.	01/11/18	Auberchicourt British Cemetery
Mason, Percy	Pte.	19/12/15	Ypres (Menin Gate) Memorial
Mason, Arthur	Pte.	09/10/17	Tyne Cot Memorial
Mason, James	Pte.	03/09/16	Thiepval Memorial
Mayall, Tom	Pte.	11/10/18	Drummond Cemetery, Raillencourt

McGregor, Donald	Pte.	29/09/16	Thiepval Memorial
McGuckin, Lionel	Pte.	21/03/18	Nine Elms British Cemetery
McNichol, Daniel	Pte.	18/11/15	Lijssenthoek Military Cemetery
McQuade, John	Sgt	01/11/18	Auberchicourt British Cemetery
McTierman, James	Pte.	21/11/15	Essex Farm Cemetery
Melvin, John	Pte.	02/07/16	Thiepval Memorial
Merrifield, Ernest	Pte.	25/04/18	Tyne Cot Memorial
Metcalfe, Charles	Pte.	05/05/18	Harlebeke New British Cemetery
Micklethwaite, Arthur	Pte.	09/10/17	Tyne Cot Memorial
Middleton, John	Pte.	25/04/18	Tyne Cot Memorial
Middleton, Orlando	Pte.	29/07/18	Poznan Old Garrison Cemetery
Midgeley, Harold	Pte.	25/04/18	Tyne Cot Memorial
Midgley, Ronald	L/Cpl	25/04/18	Tyne Cot Memorial
Milburn, Stanley	Pte.	23/09/18	Vis-en-Artois Memorial
Miller, Harry	Pte.	23/09/18	Vis-en-Artois Memorial
Miller, Herbert	Pte.	27/09/16	Thiepval Memorial
Millins, John T.	Pte.	28/09/16	Mill Road Cemetery, Thiepval
Mills, Alfred	L/Cpl	09/10/17	Tyne Cot Cemetery
Mills, George	Pte.	13/11/18	Walthamstow (Queen's Road) Cemetery
Milner, James W.	Dr	21/05/15	Rue-Petillon Military Cemetery, Fleubaix
Mitchell, Henry	Pte.	25/04/18	Tyne Cot Memorial
Mitchell, John	Pte.	03/07/16	Warloy-Baillon Communal Cemetery Extension
Mitchell, Lewis M.	2/Lt	11/08/18	Hagle Dump Cemetery
Mitchell, William	Sgt	03/04/18	Menin Road South Military Cemetery
Moore, Vincent	Pte.	25/04/18	Tyne Cot Memorial
Morgan, George	Pte.	09/10/17	Tyne Cot cemetery
Morrell, John	Pte.	03/05/18	Wytschaete Military Cemetery
Morris, Douglas	L/Cpl	11/10/17	Tyne Cot Memorial
Morrison, Albert	Pte.	01/11/18	Vis-en-Artois Memorial
Morton, Charles	Pte.	25/04/16	Tyne Cot Memorial
Mosby, Fred	Pte.	25/04/18	Sanctuary Wood Cemetery
Mosley, John	Pte.	09/10/17	Tyne Cot Memorial
Mosley, Thomas	L/Cpl	15/07/16	Authuille Military Cemetery
Moss, Herbert	Sgt	31/08/18	Cologne Southern Cemetery
Mounsey, Fred	Pte.	25/04/18	Tyne Cot Memorial
Moxon, Victor	Pte.	10/08/16	Forceville Communal Cemetery and Extension
Moyser, Hubert H.	Pte.	20/02/16	Thiepval Memorial
Mulry, Victor	Pte.	25/04/18	Tyne Cot Memorial

Mumford, William	Pte.	13/10/15	Essex Farm Cemetery
Munday, Herbert	Pte.	20/02/16	Mill Road Cemetery, Thiepval
Murthwaite, Sydney	Pte.	27/05/18	Kortrijk (St Jan) Communal Cemetery
Naylor, Arthur	Rmn	07/08/16	Authuille Military Cemetery
Neal, Thomas	Pte.	16/10/17	St Sever Cemetery Extension, Rouen
Needham, Ernest	Pte.	25/04/18	Wytschaete Military Cemetery
Nelson, Albert	Pte.	14/09/18	Berlin South-Western Cemetery
Nelson, Ernest	Pte.	25/04/18	Tyne Cot Memorial
Nendick, Robert	Pte.	12/11/18	Douai British Cemetery, Cuincy
Newby, Arthur	Pte.	09/10/17	Tyne Cot Memorial
Newman, Leonard	Pte.	26/04/17	Laventie Military Cemetery, La Gorgue
Newton, Thomas	Pte.	05/09/16	Doullens Communal Cemetery, Extension No.1
Nichols, Fred	Pte.	01/11/18	Auberchicourt British Cemetery
Nichol, William	Pte.	25/04/18	Tyne Cot Memorial
Nicholson, Arthur	RSM	01/11/18	Vis-en-Artois Memorial
Noble, Frank	Pte.	25/04/18	Tyne Cot Memorial
Nolan, Gerald	Pte.	25/04/18	Tyne Cot Memorial
Nolan, Rutherford	L/Cpl	11/08/18	Hagle Dump Cemetery
Norris, Fred	Pte.	25/07/17	Longuenesse (St Omer) Souvenir Cemetery
Northrop, Herbert	Pte.	10/04/18	Menin Road South Military Cemetery
Norton, Harry	L/Cpl	09/10/17	Tyne Cot Memorial
Oakes, Fred	Pte.	01/11/18	Auberchicourt British Cemetery
Oddy, Joseph	Pte.	10/08/18	Hagle Dump Cemetery
Ogden, Halstead	Pte.	09/10/17	Tyne Cot Memorial
Oliver, John T.	Pte.	28/09/16	Thiepval Memorial
Osbaldeston, Walter	Pte.	13/10/18	Cambrai Memorial, Louverval
Otter, Frank	Pte.	25/10/18	Belgrade Cemetery
Owen, Herbert	Pte.	25/04/18	Tyne Cot Memorial
Parker, Henry	Pte.	21/07/15	Ypres (Menin Gate) Memorial
Parker, James	Sgt	25/04/18	Tyne Cot Memorial
Parker, Richard	Pte.	07/08/18	Hagle Dump Cemetery
Pattison, Harold	CSM	09/10/17	Tyne Cot Memorial
Peacock, Alec	Pte.	15/06/16	Abbeville Communal Cemetery
Peacock, Francis W.	Pte.	07/09/15	Essex Farm Cemetery
Pearson, Dick	Pte.	03/09/16	Thiepval Memorial
Peet, George	Pte.	22/07/16	Ste.Marie Cemetery, Le Havre
Pennington, Frank	Pte.	06/08/15	Étaples Military Cemetery

Penrose, Samuel	Pte.	20/12/15	Essex Farm Cemetery
Pheasey, Ernest	Pte.	17/08/15	Lijssenthoek Military Cemetery
Philips, Frederick G.	Capt	25/04/18	Tyne Cot Memorial
Pickard, Victor	Pte.	03/09/16	Thiepval Memorial
Pickles, George	Sgt	03/11/18	Berlin South-Western Cemetery
Pickles, Harry	Pte.	29/10/18	Valenciennes (St Roch) Communal Cemetery
Pickles, Joseph	Sgt	01/07/16	Thiepval Memorial
Pickles, Joseph L.	Pte.	28/09/16	Thiepval Memorial
Pierce, John Hugh	Pte.	30/10/18	Stanley (Outwood) Cemetery
Pinchen, John	L/Cpl	30/07/17	Mont Huon Military Cemetery, Le Treport
Pink, George	Pte.	22/12/15	Wimereux Communal Cemetery
Pintches David	Pte.	25/04/18	Tyne Cot Memorial
Platt Archibald T.	Pte.	11/10/18	Vis-en-Artois Memorial
Plows, Charles	Pte.	12/10/18	Vis-en-Artois Memorial
Poe, W.A.	Pte.	23/04/18	Klein-Vierstraat British Cemetery
Polikoff, Isaac	Pte.	18/04/18	Tyne Cot Memorial
Pook, Albert	Col/Sgt	12/10/18	Bucquoy Road Cemetery, Ficheux
Porter, Frank	L/Cpl	09/10/17	Tyne Cot Memorial
Potter, Fred	Cpl	01/11/18	Cambrai East Military Cemetery
Potts, Leonard	Pte.	25/04/18	Tyne Cot Memorial
Pound, Harold	Pte.	09/10/17	Tyne Cot Memorial
Pounder, Alfred	L/Cpl	27/12/15	Lijssenthoek Military Cemetery
Pounder, George	Cpl	04/10/16	Abbeville Communal Cemetery
Prendergast, Thomas	Pte.	25/04/18	Somer Farm Cemetery
Prest, John	Pte.	25/04/18	Tyne Cot Memorial
Prest, William C.S.	2/Lt	17/08/16	Authuille Military Cemetery
Price, Henry	Pte.	22/04/18	Haringhe (Bandaghem) Military Cemetery
Priestley, William	Pte.	25/04/18	Tyne Cot Memorial
Prout, Edward	Pte.	23/11/17	Longuenesse (St Omer) Souvenir Cemetery
Pryor, Harold	Pte.	17/07/16	Authuille Military Cemetery
Pybu,s William H.	Pte.	19/12/15	Hagle Dump Cemetery
Race, William	L/Cpl	12/10/18	Vis-en-Artois Memorial
Raftery, John	Sgt	25/04/18	Tyne Cot Memorial
Ramsden, James F	Pte.	23/07/16	Puchevillers British Cemetery
Ramsey, Edward	Pte.	18/06/15	Le Trou Aid Post Cemetery, Fleurbaix
Rands, Charles	Pte.	03/09/16	Thiepval Memorial

Raw, George	L/Cpl	11/10/15	Essex Farm Cemetery
Raynor, Fred	RSM	01/05/18	Harrogate (Grove Road) Cemetery
Reddin, William	Pte.	01/05/18	Larch Wood (Railway Cutting) Cemetery
Reed, John	Pte.	05/05/18	Ghent City Cemetery
Regan, Arthur	Pte.	14/04/18	Outtersteene Communal Cemetery Ext., Bailleul
Rennie, Wallace S.	L/Cpl	15/07/16	Authuille Military Cemetery
Reynard, Joseph	Pte.	19/03/18	Nine Elms British Cemetery
Rhodes, Kenneth	Pte.	25/04/18	Tyne Cot Memorial
Richards, Albert	Pte.	30/04/18	Harlebeke New British Cemetery
Richardson, Norman	Pte.	16/09/16	Wimereux Communal Cemetery
Richmond, George	Pte.	25/04/18	Tyne Cot Memorial
Ridsdale, Frank	Pte.	18/04/18	Harlebeke New British Cemetery
Roberts, Walter	Pte.	11/03/18	Perth Cemetery (China Wall)
Roberts, William	Pte.	30/07/18	Sissonne British Cemetery
Robins, Joseph	Pte.	09/10/17	Tyne Cot Memorial
Robinson, Edward A.	Pte.	03/09/16	Thiepval Memorial
Robinson, Ernest	Pte.	28/09/16	Thiepval Memorial
Robinson, Harold	Pte.	25/04/18	Tyne Cot Memorial
Robinson, James	Pte.	29/09/16	Mill Road Cemetery, Thiepval
Robinson, John Cheer	Pte.	01/02/16	Calais Southern Cemetery
Robinson, Richard	Pte.	20/02/16	Mill Road Cemetery, Thiepval
Robson, John	Pte.	09/10/17	Tyne Cot Memorial
Rodgers, Stephen	Pte.	16/07/16	Warloy-Baillon Communal Cemetery Extesion
Rodgson, John	L/Cpl	25/04/18	Tyne Cot Memorial
Ronksley, William	Pte.	07/07/18	Sheffield (Crookes) Cemetery
Rose, Samuel	Pte.	03/08/18	Menin Road South Military Cemetery
Royce, Stephen	Pte.	03/09/15	Ste. Marie Cemetery, Le Havre
Rumboldt, Charley	Pte.	08/05/17	Laventie Military Cemetery, La Gorgue
Rushton, George	Pte.	09/10/17	Tyne Cot Memorial
Rushworth, Albert	Pte.	25/04/18	Tyne Cot Memorial
Russell, Joseph	Pte.	27/07/17	Mont Huon Military Cemetery, Le Treport
Rymer, Horace	Pte.	29/07/16	Wimereux Communal Cemetery
Sabine, William E.	Pte.	25/04/18	Tyne Cot Memorial
Sandbrook, Bertram	Pte.	08/07/16	Authuille Military Cemetery
Sanger, William	Pte.	11/10/18	Niagara Cemetery, Iwuy
Sanofski, Israel	Pte.	25/04/18	Oosttaverne Wood Cemetery

Sawbridge, George C.	L/ Sgt	25/04/18	Sanctuary Wood Cemetery
Saynor, John	Pte.	27/04/18	Harlebeke New British Cemetery
Scaife, William	Pte.	09/10/17	Tyne Cot Memorial
Scaum, John H	Pte.	25/04/18	La Laiterie Military Cemetery
Schofield, James	Pte.	11/10/17	Oxford Road Cemetery
Schofield, Walter B.	Pte.	09/10/17	Tyne Cot Memorial
Scott, Charles	Pte.	02/05/18	Pont-du-Hem Military Cemetery, La Gorgue
Scott, Thomas	Pte.	01/11/18	Vis-en-Artois Memorial
Scurrah, Edgar	Pte.	29/04/18	Pont-du-Hem Military Cemetery, La Gorgue
Seal, Albert	Pte.	23/07/15	Hospital Farm Cemetery
Secker ,Wilfred	Pte.	25/04/18	Tyne Cot Memorial
Sedgwick, Fred	L/Cpl	21/07/18	Malbork Commonwealth War Cemetery, Poland
Sefton, William	Pte.	09/10/17	Tyne Cot Memorial
Senior, Amos	Pte.	14/12/18	Berlin South-Western Cemetery
Sergeant, John H.	L/Cpl	01/11/18	Aulnoy Communal Cemetery
Sharp, William	Pte.	21/08/16	Puchevillers British Cemetery
Sharpe, Alfred	Pte.	25/04/18	Tyne Cot Memorial
Shaw, Fred	Pte.	09/10/17	Tyne Cot Memorial
Shaw, Fred	Pte.	25/04/18	Tyne Cot Memorial
Shepherd, Lawrence	Pte.	01/11/18	Aulnoy Communal Cemetery
Shillito, Alfred	Pte.	25/04/18	Tyne Cot Memorial
Simpson, Charles	L/Cpl	28/07/16	Blighty Valley Cemetery, Authuille Wood
Skinner, George H.	Pte.	01/07/16	Connaught Cemetery, Thiepval
Slack, Percy	Pte.	09/10/17	Tyne Cot Memorial
Smailes, John R.	Pte.	17/04/18	Tyne Cot Memorial
Smillie, Joseph	Pte.	12/01/17	Warlincourt Halte British Ceetery, Saulty
Smith, Alexander	Pte.	04/12/17	Peterculter Churchyard
Smith, Harold	Pte.	06/05/18	Larch Wood (Railway Cutting) Cemetery
Smith, Harry	Pte.	26/04/18	Haringhe (Bandaghem) Military Cemetery
Smith, Harry	Pte.	09/10/17	Tyne Cot Memorial
Smith, Joseph		04/06/17	
Smith, Joseph R.G.	Pte.	25/04/18	Tyne Cot Memorial
Smith, John W.	Sgt	01/11/18	Auberchicourt British Cemetery
Smith Percy	Pte.	12/07/16	Authuille Military Cemetery
Smith, Leonard	Pte.	09/10/17	Tyne Cot Memorial
Smith, Thomas	L/Cpl	07/08/18	Hagle Dump Cemetery

Smith, William	L/Cpl	31/10/15	Lijssenthoek Military Cemetery
Smithson, Herbert	Pte.	15/11/17	Tyne Cot Memorial
Smithson, Thomas E.	Pte.	09/10/17	Tyne Cot Memorial
Snow, Fred	Pte.	25/04/18	Tyne Cot Memorial
Souter, Joseph	Pte.	26/09/18	Worms (Hochheim Hill) Cemetery
Southwell, Edward	Pte.	02/05/18	Ghent City Cemetery
Sowden, Leonard	Pte.	11/10/18	Vis-en-Artois Memorial
Sowden, Tom	L/Cpl	11/10/18	St Aubert British Cemetery
Sowerby, Charles B.	Pte.	13/12/18	Mont Huon Military Cemetery, Le Treport
Spinks, William	Pte.	03/09/16	Connaught Cemetery, Thiepval
Stephenson, George	Pte.	22/04/18	Tyne Cot Memorial
Stairmand, Ernest W.	Pte.	25/04/18	Sanctuary Wood Cemetery
Stead, Edwin P.	Pte.	11/10/18	Niagara Cemetery, Iwuy
Stead, Frank	Pte.	18/08/15	Hospital Farm Cemetery
Stead, Leonard	Pte.	09/10/17	Tyne Cot Memorial
Stead, Thomas	Pte.	25/04/18	Tyne Cot Memorial
Stewart, Charles	Pte.	11/10/18	Glageon Communal Cemetery Extension
Stockell, James	Pte.	28/04/18	Tourcoing (Pont-Neuville) Communal Cemetery
Stokes, Martin	Pte.	28/09/16	Bray Vale British Cemetery, Bray-Sur-Somme
Stones, Herbert	Cpl	25/04/18	Tyne Cot Memorial
Stout, John W.	Sgt	09/10/17	Tyne Cot Memorial
Street, Arthur	Pte.	03/09/16	A.I.F. Burial Ground, Flers
Strudwick, Harry J.	Sgt	28/09/16	Connaught Cemetery, Thiepval
Sunley, James	Pte.	20/07/16	A.I.F. Burial Ground, Flers
Surbuts, Ernest	Pte.	09/10/17	Tyne Cot Memorial
Sutcliffe, Thomas	Pte.	25/04/18	Sanctuary Wood Cemetery
Swaine, Mellin	Pte.	25/04/18	Sanctuary Wood Cemetery
Swale, Charles L.	Pte.	03/09/16	Thiepval Memorial
Swales, John	Pte.	09/10/17	Tyne Cot Memorial
Swales, Leonard	Pte.	07/08/16	Pateley Bridge Cemetery
Swires, Edwin	Pte.	09/10/17	Tyne Cot Memorial
Sykes, Harold	Pte.	25/04/18	Tyne Cot Memorial
Tate, Dennis	Pte.	20/02/16	Mill Road Cemetery, Thiepval
Taylor, Albert	Pte.	25/04/18	Tyne Cot Memorial
Taylor, Daniel	Pte.	19/04/18	Tyne Cot Memorial
Taylor, Ernest	L/Cpl	24/07/18	Cologne Southern Cemetery
Taylor, Harold	Pte.	25/04/18	Wytschaete Military Cemetery
Taylor, Joseph	Pte.	03/09/16	Mill Road Cemetery, Thiepval

Taylor, Kenneth	Pte.	01/11/18	Vis-en-Artois Memorial
Taylor, Samuel	Pte.	27/09/16	Thiepval Memorial
Taylor, Stephen	Pte.	25/04/18	Tyne Cot Memorial
Terry, Frederick	Sgt	29/09/16	Thiepval Memorial
Tetley, Thomas	Pte.	11/03/18	Perth Cemetery (China Wall)
Thirkell, Alfred	Pte.	01/07/16	Thiepval Memorial
Thomas, Joseph W.	Pte.	29/11/18	Douai British Cemetery, Cuincy
Thompson, Frederick C.	Maj	02/07/16	Thiepval Memorial
Thompson, George R.	L/Cpl	31/05/15	Estaires Communal Cemetery and Extension
Thompson, Harry	Pte.	06/04/17	Merville Communal Cemetery Extension
Thompson, Herbert	Pte.	25/04/18	Tyne Cot Memorial
Thompson, Leonard	Pte.	01/11/18	Aulnoy Communal Cemetery
Thompson, Thos. W.W.	Pte.	03/09/16	Mill Road Cemetery, Thiepval
Thompson, William H	Pte.	09/10/17	Tyne Cot Memorial
Thomson, Peter	Pte.	25/04/18	Tyne Cot Memorial
Thornton, Alfred H	Pte.	11/07/15	Ypres (Menin Gate) Memorial
Thornton, William	Pte.	03/09/16	Thiepval Memorial
Thundercliffe, Henry F.	Pte.	09/10/17	Tyne Cot Memorial
Tiffney, Edwin	Pte.	27/09/16	Thiepval Memorial
Timmins, George	Pte.	23/07/15	Ypres (Menin Gate) Memorial
Tindle, John W.	Pte.	25/07/17	Coxyde Military Cemetery
Talbot, Wilfred V.	Pte.	01/11/18	Aulnoy Communal Cemetery
Todd, William S.	Pte.	25/04/18	Tyne Cot Memorial
Tolley, William H.	L/Cpl	03/04/18	Menin Road South Military Cemetery
Tolmie, George	Pte.	27/07/18	Chauny Communal Cemetery British Exension
Topham, Christopher	CSM	09/10/17	Tyne Cot Memorial
Townend, Albert	Pte.	01/09/16	Puchevillers British Cemetery
Treleaven, Noel H.	2/Lt	23/11/16	Hannescamps New Military Cemetery
Triffitt, Thomas	Pte.	02/07/16	Bouzincourt Communal Cemetery Extension
Trumble, Bernard F.	L/Cpl	11/08/18	Hagle Dump Cemetery
Tunnicliffe, Ernest	Pte.	13/10/18	Vis-en-Artois Memorial
Tuppen, Alexander D.	Cpl	01/08/15	Ypres (Menin Gate) Memorial
Turner, Harry G.	L/Cpl	25/04/18	Mendinghem Miitary Cemetery
Tute, Richard	Pte.	20/12/15	Ypres (Menin Gate) Memorial
Tyrell, Leonard C.	2/Lt	09/10/17	Tyne Cot Memorial
Urquhart, Thomas	L/Cpl	09/10/17	Tyne Cot Memorial
Vast, Charles	Pte.	26/07/17	Coxyde Military Cemetery

Vause, Charles	L/Cpl	09/10/17	Tyne Cot Memorial
Vickerman, John S.	Pte.	25/04/18	Tyne Cot Memorial
Wailes, Gilbert	Pte.	08/10/16	Whitcliffe Cemetery
Wain, Ernest	Sgt	11/01/17	De Cusine Ravine British Cemetery, Basseux
Waine / Wain, John R.	Pte.	10/05/15	Fauquissart Military Cemetery, Laventie
Waite, Wilson	L/Cpl	01/07/16	Thiepval Memorial
Walker, Alan	Cpl	28/09/16	Thiepval Memorial
Walker, Ernest	Pte.	01/07/16	Thiepval Memorial
Walker, Henry	Pte.	15/07/16	Authuille Military Cemetery
Walker, Frederick G.	Cpl	20/07/15	Ypres (Menin Gate) Memorial
Walker, Herbert	Pte.	25/04/18	Tyne Cot Memorial
Walker, John C.	2/Lt	19/12/15	Essex Farm Cemetery
Walker, Leonard	Pte.	09/10/17	Tyne Cot Memorial
Walker, Lister W	Sgt	09/10/17	Tyne Cot Memorial
Walker, Percy	Pte.	25/04/18	Sanctuary Wood Cemetery
Walker, Reginald	Lt	25/04/18	Poelcapelle British Cemetery
Walker, Thomas	Pte.	01/07/16	Thiepval Memorial
Walker, Thomas G.	Pte.	09/10/17	Tyne Cot Memorial
Wallace, Dudley W.	Capt	09/10/17	Tyne Cot Memorial
Walsh, William	Pte.	25/04/18	Tyne Cot Memorial
Walshaw, Seth H.	L/Cpl	25/04/18	Tyne Cot Memorial
Ward, Francis E.	Cpl	22/03/17	Laventie Military Cemetery, La Gorgue
Wardle, Joseph H.	Pte.	03/05/18	Tyne Cot Memorial
Warhurst, Ernest	Pte.	09/10/17	Tyne Cot Memorial
Waring, Harry	Pte.	09/10/17	Tyne Cot Memorial
Watson, Allan W.	Pte.	29/04/18	Harlebeke New British Cemetery
Watson, Alfred C.	Capt	03/09/16	Lonsdale Cemetery, Authuille
Watson, John R.	Sgt	25/04/18	Tyne Cot Memorial
Watson, Thomas	Pte.	04/09/16	Thiepval Memorial
Watts, Isaac	Pte.	09/10/17	Tyne Cot Memorial
Watts, William	Pte.	09/10/17	Tyne Cot Memorial
Waugh, Adam W.	Pte.	02/05/18	Larch Wood (Railway Cutting) Cemetery
Weatherhead, Arthur	L/Cpl	28/09/16	Connaught Cemetery, Thiepval
Webster, Frank	Pte.	11/07/16	Forceville Communal Cemetery and Extension
Webster, George	Pte.	25/04/18	Tyne Cot Memorial
Wegg, Richard	Pte.	25/04/18	Tyne Cot Memorial
Wells, Charles W.	Pte.	28/07/16	Blighty Valley Cemetery, Authuille Wood

West, Harry	Pte.	26/05/15	Le Trou Aid Post Cemetery, Fleurbaix
Westerman, Harry	Sgt	09/10/17	Tyne Cot Cemetery
Wetherill, Henry	L/Cpl	24/09/16	Puchevillers British Cemetery
Wetherill, John	Pte.	11/07/15	Ypres (Menin Gate) Memorial
Wharton, Fred	Pte.	03/09/16	Connaught Cemetery, Thiepval
Wharton, Fred Percy	L/Cpl	01/07/16	Fricourt New Military Cemetery
Wheeldon, Joseph	Pte.	25/04/18	Tyne Cot Memorial
Whelan, John	Pte.	09/10/17	Tyne Cot Memorial
White, Albert	Pte.	17/06/18	Tyne Cot Memorial
White, James A.	Pte.	03/09/16	Connaught Cemetery, Thiepval
Whitehead, Tom	Pte.	25/04/18	Tyne Cot Memorial
Whiteley, Joseph	L/Cpl	16/10/18	St Aubert British Cemetery
Whitfield, Albert E.	Pte.	10/02/17	Mont Huon Military Cemetery, Le Treport
Whittaker, Thomas	L/Cpl	02/08/17	Mont Huon Military Cemetery, Le Treport
Wilcock, Henry	Pte.	20/08/15	Essex Farm Cemetery
Wilde, Arthur H.	Pte.	11/05/15	Merville Communal Cemetery
Wilde, James G.	2/Lt	01/11/18	Maing Communal Cemetery Extension
Wildgoose, Alfred	Pte.	19/10/18	Étaples Military Cemetery
Wilkinson, William	Cpl	25/04/18	Tyne Cot Memorial
Wilkinson, William H.	Pte.	25/04/18	Tyne Cot Memorial
Williams, Evan P.	Pte.	24/04/18	Crucifix Corner Cemetery, Villers-Bretonneux
Wilmot, Robert	Pte.	19/12/15	Essex Farm Cemetery
Wilson, Albert	Pte.	03/09/16	Thiepval Memorial
Wilson, George F.	Pte.	27/09/16	Thiepval Memorial
Wilson, Henry B.	Pte.	25/04/18	Sanctuary Wood Cemetery
Wilson, James	Pte.	25/04/18	Tyne Cot Memorial
Wilson, Richard	Pte.	19/12/15	Lijssenthoek Military Cemetery
Wilson, Robert	Sgt	15/07/16	Authuille Military Cemetery
Wilson, Samuel	L/Cpl	25/04/18	Tyne Cot Memorial
Wilson, William N.	Pte.	09/10/17	Tyne Cot Memorial
Wilson, William W.	Pte.	28/09/16	Thiepval Memorial
Winter, George W.	Sgt	03/11/18	Cambrai East Military Cemetery
Winter, Joseph	Pte.	22/02/18	Perreuse Chateau Franco British National Cemetery
Winterbottom, Austin	Pte.	27/07/17	Mont Huon Military Cemetery, Le Tréport
Withers, Samuel	L/Cpl	25/04/18	Tyne Cot Memorial
Wood, James Robert	Pte.	15/05/18	Tournai Communal Cemetery Allied Extension

Wood, Joseph	Pte.	09/10/17	Tyne Cot Memorial
Wood, William	CSM	01/11/18	Auberchicourt British Cemetery
Worth, Harold	Pte.	03/09/16	Mill Road Cemetery, Thiepval
Wrather, Joseph	Pte.	27/09/16	Thiepval Memorial
Wray, Harold	Pte.	20/09/16	Aveluy Wood Cmtry. (Lancashire Dump), Somme
Wright, Arthur	Pte.	26/07/17	Coxyde Military Cemetery
Wright, Ernest	Pte.	12/10/18	Vis-en-Artois Memorial
Wright, Harold	Pte.	18/06/18	Esquelbecq Military Cemetery
Wright, Percy	Pte.	26/04/18	Harlebeke New British Cemetery
Wright Robert	Pte.	22/04/18	Wytschaete Military Cemetery
Wye, George W.	Pte.	25/04/18	Tyne Cot Memorial
Yates, Francis C.	Pte.	28/09/15	Essex Farm Cemetery
Yeldham, Edgar C.	Pte.	01/11/18	Vis-en-Artois Memorial
Young, Stanley	Pte.	25/04/18	Tyne Cot Memorial

Appendix 4

Awards and Honours

Order of St Michael and St George – CMG
Wood, Cecil Ernest	Lt. Col	14/01/16	
[Bousfield, Hugh Delabere DSO	Lt. Col	01/01/18]	

Distinguished Service Order DSO Bar
Oddie, William	Lt. Col.	03/06/18	16/09/18

Legion D'Honneur (France)
Friend, Charles MC	Lieut.	27/10/19 (*Etoile Argent*)
Gilsenan, Terence Dermot Cole	2/Lieut.	14/07/17 (*Croix de Chevalier*)
Heaton, Hedley Francis MC	Capt.	07/10/19 (*Etoile Argent*)

Medaille Militaire (France)
Pattison, Harold 200593	CSM	14/07/17

Croix De Guerre (Belgium)
[Bousfield, Hugh DSO, CMG		Lt. Col	15/04/18]
MacKay A.	307593		
Waind, William	200271	Sgt.	15/04/18

Croix De Guerre (France)
Gilsenan, Terence DC	2/Lieut.	14/07/17

Order of the British Empire – OBE (Military Division)
Baines, George Norman	Lieut.	03/06/19	(Member)
Cope, Noel Harwood	Lieut.	01/01/19	(Member)
Gaunt, Arthur	Capt.	07/06/18	(Member)
Stoddart, Dr. John Wilkie	Lieut.	07/06/18	(Member)
Veal, Frank	Q.M. Capt.	07/06/18	(Member)
Whitworth, Charles Warwick	Capt.	03/06/19	(Member)

Decoration Militaire (Belgium)

Green, Robert	202217	Pte.	21/08/19

Meritorious Service Medal – MSM

Adams, G.	203951	R.Q.M.S.	16/10/19
Akers, J.	200350	Sgt	18/01/19
Calder, G.	200025	C.Q.M.S.	18/01/19
Clark W.P.	268550	Sgt	16/10/19
Clements, D.	203277	C.S.M.	22/02/19
Varey, N.	200558	R.Q.M.S.	03/06/19
Walker, G.	200744	Pte.	18/01/19
Wheeler, H.T.	203877	Pte.	15/03/19
Whinn, J.D.P.	200065	Sgt	17/06/18
Wright, F.	305504	Cpl	03/06/19

Military Cross – MC

			Bar
Ablitt, Bernard E	Capt.	16/11/16	16/09/18
Berghoff, Henry	2/Lieut.	10/12/19	
Birbeck, Leonard Sanderson	Lieut.	01/10/17	
Foxton, John Alexander		03/06/19	
Freeman, Walter Hanson	Capt.	01/01/17	16/09/18
Gilsenan, Terence DC	2/Lieut.	14/11/16	
Green, Douglas	Capt.	18/01/18	25/04/18
Hardwick, Thomas William	2/Lieut.	01/01/18	
Heaton Hedley	Capt.	02/04/19	10/12/19
Irish, Harry	2/Lieut.	05/02/18	05/07/18
Jameson, James Leslie	Lieut.	15/03/16	
Jones, S/L/	2/Lieut.		
King, Bryan Ashfield	2/Lieut.	16/09/18	
Mackay, Kenneth	Lieut.	14/11/16	
Parker, John W	2/Lieut.	23/04/18	
Peters, John Cecil	Capt.	25/11/16	
Pinder, John (RAMC)	Capt.	23/04/18	
Rushforth, John William	Lieut.	10/12/19	
Saxby, Frederick	2/Lieut.	14/11/16	
Shillaker, Eric Charles H	2/Lieut.	25/08/16	
Sowerby, Geoffrey	Capt.	14/01/16	
Todd, George Leslie	2/Lieut.	10/12/19	
Wallace, Dudley Whistler	2/Lieut.	16/08/17	
Williamson, Percy Gordon	Capt.	14/01/16	
Wilson, Maurice	2/Lieut.	16/09/16	
Wycherley, Robert Bruce	Capt.	16/09/18	10/12/19

Distinguished Conduct Medal – DCM

Name	Number	Rank	Date	Bar
Atkinson, J.	1488	L/Cpl	15/3/16	
Baldison, Charles H.	200794	Sgt	25/11/16	
Beech Norman W.	2158	Pte.	15/3/16	
Carr, Herbert	36959	Pte.		
Cooke, A.W.	1790	Pte.	15/3/16	
Emerson, J.	6494	Sgt		
Farnhill, Albert W	3402	Pte.	25/11/16	
Grice, E.W.	1540	Cpl		
Henderson, Joseph	200510	Sgt	21/10/18	
Kavanagh, P.	265375	Sgt	11/10/18	
Kitchen, G.	900	Sgt	25/11/16	
Ledgard, Edward	200875	Sgt	17/04/18	
Lund, Gordon	1931	CSM	11/03/16	
McQuade, John C.	200788	Sgt	11/10/18	
Morton, Matthew C.	1470	Sgt	15/03/16	
Nicholson, John C.	2210	CSM	11/03/16	
Pascoe, N.	5968	L/Cpl	14/11/16	
Pattison , Harold	200593	CSM	25/11/16	
Raynor, Fred	4713	RSM	13/02/17	
Tolley, Gilbert	1161	Sgt	11/03/16	6/02/18
Usher, Harry	2168	Pte.	11/03/16	

Military Medal – MM

Name	Number	Rank	Date	Bar
Allen, A.J.	1817	Pte.	03/06/16	
Avery, S.G.	62512	Pte.	17/06/19	
Baldison, A.	540	L/Sgt	19/02/17	
Belcher, R.	40770	L/Sgt	09/07/17	
Benson, W.	2130552	L/Cpl	19/03/18	
Birbeck, J.	9547	Pte.	20/08/19	
Blanchard, J.	200670	Pte.	13/09/18	
Bland, R.	200946	Pte.	19/03/18	
Brooks, A.	3928	Pte.	09/12/16	
Broughton, W.	1643	Sgt.	03/06/16	
Brown, F.	1666	Pte.	03/06/16	
Buckroyd, J.	26205	L/Sgt	23/07/19	
Butler, B.	2518	Pte.	11/11/16	
Butterfield, H.	16/1553	Pte.	17/06/19	20/8/19
Cairns, E.	304042	Cpl	23/07/19	
Carney, T.	202721	Cpl	19/03/18	
Carr, H.	36959	Pte.	21/08/17	
Chadwick, G.H.	5512	Pte.	09/12/16	
Chandler, A.J.	62513	Pte.	17/06/19	

Clark, J.W.	1289	Pte.	11/11/16	
Currell, R.	2588	Pte.	19/02/17	
Dickens, H	58951	Pte.	17/06/19	
Dixon, F.W.	2552	Pte.	09/12/16	
Fawcett, H.	235031	Pte.	13/09/18	
Fearn, W.H.	200010	Sgt	17/06/19	
Gatenby, W.A.	2485	Pte.	03/06/16	
Grayson, J.	201434	Pte.	16/08/17	
Green, E.J.	62503	Pte.	23/07/19	
Harrison,W.	63020	Pte.	23/07/19	
Haynes, H.	2379	Sgt	11/11/16	
Hewson, A.	200630	Sgt	18/07/17	
Holford, J.T.	54131	Pte.	17/06/19	
Howarth, H.	18/411	Pte.	13/09/18	
Ingleby, A.	201114	Sgt	13/09/18	
Iredale, E.E.	1588	L/Sgt	19/02/17	
Jowett, W.H.	21/983	Pte.	13/09/18	
Kitson, T.R.	200703	L/Cpl	13/09/18	
Lee, R.J.	200575	Cpl	13/09/18	
Light, R.	200221	Sgt	13/09/18	
Lockwood, L.	202759	Pte.	19/03/18	
Long, A.	202759	Pte.	19/3/18	
Marriott, E.	241408	Cpl	17/6/19	20/8/19
Maw, T.V.	2583	Pte.	11/11/16	
McAndrew, B.	2220	Pte.	11/11/16	
Metcalfe, A.	1780	L/Sgt	11/11/16	
Miller, J.	54901	Pte.	17/6/19	
Mitchell, C.H.	202162	Pte.	19/3/18	
Paget, H.	202967	Pte.	19/3/18	
Partidge, H.	200708	Cpl	20/8/19	
Payne, H.	54171	Pte.	17/6/19	
Pickard, S.	41282	Pte.	19/3/18	
Pickles, H.	18/1288	Pte.	13/9/18	
Plant, A.E.	200075	Sgt	20/8/19	
Radband, E.	201125	Cpl	18/7/17	
Raftery, J.	200789	L/Sgt	18/7/17	
Rastrick, W.	21/394	Sgt	17/6/19	20/8/19
Render, R.	816	CQMS	11/11/16	
Richardson, J.	1441	Cpl	1/9/16	
Rogers, N.	200726	Pte.	13/9/18	
Shepherd, W.	202152	Pte.	13/9/18	
Shillito, J.W.	2688	Pte.	11/11/16	
Smith, C.	3506	Pte.	1/9/16	

Smith, F.	2755	L/Cpl	11/11/16	6/1/17
Thompson, J.W.	200049	Sgt	18/7/17	
Thornhill, R.	203143	Sgt	18/6/17	
Tomlinson, F.	130953	ACPL	14/12/16	23/2/18
Trousdale, L.	1709	Pte.	11/11/16	9/12/16
Twineham, C.	3201	Pte.	9/12/16	23/2/18
Uttley, A.E.A.	202714	Pte.	23/7/19	
Watson, W.	240888	Pte.	17/6/19	20/8/19
Wellington, H.H.	66507	Cpl	17/6/19	
Willis, A.	200610	Sgt	19/3/18	
Wilson, H.	201172	L/Cpl	13/9/18	
Wilson, J.W.	203134	Pte.	13/9/18	
Wilson, T.	202817	Sgt	23/7/19	

Appendix 5

Other Nominal Rolls

Officers of the 5th Battalion on 1 April 1908
Lt. Colonel John C. Husband
Major George Lumsden.
Major Arthur Robert Morrell.
Captain (Honorary Captain in the Army) Cecil Ernest Wood.
Captain William Waldon. (supernumerary.)
Captain William Oddie.
Captain (Honorary Captain in the Army) Robert Cattley.
Captain Charles Warwick Whitworth (supernumerary.)
Captain Frederick Charles Thompson.
Captain Matthew Burrow Ray.
Captain John William McConnell.
Captain Edward Peel Cross.
Captain Henry Maurice Platnauer.
Lieutenant Alwyne Percy Dale.
Lieutenant Donald Paley Mackay.
Lieutenant Henry Cooper Scott.
Lieutenant Rupert Rowlance Lansdale.
Lieutenant Percy Gordon Williamson.
Second Lieutenant Charles Harry Moody.
Second Lieutenant Claude Bulmer.
Second Lieutenant Francis Samuel Bastow.
Second Lieutenant Francis Gerald Scott.
Second Lieutenant Geoffrey Sowerby.
Second Lieutenant John Alexander Foxton.
Second Lieutenant John Cecil Peters.
Quartermaster and Honorary Lieutenant
James Richard Hill.

122 Officers and men known to have been taken prisoner on 25 April 1918

A Company	Bennion, J.H.	Docherty, George
Ambler, Robert	Bielby, John	Greenwood, Charles
Adams, Alfred	Davey, P.	Greenwood, Norris
Bates, Walter	Dickinson, Ernest	Hinton, Jack D.

Holbrey, J.W.
Hopkin, Horace
Jackson, John
Johnston, Thomas
Keenan, James
Mee, F.T.
Moore, S.B.
O'Shaughnessy, Amos
Park, Harry
Pinder, Harold
Scott, J.A.
Sykes, J.W.
Taylor, J.T.
Tinsdeall, C.
Walker, Herbert
Walker, Wilfred
Whitehead, Tom
Winter, Joseph
Yeoward, D.

B Company
Altoft, F.
Austwick, T.
Beattie, J.W.
Bell, T.W.
Brown, Webster
Bulmer, G.W.
Cundall, J.
Cust, Richard
Eccles, Percy
Fieldhouse, Fred
Heaton, J.
Hyde, J.
Leck, Horace
Leigh, A.
MacDonald, Paul
Mason, F.W.
Nelson, A.C.
Parker, Edward
Payne, Fred
Reading, W.

Roberts, William
Swaine, Willie
Toomie, George
Wilkinson, Leonard

C Company
Adamson, R.
Atkinson, R.
Crabtree, Allen
Ellis, Thomas
Gibson, Leonard
James, Wilmott
Jowett, W.H.
Keen, E.H.
Leak, Edwin
McNally, J.R.
Marston, J.W.
Metcalfe, Charles
Middleton, John H.
Molloy, J.
Murray, George
Ogden, John
Park, John
Parker, S.
Pollitt, A.
Rayner, W.
Robson, Arthur
Scott, C.
Sharp, A.A.
Smith, Ernest
Smith, Leonard
West, Edmund
White, Wilfred
Wilkinson, T.W.
Wooler, Ernest

D Company
Aylott, E.
Barlow, Sydney
Beard, Arthur
Beckett, Russell

Blagden, J.
Caddick, William H.
Clinton, Frank
Delaney, Thomas
Goldthorpe, A.
Hall, Fred
Hanson, L.
Horner, Wilfred
Jackson, William
Moss, H.
Priestley, Albert
Rodwell, E.
Sands, Thomas A.
Saynor, John
Smith, W.J.
Steer, Joseph
Stokell, J.
Wood, W.E.

Others
Bagnall, E.J.
Brannan, J.
Curtis, William
Faricy, John
Lawty, Percy
Marshall, William
Nelson, E.
Rhodes, Albert
Watson, W.J.

Officers
Blacker, R(ichard)
Hatton, John
Dunnington, John W.
Firth, Charles
Mardon, Stanley R.
Clubb, Andrew
Cheesman, Percy
Sayes, John

Index

Name in *italics* denotes a 1/5th Battalion soldier listed in the Appendices.

337

Croisette, 181
Croix de Guerre, 167, 170, 214
Cromer, 249
Cross, Capt. E.P., 243
Cross of St Michael and St George, 214
Crossley, Joseph, 187, 288
Crowe, Gilbert B., 155–6, 289
Crust, William, 156, 289
Crystal Palace, 270
Cumberland:
    St Bee's School, 243
Cussons, Benjamin J., 236, 280

Dalby, Alfred, 120, 264, 289
Dalby, Col. Sgt., H, 39
Dale, Capt. Alwyne, 48
Daniel, Robert, 108, 110, 289
Dardanelles, 70
Darley, 144
Darlington, 192
Dawson, Sidney T., 177–8, 280
Dawson, Walter, 109, 111, 289
Day, Arnold E., 81–3, 89
De Groot, Walter, 178, 280
DeMersey, Daniel, 155, 289
Derby, Lord, 44
    Hospital (Warrington), 104–107, 140,
    158
Devonshire Camp *see* Ouderdom (Ypres)
Dickens, H., 265, 289
Dickinson, Benjamin, 273, 289
Distinguished Conduct Medal (DCM), 87, 90,
    98, 102, 124, 169, 173, 181, 196, 200, 257–
    60, 264–5
Distinguished Service Order (DSO), 214, 265
    bar, 241
Dixon, F.W., 171, 196
Doberitz camp, 248
Dobson, QM Sgt. John, 87, 289
Doherty, L/Cpl. T.H., 60
Dolfus, Jean, 50
Doncaster Racecourse, 76
Douai, 247, 266
Douchy, 261
Doullens, 178
Dover, 247
Dragoon Camp, 222
Draper, Arthur, 219, 289
Dresser, W., 118, 123, 137, 280

Dublin:
    Trinity College, 148
Dudley, George, 250, 289
Dufton, William, 187, 289
Dunkirk, 200, 202
Durham, 138–9, 144, 181
    School, 171
Dury, Henry, 23
Dyson, Richard, 23

Easington, 177
Eastern Front, 60
Eastleigh, 173, 250
Eastwood, Robert, 111, 289
Edwards, Capt., 177
Edwards, Lt. F., 192–3, 195, 268, 280
Edwards, Pte. Fred, 224, 289
Ellison, Lt. George, 84
*Ellison, Capt. Charles C., 84, 145, 177, 200,
    280*
Elsworth, George, 38, 290
Elsworth, James, 142, 290
Elton, Walter, 182, 290
Elverdinghe, 77, 110, 113
Escaudoeuvres, 252, 258
Escaut, River, 252
Estaires, 57, 60, 63, 65, 72, 74, 197
Étaples,
    No.1 Training Camp, 200, 231, 249
Everest (Mount), 271
Exelby, George H., 69, 158, 290
Exelby, John H., 175, 290
Exeter, 115, 177
Exminster, 265

Fairburn, B., 222
Fairburn, Pte. Charles, 222
Fairburn, Fred, 49, 139–40, 222, 290
Fairburn, Spr. H., 222
Famars, 33, 201, 261–2
Farnhill, Albert, 167, 196, 290
Fauquissart (1915), 56–9, 68–9
Fearn, William Henry, 21, 271, 290
    see also Laventie, Fauquissart (1917)
Felstead School, 218–19
Ferdinand, Archduke Franz, 34
Ferguson, William, 109, 290
Fernie, Pte. R, 38
Field, Harold, 72, 290